THE INDIGENOUS EXPERIENCE

THE INDIGENOUS EXPERIENCE

Global Perspectives

EDITED BY

ROGER C.A. MAAKA
CHRIS ANDERSEN

Canadian Scholars' Press Inc.
Toronto

The Indigenous Experience: Global Perspectives
Edited by Roger C.A. Maaka and Chris Andersen

First published in 2006 by
Canadian Scholars' Press Inc.
180 Bloor Street West, Suite 801
Toronto, Ontario
M5S 2V6

www.cspi.org

Every reasonable effort has been made to identify copyright holders.
CSPI would be pleased to have any errors or omissions brought to its attention.

Canadian Scholars' Press gratefully acknowledges financial support for our publishing activities from
the Government of Canada through the Book Publishing Industry Development Program (BPIDP).

Library and Archives Canada Cataloguing in Publication

The indigenous experience : global perspectives / edited by Roger C.A. Maaka, Chris Andersen.

Includes bibliographical references and index.
ISBN 978-1-55130-300-0

1. Indigenous peoples—Colonization. 2. Indigenous peoples—Government relations.
I. Maaka, Roger II. Andersen, Chris, 1973–

JV305.I53 2006   305.8   C2006-904362-0

Cover design, interior design and layout: Susan MacGregor/Digital Zone
Cover photo: "Photo 'tree,'" by Emin Ozkan/stockxchng. Reprinted by permission of Emin Ozkan.

Printed and bound in Canada

TABLE OF CONTENTS

PREFACE

ADVANCED STUDIES OF INDIGENOUS PEOPLE in the modern world require more than the study of a particular indigenous group in isolation from others, and more than the conventional comparative study of different indigenous groups. They require an understanding that indigenous people collectively constitute a global mosaic of peoples who, in spite of their diversity, share a common experience of colonization and are considered a distinct and increasingly important sector of humanity. International networks play an important role, as Indigenous Peoples have looked to each others' struggle and progress for inspiration in articulating their own concerns. This collective effort has raised public consciousness and has created a global movement (indigeneity) that, while affirming local indigenous rights and identities, concomitantly globalizes them.

Indigenous Studies is a dynamic and changing field that seeks to understand colonialism, which denied and continues to deny Indigenous Peoples their political autonomy. Indigenous Studies also monitors contemporary developments as Indigenous Peoples regain their power of agency and nation-states react to the aspirations of the indigenous populations that live within their borders. Nation-building and indigenous identity politics intersect around ideas of citizenship, political rights, inclusion, and exclusion. Indigenous citizenship, shared citizenship within national boundaries, needs to be understood from an international and global perspective; national and regional perspectives are inadequate in scope, and perpetuate the premise that indigenous people lost their rights of autonomy through secession via treaties, conquest, and demographic displacement.

Because of the fluid and evolving nature of Indigenous Studies, course instructors often find it difficult to readily provide students with a range of suitable readings, and currently there is no single text that adequately covers the area. This book is in part an attempt to remedy this void. Such is the incredible diversity of the Indigenous Peoples that a single book of readings cannot realistically cover the circumstances of each indigenous group or every issue of importance to Indigenous Peoples. However, this book is aimed at offering the reader an insight into the richness and heterogeneity of indigenous experiences, which will hopefully spur further interest in the field. Examples are drawn from indigenous experiences in the North American nations of Canada and the USA; the Hispanic nations of Latin America; Australia, New Zealand, Hawai'i and Rapanui from Oceania; from Northern Europe and the circumpolar region, Norway; the Asian country of Japan; and from the continent of Africa, an example from Nigeria.

Despite the fact that contemporary scholarly discussion about the experiences of indigenous societies around the globe inevitably includes some reference to "colonialism," the term seems to be used less as an invitation to further research and more as an explanatory concept whose invocation is used to end debate. Also, since discussions of colonialism in different disciplines naturally occur on different registers that engage in different theories and ask different questions, the readings focus both on the experiences of specific indigenous groups and on broader issues of indigeneity in a global setting. The readings are collated into thematic areas considered essential to the understanding of the situation of contemporary indigenous populations. These include local experiences of, and global perspectives on, colonization; the mapping of its negative consequences; colonialism's "truths"; and contemporary indigenous struggles. Each part contains readings intended to present the diversity of indigenous experiences. The readings vary in degree of difficulty; some are largely historical and descriptive, and others introduce the reader to more complex conceptual issues. The book is therefore most suited for readers who have a knowledge of at least one national grouping of indigenous people, for example the Aboriginal peoples of Canada—that is, for students in their third or fourth year of a Native Studies or cognate disciplinary program.

A NOTE FROM THE PUBLISHER

Thank you for selecting *The Indigenous Experience: Global Perspectives* edited by Roger C. A. Maaka and Chris Andersen. The editors and publisher have devoted considerable time and careful development (including meticulous peer reviews) to this book. We appreciate your recognition of this effort and accomplishment.

TEACHING FEATURES

This volume distinguishes itself on the market in many ways. One key feature is the book's well-written and comprehensive part openers, which help to make the readings all the more accessible to undergraduate students. The part openers add cohesion to the section and to the whole book. The themes of the book are very clearly presented in these section openers.

The general editors have also greatly enhanced the book by adding pedagogy to close and complete each section. Each part ends with critical-thinking questions pertaining to each reading and detailed annotated further readings. The Appendix also contains annotated relevant websites.

INTRODUCTION

As this book is focused on the "indigenous experience," some consideration is offered in this Introduction of the complexity of the category itself. Because of the extreme diversity of indigenous language, culture, location, and history, defining who indigenous people are can be a perplexing task. In light of this complexity, rather than getting bogged down in the search for a precise definition, we find it more useful to consider how Indigenous Peoples may be understood, and how they have been positioned in the colonialism literature. Although individual indigenous collectivities represent a specific, localized manifestation of indigeneity, they need also to be understood against the larger (usually both in population and material resources) nation-state/colonial society within which they are situated. In this context, Indigenous Peoples are positioned here in two geopolitical dimensions: the national—that is, in the context of the nation-state in which they reside—and the global, as a component of the global mosaic of Indigenous Peoples.

All indigenous collectivities possess local centres of distinctive cultural traits and mores manifested in common dialect, custom, and symbols. A "local" perspective focuses on the distinctiveness of collectivities, which are bound by kinship, language, history, and sense of place; this is the heart of indigenous identity. The paradigm of Local encompasses notions of traditional societies and communities that are interpreted and manifested differently not only between different countries, but even within different regions of the same country. The power of local interests and expressions of collective identity (often characterized as "tribalism") are considerable, and shouldn't be underestimated. Indeed, they often become an obstacle to the formation of collective political representation at national or even regional levels.

Although perhaps controversial, the assumption of this reader is that most contemporary nation-states are also colonial ones. That is to say, they were formed—sometimes violently, sometimes more peacefully—on and over the traditional territories and jurisdictions of pre-existing Indigenous Peoples who, as a result, have come to be positioned as marginalized minorities; the social, political, and economic framework of indigenous collectivities are irreducibly framed by past colonial experiences that have further been refined and entrenched by subsequent nation-building projects. While the National paradigm does not exclude considerations of the local, the dominant tendency in academic writing has been to lump national indigenous groups together under a single label (for example, Aboriginal, Indian, Autochtone) despite wide disparities in language, custom, and history. Although this has some merit as an analytical strategy, it hides as much of the richness and distinctiveness of different indigenous collectivities as it reveals about the centralizing bureaucratic tendencies of nation-states. Still, while these labels originally reflected an outsider's perception and as such were (and still are) regarded by indigenous people as pejorative, they have also been generationally entrenched into the national mindset of the Indigenous Peoples who are obliged to use them in their interactions with state authorities and with non-indigenous settler society.

If the local and national perspective is focused on exploring some of the richness and diversity of indigeneity around the globe, the global perspective is more analytically oriented around the struggle for human rights for and by Indigenous Peoples. This struggle has slowly evolved into a growing philosophical jurisprudence on the specific indigenous rights as a distinctive category. Increasingly, international institutions like the United Nations (UN), the International Labour Organization (ILO), and the World Bank have begun to consider Indigenous Peoples as a special category of humanity with common characteristics going beyond the conventional anthropological understandings. The result of this activity has been an emerging consciousness of a global indigenous identity in which common-to-all characteristics are identified, articulated, internalized, and now conceptualized. It is no accident that this seminal definition of Indigenous Peoples came from a report commissioned by the United Nations, as only a global perspective could overcome nationalistic tendencies to regard and categorize Indigenous Peoples as minorities rather than as peoples with unique cultures and citizenship rights.

> Indigenous communities, peoples and nations are those which, having a historical continuity with pre-invasion and pre-colonial societies that developed on their territories, consider themselves distinct from other societies now prevailing in those territories, or parts of them. They form at present non-dominant sectors of society and are determined to preserve, develop and transmit to future generations their ancestral territories, and their ethnic identity, as the basis of their continued existence as peoples, in accordance with their own cultural patterns, social institutions and legal systems. (Jose Martinez Cobo (1987) Study of the Problem of the Discrimination against Indigenous Populations, Vol 5, UNESCO)

Thus, Indigenous Peoples in the 21st century are those who

- claim historical continuity to a formerly independent, self-governing society;
- were and continue to be socially and economically marginalized through the varied processes of colonization;
- are committed to surviving as distinct cultural and social entities, in the context of struggling over:
  - Land (as territory, history/identity, and sustenance)
  - Political rights (of citizenship and self-government)
  - Recognition and preservation (of language and culture)
  - Economic parity (the abolition of poverty and the right to development)

Bearing in mind the tension between, on the one hand, properly acknowledging local indigenous difference and on the other, demonstrating each group's unity with other indigenous collectivities, we have divided the book in four broad themes:

1) local views and global perspectives on colonization;
2) mapping its negative consequences;
3) colonialism's "truths"; and
4) contemporary indigenous struggles.

Each part contains readings intended to present the diversity of indigenous experiences. *Part I: Colonization and Indigenous Peoples* examines the colonial experience of the Ainu, Rapanui, and Hawaiian peoples, as well as global perspectives on colonization. *Part II: Colonialism, Genocide, and the Problem of Intention* explores the negative impacts of colonial intrusion on indigenous societies and the ways that contemporary nation-states attempt to deal with these past interactions. *Part III: Social Constructs of Colonialism* presents a number of different geographical and temporal contexts that challenge the seemingly natural divisions between indigenous and settler societies so central to colonial nation-states. *Part IV: The Indigenous Struggle and the Politics of Indigeneity* consists of readings that focus on the indigenous aspirations to regain the autonomy lost as a result of colonization. This section explores the challenges that such aspirations pose for both the indigenous communities and the nation-states that have been established on their former homelands.

PART I:

COLONIZATION AND

INDIGENOUS PEOPLES

IN THE FIRST SECTION OF *THE INDIGENOUS EXPERIENCE*, the readings offer insights into the relationships between colonization and indigenous people. In the literature, colonization is often used to refer to three distinctively different and yet interrelated eras. The first era is the period of initial contact and the establishment of colonies. The second era encompasses the nation-building exercises undertaken by the colonizing powers, and, in many cases, the settler societies that replaced them; this is the transformation of former colonies into nation-states. The third era includes the ongoing and emergent colonialisms and neo-colonialisms of the contemporary post-colonial world. This final era explores those forces that work to either assimilate Indigenous Peoples into the dominant culture or keep them in a state of marginalization.

Understanding both historical and contemporary forms of colonization is essential to understanding Indigenous Peoples, as their place in both national and global societies has been framed by their displacement by other more dominant political-ethnic groups, a process commonly referred to as colonization. The shift in status from being socially and politically autonomous societies to socially and politically subordinate and marginal societies underpins the "indigenous experience." The domination of one group of humans over another is as old as human society itself; however, the systematic military and commercial dominance over vast areas of the globe by Western European powers has set the boundaries of the modern world, and is the form of colonization that still dominates contemporary understandings of Indigenous Peoples.

From the 15th century to the end of World War II, European colonial imperialism was a process that first explored lands beyond the shores of continental Europe, then exploited local resources and established settlements to manage and handle these resources. It was a vast economic exercise motivated by the quest to find resources that would increase the wealth and power of European nations. The seminal event was the voyages of the Genoese explorer, Christopher Columbus, across the Atlantic to the lands that became known as the Americas. In his history of

Europe, Norman Davies describes the motivation for European colonial imperialism in this way: "They sailed for reasons of trade, of loot, of conquest and increasingly of religion"[1] (p. 511). This colonial imperialism was disastrous for indigenous people, as Grant McCall recounts in the story of the Rapanui people and their experience with colonial forces. Rapanui, or Easter Island as it is more commonly known, is a small island in the Pacific ocean off the coast of Chile.

After often very chequered histories, including the change of control between various European powers, many of these temporary settlements evolved into permanent settlements, and the colonial presence—or its descendant societies—became entrenched. For Indigenous Peoples, the change in status of their former homeland from colony to nation made very little difference to their situation. Indeed many of the former colonies developed imperialistic aspirations of their own. This phenomenon is illustrated in the stories on Rapanui and Hawai'i, respectively dominated by former colonies Chile and the USA. In their story of Hawai'i, Michael Kioni Dudley and Keoni Kealoha Agard show that even where an indigenous people were able to adjust to contact with the outside world and flourish in a capitalist society, it remained a target of colonial domination. Despite the fact that Hawaiian people created their own independent monarchy supported by a Western-style economy, they were still overtaken by a Western power (the US) that had itself begun as colony.

Of course, the marginalization of Indigenous Peoples is not exclusive to the West. In such diverse locales as Asia, Africa, and Siberia, large numbers of Indigenous Peoples were and continue to be marginalized by the dominant societies of the nation-states that were established on the lands of their forebears. For example, Brett L. Walker's article shows the Ainu people of Northern Japan's experiences of colonization through the colonial expansion of an Asian nation.

Although the era of Western European colonial imperialism has passed, its legacy continues and is global in effect and influence. For example the United Nations, the World Bank, and the International Labour Organization are Western European-conceived political and economic institutions which continue to dominate conceptualizations of Indigenous Peoples. The physical dominance of Indigenous Peoples by colonizing powers is never enough on its own; this is always accompanied by an intellectual rationalization for this dominance. The David Maybury-Lewis reading traces some of the history of ideas on how the West constructed "the Native" or "the Indigene" by placing indigenous people in dichotomy with Europeans, and finding them lesser beings. Hence, colonization was often justified through proclaiming a civilizing mission. Establishing the notion of intellectual superiority is very much part of colonization, as Linda Tuhiwai Smith discusses in her consideration of the establishment of the positional superiority of Western knowledge.

Colonization frames the indigenous experience, and for Indigenous Peoples the post-colonial era is unfortunately not one in which colonization in its many guises has disappeared. That is yet to come.

NOTE

1. Davies, Norman. *Europe: A History.* London: Pimlico, 1997.

CHAPTER I

INDIGENOUS PEOPLES

David Maybury-Lewis

INDIGENOUS PEOPLES HAVE ALL TOO OFTEN been the victims of genocide. As Charles Darwin noted, "Wherever the European has trod, death seems to
pursue the aboriginal" (Merivale 1842: 204). Nowhere is this more true than in the
Americas, whose native inhabitants have been intermittently slaughtered by invaders
and their descendants since the conquest. In fact the demographic consequences
of that invasion are the most drastic that the world has ever known. They were
heightened by the unique circumstances of the encounter, which was the most
extraordinary meeting in the history of humankind. It brought together two large
portions of the human race that had virtually lost touch with each other and been
separated for at least 40,000 years.

Eduardo Galeano, a distinguished Uruguayan writer, captures the surreal quality of that encounter in a brilliant description at the beginning of his quartet entitled *Memory of Fire:*

> He falls on his knees, weeps, kisses the earth. He steps forward, staggering because
> for more than a month he has hardly slept, and beheads some shrubs with his sword.

> Then he raises the flag. On one knee, eyes lifted to heaven, he pronounces three
> times the names of Isabella and Ferdinand. Beside him the scribe, Rodrigo de
> Escobedo, a man slow of pen, draws up the document.

> From today everything belongs to those remote monarchs: the coral sea, the beaches,
> the rocks all green with moss, the woods, the parrots, and these laurel-skinned people
> who don't yet know about clothes, sin, or money and gaze dazedly at the scene.

The killing of indigenous people is usually resorted to when outsiders wish to seize
the lands and resources they control or when indigenous populations are simply
considered to be "in the way" of national destiny, development, resource extraction, dam building, or anything else. Genocide is, for obvious reasons, not the policy

of choice where outsiders need indigenous labour, although there are exceptions to this. The most notorious exception in the Americas is the treatment, bordering on genocide, of the rubber tappers in the Amazon region.

Unfortunately for the indigenous peoples of the region, rubber trees grow wild throughout the Amazon basin. When the development of rubber tires in the 19th century sent the price of wild rubber soaring, it set off a rubber frenzy in large areas of Brazil, Colombia, Peru, and Bolivia. Fortunes could be and were made by those who controlled the collection and marketing of rubber, but for this they needed a docile labour force. Rubber gatherers had to walk through the forests, tapping the trees along their route and then bringing the latex back to a collection point, a highly labour-intensive operation. Rubber collectors were thus faced with the problem of acquiring a large labour force and preventing their wandering labourers from running away if they did not like their conditions of work. They solved it by seizing whole communities of indigenous peoples, forcing some of them to gather rubber and holding the others hostage to guarantee the tappers' return. This control, never lenient, degenerated in some areas to a level of sadism that is horrifying to contemplate. A traveller along the Ucayali river in the Peruvian Amazon wrote in 1874 that "On these rivers all is fright, shock, dread and panic-terror; no one on them thinks himself secure and not even life is guaranteed here" (Brown and Fernández 1991: 99). The notorious Peruvian Julio Arana set himself up with British capital on the Putumayo River (which now forms the boundary between Peru and Colombia). There he and his henchmen killed, tortured, raped, and otherwise mistreated his indigenous captives as much to amuse themselves as to instill in them the terror necessary for the extraction of the last ounce of rubber. The horrors along the Putumayo were finally exposed by a courageous Peruvian. They were investigated and publicized by Roger Casement, a British consular official who provoked a parliamentary investigation in London into what was being done with British capital and by British subjects (many of Arana's overseers were imported from Barbados) in the wilds of Peru. Arana was too influential a man to be punished, however; besides, the Peruvian government was not unhappy to support his brand of "development" in the wilds, especially when the developers safeguarded the nation's frontier by chasing away the Colombians in the region. So Arana lived out his days in the Amazonian town of Iquitos. The Amazonian rubber boom and the related sufferings of the Amazonian Indians were eventually brought to an end by the British, but for commercial rather than humanitarian reasons. An Englishman succeeded in smuggling rubber seedlings out of Brazil. These were carefully tended at Kew Gardens in London and then sent out to be replanted in southeast Asia. By the 1920s, rubber could be produced more cheaply and in larger quantities in the plantations of southeast Asia than by the collectors in the South American jungles, so the Amazonian rubber industry collapsed.

The massacre of indigenous peoples during the rubber boom is an extreme case, for it risked destroying the very labour force on which the wealth of the collectors depended. One can only surmise that Arana and his henchmen wished to control their indigenous workers through sheer terror, and that eventually they created a regime in which cruelty was piled on cruelty, simply because there was no one to stop it (see Taussig 1986). Much more common throughout the Americas, in areas where there is a substantial indigenous population whose labour is needed by its overlords, have been policies designed to force the Indians to do the work required of them. Even after the colonial policies of slavery and forced labour had been abolished, other mechanisms were put in place to accomplish the same ends. Indian lands were systematically taken away from their owners, who became a source of cheap labour once they were living in poverty on reduced holdings. Strenuous efforts were made to destroy indigenous communities by forcing them to divide up their common lands and hold them in individual parcels. Systems of debt peonage were institutionalized, especially in the Andean countries, under which Indians were tricked or forced into accepting contracts that they did not understand and often tried unsuccessfully to repudiate—contracts that required them to work for long periods of time for miserable wages or for payment in kind. Alternatively, laws were passed, as in Guatemala and El Salvador, requiring indigenous peoples to work a certain number of days each year for private employers and to carry passbooks to show that they were doing so. If all this was not enough, Indians were simply required to perform certain kinds of forced labour. Unpaid work on the roads was, for example, compulsory for all Indians in Peru well into this century.

The Americas furnish the oldest and most dramatic example of the treatment of indigenous peoples. It was the invasion of the Americas that marked the beginning of European expansion and it is the Indians of the Americas who have borne the brunt of their indigenous status for the longest time, but similar processes have taken place all over the world.

When the Spanish landed in the Americas they referred to all the natives of the New World as *Indians,* following Columbus's famous confusion. It was clear, though, that the Indians were indigenous to the Americas and the Europeans were not. It was some time later that people of European descent, but born in the Americas, started to think of themselves as "indigenous" to the Americas too. Nevertheless, Indians or Native Americans are to this day still considered the truly indigenous Americans as opposed to others born in the Americas whose ancestors, however distant, came from overseas.

This ambiguity is not peculiar to the Americas. The very term *indigenous peoples* is confusing because most people in the world are "indigenous" to their countries in the sense of having been born in them or being descended from people who were born in them. Indigenous peoples are clearly native to their countries in this sense too, but they also make another claim, namely that they were there first and are still there, and so have rights of prior occupancy to their lands. This criterion discriminates clearly enough between, for example, Native Americans and all those who came to the Americas after Columbus's invasion. It also distinguishes well enough between indigenous peoples and later comers in other parts of the world that have been colonized from overseas. There is no problem in distinguishing the Aborigines of Australia or the Maoris of New Zealand as "indigenous" in contrast to the settlers who came later to those lands; but such distinctions are not so easy to draw in Europe or Asia or Africa. In those continents, peoples have eddied this way and that, often for thousands of years, leaving in place a mosaic of different peoples who dispute the land and sometimes dispute the claim to prior occupancy of it. Additional criteria must therefore be used to define indigenous peoples for the purposes of any general discussion.

Indigenous peoples claim their lands because they were there first or have occupied them since time immemorial. They are also groups that have been conquered by peoples racially, ethnically, or culturally different from themselves. They have thus been subordinated by or incorporated into alien states that treat them as outsiders and, usually, as inferiors. Isolated or marginal groups that have not yet been conquered by a state are also considered indigenous, because it is only a matter of time before they are subordinated. Indigenous peoples maintain their own languages, which normally differ from those spoken by the mainstream populations, and their own cultures, which invariably differ from the mainstream. They are conscious of their separate identities and normally struggle to retain them. The salient characteristic of indigenous peoples, then, is that they are marginal to or dominated by the states that claim jurisdiction over them.

Since they have not developed their own states and are not integral to the states that now actually or potentially rule over them, indigenous peoples are often referred to as *tribal*. The phrase *tribal peoples* is unfortunately imprecise, but it is often used nowadays as a kind of shorthand to refer to small-scale, pre-industrial societies that live in comparative isolation and manage their affairs without any centralized authority such as the state. The worldwide tendency is for such peoples sooner or later to be conquered by states. Since the states then consider them aliens and inferiors, indigenous or tribal peoples are among the world's most underprivileged minorities, facing the constant threat of genocide or ethnocide.

Genocide (the physical extermination of a defined category of people) is today universally condemned. In fact, one of the first acts of the newly created United Nations, acting in response to the horrors perpetrated by the Nazis during World War II, was to approve a Convention on Genocide in 1948. The problem is that genocide is extremely difficult either to prevent or to punish. It requires international action against the perpetrators and that is very rarely possible to organize. Genocide, therefore, continues to take place, and indigenous peoples are especially at risk because they are so vulnerable.

Ethnocide (the destruction of a people's way of life) is, on the other hand, often not even condemned when it comes to indigenous peoples. On the contrary, it is advocated as an appropriate policy toward them. Indigenous peoples are normally looked down on as "backward," so it is presumed that their ways of life must be destroyed, partly in order to civilize them and partly to enable them to coexist with others in the modern world.

A people's way of life is often referred to by social scientists as its *culture,* a term that indicates the totality of ideas, attitudes, customs, and ways of doing things that people acquire as members of a society. Often the institutions of a society are also considered part of its culture, although some scholars prefer to make a distinction between *culture,* which is largely ideational, and *social structure,* which refers to the institutional arrangements made by people who share a given culture. I use the term *culture* to refer generally to the distinctive way of life of a given people. It is the cultures of indigenous peoples that are regularly threatened, even when their lives are not at risk, and it is to their cultures that they often cling in order to give meaning and dignity to their lives.

As we shall see, there is no hard and fast distinction between indigenous peoples and other kinds of localized ethnic groups. Who then are the peoples generally considered "indigenous" and how many of them are there? The second question is even harder to answer than the first one, for it obviously depends on who is considered indigenous (see Table 1.1). Even in the Americas, where the indigenous category is relatively easy to define, indigenous peoples are very hard to count. In places where it is a stigma to be considered "Indian," people will be reluctant to admit to it and will claim that they are of mixed blood or that they are participants in the mainstream national culture. Recently, as the indigenous rights movement has gathered steam internationally, people who once claimed not to be Indian now claim that they in fact are. There may also be political considerations that influence the over- or undercounting of Indians. At certain times in the history of the Americas, individual countries have decided that Indianness was a stigma that should be abolished in the name of egalitarianism and democracy. They have therefore abolished the category of "Indian" altogether and proclaimed that there were no more Indians in the nation. A reasonable guess as to the indigenous population of the Americas at the end of the 20th century would put it at about 31.5 million, with something less than a million in Canada, about 1.75 million in the United States, somewhat less than 13 million in Mexico and Central America, and about 16 million in South America. In addition, there are about 58,000 Inuit (Eskimo) in Greenland.

TABLE I.I

World Indigenous Population by Region of the World

REGION	POPULATION
Canada	935,000
United States	1,783,600
Central America and Mexico	12,713,000
South America	16,000,000
Greenland	58,000
Total of the Americas	**31,489,600**
China	91,000,000
Philippines	6,500,000
South Asia	60,000,000
Southeast Asia	20,000,000
Japan/Pacific Islands	750,000
Total Asia	**178,250,000**
Australia	250,000
New Zealand	325,000
Scandinavia	58,000
Former Soviet Union	28,000,000
Africa	14,200,000
Arabia	5,000,000
Total World Indigenous Populations	**257,572,600**

In other parts of the world, it is difficult even to define the category of "indigenous," let alone determine how many people belong to it. The best we can do is to give rough estimates of how many people are thought to belong in the categories that are locally considered indigenous or equivalent to indigenous. The major indigenous group in Europe are the Saami (previously known as the Lapps), who inhabit the far northern reaches of Norway, Sweden, Finland, and Russia and number about 58,000. There are about 28 million indigenous people in the former Soviet Union, and perhaps 5 million more in Arabia and the Near East. China has 91 million people classified as belonging to national minorities (see Chapter 2). Indigenous people are also found in South Asia (about 60 million), Southeast Asia and Indonesia (about 20 million), and the Philippines (about 6.5 million). Japan contains one sizeable indigenous group, the

Ainu of the far north. These, together with the indigenous peoples of the Pacific islands, total perhaps 750,000. The Aborigines of Australia (about a quarter of a million) and the Maoris of New Zealand (over 300,000) are also clearly indigenous. In Africa it is particularly difficult to distinguish between indigenous peoples and other ethnic minorities, but I have here included in the indigenous category some African peoples who are conventionally considered to be tribal outsiders in their own countries, such as the San and related peoples (Bushmen) of the Kalahari desert, the Efe and related peoples (Pygmies) of the Ituri rainforest in Zaire, and the nomads who roam the Sahara or who follow their herds in East Africa, all of whom add up to something over 14 million.

Though they are difficult to define or to count and are largely ignored by the world, indigenous peoples in fact make up about five percent of the total population of the globe. They are the descendants of peoples who were marginalized by the major powers and especially the expanding empires in their regions of the world—the European overseas empires in the Americas, Africa, Asia and Australasia, and the Russian and Chinese land empires in the heartland of Eurasia.

The expansion of these empires routinely led to the mistreatment of indigenous peoples. This is not the place to go into detail about the drastic consequences of colonial rule[1] for indigenous societies. Some examples establish the main line of my argument. The demographic consequences were disastrous everywhere. Indigenous peoples were conquered by superior weaponry. Sometimes they were subject to campaigns of extermination. More often they were driven off their lands or confined to a portion of them, if they did not flee. Meanwhile they were highly susceptible to infections transmitted by their more cosmopolitan conquerors. The results were impoverishment, starvation, and disease, which also took a fearful toll on their populations. It is difficult to calculate the exact extent of this indigenous depopulation, but Bodley combed the most reliable sources and came to the startling conclusion that indigenous peoples in the Americas, Oceania, and Africa lost about 90 percent of their population between the time of first contact and the lowest population levels experienced in the 19th century (1975:39).

These figures are easier to believe if we remember the circumstances and, above all, the attitudes that accompanied the imperial conquests. Australia under the British was considered in law to be *terra nullius,* a no man's land, technically uninhabited, in which settlers on occasion hunted Aborigines for sport as if they were game animals. The original inhabitants of Tasmania were systematically exterminated. When the authorities grew tired of their "attacks on the settlers," they arranged for a line of armed men to advance across the island, like beaters in a hunt, to flush out the remaining natives so that they could be shot down. When the Belgians administered the Congo, atrocities were committed against native peoples that paralleled those of the Peruvian Putumayo and exceeded them in scale. It was the events in the Congo that inspired Joseph Conrad's novel *The Heart of Darkness*. It was also in the Congo that Roger Casement had his first experience of investigating horror, before he was sent across the world to look into the brutalities on the Putumayo. The Germans in Southwest Africa ordered the Herero off their grazing lands and into the desert, where they would certainly have starved. When the Herero refused, the German army carried out a war of extermination against them.

Darwin's comment about death following in the footsteps of the European told a bitter truth, but it was not the whole truth. The imperialist expansion that changed the face of the globe in the centuries since Columbus's invasion of the Americas was largely, but not entirely, a European affair. When, for example, the Japanese began to take colonies, the marginal, indigenous people in them were treated in much the same way as they were in European-ruled territories. Furthermore, countries that have not known European colonial rule, such as China, or that have thrown it off, like India, Indonesia, and various nations of Africa, still practice a kind of internal colonialism toward their own marginal populations.

The 19th-century racism of Europeans and their descendants in the Americas was peculiarly virulent because it was buttressed by the theories of evolution and social Darwinism, which seemed to provide scientific support for what otherwise might have been recognized as naked prejudice. It had not always been so. From the earliest days of the European expansion into the Americas, the justification of conquest and imperialism had been much discussed. In fact, the issues were formally debated before King Charles V of Spain and a council of 14 leading theologians who were summoned to Valladolid in 1550 to hear Bartolomé de las Casas argue the case for indigenous rights against Juan de Sepúlveda. Sepúlveda invoked Aristotle's doctrine of "natural slavery" to argue that some peoples are naturally inferior to others, who therefore have a right to enslave them and to make war on them, should they refuse to submit. Las Casas replied with a massive rebuttal of Aristotle's thesis, and arguments to the effect that Spanish condemnation of indigenous customs was ill-informed, prejudiced, and, as we would now say, ethnocentric.[2] Las Casas was not alone in taking such a tolerant and enlightened view. Jean de Léry, a French Calvinist pastor, wrote a sympathetic account of the Tupinambá Indians in his *History of a Voyage to the Land of Brazil* (1578). His tolerance for Tupinambá custom was all the more remarkable because the Tupinambá, who were redoubtable warriors, practiced ritual cannibalism. This horrified the Europeans, even though they themselves routinely used judicial torture and practiced unspeakable cruelties on each other at the time (and had even been known to kill and eat each other in the religious wars that were then raging). Jean de Léry concluded that the conditions of life for the Tupinambá were somewhat better than they were for ordinary people in France. Later writers such as Montaigne and Rousseau displayed a similar rational tolerance toward the customs of exotic peoples. When such ideas carried the day and were reflected in the opinions and the laws of kings, they always encountered opposition at the frontier, but even this tension, which could on occasion be protective of indigenous rights, evaporated in the 19th century.

In the 19th century, learned opinion increasingly came to be scientific opinion, and scientific theory seemed at last to have resolved the question of the status of indigenous peoples. This was made possible by the new data that had become available. As the European powers consolidated their empires over most of the globe, they gathered enormous amounts of information about the distant peoples of the earth. Better still, this information could be ordered in terms of a theory that would enable western scholars to analyze the whole march of human history on scientific principles. This theory (or rather these theories, for there were innumerable variants) was a theory of social evolution, modelled on Darwin's theory of the evolution of the species and claiming to do for the social development of humankind what Darwin's theory had done for its physical development. A spate of books followed Darwin's *On the Origin of the Species,* all claiming to elucidate human history in a scientific and evolutionary framework. All of them placed tribal societies and indigenous peoples at or close to the bottom of the ladder of development. The writers' own societies (often simply glossed as "civilization") were invariably found at the top. Europeans and their descendants tended in any case to think that it was in the natural order of things for stronger and more "advanced" peoples to conquer and rule over weaker and more "backward" ones—a variation on Aristotle's argument cited earlier. Now they felt they had the scientific evidence that proved their superiority and justified their imperialism. The reasoned tolerance that had sometimes characterized the thinking of earlier scholars, as they tried to understand societies very different from their own, gave way in the 19th century to evolutionary disdain.

Once it was accepted as scientific truth that colonists and settlers represented societies that were on higher rungs of the evolutionary ladder than the savages they confronted, then this provided moral justification for almost anything that the former might do to the latter. If the settlers and the pioneers "had justice on their side," as Teddy Roosevelt insisted, then they need have no qualms about dispossessing the Indians. If the Indians were in any case no better than "squalid savages," as Teddy Roosevelt also said, then it followed that they could be severely treated by the bearers of civilization who came to take their lands and, if necessary, their lives. Such attitudes naturally bred others that were summed up in General Sheridan's notorious comment that "The only good Indian is a dead Indian."

The attitudes of 19th-century racism and evolutionism are no longer unquestioningly accepted throughout the world, but a certain neo-evolutionism has taken their place. Indigenous (or tribal) societies are rarely called "savage" these days, at least not in public, but they are normally considered "backward." It may no longer be considered acceptable to remove them by massacring them (though this still happens), but it is everywhere the case that governments feel that such peoples should be helped or forced to overcome their "backwardness." To overcome its backwardness, an indigenous society is urged to abandon its traditional way of life and often its language as well, usually in the hope that in so doing it will cease to exist as a society altogether. Its individual members, now no longer embedded in their "backward" society, will disappear into the population of the rest of the country.

States regularly justify their attempts to eradicate indigenous cultures with a series of arguments. The invaders of the Americas argued at first that the indigenous peoples were not fully human. Because they lacked the essential attributes of humanity—souls or a belief in Christianity—they were not entitled to what we would nowadays call "human rights" and were certainly thought to be in need of education to make them see the error of their ways and to induce them to abandon them. Later, the mission of conquest was justified in evolutionary terms. The conquerors brought civilization to the backward natives, if only the latter could be forced or induced to accept it. Nowadays some people may be hesitant to insist on the civilizing mission of the powerful. The grim history of the 20th century has made us wary of such claims. Development, however, is another matter. Indigenous peoples are usually accused of standing in the way of development, and that is normally sufficient grounds for dispossessing them and destroying their ways of life. If they are unable or unwilling to abandon their separate identities and disappear into the mainstream of the nations in which they live, they are also said to undermine the state and to impede modernization. Hence, it is argued, indigenous cultures must disappear. Sometimes we are told that the disappearance of such archaic cultures may be regrettable, but that it is also inevitable, since they cannot survive in the modern world. In short, stronger societies are bound to extinguish weaker ones and there is not much that can be done about it, since this is the result of some sort of Darwinian process where only the fittest survive.

These arguments are plausible and are certainly part of the conventional wisdom today, but they are false. We would do well to remember here that it was not only Sepúlveda who argued before the king of Spain in 1550 that slavery was part of the human condition and that indigenous peoples were destined for it. As recently as the 19th century, scholars were quoting learned arguments to the effect that the differences in the natural endowments of individuals and races, coupled with the unavoidable differences of power in human affairs, made slavery inevitable. We now realize that those arguments were false, although widely believed. How about some of the falsehoods that are widely believed in our own day?

Consider the argument that indigenous peoples must abandon their cultures because they are "backward" and, for good measure, that they "stand in the way of development." What exactly does this mean? Usually that they do things of which governments disapprove, as is the case with the few remaining nomadic peoples left on earth.

There is another line of argument that maintains that indigenous cultures should not be allowed to endure because they undermine the state. This argument normally runs that, if indigenous cultures were legitimated within the state, this would alter the social order in ways that the elite would find unacceptable. This is not the same thing as "undermining the state," although the elites would certainly have us think so. As we saw earlier, Mariategui in the 1920s called for Peru to recognize and cele-brate its indigenous roots. The idea was forcefully opposed by those in power because it would have involved changes amounting to a social revolution. On the other hand, indigenous societies with comparatively small populations are said to under-mine the state because, if their right to be different were accepted, then that would change the nature of melting-pot states.

Alternatively, indigenous societies are said to threaten the state by wishing to secede from it, yet the majority of indigenous peoples who are demanding their rights today have no interest in secession. What they ask for is a recognition of their rights *within the state*. Ironically, it is more usual for states to shift position than for the indigenous peoples at their edges to do so. Maps are redrawn (or sometimes drawn for the first time) that divide up indigenous peoples between states, or assign them to this state or that with little consideration of their past history or of their relations with local rulers. Under these circumstances, the conventional accusation that indigenous peoples at the frontiers are anxious to secede is often a classic example of projection (imputing to others what is running through one's own mind). There are, of course, some indigenous groups that have made their desire to secede quite clear. The point is that such desires are regularly imputed to the major-ity of indigenous societies, which have no such wishes, in order to avoid having to deal with their genuine demands for local autonomy.

At the heart of the prejudice against indigenous societies are the twin issues of modernization and development. States feel they cannot modernize effectively if they tolerate indigenous cultures in their midst. They feel even more that they cannot exploit the resources that lie within their territories if access to them is impeded by indigenous peoples.

In this article we have seen that indigenous peoples are defined as much by their relations with the state as by any intrinsic characteristics that they may possess. They are often considered to be tribal peoples in the sense that they belong to small-scale pre-industrial societies that live in comparative isolation and manage their own affairs without the centralized authority of a state. But we have also seen that the terms *tribal peoples* and *tribalism* are used much more broadly than that. Many peoples are stigmatized as "tribal," not because they fit the definition given above, but because they reject the authority of a state and do not wish to adopt the culture of the mainstream population that the state represents. They are in fact stigmatized as being "tribal" because they insist on being marginal.

Indigenous peoples are always marginal to their states and are often tribal in the technical sense. Marginal peoples, though, as Asian examples suggest, are not necessarily either indigenous or tribal. The point is that there are no hard and fast distinctions that enable us to place societies unambiguously within these categories. Instead, we are dealing with a continuum that ranges from *indigenous/tribal* peoples to *indigenous* (but not tribal) peoples, to peoples *stigmatized as tribal,* to peoples considered *ethnic minorities,* to peoples considered *nationalities,* though they coexist in a single state.

This last usage was employed in the former Soviet Union and still is used in the People's Republic of China. In China it is clear that not all nationalities are equivalent. The Han Chinese nationality is dominant, both culturally and numerically within the state. Other nationalities are minorities. Indeed, they are sometimes referred to in English as *national minorities,* which is also the official term used in the Philippines for all their minorities—indigenous, tribal, or otherwise. Chinese national minorities resemble indigenous peoples in that they tend to be marginal to the state, which in its turn makes sporadic efforts to assimilate them both politically and culturally. In most other ways, however, they are more like ethnic minorities.

There is another way in which the concept of *tribalism* is much in use nowadays—when it refers to the tendency for people of the same ethnicity to band together in modern societies. There has been much discussion in the world's press about the dire effects of tribalism in Europe and serious writers in the United States have urged Americans not to be lured down the slippery slope of multiculturalism into their own kind of tribalism. This kind of tribalism is usually thought to be the consequence of an innate tendency in human beings to band together with their own kind and fight all those who are different. I mention it here just to complete the discussion of the various uses of the term *tribalism.*

In spite of all these definitional difficulties, the indigenous peoples who are the focus of this article have a sufficiently clear sense of themselves, their problems, and their place in the world to have finally succeeded in getting their issues onto the agenda of the United Nations. A Working Group on Indigenous Rights has been meeting under the auspices of the United Nations and has issued a draft declaration on what those rights should be. Some of the terms of that declaration are instructive. The indigenous peoples ask for 1) self-determination within existing states, 2) protection against genocide, 3) protection against ethnocide, 4) protection of their own cultures, 5) protection of their own institutions of governance, 6) protection of their own special relationship to the land, 7) protection of their traditional economic activities, and 8) representation on all bodies making decisions about them.

The declaration makes it clear once and for all that secession and separatism are not on the mainstream agenda of indigenous peoples. What they want is a recognition of their rights within existing states, but the rights they want recognized are far-reaching. To ask not to be massacred (protection against genocide) is hardly remarkable. All peoples should have such a right. It is only significant that indigenous peoples should feel that they need specifically to ask for it and to have it guaranteed. The other rights demanded are cultural, political, and economic. Indigenous peoples ask that they be allowed to maintain their own traditions, their own ways of governing themselves, and their own ways of making a living off the land. They also ask that they have a chance to ensure that these rights are respected by being represented on all bodies that make decisions about them. These requests, if granted, would entail a rethinking and reorganization of most states in the world, as well as a rethinking of the ways in which economic activities are organized within them. The indigenous charter thus poses a direct challenge to the state as we have come to know it.

NOTES

1. Which, of course, includes the continuing rule of American countries over their indigenous inhabitants.
2. This historic debate is well described in Hanke 1959.

REFERENCES

Bodley, John H. 1975. *Victims of Progress*. Menlo Park, CA: Cummings Publishing Company.

Brown, Michael F. and Eduardo Fernández. 1991. *War of Shadows: The Struggle for Utopia on the Peruvian Amazon*. Berkeley: University of California Press.

Galeano, Eduardo. 1985. *Memory of Fire: I. Genesis*, trans. Cedric Belfrage. New York: Pantheon Books.

Hanke, Lewis. 1959. *Aristotle and the American Indians: A Study in Race Prejudice in the Modern World*. London: Hollis & Carter.

Merivale, Herman. 1842. *Lectures on Colonialism and the Colonies,* vol. 2, London: Longman, Orine, Brown, Green, and Longmans.

Taussig, Michael. 1986. *Shamanism, Colonialism, and the Wild Man: A Study In Terror and Healing*. Chicago: University of Chicago Press.

CHAPTER 2

TRADE, SLAVERY,

AND COLONIALISM

Grant McCall

W HEN DOES ONE GROUP OF PEOPLE fall under the control of another? When does a tribal autonomous nation become the subjugated property of a colonial power?

Much has been written about colonialism and what those lively centuries of European conquest and annexation did to the peoples of the rest of the world. The movement of the Europeans, that crafty group who inhabit the small peninsula perched on the western tip of Asia, which led them to become dominators of all of the other world's populations, has been written many times, by many people. Schoolchildren in Europe hear of the courage and rectitude of their ancestors, who ventured out to unknown seas, bringing the word of God and the rule of the rifle to the nations and natives they found at the ends of their long voyages.

By the 18th century, Spain, the vanguard power of the European conquest, had realized that her avaricious northern neighbours, France and England, coveted the Spanish lake that was the Pacific. The plan to try to recapture some ground for waning Spanish fortunes evolved in that most luxurious of colonial outposts, Lima. Peru was the jewel of the Spanish empire. Its precious metals filled Castilian vaults and provided trade goods for ports in the Philippines and elsewhere in Asia. There also, to Callao harbour, a few miles from the splendour of the Peruvian outpost court, came the greatest navy in the world on its voyages of trade and defence of the interests of the successive Philips of Spain. In 1770, the Viceroy of Peru, Don Pedro Amat, proposed to launch a goodwill mission to Oceania, particularly to Polynesia. Three years before, the English navigator Wallis had touched down at Tahiti, followed the next year by the Frenchman Bougainville. The exploits of James Cook were much discussed in the Peruvian capital. Perhaps the Spanish Dons knew of Cook's landing at Matavai Bay in Tahiti in April of 1769?

The Spanish hoped to make up for their oversights in the Pacific by sending a goodwill mission to Tahiti with the aim of establishing friendly relations and arranging for the arrival of Spanish colonists. The envoys' political duties were defined in detail and, moreover, the envoys had stern instructions to make friends with whatever island peoples they encountered. In this anxiously amiable frame of mind, Captain Don Felipe Gonzales charted a course for his two ships from Callao to the South Seas. Whether or not he knew any detail of the Dutchman Roggeveen's visit to Rapanui in 1722, he dropped anchor at the Island at much the same place that the Dutch had used half a century before. Then Gonzales waited for his first contacts with the Islanders, with whom he was grimly determined to be friendly.

The Rapanui had been anxiously awaiting the next European visit, eager to continue the trade in rare objects that had ended after so short a period. The eager friendliness of the Rapanui and the policy of goodwill on the part of the Spaniards fortuitously coincided. Not surprisingly, the result was the acquisition by the Rapanui of large quantities of trade goods. In return, the Spaniards mapped the outline of Easter Island, eventually claiming it for the King of Spain through an elaborate ceremony of annexation. The great expectations of both foreigner and local were fulfilled, and exceeded their respective hopes. The Spaniards even sent a small reconnaissance boat around the Island, and friendly trade continued. No unpleasant incidents occurred and the Spanish quelled even minor scuffles, so as not to create a poor impression with their hosts. Spain, the first European country to claim Rapanui as a possession, was also the first to abandon it. No ship from the Spanish navy has ever called at Rapanui since the 18th century, though ships from Peru were to play a decisive role in Rapanui history in the mid-19th century.

The success of the Spanish visit, though it was mainly to the east coast, had implications throughout the Island. The previously rare European objects became more familiar, and the Rapanui began to know what it was that the foreigner wanted and what he was prepared to give for local objects. Fascination with the exotic character of European goods changed to an appreciation of their utility. For example, European clothing gave better protection than traditional garments.

Rapanui discovered certain points around their Island that only with the coming of Europeans came to be appreciated. Anchorage for European ships rarely relates to Pacific Islander requirements of land and sea use; in fact, they are at odds. Local exploiters of the sea coast, such as the Rapanui (and other Polynesians) using minimum draft canoes, covet a shallow, sloping shore with many rocks and reefs, where abundant sea resources await harvesting by careful gatherers. The European, on the other hand, favours relatively deep waters in which to anchor his large ships. Hanga o Hoonu (Turtle Bay), charted by both the Dutch and Spanish expeditions, was one such good anchorage. It was James Cook in 1774 who discovered the potential of Hangaroa (Long Bay) for his ships' anchorage. After Cook, most of the 100 vessels which came to Rapanui in the late 18th century and early 19th century made for one of these two harbours. Hanga o Hoonu was firmly in Hotuiti hands, while Hangaroa was ruled by Tu'uaro.

Because Hangaroa became the most frequent anchorage, balance between the belligerent clans was maintained. True, the outsiders arrived in Tu'uaro territory, but most of these visitors were seeking supplies of fruit and vegetables—and these had to come from Hotuiti. Even if the foreigners turned up in the Hotuiti Hanga o Hoonu, the local clans did not possess the canoes controlled by the Tu'uaro. Potentially at least, balance was possible in the exploitation of the outsider resources.

But the delicate thread that bound Hotuiti and Tu'uaro in their contracts in kinship, strengthened by the cathartic annual Orongo had been frayed, first by famine, then by competition for trade with outsiders. However, its breaking did not mean death, although at times the disturbance did bring death to individual groups. The Rapanui were able, again, to transform their traditions and survive in their changing circumstances.

Throughout this period of constant internal strife, European ships came and went, for a variety of purposes, adding to the opportunities for trade and experiences of contact with the outsiders.

The main attraction that Rapanui held for the various ships' captains was that fresh fruit and vegetables could be obtained in exchange for a few trade goods. Throughout the first half of the 19th century, barrels sent ashore with landing parties were filled by the Rapanui merchants with sweet potatoes and yams. Bunches of bananas also formed a part of the trade from time to time. When a European ship was sighted from one of the towers used especially for the purpose, people gathered along the shore, displaying what they had to offer. They knew that the Europeans had a way of seeing long distances with more accuracy than even the best Rapanui warrior, so often the locals lit signal fires to attract the foreign seamen.

A few of the people who called at Rapanui tried to encourage the Islanders to grow European crops or breed larger meat animals. There were few chickens on Rapanui, and European taste did not run to the locally valued rat. These samples became part of the trading network and acquired a value above their practical worth. But the seeds to be planted were put on display, and the animals to be propagated remained mere symbols of prestige, to be eaten when it seemed most opportune for alliance or advantage.

To the first visitors, the Rapanui had offered their produce as a gesture of hospitality and goodwill, receiving in return a series of items, apparently random. Particularly during the first 60 years of the 19th century, the Rapanui learned what kinds of goods and services the outsiders had to offer. Pendants, either of cheap plate or minted coin medallions, enjoyed a vogue. Bottles on a string, sometimes with messages inside, could be hung around the neck. Strong, thin nails and even steel tools could be obtained from some ships, while some members of the larger crews traded items of their clothing for what they wanted. On a few occasions, when there had been a disastrous feud or famine, the Rapanui even had to ask for food from calling whaling ships, who had sailed to the Island for provisions for themselves.

For a while, Europeans offered to shave the beards of Rapanui men who came on board, but the impermanence of the operation did not suit Rapanui temperament, and material goods remained in favour as trade items.

Early on, the outsiders had shown an interest in the small carvings that many Rapanui made for amusement and decoration. These small bits of wood, that a man might work on in his spare time or while sheltering in a cave in a time of hostilities, fetched very good returns from individual sailors. The Rapanui took to carrying their statuettes on cords, so that they could show a number of samples to their prospective clients. Deals for the little figures could be struck on board the ship or when the sailors landed to obtain their vegetables and fruit. Some difficult ships did not send in boats but kept some distance from the shore, so imposing on a prospective trader the need for a dangerous paddle or swim out to the anchored vessel. From time to time, some Rapanui became hostile to these occasional and unpredictable outsider visits, especially if visitors had misbehaved, and would repel any attempts to land. Once or twice, old scores with outsiders were settled—on one occasion a crowd bludgeoned a seaman to death in full view of his shipmates. With the decline in power of both hereditary ruler and ordeal-selected prime warlord, island-wide coordination and cooperation did not exist; each group acted only for itself, and if any group's behaviour threatened the goodwill of the outsiders, then it was a local matter, not one that anyone else could do anything to alter.

The Europeans were at first an undifferentiated group for the Rapanui, all being referred to as *Tangata hiva,* man from elsewhere, outsider. For the most part, the Rapanui did not trouble to tell one foreigner from another. If the crew of one ship was kind to one group of Rapanui, that group received the next ship with courtesy. But if an outrage was committed by even one crewman, visitors on several subsequent ships might be made to suffer. The Rapanui remembered a man who shot at them from the deck of his ship, shouting with triumph each time a Rapanui's flesh was torn open by a pellet from his banging rifle. They remembered another time, when a group of Islanders had gone to a ship as usual, and had been welcomed with food and drink. Members of the crew invited the Rapanui, all of them, to come inside their ship, with the promise of more food. Suddenly the hatch was closed and the score of scared Islanders felt the ship get under way. After a while, the outsiders came and opened the room where the Islanders lay, some now desperate not to leave their Island. Once out on deck, the more determined leapt overboard, even though the Island was no longer in sight. Only one managed to survive the swim of several days to tell the story to his family.

Not all Rapanui, however, would have been so determined to escape, for Islanders at various times had asked, even begged, to be taken off their miserable and strife-torn little land. The idea first arose in 1774, when Captain James Cook visited the Island with two ships. Cook had taken the Tahitian Mahine on board as interpreter. Just as the Rapanui were getting used to seeing short, pale-skinned outsiders, they were surprised to find a man very much like themselves among this odd company. Mahine spent much time with the Rapanui. Tahitian traveller and Rapanui local struggled to understand each other, and succeeded well enough for the Rapanui to learn about Tahiti, as well as that other distant island of many wonders, "Britanee." Mahine's predecessor as Polynesian companion to the first Cook expedition, the handsome Omai, had returned to Tahiti laden with fine European goods bestowed upon him by his European hosts and hostesses. Mahine hoped for the same rewards in return for assisting Cook in his contacts with the various island groups. While Mahine's tales of Tahiti interested them, it was the rich and wonderful land of "Britanee" that caught some Rapanui imaginations.

Among the favours Rapanui asked from their European visitors, there were always a few requests to be taken to "Britanee." Most of the Europeans' leaders refused the request, but more than three decades after Mahine's description had enthralled some of his Rapanui listeners, one did agree. Benjamin Page, an experienced whaler, when trading for food, was offered the care of a young man in his late teens. Page, who operated out of New as well as old England, knew about the more celebrated 18th-century Pacific visitors to England, the first brought by Cook. In 1806 he took the young Rapanui on his ship and named him Henry Easter. Five years later, Henry asked to be returned to Rapanui. Before Page arranged to have his adopted son returned to Rapanui, he took the young man to Rotherhithe Church, in the dock area of south London and there, at a baroque font in the church from where the Pilgrim Fathers had departed for America, (and where an 18th-century Micronesian visitor was buried) had him formally baptized a Christian. Henry Easter was the first Rapanui convert.

On the Island, the practice of parading light-skinned young boys and girls in seasonal ceremonial was influenced by European visitors. From the first visit, the outsiders, when they could be separated from their leaders, showed a great interest in Rapanui women. Although clearly familiar with females, the outsiders never seemed to have any of their own. In return for sexual pleasure, the outsiders were willing to part with the much-desired goods. The results of the first encounters with the Dutch were children who had, by Rapanui standards, very light skin. The production of light-skinned offspring, who could be used in the display ceremonies, was an added benefit of the trade, along with the goods received at the time of the intercourse. Not all women were offered, and each time the European ships came over the horizon, only a few would be selected to satisfy the sailors' appetites, the others being concealed from view, as some disappointed visitors reported in their logbooks and published accounts.

By the mid-19th century, conditions seemed to be getting better on Rapanui. The weather was improving; the European visits, although fewer, seemed to be better managed; and ceremonial at a kind of resuscitated court at Anakena was becoming more elaborate. The long-standing enmities still existed and new ones were created, but the Island was recovering from its past calamities. A trio of Rapanui men had been engaged on a European whaling vessel, and others may have been waiting their chance for adventure and profit away from the Island.

It was the activities of Britain, Peru, and France that created Rapanui's commerce from the 18th century. The British and the French were jockeying for influence in Tahiti, and the Spanish, operating out of Peru, hoped to foil those plans, to their own belated advantage. European squabbling over Tahiti had predisposed the Spanish expedition of 1770 to be especially amicable during their Rapanui sojourn. Britain, Peru, and France affected Rapanui history in another way. Republican Peru, still cowering when Spanish gunboats appeared at her ports and along her coasts, was a labour-starved country. Indigenous Indian labour had been exhausted early on and, with the fight for political independence from Spain, Peru, together with most of the other American states, had abolished slavery, thus terminating the cheap labour supply from Africa. In the 1850s, Peru sought to tap that rich source of labour bursting out of over-populated and impoverished China. Huge clipper ships each brought more than 500 coolies to work on the plantations, as domestic servants, and in the mines of Peru. The British interests in China, newly won through political connivance, conspired to terminate Peru's even slight poaching on Victorian interests in Asia. As a result of a blockade, Peruvian merchants could no longer dock at Chinese ports, and the Peruvians were left with the problem of keeping up with the ever-growing need for menial labourers in their developing economy.

A Dubliner called Byrne, who had had a chequered career in Natal, New Caledonia, and Australia, came to Peru in 1861 with a proposal. According to him, the islands of the Pacific were heavily populated with Polynesians wanting to migrate as colonists to labour in the rich fields of Peru. Byrne stressed that many of these peoples were pagan and would welcome release from the boredom of their lives and the tyranny of their rulers. He persuaded the not-very-sceptical Peruvian government to grant him a licence to recruit indentured servants, under short-term contract. It would be these contracts, not the people, he assured his credulous official contacts, that would be sold to the highest bidder at public auction.

Bryne himself died during the first recruiting voyage in 1862, but the profits his surviving partners made at the dock-side auctions impressed several Lima businessmen, and within a few weeks a number of ships had been outfitted for the trade,

FIGURE **2.1.**

A not-very-flattering portrayal by La Pérouse of the Rapanui character. From La Pérouse, Jean François de Galoup. 1798. A Voyage Round the World ... London: J. Johnson. Vol. 2.

FIGURE **2.2.**

Alphonse Pinart portrays the Rapanui royal court, with Jean Baptiste Dutrou-Bornier's widow as queen. From A. Pinart, 1878, "Voyage à l'île de pâques," *La Tour du monde* Vol. 36: 225–240.

complete with parcels of paper contracts in Spanish and "Polynesian." The fields for the recruitment were those islands of Oceania that were not fully under the protection of a European power and closest to the Peruvian port of Callao, from where most of the ships set sail. About a third of the ships eventually contracted for this trade made directly for Rapanui, one of the nearest islands.

In early December, summer begins on Rapanui. It is a warm and moist time, full of light and promise. On such a summer day, a number of ships weighed anchor at various points around Rapanui's coast, the captains all with common goals but different ideas of achieving them.

One captain made a straightforward appeal to the Islanders he contacted, explaining as best as he could that he was willing to take Rapanui to Peru, though the details of the contract were probably lost in the rough translation. Another captain, despite observing the first's calm recruitment, chose a more direct method. He had heard that Rapanui would swim out to visiting ships to trade and so he waited until some came to his vessel. He entertained his guests with food and strong drink, sending one or two back to bring out more. When he had his hold full, he ordered the hatches closed and lashed secure, setting sail with his surprised and agonized human cargo for the Peruvian labour markets.

By the time nearly a dozen ships had arrived, the supply of Rapanui who genuinely volunteered to leave their land, and those gullible enough to be entrapped into doing so, had been exhausted. There were still other captains who wished to take part in the lucrative trade, and their methods were much more severe. The remaining ships cooperated to send a landing party ashore at Hangaroa, the Long Bay that bore Cook's name on European charts. Upon landing, the armed invaders showered handfuls of trinkets onto the sand and rocks, and were able to see where the victims came from and how many there were. As soon as enough Rapanui had gathered on the quiet beach, the sailors threw nets over their prey or roped and tied their captives, tossing them like trussed-up sheep, an eyewitness remembered, into their boats. Then, not satisfied with the initial numbers, men chased the Rapanui and their women and children, until they either caught their captives or murdered them in the pursuit.

The Rapanui warriors, who had so eagerly fought one another, struggled bitterly against the invaders. Although the outsiders had superior weapons, the warriors attacked and slew as avidly as they did during their intertribal battles. One warrior, who succeeded in disarming a Peruvian, chased him with raised spear across the landscape, but since, unlike the slavers, the Rapanui would not kill an assailant from the back, eventually the Peruvian escaped, unharmed. A few other Peruvians in the attack fell to expertly aimed spears.

The outsiders' devastating firepower allowed them to subdue Rapanui opposition, and within a few weeks the place became a staging area where Polynesians collected from other islands were brought. Though this terrible period lasted only a few months, the Rapanui learned three lessons that they would never forget and which still influence their attitudes to outsiders over a century later.

Firstly, they learned that outsiders could overwhelm their little Island and dominate the few people living there. The only alternative to submission was death, a choice taken by dozens of Rapanui in the decade following the raids in 1862–63. Secondly, they met other Pacific Islanders, both as fellow prisoners on board ships and as co-labourers in the elegant homes and sweltering coastal hacienda fields of Peru. From this encounter, the first since Mahine's visit almost a century before, they acquired for the first time a name for themselves: Rapanui, people of the big island. Polynesians, fellow victims of the trade, provided the name. Rapanui learned that there were islands near and far to be explored and peoples similar to themselves to learn to know. Though some few Rapanui had visited other places, they had always returned, never really having seriously considered any alternative to their home Island.

Finally, Rapanui learned what they had suspected before—that the ways of the outsider could be understood, and that if they observed closely and carefully the actions of the foreigner, no matter how strange or ridiculous they might seem, those actions could be mastered and turned to their own benefit in subsequent dealings. Slavery, if it is short-term, which it was for the Rapanui, can give a perspective on life unlike any other experience.

Because of the concerted December 1862 attacks on the Island, all Rapanui experienced the shock and the naked horror of the brief Peruvian episode. Of the 1,500 or so Islanders taken from Rapanui by force, there were only a dozen or so survivors, of whom all but a few had been returned to their Island by August 1863. French opposition to Peru's support of the then-raging Mexican insurrection lay behind the cessation of the Peruvian trade. Even though Government offices and leading newspapers in Lima had questioned the importation of so-called Polynesian colonists almost from the beginning of the short episode, it was French insistence which led to the cancellation of the import licences and the rounding up of the Polynesian survivors, including the Rapanui ones, for transport back to their widely scattered islands. And it was a French ship that carried the Rapanui and other Polynesians home.

In September 1862, there had called at Rapanui a French warship, whose main mission was to make a show of strength along the South American coast to remind the new Latin republics that it wished to replace Spain as the major force in the area. Captain Lejeune stopped at Rapanui mostly out of curiosity, but also to check and report on the situation there. His relations with the Rapanui were amicable, and the usual vegetable and fruit trading took place, though the group with whom he traded produced only a solitary chicken, more as a token of friendship than as part of the victualling trade. Lejeune was impressed with the Rapanui, but he was more impressed that the Island, no matter how inconsequential it might be, was still without a European protector. As a first step in that process, he visited a French missionary order in Valparaiso, the Sacred Hearts Congregation house. In addition to work in Chile, the missionary fathers were also in charge of spreading the Christian message in Eastern Oceania, an area of great strategic interest to the French then, as now.

Captain Lejeune's suggestion to the French Catholic missionaries that they should establish themselves on Rapanui was made a few months after the end of the Peruvian raids. A few more months after Lejeune's advice, Frenchman Eugène Eyraud, a motor mechanic turned soul saver, landed on the Island. A zealous lay member of the Sacred Hearts Congregation who had made his fortune in South America, Eyraud came equipped with the accoutrements of a proper mission, even a bell, and a degree of naïveté that permitted the local Rapanui to strip him in a few months' time of all his possessions, including his clothes. Eyraud's avaricious Rapanui sponsor, the warrior Torometi, clearly enjoyed degrading an outsider within a few months of his own humiliation at the hands of marauding Peruvians, as Eugène Eyraud later reported in his letters to his Ecclesiastical Superiors. Lay Brother Eugène was led about by Torometi like the paschal lamb, as the Frenchman tried to understand the rising and eventually falling fortunes of his erstwhile captor. Only the visit of some fellow missionaries saved the ailing Eyraud, after a nine-month ordeal.

At about that time, a highly spirited priest of the Sacred Hearts order, Father Hippolyte Roussel, was removed from his position at Mangareva, due to his strident pronouncements and inconvenient actions which interfered with French trading in the area. When the recovered Lay Brother Eugène insisted that he be allowed to return to Rapanui, the Sacred Hearts took the opportunity to exile Roussel to that mission as well. In order to keep an eye on the situation, they subsequently sent another priest, Father Gaspar Zumbohm, and a lay assistant, Théodule Escolan. After the first failure with the solitary Eyraud, deserted by his fearful Polynesian assistants, the Sacred Hearts launched a full scale four-man mission in 1866.

By this time, four years after the Peruvian raids, smallpox, respiratory ailments, measles, and other diseases caught in Peru were affecting the whole Island. There were now just over 1,000 people left. The departure and death of so many persons had left Rapanui in chaos. With day-to-day wants being uppermost in people's minds, the longer-term fishing or farming activities declined in the uncertain times. Though by the mid-1860s less vegetable, fruit, and fish production was needed than in earlier, more populous times, the food the missionaries brought with them provided an added incentive for the mass conversions that took place. In exchange for the Rapanui saying some strange sounds and performing some peculiar actions, the missionaries would give food, shelter, and medicines. After some months, it became clear that these new resident outsiders could call on ships to provide them with more supplies. Moreover, the missionaries brought with them ideas for local food production and effective instruments for caring for the new crops. The fishermen too were satisfied, for the outsiders gave of their supplies of articles for shore fishing, in exchange for conversion. In common with other Evangelists elsewhere in Polynesia, the missionaries pursued a stategy of sustaining both the material and spiritual needs of their struggling flock.

Rapanui sought to reassure the powerful foreigners of their confidence by mimicking whatever they did. One built a European-style bed, while another constructed a copy of Eyraud's house. Others wore the European clothes they had obtained, especially for church services.

Though Brother Eugène had landed at Hanga o Hoonu, in Hotuiti territory, Torometi persuaded the missionaries to establish their headquarters at Hangaroa, on his Tu'uaro land. Torometi used the missionaries skillfully, even convincing them that they should move their first mission inland, building it on the site of a large Tu'uaro meeting house. The Church, Torometi wanted it to be quite clear, was firmly in Tu'uaro hands. Eyraud must have recalled that during his captivity with Torometi, that ambitious warlord had been thrown out of Hangaroa and ingloriously stripped of his power. Now, with the Church building on Torometi's land, his triumphant return was displayed to all.

Another factor comes into the Rapanui story in the person of a former officer in the Crimean Army, Jean Baptiste Onèsime Dutrou-Bornier. The man with the splendid name and equally splendid demeanour had first come to Rapanui to deliver the French missionaries in 1866. Only a few years later, Bornier had lost all his money and his fine ship, and was seeking to anchor his borrowed scruffy little yacht at Hangaroa, his only crewman an aging Danish carpenter who called himself Christian Smith. Zumbohm welcomed Bornier, but Roussel was more reticent with the new arrival, in spite of the fact that the French captain was ostensibly in partnership with the Church for the development of Rapanui.

Torometi was not slow to recognize the advantages to be gained by leaving the missionaries and taking up with the more audacious Bornier. Quite apart from practical value, the two men must have recognized in each other a closeness in temperament and attitude which they could not find amongst the more pious and reserved missionaries. On the practical side, however, Bornier had managed to salvage a cannon and some rifles from his tiny yacht before it sank in a storm shortly after his arrival.

Torometi's alliance with Bornier threw Torometi's old antagonist Roma, also a convert, further into the missionary camp, while the conversions and the deaths from disease continued. Eyraud himself fell ill with tuberculosis and died. Zumbohm, who had tried to arouse interest in Chile to finance the work of the mission, felt his health was deteriorating. Torometi and Roma renewed their old conflicts, and their outsider sponsors, Bornier and Roussel respectively, were drawn into conflict.

There ensued three years of conflict, beginning with Eyraud's death in 1868, with Bornier taking potshots at Roussel with the salvaged cannon, Roma attacking Torometi. The reciprocal feuds of old returned.

Though Torometi's reasons for fighting Roma were traditional, based in clan enmities that went back centuries, his methods, owing to Dutrou-Bornier's armoury, were modern. One of Roma's allies, a chief called Mini, challenged Torometi to a duel on the plain at Mataveri. Mini arrived with his lance, ready to face his adversary, practising the complicated and agile dodging he would use to avoid Torometi's weapon. But, to Mini's surprise, Torometi did not carry the familiar obsidian-topped Rapanui spear, but bore instead a curious staff of carved wood and shiny metal. Mini threw his lance first, waiting until he thought Torometi was off guard, but in spite of the heavy object he held in his arms, Torometi easily avoided the throw. Then Mini waited to see when Torometi would throw his projectile, rocking, poised to dart this way or that when the peculiar object left his adversary's hands. Instead, Torometi put the staff to his shoulder and pointed it at Mini. Mini's last memory must have been a flash of powder and light, and sharp pain as the bullet found his heart.

Zumbohm eventually left Rapanui a sick man, leaving Escolan and Roussel to fend for themselves against the growing numbers of Torometi's band who all camped around the house Bornier had built for himself a few kilometres from the missionary settlement. Just as Torometi had once convinced the missionaries to put up their church over the Tu'uaro meeting place, he influenced Bornier to build his rival camp at Mataveri. The Mataveri plain, with its Orongo associations, the yearly choosing of a king, the centre for Rapanui island-wide activity, was a perfect setting, from both Torometi's and Bornier's point of view.

Eventually, Bornier succeeded in his campaign against Roussel, and the priest who had been branded a troublemaker in Mangareva was told to leave Rapanui as well. He did so with a few hundred Rapanui accompanying him, bound for Mangareva and labouring jobs in the Catholic mission's coco-palm plantations.

By the end of 1872, Dutrou-Bornier felt sufficiently in command of the Rapanui situation to leave the Island, stopping briefly in Papeete on his way to Australia. There he obtained over 400 merino sheep, some probably from the Darling Downs and the area around the Namoi River Valley in New South Wales. When this flock arrived on Rapanui to supplement the sparse stock first imported by the missionaries from Chile a few years earlier, the Islanders called these Namoi sheep "Mamoe," the name they still use to refer to all sheep. Dutrou-Bornier, with Torometi as his first lieutenant, allowed the missionary buildings to fall into disrepair, and maintained his homestead at Mataveri. Under local influence, Bornier established a

Polynesian monarchy with his Rapanui wife, Koreto, as queen and himself as prince regent and father of her two daughters.

Bornier sent his two little girls to stay with his other wife in Tahiti for a time, but the two princesses-who-never-would-be were to spend the rest of their lives on Rapanui, as the founders of two important Rapanui families. The Orongo returned as a yearly practice, and Rapanui under Torometi's control returned to their homesteads in Tu'uaro territory at Anakena and Hotuiti land at Vaihu, where they built small, European-style huts. Once banned by the missionaries, the carvings in wood were again produced and traded to the ships who plied between Rapanui and Tahiti, 3,500 kilometres (2,187 miles) away. Bornier settled down to his pseudo-regal plantation life, causing the wreck of the occasional non-French ship when he needed more building materials for his ranch's outbuildings.

Koreta was a strong-willed woman and insisted upon the few remaining Rapanui paying suitable deference to her, which caused occasional conflict. In 1876, Dutrou-Bornier commissioned a dress to be made for his queen, and when the result was not to her liking, the French captain picked up his rifle and paid a stern visit to the house of the seamstress. But she was not there. Instead, warned of Bornier's anger, three Rapanui waited inside the hut, with the low traditional door. As the foreign king poked his head inside to inflict the punishment he had intended, three of his Islander subjects attacked and killed him in the ensuing struggle.

A nervous few months passed until a French ship called, asking the whereabouts of Bornier. The French tricolour flew over the Mataveri property and the visitor, fashionable Alphonse Pinart, was informed that Bornier had died when he fell from his horse drunk, a story that still appears in some books.

The Tahitian-English-French consortium that had been Bornier's partner in the Rapanui ranch sent one of their number, Alexander Salmon, to take Bornier's place. Shortly after that, Torometi, his sponsor gone, left for the richer fields of Tahiti, where he died in the Rapanui settlement in Pamata'i sometime in the 1880s. For more than a decade, frequent ships, French and foreign, took regular shipments of trade goods to Rapanui, and wool and meat from there to Papeete. Like the deceased Bornier, Salmon was sympathetic to local beliefs and encouraged the figure-carving as valuable and useful for trade. Instead of living at Mataveri, Salmon preferred the Hotuiti Vaihu base, where traditional clothing prevailed except when foreign ships came to call. Father Hippolyte Roussel, with only a few of his Rapanui converts in Mangareva, still maintained an interest in developments on the Island and returned from time to time to baptize, to marry former parishioners, and to report on affairs to his superiors. The remaining, dwindling population on the Island applied several times for annexation to France, so as to be closer to their relatives working in Tahiti. A delegation of family heads went to Papeete in the early 1880s where they obtained the promise of a gendarme for their little Island. Although Rapanui supplied several tonnes of meat and agricultural products to Tahitian markets, the French Government in Paris never took a serious interest in acquiring the Island.

The first Chilean ship to stop at Rapanui was the Colo-Colo in 1837, on the way to Sydney with a political prisoner. Nearly four decades passed before another official Chilean visit transpired, in 1870; officers of the vessel prepared a detailed map of the European-style settlements. During the brief Chilean visit, Bornier gratefully received a barrel of gunpowder from ship's stores, and at least one Rapanui obtained an 1851 souvenir peso, which turned up in archaeological digs in 1980. It was not long after that that the Chilean government, with strong support from British phosphate interests, declared war on Peru and Bolivia in one of many skirmishes between the Latin American states over the redefinition of old colonial borders. Chile had been the Cinderella colony of Spain, denigrated as rough and worthless, denied the favoured position of her northern neighbour. In the aftermath of the ferocious War of the Pacific, Chile's navy had on paper the largest number of warships in the Pacific, and her desire to acquire other symbols of world-power status grew. Unfortunately for Chile, most of the inhabited islands of the South Pacific had been claimed by the end of the War of the Pacific, except for nearby Rapanui.

An ambitious naval officer, Captain Policarpo Toro Hurta-do, with hopes of a private and profitable plantation on Rapanui, urged the Chilean government to acquire the rejected French colony from the Tahiti-based company that ran it, promising for his country the glory of empire that figured so large in 19th-century nation-state ambition. It was land only he had in mind, for by 1877 the population had been reduced to a mere 110. In 1888, with a flag-raising ceremony of annexation, Rapanui formally became a part of Chile, as it is still today.

The parents of some of the older people in the population today were alive to witness the missionary and commercial exploitation of Rapanui in the late 19th century. If you ask modern Rapanui to tell you about *matamu'a,* to cast their minds back to the past, they will not tell you about Dutrou-Bornier, Torometi, the impetuous Roussel, or the kindly Eyraud. They will recount instead their scant knowledge of their heritage when their ancestors raised memorial monoliths or gathered yearly at Orongo to watch young men risk life and limb for an egg at Easter. Like adherents of some ecstatic religious cult, the Rapanui were born again in the last century, and the bases for association, for love and hate, come from events over the last seven generations—the decades during which a handful of conquered but clever individuals formed the Rapanui of today.

NOTE

1. This material derives from my archive research in Chile, Peru, France, Tahiti and Italy, as well as from background on international events from Glen Barclay's *A History of the Pacific from the Stone Age to the Present* (London: Sidgwick and Jackson, 1978) and K. R. Howe's *Where the Waves Fall: A New South Seas Islands History from First Settlement to Colonial Rule* (Honolulu: University of Hawai'i Press, 1979).

CHAPTER 3

THE ECOLOGY OF AINU
AUTONOMY AND DEPENDENCE

Brett L. Walker

Trade and other forms of contact with Japanese sparked the changes in Ainu society that provided the dangerous kindling for the outbreak of Shakushain's War. Powerful chiefdoms such as the Hae and Shibuchari, who shared a common border along the upper section of the Shibuchari River, fought sporadically over access to animals for subsistence, ritual, and trade. In the midst of the fighting, Matsumae generals understood that their trade embargo in Ezo remained the single most effective means to bring the defiant Shakushain to his knees; and as reported by Maki Tadaemon, the embargo had left groups around Yoichi on the verge of starvation at the conclusion of the conflict. If Shakushain's War exposed the tears in Ainu autonomy that existed even in the late 1660s, the aftermath of the war enlarged the tears, as the rapid construction of trading posts throughout the late 17th century made Ainu even more dependent on these posts for their livelihood. Throughout Matsumae's tenure as overseer of the trade with Ainu, threats to halt trade remained the most effective method to wield influence over even the most powerful chiefs. When the shogunate dispatched officials to investigate the "secret" Russian trade in the 1780s, Matsumae officials warned Ainu elders that if they spoke openly about the trade with shogunal officials, the elders would be gouged to death with spears; but equally damaging, at least from the perspective of Ainu communities, was the threat that Matsumae would stop dispatching trade ships. It appears that with Japanese goods so readily available, Ainu became reliant on imported grains and fabrics to feed and clothe their families; and other merchandise became tied to Ainu political hierarchies, perceptions of personal wealth, and ritual life. Subsequently, at the same time that Ainu came to depend on and draw personal prestige from trade goods, we will see later that they overexploited animals and fisheries that were critical to their survival and were needed to pay for imports.

AINU SUBSISTENCE PRACTICE AND DEPENDENCY

Any analysis of Ainu dependency must begin with a brief discussion of the term "dependency" as it is used in this study. Richard White applies dependency theory to the history of three North American Indian nations in his signal work, *The Roots of Dependency.* He identifies social changes that occurred in the Choctaw, Pawnee, and Navajo nations as a result of trade with Europeans. He argues that dependency among Native Americans meant that people "who had once been able to feed and clothe themselves with some security became unable to do so. Environments that had once easily sustained Native American populations underwent increasing degradation as familiar resources could not support the peoples who depended on them."[1]

White concludes that the cultural and economic impact of the market economy, more than any other single force, destroyed Native American subsistence systems and undermined their autonomy. The "productive systems" of these peoples, he notes, were "geared toward subsistence rather than the market," and as Native Americans overextended hunting to meet market demands, they became dependent on Europeans for their survival.[2] He cautions, however, that dependency should not be viewed as simply an economic or material condition. Instead, because Native Americans projected their relationship with the environment through their own cultural lens, dependency also meant deep and, ultimately, fatal cultural and political changes among Native American nations.

Ainu subsistence practice and material culture underwent a similar transformation in the 17th and 18th centuries. Matsumae vassals, under the trade-fief system, built trading posts in the most potentially lucrative parts of Ezochi, strategically choosing watersheds, coastal streams, bays, and other places near Ainu communities. At these sites they gradually commodified local fauna—that is, they identified what White calls the "animals of enterprise," resources upon which Ainu subsistence and social autonomy had depended for centuries, but which would now serve the growing market economy in Japan.[3] Consequently, Ainu productive systems changed, and the purpose of hunting and fishing became the acquisition of the political power and personal prestige that animal skins bought at trading posts. These changes were accompanied by shifts in deeper sentiments about killing animals. In time, deer and salmon, critical to Ainu survival, became overhunted and over-fished. Pressure from hunting, combined with other environmental factors such as pestilence and hard weather, drove game from habitual feeding grounds. Ainu became dependent on goods acquired in trade to supplement their weakening subsistence system as the salmon and deer, which had once fed and clothed their communities, were exported to satisfy new Ainu wants, as well as commercial demand in Japan.[4]

Historically, the distribution of animal life on the island known today as Hokkaido was shaped by regional plant and climatic diversity, and so, therefore, was the distribution of Matsumae trading posts in the 17th and 18th centuries. Generally speaking, the western section of Hokkaido receives heavy snowfall in the winter, whereas the eastern section receives a comparatively moderate blanket. Such animals as deer, brown bear, marten, red fox, and the Steller's sea eagle, all important products in trade, migrated to eastern Ezo every winter in search of food.[5] There, Ainu hunters trapped and shot them for their hides and feathers.

Trade records note that with the exception of posts located at Sya in the north, and on the lower section of the Ishikari River, where "Ainu brought animal skins down from the headwaters," furs and feathers were not major trade items at the other 26 posts in western Ezo. Posts there were almost exclusively for fisheries. Posts east of Lake Shikotsu, however, handled a variety of pelts, feathers, and other goods, as well as fish products.[6] The Steller's sea eagle, for example, which bred on the coasts of the Okhotsk Sea as far north as the Kamchatka Peninsula and then migrated to the inland marshes near Kusuri (present-day Kushiro) to winter, was a valuable trade commodity because Japan's warrior elite used its feathers, called *maba,* as fletching on their arrows.[7] Although there was some trade in eagle feathers on Sakhalin Island, most of them moved through posts at Kusuri, Akkeshi, and Kiitappu, all in eastern Ezo.[8]

The type and distribution of natural resources in Ezo shaped Matsumae's economy in other ways as well. Sakakura Genjirō, an official from a Japanese mining house, pointed out that Matsumae's economy differed radically from that of other early-modern domains. For example, the Matsumae family did not encourage wetland rice cultivation, as other warrior houses did. Sakakura explained that this was not because of poor land quality but because rice cultivation would have interrupted harvesting of the more lucrative fisheries. He remarked that most settlers in Wajinchi devoted the majority of their time to herring and salmon.[9] Matsumae vassals, however, collected their stipends from trading with Ainu, much as vassals from Tsushima domain survived on trade with Korea.

Ainu subsistence, as well, was shaped by the distinctive landscape of Ezo. No two Ainu communities undertook exactly the same subsistence activity, so it is important to explore the political and environmental factors that determined inter-community variation. Although Ainu today sometimes use the term *Aynu-mosir,* "human land," to harken back to a day when Ezo was the "last free land of the Ainu,"[10] the term, however appealing, belies the linguistic regionalism and political disunity that actually prevailed in Ezo. Kaiho Mineo argues that the Ainu of the early Tokugawa years can be divided into five broad political spheres united under figures called "greater generals" *(sōtaishō)* in the Japanese sources: (1) the Shumukuru (Ainu, Sarunkur) group, inhabiting the region roughly between Niikappu and Mukawa; (2) the Menashikuru (Ainu, Menas-kur) group, located between Shizunai and Urakawa; (3) the Ishikari group, inhabiting the Ishikari plain; (4) the Uchiura group, inhabiting the region between Shirikishinai and Otoshibe; and (5) the Sōya group of northern Ezo.[11] Kaiho draws almost exclusively on political and social dissimilarities when demarcating these spheres, and his divisions correspond to those identified by Kono Hiromichi. Kono, who conducted studies of Ainu burial rituals in the 1930s, divided Hokkaido Ainu into spheres that closely resemble Kaiho's.[12]

However, even more central than abstract political spheres in shaping Ainu identity were patrilineal political alignments called *petiwor,* or river-based chiefdoms, which were composed of several villages situated along major watersheds or coastal rivers and their tributaries. These Ainu chiefdoms were basically spatial units demarcated by the boundaries of such subsistence practices as hunting, fishing, and plant gathering. Inhabitants of a particular *petiwor* also linked their identity to a powerful *sine itokpa,* or a patrilineal household, with a single-male ancestral symbol such as markings on an arrow shaft; and this household served as the political center of the chiefdom.[13] In any given chiefdom, moreover, Ainu had self-declared rights to exploit resources within that productive space. These rights were articulated and sanctioned metaphysically rather than economically or politically, and chiefdom borders were authenticated by a sacred relationship that Ainu groups cultivated with local *kamuy,* or gods, which largely took animal forms.

Ainu viewed the natural environment of Ezo as a sacred space teeming with *kamuy* in the form of animals, plants, fish, and even contagions. To kill an animal to feed and clothe one's family was to free the *kamuy* from its ephemeral temporal guise, a process that involved the active participation of the animal and that was construed by Ainu as a spiritual act which legitimized their place in the natural landscape. Only worthy hunters killed game (see figure 3.1.). Gestures of atonement for animal slaughter, which took the form of sacred acts directed at animals and fish, appeared both in the hunt and later in ceremony. In the most idealistic sense, animals were often seen as willing participants in the kill. Drawing on Ainu folklore, for example, Honda Katsuichi emphasizes this point through a fictional Ainu orator, or *ekashi,* who transports us into the mind of the bear god. "Even the highest-ranked gods must visit the land of the *ainu* [humans] every few years," the bear god explains. "They don't visit just any *ainu,* of course, but they pick one who's skilled at making *inau* [ceremonial fetishes] and is good-natured."[14]

In Honda's story, having found such a worthy Ainu, the bear god describes his encounter with the Ainu hunter: "[I] wandered out purposefully to be seen by him, whereupon he swiftly hid behind a tree and put an arrow to his bow as he waited for me. Pretending not to notice, I passed by him. The twang of the bowstring sounded, and the god of the arrow pierced me. As I heard the bowstring sound two or three times more, I lost consciousness." The hunter then brings the large bear back to his *kotan,* where "songs and dances were performed," and the bear is struck by the dancing of a youth. Exposing Ainu attitudes about the kill, the bear explains, "I again received many gifts and was sent back to the land of the gods, but still

FIGURE 3.1

Ainu hunting a bear. Ainu folklore often stressed that only virtuous hunters, those who had high moral character and conducted rituals aimed at the myriad deities, were able to kill game such as brown bear. It was, suggests this folklore, the bear god that willingly made itself available to hunters of such worthy character. Ainu hunted these larger animals with handheld bows, or *caniku,* using poison arrows called *surkuay. Tōkai yawa* [Night talk from eastern Ezo]. Courtesy of the Resource Collection for Northern Studies, Hokkaido University Library.

remained in the dark about the youth. I went down to Ainu Moshir repeatedly in order to be shot by an arrow and invited to the *kotan* so that I could find out about him and see more of his mesmerizing dances."[15] Ainu hunters killed these animal-gods, in other words, because they chose to be killed. James Serpell, writing of hunting peoples in general, makes this point as well. He explains that the "successful hunter achieves his goal, not primarily through practical knowledge or skill, but rather by virtue of his respectful attitudes and behavior toward the quarry." Only then, Serpell continues, "will the animals consider him worthy of the gift of meat and allow themselves to be killed."[16] These observations, for the most part, hold true for Ainu as well, as highlighted by the above ethnographic account.

The identities of local Ainu groups, furthermore, were taken from these river-based chiefdoms. Ainu from the Saru River were known—and knew themselves—as Sarunkur, "people of the Saru River" (the term *kur* means "people"). The strong ties to the region around the Shibuchari River felt by both the Shibuchari and Hae

Ainu prior to Shakushain's War stand out as an example of local identity. Sources such as the *Tsugaru ittoshi* specifically referred to the two groups involved in the war as the Menashikuru (Shibuchari) and the Haekuru (Hae), suggesting that they had forged local identities that they had communicated to Japanese. So does a later instance observed by Matsuura Takeshirō, a shogunal official. He noted that in eastern Ezo, where competition over resources was most acute, chiefdoms even erected boundary poles to demarcate their territorial base.[17] Most of these river-based chiefdoms appear initially to have been self-sustaining, under normal circumstances providing the salmon and deer necessary to feed and clothe their inhabitants.[18]

Hunting was critical to the survival of all Ainu chiefdoms, and they divided deer- and bear-hunting into spring and autumn tasks. The autumn deer hunt, called *yuk iramante,* played a particularly valuable role in Ainu subsistence because dried venison butchered in the autumn sustained them throughout the winter months.[19] Excellent hunters, Ainu used a variety of methods to kill deer, bear, and small game.

FIGURE 3.2

A spring-bow trap. Ainu hunters used these traps, called *kuari* or *amappo,* to kill the more crafty fur-bearing animals such as the northern fox. The skins of these animals were traded with Japanese at trading posts for rice, tobacco, saké, and other goods. *Ezoto kikan* [Strange sights from Ezo Islands]. Courtesy of the Resource Collection for Northern Studies, Hokkaido University Library.

However, the handheld bow *(caniku)* and the spring-bow trap *(kuari* or *amappo)* remained the weapons of choice until the Meiji government prohibited their use and modified deer-hunting regulations throughout Hokkaido in the 1870s (see figure 3.2).[20] Ainu hunters equipped the spring-bow trap with bamboo arrowheads laced with an aconite poison *(surkuay),* using it in coordination with a deer fence built along game trails to steer deer toward the loaded traps.[21]

FIGURE 3.3

Ainu fishing for salmon, the "divine fish," with a *marep,* a traditional harpoon-like instrument. *Ezoto kikan* [Strange sights from Ezo Islands]. Courtesy of the Resource Collection for Northern Studies, Hokkaido University Library.

Also critical to Ainu subsistence were the watersheds and coastal rivers of Ezo. In the summer and autumn months they filled with spawning trout and salmon, providing a variety of fish that were inseparably tied to the survival and ritual life of all river-based Ainu chiefdoms. In the summer, Ainu fished for diadromous trout *(icaniw* or *icanuy;* trout that migrated between salt and fresh waters), undertaking no major hunting trips that might divert their energies. Similarly, salmon—which Ainu believed to be *kamuy-cep,* the "divine fish"—began moving upstream in large numbers in the autumn to spawn. Ainu fished for salmon and trout using nets worked from small boats *(yasya)* and basket traps *(uray)* placed in holding waters. They also hunted from small huts *(oruncise)* using a *marep,* a harpoon-like instrument with a hook at the end (see figure 3.3).[22]

Of course, these fish and game, which were most important to Ainu survival and ritual, never stayed in one location; and chiefdom boundaries tended to be elastic or overlap to accommodate game migration. When spawning salmon first entered major rivers such as the Tokachi or Saru in eastern Ezo, for example, many Ainu from chiefdoms upstream would travel down to the mouth of the river, seeking permission from local elders to fish salmon fresh from the ocean. Later, as the salmon approached their upstream spawning beds, Ainu from chiefdoms near the mouth of these same rivers might travel upstream to fish salmon there. Chiefdoms negotiated access to these resources. It was also at these fluid and poorly defined boundaries where the rights to resources were sometimes disputed, and chiefdom wars, such as that between the Shibuchari and Hae Ainu, erupted when animals or fish became scarce or when pressure for trade increased. Trading posts further aggravated these border relations by increasing the value of the resources that lay within chiefdom boundaries.

EARLY MINING ACTIVITY AND ENVIRONMENTAL DEGRADATION IN EZO

Early on, Matsumae economic activity began to disrupt Ainu subsistence practice. Shortly after its investiture with exclusive rights to trade with Ainu, the Matsumae family sought to diversify the kinds of resources it exploited in Ezochi. In 1604, as noted, the shogunal official Honda Masanobu spoke with Matsumae Yoshihiro about the possibility of mining gold in Ezo. By 1617, gold miners, using placer techniques, had begun extracting gold from streams in Sotsuko and Ōsawa on the Oshima Peninsula, and in 1620, the Matsumae lord, Kinhiro, presented one hundred *ryō* in gold, which Japanese had extracted from these sites, as a gift to shōgun Tokugawa Hidetada. At that time, the Matsumae lord received approval from shogunal officials Doi Toshikatsu, a senior councillor, and Aoyama Tadatoshi to continue opening new mining sites in Ezo.[23] By then, Matsumae's gold-mining operations and salmon fisheries were starting to disrupt Ainu seasonal fishing in eastern Ezo, placing new pressure on chiefdom boundaries and Ainu-Japanese relations.

Under the direction of domainal officials Kakizaki Hiroshige and Satō Kaemon, Fukuyama Castle intensified placer mining, moving deeper into Ezochi. By 1628, miners were extracting large amounts of gold from the headwaters of the Shiriuchi River in western Ezo. Only three years later, they were also extracting gold from Shimakomaki, also in western Ezo, and by 1633, they had moved into the Shibuchari and Kenomai Rivers in eastern Ezo. By 1635, miners had taken gold from streams in Tokachi and Unbetsu (near Samani), in the Hidaka region of eastern Ezo, and from Kunnui and the headwaters of the Yubari River.[24] It was at one of these mining camps that Bunshiro worked, and there he fostered the strong ties to Onibishi that so frustrated and, ultimately, angered Shakushain, helping to spark Shakushain's War.

The 17th century also witnessed the expansion of mining in Japan. One reason was that precious metals—gold, silver, and copper—were the major Japanese export commodities in the early Tokugawa years. Facilitating both the expansion of the mining industry and the exploitation of these valuable resources were technological innovations in excavation, drainage, surveying, and smelting.[25] In fact, foreign trade "speeded the pace of innovation by increasing the demand first for silver and later for gold and copper."[26] The Matsumae family used a variety of techniques to extract gold from Wajinchi and, later, Ezochi; and most techniques involved redirecting the river's current to flush out or expose metal deposits.[27]

In Japan, as elsewhere, such placer mining techniques had the potential to devastate rivers and local fisheries. While in Wajinchi, Portuguese missionary Diego Carvalho observed some local mining operations:

Their way of extracting gold from these mines is as follows. When they have decided on the mountain range in which, according to experts, there ought to be gold, friends and acquaintances get together and unite in a body purchase from the *tono* [lord] of Matsumae so many *ells* [one *ell* is about forty-five inches] of one of the rivers which flow through the said range, for so many bars of gold, and they must needs pay these bars whether they find gold or not. And when a great number of such groups come to the river, they divert the flow of water along a different course and then dig into the sand which remains, until they reach the living stone and rock beneath the river bed. And in the sand lodged in the rents and fissures of the rock is found gold as fine as beach gravel.[28]

Tawara Hiromi, pointing to the impact of this process, argues that altering the flow of streams and depositing large quantities of sediment in the water likely disrupted migrating salmon and destroyed spawning beds.[29] In 1724, for example, merchants reported that more than 200 Ainu had starved to death in the Ishikari region because of poor salmon runs. That same year, moreover, widespread starvation was reported in the Lake Shikotsu area.[30]

Indeed, one Ainu *yukar,* or epic poem, from the Hidaka region suggests that gold mining—under the auspices of Bunshiro, who, as mentioned, oversaw the Japanese camp established along the Shibuchari River—sparked Shakushain's War.[31] Bunshiro and his miners had badly churned up the Shibuchari River, preventing salmon from ascending the river to spawn. Local Ainu from Peppana, Ichipu, and Rupeshipe, all in the Shibuchari area, found themselves with a dangerously limited supply of fish for the coming winter. Ainu chiefs protested but were treacherously murdered. The *yukar* indicates that when Shakushain heard this, he launched an attack against Japanese, killing hundreds, many of them miners.[32] No doubt this story oversimplifies the origins of the conflict, but it is known that Shakushain's attitude toward Japanese miners, who disrupted his streams and allied themselves with Onibishi, was less than congenial. It is important to remember that he had burned Bunshiro's house to the ground. Matsumae's financial needs had thus already had an impact on Ainu living in the early 17th century, weakening their subsistence practice through environmental degradation. Whether the Hidaka poem accurately describes events leading up to Shakushain's War is less important than the fact that poor salmon runs were clearly disastrous for Ainu.

Gold mining, however, was not the only Japanese enterprise that degraded salmon fisheries. In 1670, Maki Tadaemon, the Hirosaki domain spy who had clandestinely entered Ezochi to gather information, made stops at Horomoi, Oshoro, and Nomanai and spoke with local Ainu elders.[33] He directly solicited reports from elders as far north as Rishiri and Sōya, in northern Ezo, about the causes of Shakushain's War. Kannishikoru, the elder from the Shirifuka region, complained that Japanese merchants in search of salmon had recently entered Ezochi in large numbers. He explained that "they cast huge nets in the rivers and the salmon that they catch are all taken to markets in Kamigata [Kyoto and vicinity] for sale."[34] Kannishikoru also noted that Ainu had approached Matsumae officials, pleading that if they took all the salmon, Ainu would be unable to feed themselves. Officials answered by beating them and accusing them of being greedy. The officials explained to Kannishikoru that these rivers were now trade fiefs *(chi-gyo-sho),* which must have surprised Kannishikoru, who considered himself chief of Shirifuka.[35]

GRAIN IN AINU SUBSISTENCE AND DEPENDENCY

The regional disappearance of resources such as salmon was not the only result of Matsumae's economic activity; trade proved a double-edged sword for most Ainu. At the same time that trade provided Ainu with the impetus to increase their hunting and fishing activity, it also introduced Japanese grain, which began to supplement their diet, further nurturing dependency. With the intensification of trade with Japanese, the importance of Japanese grains in the Ainu diet appears to have increased markedly.[36] Matsumae Norihiro, for example, wrote to Edo senior councillors in 1715 that Ainu predominantly subsisted on bear, herring, whale, fur seal, and a variety of fisheries. He also included rice among common Ainu foods, noting that with the exception of millet and lily grass, Ainu raised few grains but ate a substantial amount of rice acquired in trade. He remarked that they were also extremely fond of tobacco and saké.[37]

Yamamoto Tadashi argues that one reason 18th-century Ainu ate so much rice was that Fukuyama Castle prohibited them from raising their own grains. Pointing to archaeological evidence from the Usujiri site in Minamikayabe, he speculates that Ainu had long cultivated simple grains but that the Japanese prohibited them from raising traditional crops, as well as rice.[38] With rice and saké being lucrative export products in domainal trade, Matsumae officials used local prohibitions to nurture Ainu dependency on Japanese cereals and saké, thus bolstering activity at trading posts. In 1786, shogunal official Matsumoto Hidemochi recorded that Matsumae lords prohibited Ainu from raising grain. One of the explanations given was that Matsumae's "financial circumstances" necessitated the prohibition. And around 1790, Mogami Tokunai, another shōgunal official, wrote that the local regulations of Fukuyama Castle prohibited Japanese from bringing seeds, for rice or any other grain, into Ezochi. He remarked that because of these prohibitions, "Ainu do not understand the way to cultivate grains, and would not even know a rice field if they saw one." This was why, he concluded, erroneously it appears, "they eat only fish and animal flesh."[39] Maintaining the vitality of Matsumae's trading posts required that trade regulations be aimed at fostering demand for Japanese goods. It was clear to the domain's officials that the demand for Japanese grain was central to their survival in the early-modern polity and to commercial expansion into Ezochi.

During the same 1780s investigation that produced Matsumoto Hidemochi's comments, Satō Genrokurō, a shogunal official, wrote that at one point Ainu from the upper section of the Ishikari River had successfully cultivated a plot of rice, but when Fukuyama Castle caught wind of the enterprise, Matsumae officials were dispatched, and they ripped up the seedlings and forced the Ainu involved to offer amends. On another occasion, Satō was asked by Shonko, a chief from eastern Ezo, for seeds and information on how to cultivate them. He explained that Matsumae regulations prohibited Ainu from learning how to cultivate these important crops.[40] It is unlikely that Shōnko received any seeds, but there was no shortage of rice being shipped to Ezo, both for trade and for consumption by Japanese in Wajinchi. A shogunal inspector was informed in 1761 that 40,291 *koku* of rice entered Ezo from Japan.[41] In 1788, only 27 years later, Mogami recorded that the Matsumae family imported 66,700 *koku* of Morioka, Hirosaki, Sendai, Echigo, Sakata, Shirakawa, and Shi-bata rice. Of this total, Matsumae vassals used 10,000 *koku* for trade (5,000 *koku* in eastern Ezo and 5,000 *koku* in western Ezo).[42]

A second explanation for agriculture's role in the development of Ainu dependency has to do with the gender dynamics of Ainu productive systems. Tessa Morris-Suzuki argues that there were actually two types of farming in Ainu communities: dog farming and small-scale shifting cultivation. Dog farming was largely confined to Sakhalin Ainu, who raised dogs for hunting, sled hauling, companionship, and food.[43] In shifting cultivation, crops such as sorghum, millet, beans, barley, and some vegetables were cared for largely by women in the summer months. Women collected wild plants as well. The notion that Ainu ate only flesh, Morris-Suzuki submits, is part of a deeply rooted intellectual misconception. If Ainu are in fact the descendants of the Epi-Jōmon culture, or even the slightly later Yayoi and Kofun cultures (200–650 C.E.), that would make their ancestors participants in the earliest forms of "Japanese" agricultural society. She continues that when Ainu women, the backbone of Ainu agriculture, left their plots to work in nearby fisheries, their community's subsistence system weakened as a result. Thus, agriculture, although small-scale compared to some Japanese standards, was a crucial component in the emergence of Ainu dependency.[44]

With declines in game supplies, prohibitions against cultivating grain or even importing seeds into Ezochi, and changes in the gender dynamics of community agriculture, Ainu became increasingly dependent on rice acquired in trade. Matsumae's rice and yeast *(koji)* were essential ingredients in making saké, which in the 17th century became an ever-present feature of Ainu rituals and daily life. These prohibitions were aimed at preserving, or even creating, Ainu demand for Japanese products. To what degree Ainu actually became dependent on Japanese grain is in truth impossible to determine. Most likely, grain never constituted a large enough portion of the Ainu diet to seriously undermine their ability to subsist. But Japanese prohibitions such as these expose both the Matsumae reliance on trade and officials' halfhearted attempt to organize a conscious policy geared toward engendering dependency. Matsumae officials nurtured Ainu dependency with strict regulations because they believed that their own economic survival, and political autonomy in Ezo, were contingent upon it.

AINU EXPORTS TO JAPAN
HUNTED COMMODITIES

Prior to the early 1620s, trade between Ainu and Japanese was conducted only at Fukuyama (see figure 3.4). Once a year different Ainu groups traveled to Fukuyama Castle in small Ainu crafts called *nawatojibune* in Japanese to trade with merchants and Matsumae lords. While in Fukuyama, the traders stayed in temporary huts *(marugoya)* built along the beaches.[45] These huts, which Ainu traders built just outside of Fukuyama, highlighted the temporary character of this trade, with Ainu traveling long distances for a limited season of exchange. Although the volume of this trade was modest, it brought into the castle town many of the goods that Japanese later exported via trading posts.

However, after Shakushain's War, Matsumae leaders expanded trade by distributing trade fiefs, strategically placing them along coastal rivers in Ezochi. The locus of trade, now the trading post, was thus brought closer to traditional Ainu hunting and fishing grounds. This change laid the foundation for the rise of the market

FIGURE 3.4

Archaeological remains from the old port at Matsumae (Fukuyama). The land mass visible in the distance is Honshu Island as seen from southern Hokkaido.

culture that surrounded the trading post and helped engender Ainu dependency. Unlike in the early Fukuyama exchange, trade schedules now were, of necessity, coordinated with Ainu seasonal hunting and fishing, and commerce was now more closely synchronized with the rhythms of Ainu subsistence practice and ritual life. Many Japanese goods were readily available at these posts and were integrated into Ainu ritual and domestic life. From this point forward, Ainu subsistence practice functioned less and less independently of Japanese economic concerns in Ezo.

Satō Genrokurō recorded that in the northwest, the Matsumae trading post at Sōya was opened up in the 1680s; and in the east, Akkeshi was opened up in the 1640s, Kiitappu in the late 17th century, and Kunashir Island in the 1750s. He noted that Matsumae used these posts exclusively for trade with Ainu.[46] By the late 18th century such merchants as Hidaya Kytibei, who contracted out trading posts in the east, had transformed some trading posts from crude shacks to virtual markets, offering traders a variety of services ranging from lodging to transportation.[47]

Satō wrote that Fukuyama Castle had originally regulated trade with Japan proper through the customs houses, or *okinokuchi bugyō*, permitting trade in Ezo only once a year. However, as merchants opened up branch shops *(demise)* in such ports as Esashi and Hakodate, they began bypassing the houses and trading directly in Ezochi. When Satō questioned Matsumae vassals as to why they permitted merchants to bypass the houses, they responded evasively; merchants who did this were in "special ships" *(negai-bune)*, they argued, regulated by officials in Matsumae, Hakodate, and Esashi.[48] Leveling what became a common attack on the situation in Wajinchi, Satō argued that the Matsumae family was blurring the social distinction between merchants and warriors, one of the hallmarks of the Confucian-inspired authorizing strategy of the early-modern regime. He noted that "in Matsumae, what vassals do and what merchants do is, of course, the same thing." Domain elder Matsumae Kenmotsu, he explained, "does not have his own store, but on his trade fief he does basically the same thing that merchants do." Even the town magistrate. Kudo Heizaemon, collected his income from a nearby trading post.[49] This blurring of the line between warrior and merchant became a major bone of contention for those who wanted the Edo shogunate to take control of Ezo. They argued that domain vassals myopically concerned with buying and selling were hardly in a position to properly govern the northern boundary.

The reliance on trade, as well as the fuzzy distinction between warrior and merchant, existed further south as well, especially in Tsushima domain. In the early 17th century, Tsushima had received rights *(kayaku)* to control foreign trade with Korea, and the shogunate encouraged Tsushima-Korea relations thereafter, lest the domain come to Edo looking for financial aid during a trade slump. Profits from trade became a substantial portion of the revenues for Tsushima and its vassals, and even as late as the 19th century, the domain imported Korean beans, carrots, cotton, and rice for domain consumption and for vassal stipends.[50] Further south, inhabitants of Satsuma domain improved their lifestyles through profits from trade with China via the Ryukyu Kingdom.[51] Not only rice stipends, then, but also trade were central to supporting the vassals of Tsushima and Satsuma.

In Ezo, cooperation between warriors and merchants seems to have had more complex socio-economic repercussions than in the far south and to have transformed the fundamental nature of trade. Matsumae vassals became so indebted to merchants, who advanced them on credit the goods and grain that they traded in Ezochi, that their trade fiefs became essentially "pawned lands" to Japanese merchants, according to Satō Genrokurō. He noted that as Matsumae creditors, merchants were given a "free hand" to shape trade and that the trading posts became permanent marketplaces *(akinaigoya)*, where merchants freely exploited the Ainu in year-round trade.[52] By the mid-18th century, Matsumae finances relied on vassals' successfully securing credit by contracting out their trade fiefs to merchants from Japan. This trend not only led to an increase in the volume of trade but also fundamentally altered its character. The trading post, where these merchants set up shop, now became a local monopoly, playing a role analogous to that of Fukuyama in the 1620s. By the late 18th century, some trade fiefs in eastern Ezo—Akkeshi, for example, which had by that time been contracted out by retainer Ohara Kamegoro to Hidaya Kyubei—included not just the trading post itself but also travel inns, storehouses, shrines built for the fox god and other Buddhist and Shinto deities, guard posts, and even horse stables.[53] In 1799, the trading post at Kiitappu kept 40 horses, largely used for personnel transport.[54]

The existence of large, permanent trading posts along the rivers and watersheds allowed Ainu to quickly trade animal skins and fish products (which normally would have been used to feed and clothe their communities) for rice, tobacco, saké, and other Japanese items; and this trade sometimes created new scarcities. Moreover, the hunt, which had once dramatized the spiritual relationship between Ainu chiefdoms and their local environment, and the *kamuy* that lived there, took on more-commercial connotations. Although this transformation in Ainu productive patterns occurred from at least the mid-17th century onward, there are several accounts from the 19th century that illustrate the trend particularly well.

In the mid-19th century, Ōuchi Yoan, an Edo physician, observed that Ainu hunted and fished not simply to feed and clothe themselves but to accumulate animal skins and other products for trade with Japanese. He remarked that as a result of this trade, animals had become "hunted commodities" *(shubutsu)*—a notion similar to White's "animals of enterprise"—that is, products valued not for their spiritual presence, immediate usefulness, or worth in small interchiefdom exchange, but for the price they brought when traded with Japanese merchants. Ōuchi wrote, "Now, the Ainu, if the winter fishing months end, tour the deep mountain recesses to seize hibernating bears or deer, fox, river otter, marten, eagles, and other animals, as well as seal and sea lion that come out on the beach. This becomes their livelihood. These goods are brought to the trading post and traded for rice, saké, tobacco, cotton, and needles and thread. This is called taking "hunted commodities."[55] In 1838, Kunitomo Zen'an, from Mito domain, noted that when not working in fisheries, Ainu traveled into the mountains to hunt animals for their skins. They then traded these pelts for Japanese goods, including saké and grain. By the 1830s, in fact, Ainu hunted largely for the purpose of killing animals for trade, and had significantly less time for more productive forms of subsistence-related activity.[56]

By the 17th and 18th centuries, a wide variety of goods were clearly being traded in Ezo, but the types of products gradually changed over time as certain items accrued greater value in Japanese and Ainu societies. In the early trade between Ainu and Japanese, items tended to be those with cultural capital, such as animal skins that could be given as gifts in Edo. Precious metals such as copper remained conspicuously absent from the Ainu-Japanese trade, unlike other foreign trading in Japan.[57] Rice and saké were standard items traded by Japanese, but they also provided tobacco, salt, yeast, iron pots and kettles, thread, large knives *(debabocho)*, needles, used utensils and tools, used clothing, dye, cotton, hemp cloth and other fabrics, lacquerware *(nurimono),* gold and silver lacquer works *(makie),* various iron tools, and small swords *(makiri).*[58] As Kaiho Mineo points out, an investigation of the types of goods traded at different times throughout the 17th and 18th centuries reveals the growing place of metal products in Ainu domestic life and ritual. Because the Ainu did not manufacture their own iron products, the increased use of metal items contributed to their growing dependency, even as it led to decreased production of native earthenware goods. Thus, during the 1611–21 period Ainu received goods such as rice, clothing, yeast, saké, and some iron eating utensils, whereas between 1621 and 1739 such iron products as axes, sickles, hatchets, kettles, ceremonial swords, and pipes dominated their acquisitions (see figure 3.5).[59]

FIGURE 3.5

The inside of an Ainu home. The large amount of Japanese-manufactured clothing, lacquerware, and iron goods inside the home illustrates how Japanese items had become integrated into Ainu domestic and ritual life. *Ezo fuzokuzu* [Illustrations of Ainu customs]. Courtesy of the Resource Collection for Northern Studies, Hokkaido University Library.

Security considerations played a modest role in determining the types of goods exchanged at trading posts. Under Lord Yoshihiro, domainal officials had frequently traded weapons and armor with Ainu, but the practice petered out with Lord Kinhiro, who ruled between 1617 and 1641.[60] The exact reason for this policy change remains unclear, but Matsumae leaders likely realized that arming the Ainu threatened their own military superiority in Ezo. It was also at about this time that affairs heated up between the Shibuchari and Hae Ainu. Nonetheless, Ainu continued to possess weaponry. These weapons, however, were rarely used for military purposes. Instead, most Ainu regarded them as treasures *(ikor)*. Furukawa Koshōken, for example, remarked in 1788 that along with sword hilts and sheaths, Japanese long swords *(tachi,* or *tannep-ikor* in Ainu) were abundant in Ezo and were considered extremely valuable.[61] However, as a result of the above-mentioned policy change, Ainu began to look for new ways of obtaining these highly valued goods. Indeed, trade restrictions had been one complaint of Haukase and the Ishikari Ainu in the aftermath of Shakushain's War.

In the early 17th century, Ainu mostly offered fish products and animal skins. By 1739, however, over 25 kinds of products were commonly traded, including pharmaceuticals and exotic clothing from China.[62] The products that Ainu presented for trade changed over time, but they can be divided into four broadly defined categories: (1) animal and bird products, (2) pharmaceuticals and plant products, including kelp, (3) fisheries yield, and (4) imported goods from the Eurasian continent or the North Pacific.

The most common animal and bird products traded in Ezo were live hawks, eagle feathers, animal skins, marine mammal products, cranes, and geese, both alive and dead. Pharmaceuticals included such medicines as *takeri,* bear gallbladders, *ikema (Cynanchum caudatum), eburiko (Fomitopsis officinalis),* and *okurikankiri* (the crawfish shell and stomach area, which is enriched with calcium, carbonic acid, and phosphoric acid). Plant products included shiitake mushrooms, lumber, black lichen, a great variety of kelp, *atsushi (attus* in Ainu; a fabric made from elm bark), and *shinanawa (harkika;* rope made from elm bark). Fisheries yield included everything from large-scale salmon and herring catches to the somewhat smaller, although no less important, sea cucumber and abalone trade. Other common fisheries were salmon, herring, dried shark *(hoshizame),* dried codfish *(hidara),* trout, *kasube* fish, dried abalone *(shiraboshi awabi),* boiled and dried sea cucumber *(iriko),* and skewered shellfish *(kushigai).* Goods imported via Sakhalin Island included a variety of products manufactured by the Chinese and other continental peoples: colored beads *(mushinosudama* and *aodama),* bronze medallions, Ezo silks *(nishiki* and *jittoku),* Chinese cottons, some Russian goods, and various ornaments and other knick-knacks.[63]

In essence, the diverse goods that came from the foreign lands of Ezo and beyond found two clienteles. Some goods were prized as gifts by the Japanese ruling elite, and others carried much broader market value in cities like Osaka and Edo. The 13 tail feathers from the Steller's sea eagle could not be found in Japan, nor could skins from the Ezo brown bear. Even Ezo deer differed from their Japanese relatives. Similarly, textile products obtained in trade on Sakhalin, such as *jittoku* and *nishiki,* were frequently higher in quality than the silks imported through Nagasaki, because they were part of the official Chinese dynastic trade. These goods proved valuable as cultural capital in the form of gifts at official levels.

BALED GOODS

The *tawaramono,* or baled-goods, trade, traditionally a state-sponsored activity over-seen by the Edo shogunate because of its Nagasaki connection, remains among the best-documented commercial activities in Ezo and serves as a lucid example of how business was conducted at trading posts. As Hezutsu Tosaku noted in 1784, *tawaramono* comprised items such as dried sea cucumber, dried abalone, and Shinori kelp. They were harvested and assembled in Ezo and then shipped to Nagasaki, where they were used in the official China trade.[64] By the beginning of the 18th century, in fact, *tawaramono* and other exports such as copper had almost replaced silver in the Nagasaki trade with China.[65] Later, under senior councillor Tanuma Okitsugu, the shogunate extended licenses to merchants in Osaka and Edo to bring these goods from Ezo to the southern foreign entrepot, and then took a percentage of the profits for itself.[66]

The scale of Ezo's *tawaramono* exports was substantial. In 1788, merchants Abuya Mohei and Abuya Senpachi remarked in a note sent to their Osaka associates that 100,000 *kin* (about 132,000 pounds) of dried sea cucumber and abalone and 3,000 *kokume* (about 134,400 gallons) of Shinori kelp had been shipped to Nagasaki that year, despite the fact that "these products had become scarce." This same note records that the total licensing fees *(unjōkin)* paid to the Matsumae family for that year were 400 *ryō* in gold. In light of the growing cost of obtaining sea cucumber and abalone from Ainu, added Mohei and Senpachi, they were requesting additional cash.[67] Two other merchants, Horaiya Chobei and Otsuya Buzaemon, noted in 1788 that their total purchase of dried sea cucumber and abalone came to 8,948 *ryō* for that year.[68]

Ainu were integral in the *tawaramono* trade. Kushihara Seiho wrote in the 1790s that on a "lucky day," one net from an Ainu boat *(ibune)* took 120 to 130 live sea cucumber and that the total daily catch was about 2,000 per Ainu. The fishermen brought their catch to a fishery hut, where a Japanese manager counted them in the Ainu language. The manager grabbed five sea cucumber, and the Ainu said *shineppu* (one). In handfuls of five, the sea cucumber were counted: *toppu* (two), *reppu* (three), *inuppu* (four), and so on to 10 handfuls. The manager then made one of the five strokes of the Chinese ideograph *shō* in his notebook. When he completed one *shō,* representing 250 sea cucumber, he brushed a black stripe on the arm of the Ainu trader. For each mark on the arm, a trader received one cup of saké at the trading post, an incentive to gather more dried sea cucumber for the Nagasaki trade. For two *shō*, or 500 sea cucumber, the Ainu received one *tawara* of rice (about four gallons).[69] (One might speculate that the arm marks served as a visual reminder of Japanese superiority over the Ainu, a dehumanizing sign that placed Ainu in a subordinate position to their merchant counterparts. Indeed, tattooing carried great symbolic value in Ainu society.)

Kushihara noted that near Sōya a total of about 300 boats (400 Ainu traders) worked the northern coasts for sea cucumber. Kushihara, a mathematician by training, estimated that if each boat took 400 sea cucumber, then about 120,000 were taken in one day. Because there were 12,000 sea cucumber in one *tawaramono*, about 300 bales were put together in one month. Kushihara noted that merchants took the dried sea cucumber caught in Sōya to Matsumae, where the Nagasaki *tawaramono gakari,* the shogunal official who oversaw the *tawaramono* trade, standardized purchase rates.[70]

Kushihara observed that Ainu traded according to two basic systems: the seasonal credit system *(kashi tsukeoki)* and direct exchange *(genkin koeki)*. In the seasonal credit system, Ainu purchased items such as fishing gear, sea cucumber nets, saké, rice, and clothing from the trading post on credit. The trading-post manager recorded credit-related information in his notebook, expecting Ainu to repay their debts with dried sea cucumber the following season.[71] Managers recorded the date, the product traded, the amount, and the name of the Ainu trader. They also noted whether the trading post had any outstanding loans to Ainu.[72] Moreover, merchants standardized local exchange rates in terms of bales of rice. Of the seasonal credit system, a shogunal inspector noted in 1717 that 61 trading posts permitted Ainu to trade on credit, without bringing actual "harvests." Ainu later brought their eagle feathers, deer pelts, or salmon and traded them directly with Japanese merchants.[73]

In direct exchange, Ainu brought sea cucumber to the trading post and exchanged them directly for Japanese goods. Kushihara observed that all an Ainu had to do was bring 100 dried sea cucumber to the trading post and say that he wanted *aburashake,* and in return he received three cups of saké. If the Ainu wanted tobacco, he asked for *tanbako* and traded 150 dried sea cucumber for one bundle of tobacco. For lacquerware cups, he asked for *yayakan,* and so on.[74] Not surprisingly, trade proved lucrative for Ainu living in areas with abundant resources. At trading posts in the east, for example, a high-quality sea otter pelt or the tail feathers from a sea eagle were traded at an extremely high premium, bringing in several bales of rice and yeast, barrels of saké, and numerous bundles of tobacco.[75] The trading post had become, in this sense, a bustling market, which shaped the seasonal rhythms of Ainu hunting and fishing.

The main difference between the two trading systems was the exchange rate. Kushihara noted that Ainu who traded in small quantities by direct exchange were at a disadvantage, whereas the seasonal credit system was more equitable. For Ainu, the seasonal credit system was clearly the better deal. If the 300 *tawaramono* that could be put together in one month by Sōya Ainu were traded by direct exchange, rather than by the seasonal credit system, Ainu stood to lose 26 *koku* of rice.[76] Like some rural money-lending in Japan, which allowed peasant entrepreneurs to gain access to needed capital, the seasonal credit system also allowed Ainu of limited means to get involved in the lucrative sea cucumber trade.[77]

CONCLUSION

With trading posts situated near Ainu communities, the acquisition and use of Japanese goods became integrated into the very fabric of Ainu society. The emergence of a market culture, moreover, symbolized by the "hunted commodities" Ainu hunters and trappers brought to posts, rapidly transformed the productive rhythms of Ainu life: trade became a part of Ainu daily habits and subsistence practice. The trade, as this article has shown, grew from a small-scale exchange at Fukuyama to a broader trade system interwoven into a complex web of vassal stipends, the shogunal-sponsored Nagasaki *tawaramono* trade, and merchant interests in Ezo. As we have seen, Matsumae officials even attempted to nurture Ainu demand for rice by prohibiting the importation of seed into Ezochi. As vassal trade fiefs became "pawned lands" for powerful merchant interests to run with a "free hand," trade in Ezo intensified and quickly spread to even remote areas in the north and east.

The increased demand for Japanese goods was not, however, fueled solely by Matsumae policy or market growth in Japan but also by changes that occurred in Ainu society as a result of trade. The ever-present trading post facilitated a shift in the value of familiar natural resources; Ainu appreciated resources not simply for their direct utilitarian value but also for the price they brought at the trading post. This trend exposes the changing character of Ainu society and its growing dependency on trade with the Japanese.

NOTES

1. Richard White, *The Roots of Dependency: Subsistence, Environment, and Social Change among the Choctaws, Pawnees, and Navajos* (Lincoln: University of Nebraska Press, 1983), xiv.
2. Ibid., 239.
3. Richard White, "Animals and Enterprise," in *The Oxford History of the American West,* ed. Clyde A. Milner II et al. (New York: Oxford University Press, 1994), 238.
4. Ronald P. Toby, "Both a Borrower and a Lender Be: From Village Moneylender to Rural Banker in the Tempō Era," in *Monumenta Nipponica* 46, no. 4 (winter 1991): 483; and Saitō Osamu, *Puroto kogyoka no jidai: Seid to Nihon no hikakushi* (Tokyo: Hyoronsha, 1985). Although Thomas Smith did not use the term "proto-industrialism" in *The Agrarian Origins of Modern Japan,* as Saitō Osamu argues, Smith was in fact heading in that direction (Saitō Osamu, "Bringing the Covert Structure of the Past to Light," *Journal of Economic History* 49, no. 4 [1989]: 992–9). See Thomas C. Smith, *The Agrarian Origins of Modern Japan* (Stanford: Stanford University Press, 1959; reprint, New York: Atheneum,

1966). See also Kären Wigen, *The Making of a Japanese Periphery, 1750–1920* (Berkeley: University of California Press, 1995), 25–136; and David L. Howell, *Capitalism from Within: Economy, Society, and the State in a Japanese Fishery* (Berkeley: University of California Press, 1995), 1–23. On the protoin-dustrialists, see Anne Walthall, *The Weak Body of a Useless Woman: Matsuo Taseko and the Meiji Restoration* (Chicago: University of Chicago Press, 1998), 38–99; and Edward E. Pratt, *Japan's Proto-Industrial Elite: The Economic Foundations of the Gōnō* (Cambridge: Harvard University Press, 1999).

5. Norihisa Kondo, "Mammal Fauna and Its Distribution in Hokkaidō," in *Biodiversity and Ecology in Northernmost Japan,* ed. Seigo Higashi et al. (Sapporo: Hokkaido University Press, 1993), 83.

6. *Ezo shōko kikigaki* [1739], in MCS, 3:5–12.

7. Teruaki Hino, "Bird Fauna and Its Distribution in Hokkaidō," in *Biodiversity and Ecology in Northernmost Japan,* ed. Seigo Higashi et al. (Sapporo: Hokkaido University Press, 1993), 90–5.

8. *Ezo shōko kikigaki* [1739], in MCS, 3:5–12.

9. Sakakura Genjirō, *Hokkai zuihitsu* [1739], in NSSSS, 4:408.

10. Sannyo-Aino Toyo'oka, "The Future of Humans and the Creation of a Third Philosophy: An Ainu Viewpoint," trans. Takeshi Osanai and Richard Siddle, in *Indigenous Minorities and Education: Australian and Japanese Perspectives of Their Indigenous Peoples, the Ainu, Aborigines, and Torres Strait Islanders,* ed. Noel Loos and Takeshi Osanai (Tokyo: Sanyusha Publishing, 1993), 353.

11. Kaiho Mineo, *Nihon hoppōshi no ronri* (Tokyo: Yuzankaku, 1974), 100.

12. Kono Hiromichi, "Bohyōno keishiki yori mitaru Ainu no shokeitō," *Ezo orai* 4 (August 1931): 101–21; and Utagawa Hiroshi, *Ainu bunka seiritsushi* (Sapporo: Hokkaidō Kikaku Sentā, 1988), 314–6.

13. Takashi Irimoto, "Ainu Territoriality," *Hoppō bunka kenkyū* 21 (1992): 69–71, 78.

14. Honda Katsuichi, *Harukor: An Ainu Woman's Tale,* trans. Kyoko Selden (Berkeley: University of California Press, 2000), 124–8. For the original Japanese, see Honda Katsuichi, *Ainu minzoku* (Tokyo: Asahi Shinbunsha, 1993), 122–5.

15. Honda, *Harukor,* 124–8.

16. James Serpell, *In the Company of Animals: A Study of Human-Animal Relationships* (Cambridge: Cambridge University Press, 1986), 181.

17. Takeshirō noted, for example, that a piece of driftwood marked the border between Yamakoshinai and Abuta chiefdoms (Matsuura Takeshirō, *Shinpan Ezo nisshi: Higashi Ezo nisshi,* ed. Yoshida Tsunekichi [Tokyo: Jiji Tsūshinsha, 1984], 1:41).

18. Hitoshi Watanabe, *The Ainu Ecosystem: Environment and Group Structure* (Tokyo: University of Tokyo Press, 1972), 56, 69–70, 77–8.

19. Inukai Tetsuo, "Hokkaidō no shika to sono kōbō," *Hoppō bunka kenkyū hōkoku* 7 (March 1952): 1–22.

20. SSHS, 2:466; and Kadosaki Masaaki and Inukai Tetsuo, *Higuma: Hokkaidō no shizen* (Sapporo: Hokkaidō Shinbunsha, 1993), 272–352.

21. Deriha Kōji, "Shuryōgu kara mita Hokkaidō Ainu oyobi hokutō ajia shōminzoku no kogata mōhijū shuryō katsudō no imi," in *Kita no rekishi-bunka kōryū kenkū jigyō,* ed. Hokkaidō Kaitaku Kinenkan (Sapporo: Hokkaidō Kaitaku Kinenkan, 1995), 305–30.

22. Watanabe, *The Ainu Ecosystem,* 26–7; and Chiri Mashiho, "Ainu no saké ryō," *Hoppō bunka kenkyū hōkoku* 12 (March 1959): 245–65.

23. *Matsumae nennenki* [1742], in MCS, 1:56–7; and Matsumae Hironaga, *Fukuyama hifii* [1780], in SSHS, 5:30.

24. SSHS, 2:127.

25. Robert Leroy Innes, "The Door Ajar: Japan's Foreign Trade in the Seventeenth Century" (Ph.D. diss., University of Michigan, 1980), 533.

26. Ibid., 543.

27. Yanaga Yoshiko, *Ezo no sakin* (Sapporo: Hokkaido Shuppan Kikaku Senta, 1981), 134–46.

28. Michael Cooper, comp., *They Came to Japan: An Anthology of European Reports on Japan, 1543–1640* (Berkeley: University of California Press, 1965), 235–6; and Diego Carvalho, "Copia de huma [carta] que o Padre Diogo Carvalho me escreveo acerca da missam que fez a Yezo e outras partes" [1620], in *Hoppō tankenki: Genna nenkan ni okeru gaikokujin no Ezo hōkokushō,* ed. Hubert Cieslik

(Tokyo: Yoshikawa Kōbunkan, 1963), 13, 64.

29. Tawara Hiromi, *Hokkaidō no shizen hogo* (Sapporo: Hokkaido Daigaku Tosho Kankōkai, 1979), 66–7.

30. "Kyōhō kyūnen shichigatsu jūrokunichi Edo e Ezojin gashi tsukamatsuri sōrō nitsuki mōshitsukawashi sōrō kakitsuke" [1724], cited in SSHS, 2:301.

31. *Tsugaru ittōshi*, bk. 10 [1731], in SHS, 7:127–8.

32. Tawara, *Hokkaidō no shizen hogo,* 67–8.

33. Asakura Yūko, "Ezo ninshiki no keisei: Toku ni keiki to shite no jōhō o megutte," in *Kita kara no Nihonshi,* ed. Hokkaidō-Tōhoku Kenkyūkai (Tokyo: Sanseidō, 1990), 2:136.

34. *Tsugaru ittōshi,* bk. 10 [1731], in SHS, 7:188.

35. Ibid.

36. Yamamoto Tadashi, *Kinsei Ezochi nōsakumotsu nenpyō* (Sapporo: Hokkaidō Daigaku Tosho Kankōkai, 1996), 111–5. For an interesting look at Ainu agricultural practices in historical perspective, see Tessa Morris-Suzuki, "Creating the Frontier: Border, Identity, and History in Japan's Far North," *East Asian History* 7 (June 1994): 18–23.

37. Matsumae Norihiro, *Shōtoku gonen Matsumae Shima-no-kami sashidashi sōrō kakitsuke* [1715], in SSKS, 134.

38. Yamamoto Tadashi, "Ezo nōkō kinshi kō," *Monbetsu shiritsu kyōdo hakubutsukan hōkoku* 5 (1992): 18. For more complete studies of "Ainu plants," see Fukuoka Itoko, *Ainu shokubutsushi* (Tokyo: Sofukan, 1995); Hayashi Yoshishige, "Ainu no shokuryō shokubutsu saishū," *Hoppō bunka kenkyū* 2 (1967): 157–72; and Hayashi Yoshishige, "Ainu nōgyō no keiei keitai," *Hoppō bunka kenkyū hōkoku* 17 (March 1962): 39–60. See also John Batchelor and Miyabe Kingo, "Ainu Economic Plants," *Transactions of the Asiatic Society of Japan* 21 (1893): 197–240.

39. Mogami Tokunai, *Ezokoku fūzoku ninjō no sata* [1791], in NSSSS, 4:444.

40. *Ezochi ikken* [1784–90], in SHS, 7:87,330,333,341.

41. *Gojunkenshi ōtō mōshiawasesho* [1761], in MCS, 1:406.

42. Mogami Tokunai, *Ezo sōshi betsuroku* [1781–8], in MCS, 3:36.

43. For more on the Ainu relationship with dogs, see Hatakeyama Saburōta, "Hokkaidō no inu ni tsuite no oboegaki: Senshi jidai kaizuka ken to Ainu ken no hikaku," *Hokkaidōshi kenkyū* 1 (December 1973): 41–68.

44. Morris-Suzuki, "Creating the Frontier," 18–21.

45. MCS, 1:559.

46. *Ezochi ikken* [1784–90], in SHS, 7:483.

47. Shirayama Tomomasa, *Matsumae Ezochi bashō ukeoiseido no kenkyū* (Hakodate: Hokkaidō Keizaishi Kenkyūjo, 1961), 1:155–7.

48. *Ezochi ikken* [1784–90], in SHS, 7:335–6.

49. Ibid., 334–5.

50. Maehira Fusaaki, "'Sakoku' Nihon no kaigai bōeki," in *Nihon no kinsei: Sekaishi no naka no kinsei,* ed. Asao Naohiro (Tokyo: Chūō Kōronsha, 1991), 1:159; and Tashiro Kazui, "Bakumatsuki nitchō shibōeki to wakan bōeki shōnin: Yunyū yonhinmoku no torihiki o chūshin ni," in *Tokugawa shakai kara no tenbō,* ed. Hayami Akira et al. (Tokyo: Dōbunkan Shuppan, 1989), 300.

51. Maehira, " 'Sakoku' Nihon no kaigai bōeki," 159.

52. *Ezochi ikken* [1784–90], in SHS, 7:336–7.

53. *Higashi Ezochi kakubasho yōsu taigaigaki* [1808–11], in SHS, 7:577, 544.

54. Ibid., 544. See also Tani Gentan, *Ezo kikō* [1799], ed. Satō Keiji (Tokyo: Asahi Shuppan, 1973), 35. For paintings of trading posts in eastern Ezo, see Tani Gentan, *Ezo kishō zue* [1799], ed. Satō Keiji (Tokyo: Asahi Shuppan, 1973).

55. Ōuchi Yoan, *Tōkai yawa* [1854–59], in HMSS, 5:461.

56. Kunitomo Zen'an, *Hokusui taimon* [1838], RCNS.

57. Innes, "The Door Ajar," 77–243.

58. Mogami Tokunai, *Ezo sōshi betsuroku* [1781–8], in MCS, 3:36–7; *Ezochi ikken* [1784–90], in SHS, 7:301; and Sakakura Genjirō, *Hokkai zuihitsu* [1739], in NSSSS, 4:404.

59. Kaiho Mineo, "Shakushain no tatakai: Ainu shakaishi ni taisuru bakuhansei kokka seiritsu no igi,"

in *Kinsei no shihai taisei to shakai kōzō,* ed. Kitajima Masa-moto (Tokyo:Yoshikawa Kōbunkan, 1983). See also Fukusawa Yuriko, "Ainu Archaeology as Ethnohistory: Iron Technology among the Saru Ainu of Hokkaidō in the Seventeenth Century" (Ph.D. diss., Cambridge University, 1995).

60. Matsumiya Kanzan, *Ezo dan hikki* [1710], in NSSSS, 4:392.
61. Furukawa Koshōken, *Tōyū zakki* [1788], ed. Ōtō Tokihiko (Tokyo:Tōyō Bunko, 1964), 164–6.
62. Kaiho, "Shakushain no tatakai," 48.
63. *Matsumae Ezoki [1717],* in MCS, 1:386; Sakakura Genjirō, *Hokkai zuihitsu* [1739], in NSSSS, 4:404; Matsumiya Kanzan, *Ezo dan hikki* [1710], in NSSSS, 4:392; and *Ezo banashi* [1798], RCNS, or *Ezo Matsumae kenbunki* [1798], RCNS. (This manuscript also appears under the title *Ezo miyage.)* For salmon and herring products, see Murayama Denbei, *Matsumae sanbutsu daigaikan* [1804–17], in *Hokkaidō kyōdo kenkyū shiryō* 6 (December 1960). For a list of animal, fish, and bird products, or the general fauna of Hokkaido, mentioned in pre-1868 manuscripts on Ezo, see Kadosaki Masaaki and Seki Hideshi, "Ezochi ni okeru dōbutsu no bunken-gakuteki kenkyū," *Hokkaidō kaitaku kinenkan chōsa hōkoku* 38 (1999): 96–108.
64. Hezutsu Tōsaku, *Tōyūki* [1784], in NSSSS, 4:429.
65. Innes, "The Door Ajar," 77–243; John W. Hall, "Notes on the Ch'ing Copper Trade with Japan," *Harvard journal of Asiatic Studies* 12 (1949): 456; Kate Wildman Nakai, *Shogunal Politics: Arai Hakuseki and the Premises of Tokugawa Rule* (Cambridge: Harvard University Press, 1988), 108; and Maehira, "'Sakoku' Nihon no kaigai bōeki," 155–6.
66. Harold Bolitho, *Treasures among Men: The Fudai Daimyo in Tokugawa Japan* (New Haven:Yale University Press, 1974), 195–6; and Maehira, "'Sakoku' Nihon no kaigai bōeki," 156.
67. Abuya Mohei and Abuya Senpachi, *Nagasaki tawaramono no ikken: Tenmei hachinen saru jūgatsu Ōsaka omote e sashidasu nari* [1788], in *Hidaya Takekawa-ke monjo,* vol. 9, no. E 7, RCNS.
68. Hōraiya Chūbei and Ōtsuya Buzaemon, *Tenmei hachi saru toshi Matsumae Ezochi mawari tawaramono kaiire daikin ukeharai kanjōchō* [1788], in *Hidaya Takekawa-ke monjo,* vol. 9, no. E 1, RCNS.
69. Kushihara Seihō, *Igen zokuwa* [1792], in NSSSS, 4:491–2.
70. Purchase rates were standardized at 250 *mon* of gold per 1 *kin* per *tawaramono.* At this rate, the 300 *tawaramono* that were put together in one month were worth 1,562 *ryō 2 bu* in gold (ibid.).
71. Ibid., 492–4.
72. *Kiitappu hitsuji no haru uketori nimotsu no bun* [1788], in *Hidaya Takekawa-ke monjo,* vol. 9, no. D 6, RCNS.
73. *Matsumae Ezoki [1717],* in MCS, 1:389.
74. Kushihara Seihō, *Igen zokuwa* [1792], in NSSSS, 4:492–4.
75. Mogami Tokunai, *Ezo sōshi betsuroku* [1781–8], in MCS, 3:28–9.
76. Kushihara Seihō, *Igen zokuwa* [1792], in NSSSS, 4:491–2.
77. Toby, "Both a Borrower and a Lender Be," 486–7.

REFERENCES

UNPUBLISHED DOCUMENTARY SOURCES

Abuya Mohei and Abuya Senpachi. *Nagasaki tawaramono no ikken: Tenmei hachi-nen saru jūgatsu Ōsaka omote e sashidasu nari* [1788]. In *Hidaya Takekawa-ke monjo.* Vol. 9, no. E 7. Resource Collection for Northern Studies, Hokkaido University Library, Sapporo, Hokkaido.

Ezo banashi [1798]. Resource Collection for Northern Studies, Hokkaido University Library, Sapporo, Hokkaido.

Ezo Matsumae kenbunki [1798]. Resource Collection for Northern Studies, Hokkaido University Library, Sapporo, Hokkaidō.

Kiitappu hitsuji no haru uketori nimotsu no bun [1788]. In *Hidaya Takekawa-ke monjo.* Vol. 9, no. D 6. Resource Collection for Northern Studies, Hokkaido University Library, Sapporo, Hokkaido.

PUBLISHED DOCUMENTARY SOURCES

Carvalho, Diogo (Diego). "Copia de huma [carta] que o Padre Diogo Carvalho me escreveo acerca da missam que fez a Yezo e outras partes" [1620]. In *Hoppō tankenki: Genna nenkan ni okeru gaikokujin no Ezo hōkokusho*. Edited by Hubert Cieslik. Tokyo: Yoshikawa Kōbunkan, 1963.

Ezochi ikken [1784–90]. In *Shin Hokkaidōshi*. Vol. 7. Edited by Hokkaidō. Sapporo: Shin Hokkaidōshi Insatsu Shuppan Kyōdō Kigyōtai, 1969.

Ezo shōko kikigaki [1739]. In *Matsumae chōshi*. Vol. 3. Edited by Matsumae Chōshi Henshūshitsu. Hakodate: Daiichi Insatsu, 1979.

Furukawa Koshōken. *Toytt zakki* [1788]. Edited by Ōtō Tokihiko. Tokyo: Tōyō Bunko, 1964.

Gojunkenshi ōtō mōshiawasesho [1761]. In *Matsumae chōshi*. Vol. 3. Edited by Matsumae Chōshi Henshūshitsu. Hakodate: Daiichi Insatsu, 1979.

Hezutsu Tōsaku. *Tōyūki* [1784]. In *Nihon shomin seikatsu shiryō shūsei*. Vol. 4. Edited by Takakura Shin'ichirō. Tokyo: San'ichi Shobō, 1969.

Higashi Ezochi kakubasho yōsu taigaigaki [1808–11]. In *Shin Hokkaidōshi*. Vol. 7. Edited by Hokkaidō. Sapporo: Shin Hokkaidōshi Insatsu Shuppan Kyōdō Kigyōtai, 1969.

Kushihara Seihō. *Igen zokuwa* [1792]. In *Nihon shomin seikatsu shiryō shusei*. Vol. 4. Edited by Takakura Shin'ichirō. Tokyo: San'ichi Shobō, 1969.

Matsumae Ezoki [1717]. In *Matsumae chōshi*. Vol. 1. Edited by Matsumae Chōshi Henshūshitsu. Hakodate: Daiichi Insatsu, 1974.

Matsumae Hironaga. *Fukuyama hifu* [1780]. In *Shinsen Hokkaidōshi*. Vol. 5. Edited by Hokkaidō Chō. Sapporo: Hokkaidō Chō, 1936. Reprint, Osaka: Seibundō, 1991.

Matsumae nennenki [1742]. In *Matsutnae chōshi*. Vol. 1. Edited by Matsumae Chōshi Henshūshitsu. Hakodate: Daiichi Insatsu, 1974.

Matsumae Norihiro. *Shōtoku gonen Matsumae Shima-no-kami sashidashi sōrō kakit-suke* [1715]. In *Saisenkai shiryō*. Edited by Takakura Shin'ichirō. Sapporo: Hokkaidō Shuppan Kikaku Sentā, 1982.

Matsumiya Kanzan. *Ezo dan hikki* [1710]. In *Nihon shomin seikatsu shiryō shūsei*. Vol. 4. Edited by Takakura Shin'ichirō. Tokyo: San'ichi Shobō, 1969.

Matsuura. *Shinpan Ezo nisshi* [1856–8]. 2 vols. Edited by Yoshida Tsunekichi. Tokyo: Jiji Tsūshinsha, 1984.

Mogami Tokunai. *Ezokoku fūzoku ninjō no sata* [1791]. In *Nihon shomin seikatsu shiryō shūsei*. Vol. 4. Edited by Takakura Shin'ichirō. Tokyo: San'ichi Shobō, 1969.

———. *Ezo sōshi betsuroku* [1781–8]. In *Matsumae chōshi*. Vol. 3. Edited by Matsumae Chōshi Henshūshitsu. Hakodate: Daiichi Insatsu, 1979.

Murayama Denbei. *Matsumae sanbutsu daigaikan* [1804–17]. In *Hokkaidō kyōdo kerikyu shiryō* 6 (December 1960): 5–32.

Ōuchi Yoan. *Tokai yawa* [1854–9]. In Hokumon sōsho. Vol. 5. Edited by Ōtomo Kisaku. Tokyo: Hokkō Shobō, 1944.

Sakakura Genjirō. *Hokkai zuihitsu* [1739]. In *Nihon shomin seikatsu shiryō shūsei*. Vol. 4. Edited by Takakura Shin'ichirō. Tokyo: San'ichi Shobō, 1969.

Tani Gentan. *Ezo kishō zue* [1799]. Edited by Satō Keiji. Tokyo: Asahi Shuppan, 1973.

Tsugaru ittōshi. Bk. 10 [1731]. In *Shin Hokkaidōshi.* Vol. 7. Edited by Hokkaidō. Sapporo: Shin Hokkaidōshi Insatsu Shuppan Kyōdō Kigyōtai, 1969.

OTHER SOURCES

Asakura Yūko. 1990. "Ezo ninshiki no keisei: Toku ni keiki to shite no jōhō o megutte." In *Kita kara no Nihonshi.* Vol. 2. Edited by Hokkaidō-Tōhoku Kenkyūkai. Tokyo: Sanseidō.

Batchelor, John, and Miyabe Kingo. 1893. "Ainu Economic Plants." *Transactions of the Asiatic Society of Japan.* 21: 197–240.

Bolitho, Harold. 1974. *Treasures among Men: The Fudai Daimyo in Tokugawa Japan.* New Haven: Yale University Press.

Chiri Mashiho. 1959. "Ainu no sake ryō." *Hoppō bunka kenkyū hōkoku* 14. March: 245–65.

Cooper, Michael, comp. 1965. *They Came to Japan: An Anthology of European Reports on Japan, 1543–1640.* Berkeley: University of California Press.

Deriha Koji. 1995. "Shuryōgu kara mita Hokkaidō Ainu oyobi hokutō ajia shominzoku no kogata mōhijū shuryō katsudō no imi." In *Kita no rekishibunka kōryū kenkyū jigyō.* Edited by Hokkaidō Kaitaku Kinenkan. Sapporo: Hokkaidō Kaitaku Kinenkan.

Fukuoka Itoko. 1995. *Ainu shokubutsushi.* Tokyo: Sōfūkan.

Fukusawa Yuriko. 1995. "Ainu Archaeology as Ethnohistory: Iron Technology among the Saru Ainu of Hokkaidō in the Seventeenth Century." Ph.D. diss., Cambridge University.

Hall, John Whitney. 1949. "Notes on the Ch'ing Copper Trade with Japan." *Harvard Journal of Asiatic Studies* 12: 444–61.

Hatakeyama Saburōta. 1973. "Hokkaidō no inu ni tsuite no oboegaki: Senshi jidai kaizuka ken to Ainu ken no hikaku." *Hokkaidōshi kenkyū* 1. December: 41–68.

Hayashi Yoshishige. 1962. "Ainu nōgyō no keiei keitai." *Hoppō bunka kenkyū hōkoku* 17 March: 39–60.

———. 1967. "Ainu no shokuryō shokubutsu saishū." *Hoppō bunka kenkyū* 2: 157–72.

Hino, Teruaki. 1993. "Bird Fauna and Its Distribution in Hokkaidō." In *Biodiversity and Ecology in Northernmost Japan.* Edited by Seigo Higashi, Akira Osawa, and Kana Kanagawa. Sapporo: Hokkaido University Press.

Honda Katsuichi. 1993. *Ainu minzoku.* Tokyo: Asahi Shinbunsha.

———. *Harukor: An Ainu Woman's Tale.* 2000. Translated by Kyoko Selden. Berkeley: University of California Press.

Howell, David L. 1995. *Capitalism from Within: Economy, Society, and the State in a Japanese Fishery.* Berkeley: University of California Press.

Innes, Robert Leroy. 1980. "The Door Ajar: Japan's Foreign Trade in the Seventeenth Century." Ph.D. diss., University of Michigan.

Inukai Tetsuo. 1952. "Hokkaidō no shika to sono kōbō." *Hoppō bunka kenkyū hōkoku* 7 March: 1–22.

Irimoto, Takashi. 1992. "Ainu Territoriality." *Hoppō bunka kenkyū* 21: 67–81.

Kadosaki Masaaki and Seki Hideshi. 1999. "Ezochi ni okeru dōbutsu no bunkengakuteki kenkyū." *Hokkaidō kaitaku kinenkan chōsa hōkoku* 38: 96–108.

Kadosaki Masaaki and Inukai Tetsuo. 1993. *Higuma: Hokkaidō no shizen.* Sapporo: Hokkaidō Shinbunsha.

Kaiho, Mineo. 1974. *Nihon hoppōshi no ronri*. Tokyo: Yūzankaku.

———. 1983. "Shakushain no tatakai: Ainu shakaishi ni taisuru bakuhansei kokka seiritsu no igi." In *Kinsei no shihai taisei to shakai kōzō*. Edited by Kitajima Masamoto. Tokyo: Yoshikawa Kōbunkan.

Kondo, Norihisa. 1993. "Mammal Fauna and Its Distribution in Hokkaidō." In *Biodiversity and Ecology in Northernmost Japan*. Edited by Seigo Higashi, Akira Osawa, and Kana Kanagawa. Sapporo: Hokkaido University Press.

Kōno Hiromichi. 1931. "Bohyō no keishiki yori mitaru Ainu no shokeitō." *Ezo ōrai* 4 August: 101–21.

Maehira Fusaaki. 1991. "'Sakoku' Nihon no kaigai bōeki." In *Nihon no kinsei: Sekaishi no naka no kinsei*. Vol. 1. Edited by Asao Naohiro. Tokyo: Chūō Koronsha.

Morris-Suzuki, Tessa. 1994. "Creating the Frontier: Border, Identity and History in Japan's Far North." *East Asian History* 7. June: 18–23.

Nakai, Kate Wildman. 1988. *Shogunal Politics: Arai Hakuseki and the Premises of Tokugawa Rule*. Cambridge: Harvard University Press.

Pratt, Edward E. 1999. *Japan's Proto-Industrial Elite: The Economic Foundations of the Gōnō*. Cambridge: Harvard University Press.

Saitō Osamu. 1989. "Bringing the Covert Structure of the Past to Light." *Journal of Economic History* 49, no. 4: 992–99.

———. 1985. *Puroto kōgyōka no jidai: Seiō to Nihon no hikakushi*. Tokyo: Hyōronsha.

Sannyo-Aino Toyo'oka. 1993. "The Future of Humans and the Creation of a Third Philosophy: An Ainu Viewpoint." Translated by Takeshi Osanai and Richard Siddle. In *Indigenous Minorities and Education: Australian and Japanese Perspectives of Their Indigenous Peoples, the Ainu, Aborigines, and Torres Strait Islanders*. Edited by Noel Loos and Takeshi Osanai. Tokyo: Sanyusha Publishing.

Serpell, James. 1986. *In the Company of Animals: A Study of Human-Animal Relationships*. Cambridge: University of Cambridge Press.

Shirayama Tomomasa. 1961. *Matsumae Ezochi basho ukeoiseido no kenkyū*. 2 vols. Hakodate: Hokkaidō Keizaishi kenkyujo.

Smith, Thomas C. 1966. *The Agrarian Origins of Modern Japan*. Stanford: Stanford University Press, 1959. Reprint, New York: Atheneum.

Tashiro Kazui. 1989. "Bakumatsuki nitchō shibōeki to wakan bōeki shōnin: Yunyū yonhin-moku no torihiki o chūshin ni." In *Tokugawa shakai kara no tenbō*. Edited by Hayami Akira, Akimoto Hiroya, Tomobe Ken'ichi, Sugiyama Shinya, and Saitō Osamu. Tokyo: Dōbunkan Shuppan.

Tawara Hiromi. *Hokkaidō no shizen hogo*. Sapporo: Hokkaidō Daigaku Tosho Kankōkai, 1979.

Toby, Ronald P. 1991. "Both a Borrower and a Lender Be: From Village Moneylender to Rural Banker in the Tempō Era." *Monumenta Nipponica* 46, no. 4, Winter: 483–512.

Utagawa Hiroshi. 1988. *Ainu bunka seiritsushi*. Sapporo: Hokkaidō Shuppan Kikaku Sentā.

Walthall, Anne. 1998. *The Weak Body of a Useless Woman: Matsuo Taseko and the Meiji Restoration*. Chicago: University of Chicago Press.

Watanabe, Hitoshi. 1972. *The Ainu Ecosystem: Environment and Group Structure*. Tokyo: University of Tokyo Press.

White, Richard. 1994. "Animals and Enterprise." In *The Oxford History of the American West*. Edited by Clyde A. Milner II, Carol A. O'Conner, and Martha A. Sandweiss. New York: Oxford University Press.

———. 1983. *The Roots of Dependency: Subsistence, Environment, and Social Change among the Choctaws, Pawnees, and Navajos*. Lincoln: University of Nebraska Press.

Wigen, Kären. 1995. *The Making of a Japanese Periphery, 1750–1920*. Berkeley: University of California Press.

Yamamoto Tadashi. 1992. "Ezo nōkō kinshi kō." *Monbetsu shiritsu kyōdo hakubutsukan hōkoku* 5: 18–33.

———. 1996. *Kinsei Ezochi nōsakumotsu nenpyō*. Sapporo: Hokkaidō Daigaku Tosho Kankōkai.

Yanaga Yoshiko. 1981. *Ezo no sakin*. Sapporo: Hokkaidō Shuppan Kikaku Sentā.

CHAPTER 4

HAWAI'I UNDER

NON-HAWAIIAN RULE

Michael Kioni Dudley and Keoni Kealoha Agard

IMMEDIATELY AFTER THE OVERTHROW of the Hawaiian monarchy, the American interests involved in the overthrow appealed to have Hawai'i annexed by the United States. Administration of the outgoing President Harrison processed this request in twelve days and sent a treaty of annexation on to the Senate for approval. However, before it could be passed by the Senate, Grover Cleveland became president. Cleveland withdrew the treaty and arranged for an investigation into the overthrow of the monarchy. On receiving the report of the investigation, he sent a lengthy message to Congress explaining his actions. (Dudley and Agard, pp. 22–3). This reading describes the reaction in Congress to Cleveland's message.

In the middle of December, 1893, just about the time that President Cleveland's "Message" was given to Congress, Lili'uokalani did agree to an amnesty for the members of the provisional government. Minister Willis of the United States took her decision to the Provisional Government and asked if now they would restore the monarchy in accordance with President Cleveland's wishes. The answer was "No." Their argument was that they were now a government themselves, that they had been recognized by America and by other great powers as the government for the Hawaiian Islands, and that they would not allow President Cleveland and the American government to "interfere in the internal affairs of their sovereign nation."[1]

President Cleveland had closed his "Message" by giving Congress control over a solution to the problem. When Congress was pressed for a decision, they opted for inaction. Despite the clear case presented by the President of immoral and illegal wrongdoing by the United States in the setting up of this hollow, non-representative government, now that the situation was so favorable to American interests, Congress conveniently decided they should follow the precepts of international law and not interfere in the "internal affairs" of the "sovereign government" of Hawai'i. The provisional government was allowed to stay in power.

Like Kamehameha III before her, in his experience with Britain, the Queen had depended on the justice of a great nation to restore her throne. Unlike Britain, however, America found greed a stronger passion than justice.

The provisional government began to take steps to establish itself as a permanent government. Sanford Dole, the president, announced an election for delegates to a Constitutional Convention. But, making sure that the new constitution would reflect the goals of the revolutionaries, 19 delegates were appointed by Dole himself, and only 18 were elected. To vote, one had to sign an oath declaring allegiance to the new regime and swearing to oppose any attempt to restore the monarchy. This, of course, prevented most native Hawaiians from voting. Even among the white people, however, voting for delegates was very light.[2]

Qualifications for future voting were even more stringent when the new constitution emerged. Men had to own property, swear allegiance to the Republic and swear to oppose the restoration of the monarchy; they also had to be able to speak, read, and write English, and be able to explain the constitution—which was written in English—to the satisfaction of members of the government.

Once the new constitution was completed, it was time for a vote to adopt it and thus to establish the Republic of Hawai'i. However, as Gavan Daws notes, in the opinion of the provisional government even those few thousand voters who had elected the delegates to write the constitution could not be trusted to endorse it, and so the constitution became law not by plebiscite but by proclamation. When Lili'uokalani intended to establish a new constitution by her own royal proclamation, even though she had the support of two-thirds of the voters, the revolutionaries declared her act to be so criminal that it justified their overthrow of the monarchy. Now, fearing they could not count on the support of even their own backers, these same revolutionaries did what they had overthrown the Queen for threatening to do: they established their own Constitution by proclamation.

"Sanford Dole announced the inauguration of the Republic of Hawai'i and proclaimed himself president on Fourth of July, 1894."[3] The significance of the date was lost on no one.

In that same year the United States Congress repealed the McKinley Act, which had caused the depression and the overthrow of the monarchy. The price support on sugar produced in the United States was removed, a new tariff was placed on sugar from other countries, and Hawaiian sugar was restored to its privileged place in the American market.[4]

AN ANALYSIS OF THE AMERICAN ROLE IN THE OVERTHROW

One must ask why the McKinley Act of 1890 was ever passed. Why would America tax its own economy voluntarily, instituting a huge price support for its domestic sugar while giving up all the import tax money it had been collecting on foreign sugar? The whole thing doesn't seem to make good economic sense. It becomes even more inexplicable when it is seen that passing the Act meant turning America's back on Hawai'i and precipitating a disastrous depression in the islands at a time when the United States had just acquired such a plum—Pearl Harbor—through negotiation of the 1887 sugar treaty with Hawai'i. It is equally puzzling why this disastrous Act was in effect for only four years, and why its provisions were rescinded once the Annexationists were clearly in power and America's eventual possession of Hawai'i was assured.

There is strong evidence to indicate that the principal purpose for putting the sugar provisions of the McKinley Act into law was to topple the Hawaiian monarchy and to bring the islands under American control.

To really understand how America could be so involved—to understand how, over decades, it could have intentionally evolved a plan to engineer the overthrow—one must understand the mood and aspirations of America in the 1800s. Consider carefully the history of America's colonialistic activity. From its earliest years as a nation, America experienced an expansionist fervor. Thomas Jefferson, the writer of the Declaration of Independence and third president of the United States—in a secret deal which Congress knew nothing about until they were asked to pay the bill—doubled the territory of the United States overnight by buying almost one-third of the American continent from the French in the Louisiana Purchase.[5] That was in 1803, 16 years before the American missionaries left for Hawai'i. This is only one example of young America's lust for lands. Between 1810 and 1819, also before the missionaries' departure, America had fought the battle of New Orleans and taken the Spanish-held area west of it; it had also taken all of Florida from the Spanish; and Americans were poised and ready for their 1821 push into Texas.[6]

Were the American missionaries who came to Hawai'i in those years a part of this expansionist movement?

Researching the American Board of Commissioners for Foreign Missions, which sent the missionaries, one finds that besides the spiritual leaders, its principal backers were famous politicians: men at one time governors of Connecticut, New York, and New Hampshire; Congressmen; even a US Secretary of State for Foreign Affairs. Other backers were men who had made fortunes in merchandising and shipping, whose lives centered around expanding American horizons and boundaries.[7] The missionaries were not only sent by this American Mission Board, but also were supported by them and kept in close contact with them.

For America the missionaries would serve as goodwill ambassadors, as listening posts in the Pacific, as opinion shapers, as powerful pro-American influences, and as openers of markets. This is not to say that the missionaries intended to do anything other than sacrifice their lives to save the souls of the heathen Hawaiians, and in the process to give the Hawaiians "better lives." Their ideological colonialism destroyed the Hawaiian nation, however, with their insisting on Western-style private property until they forced the *mahele* into reality, and then their buying up and leasing large tracts of land until they or their children owned or controlled all the major business interests in the islands.

While this was happening in Hawai'i, the American nation was expanding westward and developing the philosophy of "Manifest Destiny" to support its imperialism. As America stretched westward, it found indigenous peoples in its way. What was to happen to them? Early cowboy-and-Indian movies tell the story from the American viewpoint quite accurately. The Americans were a rising people. By contrast, the Indian was necessarily a no-account, a troublemaker, a problem standing in the way. Indians had to be conquered and either moved or wiped out. This was good and necessary. This attitude was not encountered occasionally and by chance as a solution to a specific cowboy-and-Indian problem here or there. Rather, it was the carefully formulated official policy of the US government regarding native Americans: according to the doctrine of "Manifest Destiny," white Americans must fulfill their "Manifest Destiny allotted by Providence" to develop and rule the breadth of the continent. All actions to remove obstacles that stood in their way were therefore morally righteous, including the dispossession and slaughter of Indians.[8]

If the doctrine of "Manifest Destiny" was popular among the masses, it was even more fervidly embraced by those who were making that destiny fact—those in the military and the government.

As the years went on, the value of Hawai'i had become more and more obvious, not only to America, but also to other colonial powers, the British and the French. The Navy and the State Department began to plan ways to secure their ties to the islands.

It is hard to pinpoint the beginning of actual American meddling in the Hawaiian governmental activity. When Kamehameha V died in 1872, Admiral Pennock was sent to Honolulu with the following instructions:

> Go to Honolulu as soon as possible ... and in concert with [Minister Pierce], use all your influence and all proper means to direct and maintain feeling in favor of United States, and at least to secure selection of successor favorable to our interests.[9]

Lunalilo, who was favorable to America, had been elected king before Pennock arrived, and there was no need for America's interference. But aboard the same ship were Major General John M. Schofield, Commander of the US Army Pacific; and Brigadier General B.S. Alexander of the Corps of Engineers, arriving on secret mission for the US government. According to confidential orders from Secretary of War, W.W. Belknap, they were to visit the Hawaiian islands for the purpose of ascertaining the defensive capabilities of the different ports and their commercial facilities, and to examine into any other subjects that may occur to you as desirable, in order to collect all information that would be of service to the country in the event of war with a powerful maritime nation.... It is believed the objects of this visit to the Sandwich Islands will be best accomplished, if your visit is regarded as a pleasure excursion, which may be joined in by your citizen friends.[10]

Schofield and Alexander stayed in Hawai'i two months. Touring the islands, they were shown its lush mountains and valleys and its gorgeous beaches, but their colonialist eyes saw only future militarily strategic bases—one at the only large natural harbour in the northern Pacific. Returning to the US in 1873, they "subsequently prepared a report, made public twenty years later, which emphasized the value of Pearl Harbor and discussed the means of making it available for naval and commercial purposes."[11] Thus began the intense American interest in securing Pearl Harbor.

Hawai'i was interested in securing a reciprocity treaty with the United States. Among other things, such a treaty would greatly help the sugar interests. The American navy tried to secure a foothold in Pearl Harbor during negotiations for the treaty. This caused the negotiations to drag on; King Lunalilo died; and his successor Kalakaua was strongly opposed to cession of the harbour in any way, even leasing. He was successful in holding the admirals at bay. The first Reciprocity Treaty, signed in 1876, did, however, prohibit the Kingdom from leasing or otherwise disposing of any port, harbour, or territory to any power other than America during the treaty period.[12] Senator John T. Morgan of Alabama later wrote about the 1876 treaty, "The Hawaiian treaty was negotiated for the purpose of securing political control of those islands, making them industrially and commercially, a part of the United States."[13]

After the treaty of 1876, America began to take a more active role in guiding the internal politics of Hawai'i. In 1887 when the Hawaiian League and the Honolulu Rifles took over the city and forced Kalākaua to sign the bayonet constitution, the Hawaiian minister to Washington, H.A.P. Carter, although sent there by the king, convinced the Secretary of State to support the revolutionaries against the king. A letter from Carter's son, Charles, to Secretary of State Bayard tells the story:

In June 1887, my father ... came to ... Michigan to attend my graduation ... He was compelled to leave in the midst of the festivities because ... he learned that it was the intention of the United States Government to send the warship Adams to Honolulu to protect the late King Kalakaua and his government from the anticipated Revolution predicted in the then latest dispatches and **he further told me that in consequence of his assurances to you, that the revolution was being conducted by his friends and would be in the best interests of Hawai'i,**

that the orders to [US] Minister Merrill and the warships at Honolulu were not to interfere with those conducting the revolt[14] [Emphasis added.]

Following this move to withold support for the king in the revolution, the United States then pushed for exclusive rights to maintain a coaling station at Pearl Harbor, demanding that this be a part of the second Reciprocity Treaty in 1887.

The US was successful this time. The power of Kalakaua being severely limited by the new Bayonet Constitution, he was forced to sign the treaty of 1887 granting America exclusive use of Pearl Harbor. This right would end, however, when the reciprocity treaty expired.

The Admirals of the American navy were growing in power. It was the eve of their spectacular victories in the Spanish-American War, when Admiral Dewey would take the Philippines. Pearl Harbor had long been recognized as crucial to the Navy in order to promote and maintain American interests in the Pacific. The Congress, bowing to pressure from the Navy, had attempted to make use of Pearl Harbor a precondition for agreement to both the 1876 and the 1887 sugar Reciprocity Treaties. Perhaps the Navy could again use sugar as its tool in securing complete control over Pearl Harbor.

The McKinley Act was convenient. There were very few states producing sugar at that time. Opposition in Congress would not be strong. And the Congressmen from the sugar states could take home to their growers a two cents per pound price support to offset any losses. Such an Act would cause enough major problems in Hawai'i that the Annexationists would have "just cause" to overthrow the Queen. Hawai'i could then be annexed. And Pearl Harbor would then belong forever to the American naval forces.

That is the scenario. Are there additional facts to support it? First of all, the McKinley Act was no surprise when it took effect in 1891. The Hawaiian government had heard talk about it in 1888, within weeks after signing the reciprocity treaty with its lease of Pearl Harbor.[15] It certainly must be seen as strange that the United States government would sign a treaty protecting Hawaiian sugar interests and within a few weeks would be discussing a bill that would cripple it. The question must be asked, "When the United States was negotiating the treaty, did they ever really intend to protect Hawaiian sugar? Or was the treaty just another effort to secure Pearl Harbor for the Navy?"

It seems that after the treaty was signed, when the Navy was not completely happy with the impermanence of what they got, they did decide to continue using the needs of the sugar industry to get more. Congress quickly started debating a bill that would threaten Hawaiian sugar and the Hawaiian economy with disaster, so the State Department would have leverage to push the government of Hawai'i into a permanent pact securing Pearl Harbor. During these next two years, 1888–89, the US Secretary of State, James G. Blaine, attempted to negotiate two treaty proposals with the Hawaiian Minister. Both would have superseded the sugar provisions in the McKinley Act and given all Hawaiian products identical treatment with domestic American products. Both treaties also would have "guaranteed" the independence of the kingdom. This "guaranteeing" would have included a permanent American guard—which would have in effect also guaranteed the Navy permanent use of Pearl Harbor. The first treaty proposal also included "the landing of troops for this purpose if necessary." Although King Kalakaua's white annexationist cabinet urged agreement with both treaties, he realized that the native Hawaiians would be enraged over his making Hawai'i a protectorate of the US, and he refused to sign either.[16] The Reciprocity Treaty granting temporary use of the harbour was as far as he would go. He could not be budged.

If the king would not cooperate, said some, then get rid of the king, and the kingdom along with him. There were forces in the islands who wanted annexation. Give them a true rallying cause for an overthrow: a pain where it would hurt those who could be rallied most—in the pocketbook. The McKinley Act was signed into law by President Harrison in 1891. And the terrible economic depression began.

In 1892, the white annexationist leader, Lorrin Thurston, secretly visited Washington to search for support for Annexation should he and his small band of revolutionaries be able to overthrow the Queen. Thurston's *Memoirs of the Hawaiian Revolution* tell the fascinating story:

Mr. Blaine [the Secretary of State] asked, "Have you talked to anyone else in Washington on this subject?" I answered that I had, mentioning Senator Davis and Mr. Blount.

Mr. Blaine said that he considered the subject of the utmost importance, and continued, "I am somewhat unwell, but I wish you would call on B.F. Tracy, secretary of the navy, and tell him what you have told me, and say to him that I think you should see the President. Do not see Mr. Blount again. I will attend to him. Come to me after you have seen President Harrison." In accordance with the request, I immediately met Secretary Tracy and reported my conversation with Mr. Blaine.

Said Mr. Tracy: "I do not know whether you had better see the President or not. But come with me, and we will learn what he thinks." We went to the White House. Mr. Tracy had me wait in an outer room while he spoke with the President. After about a half-hour, the Secretary reappeared and beckoned me to accompany him outdoors. Then he spoke: "I have explained fully to the President what you have said to me, and have this to say to you: **the President does not think he should see you, but he authorizes me to say to you that, if conditions in Hawai'i**

compel you to act as you have indicated, and you come to Washington with an annexation proposition, you will find an exceedingly sympathetic administration here." That was all I wanted to know.[17] [Emphasis added.]

After Thurston returned home, the economic depression continued to worsen. The American Minister, John L. Stevens, who had been appointed by President Harrison and was privy to all the communications between the President, the Secretary of the Navy, and Thurston, acted as he knew his government at the time wanted him to. Stevens joined with the revolutionaries and plotted their revolution with them, as his letter of March 8, 1892, shows. He called in the American troops when the time came, and he refused to call off the landing of the Marines when the Committee of Safety got cold feet. By doing this, Stevens, the American Minister, forced the revolutionaries to complete the overthrow.

The actions of the American Minister, John L. Stevens, are said by many to be the individual actions of an overzealous minister, working alone and without the consent of the US government. Such claims ignore the reality that Minister John L. Stevens and James C. Blaine, Secretary of State during the Harrison administration, had for 37 years been close friends—sharing the same aspirations and championing the same causes—when Blaine sent him to be American Minister in Hawai'i. As far back as 1854, they had purchased and together edited a newspaper, the *Kennebec Journal*, in Augusta, Maine. Together they had worked hard to promote and develop the Republican party in that state.[18]

Another close friend and political mentor to Stevens, Luther Severance, had been editor of the *Kennebec Journal* for 25 years when in 1850 he was appointed United States Minister to Hawai'i. He served in that post for two years. Severance supported annexation and, along with Blaine, greatly influenced Stevens' views "on the 'manifest destiny' of the United States in the Pacific region."[19]

Over the years, Secretary of State Blaine himself had made no secret of his support for annexation of Hawai'i.[20] In 1881, 10 years before sending Stevens to Hawai'i, he had spoken of the necessity of

drawing the ties of intimate relationship between us and the Hawaiian islands so as to make them practically a part of the American system without derogation of their absolute independence.... If they drift from their independent station it must be toward assimilation and identification with the American system, to which they belong by the operation of natural laws and must belong by the operation of political necessity.[21]

Thus in 1891, when Blaine called upon Stevens, his close friend whom for almost 40 years he had known to share his views and aspirations, and sent him to be

American Minister to Hawai'i, Blaine knew that Stevens could be depended on to accomplish what the Secretary of State and the American President wanted done.[22] As Kuykendall concludes, "Stevens apparently thought it was his mission to see that the island kingdom did not stray from the path of its American destiny."[23]

Given all of these facts, there can be little argument that the United States did condone and support Stevens's activities as he planned and plotted the revolution with the annexationists and then forced the revolutionaries to go through with it.

For far more years than has even been imagined in the century since, America was involved in planning a takeover of Hawai'i—in the 1876 Reciprocity Treaty when America insisted on guarantees that no lease or sale of ports or lands could be made to other governments, in the bayonet revolution when America sided with the revolutionaries and withheld support for the King, in the 1878 Treaty of Reciprocity when America demanded and got exclusive use of Pearl Harbor, in the pressuring for two new treaties in 1888–89 that would permanently lease Pearl Harbor to the Navy, in moving ahead with the McKinley Act that caused the depression, in sending Stevens—who would carry out the Harrison Administration's view of "manifest destiny"—to be the American Minister to Hawai'i, in holding highest level Washington meetings with the annexationist leader Lorrin Thurston, in Stevens's planning the revolt with the annexationists, and finally in Stevens's eventual forcing the annexationists to carry through when they wanted postponement. These facts support the Hawaiian claim that America had a clear history of meddling in the internal affairs of the sovereign Hawaiian nation, and that the American government conspired to overthrow the Hawaiian monarchy and supported the actual takeover with its troops.

President Cleveland, inaugurated two months after the overthrow of the monarchy, was a political enemy of former President Harrison, and very possibly knew nothing of the involvement of Harrison, Secretary of State James G. Blaine, Secretary of the Navy B.F. Tracy, Minister Stevens, and certain members of the Congress in the whole affair. When, however, during his administration he gave Congress the opportunity to solve the problem, those in power were not about to resist plucking the pear they had nurtured over the years to such ripeness. The provisional government would stay in power.

Later, when the revolutionaries were solidly entrenched and committed to the path of annexation, the provisions of the McKinley Act were repealed. It had only taken four years from its original passage: Pearl Harbor and the rest of Hawai'i would now belong to the United States forever.

When Sanford B. Dole was inaugurated as the first Territorial governor in 1900, a huge banner stretching the length of the balcony beneath him appropriately read, "Westward the course of empire...."[24]

RESISTANCE BY NATIVE HAWAIIANS

What was the native Hawaiian sentiment towards all these happenings? Did native Hawaiians just go along? Or did they protest? Shortly after the Bayonet Constitution had been forced upon King Kalakaua in 1887, native Hawaiians formed a resistance. Robert Wilcox, a half-Hawaiian, who had been sent by Kalakaua to study politics in Italy, led an insurrection to re-establish the power of the king and to do away with the Bayonet Constitution. His troops were defeated. Seven Hawaiians were killed, and a dozen or so wounded. Wilcox was tried for high treason, but an all-Hawaiian jury acquitted him, and he became a national hero.[25] During the short reign of Queen Lili'uokalani, again Hawaiians under Wilcox plotted to take over the government and to save the islands for Hawaiians. Wilcox and other leaders were arrested but, because of their popularity, were never tried.[26]

With the monarchy overthrown, in 1895 Wilcox, having joined forces with Lili'uokalani, once more led an attempt to restore Hawaiian rule. Skirmishes went on for about 10 days before the royalists surrendered. After they surrendered, to save them from death, Queen Lili'uokalani formally abdicated her throne. No one was sentenced to death. The Queen was imprisoned in the palace. She was the last of the prisoners to be released.[27]

The native Hawaiian community had spoken with its blood. It clearly did not want annexation to the United States.[28] Hawaiians continued to speak out against it. In 1897 they sent the so-called "monster petition," signed by 29,000 native Hawaiians, to the Congress protesting annexation.[29]

ANNEXATION

The general citizenry of Hawai'i never voted for annexation. It was the all-white provisional government that in 1893 sent a committee to Washington to work out a treaty with President Harrison. That treaty was never put before the electorate. And it died when the incoming President Cleveland withdrew it from Congressional consideration.

After Grover Cleveland left office in 1897 and William McKinley was inaugurated as President of the United States, the Republic of Hawai'i sent another delegation to Washington to negotiate a treaty. President McKinley signed the Treaty of Annexation with the Republic of Hawai'i on June 16, 1897. It then needed ratification by both countries. Hawai'i was no problem: the Senate of the Republic of Hawai'i ratified it on September 9, again without the matter ever having been brought before the people for a vote.

Ratification by the United States Senate would be more difficult. The Constitution of the United States explicitly states that all treaties must be ratified by two-thirds of the members of the Senate. This treaty did not have the required support in the US Senate, so it was never ratified. Rather, it was laid aside in favour of an alternative move. Admission of Texas into the Union in 1845 had been accomplished through a joint resolution requiring only a majority vote in both houses of Congress. This avoided treaty ratification. A similar bill to annex Hawai'i was introduced. It was called the Newlands Resolution. Getting it through both houses of the Congress was no easy task, either. However, on May 1, 1898, Captain George Dewey sank the Spanish fleet in Manila harbour. Americans could see the value of holding on to the Philippines, and Hawai'i was seen as central to that move. Already passed by the Senate, the resolution for Annexation was quickly passed by the House and was signed by President McKinley on July 7, 1898.[30]

Formal annexation ceremonies took place in the islands on August 12, 1898. The Republic of Hawai'i would now be the Territory of Hawai'i, a Territory of the United States. The white community was deliriously happy. Native Hawaiians were desperately gloomy. The ceremony proclaiming the islands the Territory of Hawai'i took place in front of 'Iolani Palace,' which had been renamed "Government Building." As Gavan Daws writes, "The Hawaiian anthem, 'Hawai'i Ponoi,' was played for the last time as the anthem of an independent nation, and the Hawaiian flag was hauled down. The Stars and Stripes took its place, and the band played 'The Star Spangled Banner.' 'To the Hawaiian born, it was pathetic,' wrote the *Pacific Commercial Advertiser*. This was the ultimate dispossession."[31]

During the next two years, a constitution for the Territory of Hawai'i was hammered out and approved by Congress. That constitution is referred to as the Organic Act. It took effect on June 14, 1900, and lasted—with occasional changes made by Congress—until admission to Statehood August 21, 1959.[32]

THE CEDED LANDS

"Crown lands" and "government lands" had been set aside by King Kamehameha III at the time of the *mahele*. When the provisional government toppled the monarchy, they claimed that what remained of both sets of lands belonged to the new government. They then sold large portions of the lands during their few years of rule. There were protests at that time that the crown lands belonged to the Queen, and that the government lands were given in perpetuity to the native Hawaiian people, not to others living in Hawai'i. At annexation, however, both sets of lands were "ceded" to the United States by the Republic of Hawai'i, with the stipulation that they were to be held in trust for "the Hawaiian people." Since that time, these lands have been called the "Ceded Lands." They make up about half of the land of the eight major islands. Native Hawaiians were never asked for permission to cede their lands to the United States, and they have never surrendered their claim to them as lands belonging specifically to native Hawaiians. During the years of the Territory, almost 20 percent of these lands were dedicated for federal use—143,700 acres for military bases and 227,972 acres for national parks.[33] Another 200,000 acres were set aside for home-steading by native Hawaiians through the Hawaiian Homes Act. At the time of admission to the Union in 1959, the rest of these lands were given to the State of Hawai'i to be held in trust for the Hawaiian and native Hawaiian people.

The native Hawaiian people today still lay claim to the entire territory included in the original Ceded Lands. And it is these lands, at a minimum, they want returned to their rule.

THE HAWAIIAN HOMES COMMISSION ACT

The native Hawaiians' right to the Ceded Lands was recognized by the Hawaiian Territorial government and by the American government in the events surrounding the Hawaiian Homes Act.

Twenty years after annexation, through the efforts of Prince Jonah Kūhiō Kalaniana'ole, who was the Territory's delegate to Congress at the time, some 200,000 acres of the "crown lands" and "government lands" which had been ceded to the United States at the time of annexation were formed into a special land trust for homesteading by native Hawaiians. This was brought about by the Hawaiian Homes Commission Act, which was passed in 1921.

It had been recognized for many years that the Hawaiian people were not assimilating into Western society, and also that the Hawaiian race was fast disappearing. These had been persistent problems for nearly a century. One of the motivations for the *mahele,* 70 years earlier, had been to get native Hawaiians out of the slums in the towns and back onto the land. In the period just prior to 1920, people in Honolulu and in Washington were saying it aloud again: if the Hawaiians were to survive as a culture and as a race, they had to get back to the land and to reestablish their ties with nature. Congressional discussions of the proposed Act said it would "save the Hawaiian people from extinction by returning them to the land and to 'the mode of living that their ancestors were accustomed to.'"[34] Return of the trust lands to native Hawaiians would "rehabilitate" the people by giving them farms where they could be self-sufficient, where they could practice initiative, and where they could preserve their native Hawaiian culture.[35]

This was supportive talk, and it did get the bill passed. But, in reality, the Hawaiian Homes Act came about as a response to plantation events rather than Hawaiian needs. There was very little that was noble about the intentions of many who were its strongest supporters in Hawai'i. Between 1915 and 1920, the plantations had 213,000 acres of the islands planted in sugar cane. Most of this acreage they owned outright. But 34,000 acres of their prime agricultural lands were "government lands" which they had leased from the government over the years.[36] The Organic Act, the

Constitution for the new Territory of Hawai'i, had set a ceiling for the acreage of land that could be held by any single party in the Territory. That ceiling was 1,000 acres per individual or corporation. For years the plantations had gotten around the 1,000-acre limit by forming bogus partnerships or corporations. This was easy enough to do, with governors who were friendly to sugar. But there was always the worry that they might be taken to court where, if the circumvention were properly attacked, they knew that they would be beaten.[37] Sugar needed Section 55, with its 1,000-acre ceiling, repealed from the Organic Act, the constitution of the Territory of Hawai'i.

Sugar also had another problem: homesteading. Provisions in the Organic Act allowed Hawaiians to homestead prime "government lands" leased by the sugar plantations, but governors friendly to sugar had consistently renewed expiring leases on the sugar acreage instead of opening up the good sugar lands for homesteading. Further, the plantations had such control over supplies, transportation, and marketing that they could easily drive those farmers who did succeed in getting homesteads out of business and off their lands.[38]

In an effort by Congress to encourage the Territory to open up leased lands for homesteading, the Organic Act was amended in 1908 to require that all leases on agricultural lands read that "at any time during the term of the lease [the property could] be withdrawn from operation for homesteading or public purposes." A year later, an even more radical change was made in the Organic Act: it encouraged groups of 25 or more people to get together and apply to homestead public property, and it obliged the Commission of Public Lands to open areas of prime agricultural land leased by the sugar plantations for homesteading.[39] This was a major cause for worry on the plantation. If a governor should be appointed now who was not friendly to sugar, he could use the withdrawal clause to open up any public lands for homesteading.

Sugar was in trouble. The mission boys, as the leaders in the Territory liked to call themselves, came up with a proposal for Prince Kūhiō, the delegate to Congress who for years had been pressing for the opening of homestead lands. If he agreed to allow the Organic Act to be changed in a way to keep homesteaders off the sugar lands and also to delete the 1,000-acre ownership ceiling, they would lobby Congress to set aside 200,000 acres of the Ceded Lands for homesteading by Native Hawaiians. Land already being used for cultivating sugar would be excluded from these homestead lands. Forest preserves and lands already occupied by homesteaders under previous agreements would also be excluded. Besides lobbying for the 200,000 acres for homesteads, the mission boys would agree that 30 percent of the revenues which the territory collected in lease rents from the "government lands" it leased to the plantations would be put into a fund for rehabilitation of the Hawaiian people. Revenues would continue to be put into the fund until it reached $1,000,000. This "Home Loan Fund" was to be a fund from which native Hawaiian homesteaders could make loans to "erect buildings, purchase live stock and farm equipment, and otherwise assist in the development of tracts."[40]

The deal must have looked good to Prince Kūhiō. For years he had fought for homestead rights for his people, but friends of sugar in high places had thwarted him at every turn. He had met with almost total lack of success for so long, and there was no reason to expect anything different in the future. This deal at least guaranteed lands and money for his people.

But what native Hawaiians actually got was not much. Once sugar and forest lands were excluded from consideration, "what was left was land that no one had ever been able to make productive."[41]

For example, on the island of Maui the greatest part of the lands given to the Hawaiians for homesteading are on the desert side of Haleakalā volcano and rise up to the 9,000-foot peak—beyond the timberline, beyond the vegetation line: Hawaiians were given lands to cultivate that were so high that in the entire history of the universe no plant has ever been able to survive and grow there. On the island of O'ahu, they were given hundreds of acres on the face of sheer, 1,000-foot cliffs behind Waimānalo. Also on O'ahu they got the desert land of Nānākuli, 30 miles from town on the Wai'anae coast. One tradition says that Nānākuli, which means "Look at the deaf one," got its name because those who lived there had so little water that they pretended they were deaf when travellers passed through, so that they wouldn't have to offer traditional hospitality and give away the precious little water they had. Surveying all of the 200,000 acres set aside by the Act as Hawaiian Homes Lands, one sees that most of the lands the Hawaiians were given were among the worst in the state. And the decent lands given them were in remote, inaccessible areas.

What of the other "boon" for the Hawaiians—the 30 percent from the sugar lease revenues? With its cap of $1,000,000, this was very little money even then to accomplish a terribly big order. It was supposed to pay for roads, water lines, and power lines to distant, inaccessible areas, and it was supposed to pay all the costs of clearing land and building homes, and costs for farm equipment and livestock.

In the 68 years since the Act, even though the million-dollar limit for this fund has been lifted twice, less than $14 million has come to the Fund. To pay the huge costs for roads, water, and so forth, the Hawaiian Homes Commission has had to rent out large tracts of the land to non-Hawaiians. About 100,000 acres of Hawaiian Homes Lands are now in the hands of non-Hawaiians—68 percent of the acreage. And on that acreage, they are getting an average rent of only $16 per acre per year.[42]

In the more than 60 years between 1921 and 1984, only about 3,000 applicants received Hawaiian homesteads. That number has been doubled in the last four years, although most new applicants who have received homesteads are not yet on the land. In 1988, 18,000 applicants were still waiting, and 2,000 new names were added to the waiting list.[43] Lots that Hawaiians receive today will not bring them back to the land, because the land will not sustain crops. However, with the cost of the average home in Hawai'i hovering around $200,000, no matter how desolate and distant the Hawaiian Home Lands may be, they are the only hope many Hawaiians have for ever having a place of their own in their own land.

Disappointment and frustration were programmed into the Hawaiian Homes Lands project from the beginning. The other half of "the deal," however, was to profit the sugar growers. There was no disappointment or frustration there. The clause in the Organic Act that had limited sugar growers to 1,000 acres of lands was deleted.[44] Sugar interests were allowed to renew leases on all of the prime agricultural lands that they had held. And sugar lands no longer lay under the threat of possible homesteading. Again the mission boys had come out on top.

In the discussions that took place in Congress before passage of the Act, there might be a hidden boon for native Hawaiians, however—recognition of their claim to the Ceded Lands. Lawrence Fuchs writes in *Hawai'i Pono:*

> The first resolution passed by the territorial legislature in 1919 requested Congress to set aside certain crown lands—meaning public lands—for the special benefit of the Hawaiian people. A lobbying commission, representing interests friendly to the planters, was appointed to steer the bill through Congress. The commissioners pointed out that in the Great Mahele the commoners did not receive their just share of the lands of the Kingdom. They recalled that with the overthrow of the monarchy, the crown lands, which Kūhiō alleged had been set aside as a trust for the common people, were taken over by the Republic, depriving the natives of their rights. On this ground and on the evidence that the Hawaiian race was dying, Kūhiō and his supporters justified special treatment for the Hawaiians in the Territory's homestead policies.[45]

One wants to be clear that the Act establishing the Hawaiian Home Lands was never in any way considered a reparations act, compensating Hawaiians for lands taken in the overthrow of the monarchy. The Hawaiian Homes Commission Act was a response to needs of the sugar interests. However, a careful study of the discussions in the 1921 Congressional Record regarding the Hawaiian Homes Commission Act establishes that Congress has already recognized the rights of native Hawaiians to the Ceded Lands, and that they acted in 1921 to establish the Hawaiian Homes Lands because of that recognition. This should serve as a valuable precedent in future presentations to Congress, since Congress is the branch of government which will deliberate and formulate the re-establishment of the Hawaiian Nation.

THE ERA OF THE BIG FIVE

It was primarily missionaries and their descendants who got into sugar early. It was the mission boys who formed the core of the all-white Hawaiian League that forced the Bayonet Constitution on King Kalakaua. Again it was they who were the core of the Annexation Club. It was primarily the mission boys who composed the Committee of Safety. They headed the provisional government and, later, the government of the Republic of Hawai'i. Now, under the Territory, the mission boys who had delivered the islands to the United States prospered beyond their wildest dreams. Their companies became the "Big Five": Castle and Cooke, Alexander and Baldwin, C. Brewer and Co., Theo. Davies & Co., and American Factors. They controlled 75 percent of the sugar by 1910; by 1933 they controlled 96 percent. They eventually came to own every business associated with sugar: banking, wholesale and retail merchandising, insurance, utilities, on-island railroad transportation, shipping between the islands, and shipping to and from the continental United States.

Each of the Big Five had a least one direct descendant of a missionary on its board: Alexander, Baldwin, Smith, Castle, Cooke, Judd, Wilcox, Dole, Damon, Thurston, Hall, and Chamberlain—all missionary families—appeared on the boards of almost every important firm that did business in Honolulu. And Walter F. Dillingham, the Big Sixth, was related to the missionary families through his mother. Through interlocking directorates, the missionary families controlled everything that went on in the islands. Their wealth was fabulous.[46]

ADVERSE IMPACTS ON NATIVE HAWAIIANS

Native Hawaiians during the time of the Territory were encouraged to "become American," and many did. Any hope of ever having their own nation restored was gone.

Hawaiian language was forbidden in the schools, and many families came to forbid it at home. Passing on the culture was laid aside in many homes.

Hawaiians gave their children American names so that they could fit better into American society. They sent their children to American schools, where they were taught to pledge their allegiance to the United States.

They taught their children to abide by the white man's laws, to adopt his morality, and to try to take on his American lifestyle.

They let their children learn and accept as true the history of Hawai'i from the white man's view.

The radio, the newspaper, everything preached Americanism.

Hawaiian children were taught that their people were lazy, stupid, and worth-less, and that they should turn against their culture and make themselves into Yankee adults. With some children it worked. With most, it did not. Many heard they were lazy, stupid, and worthless often enough that they came to believe it.

With the passing of two or three generations under Territorial rule, most Hawaiians not only did not fit in—just as they had never fit into Western culture—but they had now also surrendered knowledge of their language and their culture.

Worst of all, perhaps, the brainwashing over the decades had convinced most Hawaiians that only a small injustice had been done to their people by the mission-aries and their descendants, and by the United States of America.

STATEHOOD

Hawai'i became the 50th State in the Union in 1959. Native Hawaiians again were never asked for their consent. The options available regarding statehood did not allow one to choose between having a Hawaiian nation or having Statehood. One could only choose between having Statehood or continuing the American Territorial Government. It was an American question, asked of Americans: "What kind of Americanism do you choose?" There was no box for checking "None of the above."

While Statehood has profited almost every group in Hawai'i, it has brought little for the Hawaiian.

Pōkā Laenui (Hayden Burgess) writes of events since Statehood,

We were the target of a free-for-all, "grab whatever you can get" attitude. New economic interests poured into Hawai'i to play the American financial game. Land became the play toy. Selling, trading, leasing, mortgaging, subdividing, became the craze, driving up the price with each change-over. Construction industries changed much of Hawai'i from a lush green paradise, to a cancerous, white, concrete jungle tied together by roadways of asphalt. Foreigners from the United States, Canada, Japan, China, the Arab nations, and elsewhere took "title" to large tracts of land.

Land today is bartered back and forth with no regard to its spiritual and cultural values or the economic need of the people. Much of it is investor owned, and sits locked up, waiting for price inflation to drive up the speculators' profits. There is mini-mal concern for the needs of the local people. While empty apartment units are being sold in foreign markets at prices far above our people's abilities to pay, many of our people are sleeping in cars or in parks, hoping to avoid arrest before the morning.[47]

The severe recession of the early 80's slowed American interest, but in the latter part of the decade, the weakness of the dollar and the strength of the Japanese *yen* have made Hawai'i attractive to the Japanese. The race is on again, with prices skyrocketing.

Pōkā Laenui continues,

Any attempt to bring reason to this madness under the American system fails. The people of Hawai'i cannot limit or control this investment madness for several reasons. For one, the present money interests have bought off the pillars of power in Hawai'i. But even if the present State government could be convinced of the ill effects of inter-state and foreign investments in Hawai'i, they could do nothing. For the US Congress has claimed constitutional supremacy in the area of inter-state commerce and foreign affairs, thus locking Hawai'i into America's colonization and investment policies.[48]

NOTES

1. Kuykendall, Ralph S., *A History of Hawaii,* New York: Macmillan 1928, p. 280–1. Also, Daws, *Shoal of Time,* p. 279.
2. Daws, *Shoal of Time,* p. 281.
3. Daws, *Shod of Time,* p. 281.
4. Daws, *Shoal of Time,* p. 285.
5. Cooke, Alistair, *America: A Personal History by Alistair Cooke,* a television series on the Public Broadcasting System. These notes are taken from the episode called, "Gone West." For additional support, see also footnote 6 below.
6. Calkins, Carroll C, ed. *The Story of America,* Pleasantville, N.Y.: Readers Digest, 1975, p. 71.
7. They were such people as John Jay, who among many other things was a signer of Declaration of Independence, signed the Peace Treaty with England, was US Secretary of State for Foreign Affairs, and also Governor of New York; John Langdon, delegate to the Continental Congress and Governor of New Hampshire; Elias Boudinot, elected to Congress, appointed by President Washington as Director of the Mint; John Treadwell, Governor of Connecticut; General Henry Sewell; and businessmen William Bartlett, William Phillips, and Robert Ralston. For more details see *Memorial Volume, American Board of Commissions for Foreign Missions, Half-Century,* Boston: Missionary House, 1861, pp. 116–125. Available at Mission Houses Library, Honolulu.
8. Calkins, *The Story of America,* p. 82.
9. Sec. of Navy Robeson to Pennock, Dec. 25, 1872, Navy Dept, Letters to Flag Officers and Commandants of Vessels, No. [Vol.] 7. as quoted in Kuykendall, *The Hawaiian Kingdom,* II, p. 248. Insertion of "[Minister Pierce]" by Kuykendall.
10. Belknap to Schofield, confidential, June 24, 1872, War Dept. Records, quoted in Kuykendall, *The Hawaiian Kingdom,* II, p.248.
11. Schofield and Alexander to Belknap, May 8, 1873, printed in Sen. Ex. Docs., 52 Cong., 2 sess., no. 77, pp. 150–4. Quoted in Kuykendall, *The Hawaiian Kingdom,* II, p.248.
12. *Native Hawaiian Study Commission,* Vol. I, p. 267, which cites the Act of January 30, 1875, 19 Stat. 625–626.
13. *Native Hawaiian Study Commission,* Vol. I, p. 267, which cites Charles C. Tansill, *The Foreign Policy of Thomas F. Bayard.* New York: Fordham University Press, 1940, p. 370.

14. *Native Hawaiians Study Commission,* Vol. I, p. 274. They cite Bayard MS, Foreign Relations, 1894, Appendix II, pp. 660–662, 793–817, quoted in Tansill, *The Foreign Policy of Thomas Bayard,* p. 391–2.

15. Daws, *Shoal of Time,* p. 259.

16. Daws, *Shoal of Time,* p. 260–1.

17. Thurston, Lorrin A., *Memoirs of the Hawaiian Revolution,* Honolulu: Advertiser Publishing Co., 1936, pp. 230–2. I have taken this quotation from *The Native Hawaiians Study Commission,* Vol. I, p. 289.

18. Kuykendall, *The Hawaiian Kingdom* III, p. 567.

19. Kuykendall, *The Hawaiian Kingdom* III, p. 567.

20. Kuykendall, *The Hawaiian Kingdom* III, p. 567.

21. Kuykendall, *The Hawaiian Kingdom* HI, p. 567–8.

22. Much of this information is also found in a manuscript for an article titled, "Cuba and Hawai'i," written by Carl Opio Young for the *Journal of the World Council of Indigenous Peoples,* Vol. 3. The authors are grateful to Sylvia Reck for bringing the article to their attention.

23. Kuykendall, *The Hawaiian Kingdom* III, p. 568.

24. Picture found in *Ka Mana O Ka 'Aina,* May/June 1969, p. 7.

25. Daws, *Shoal of Time,* p. 256–7.

26. Daws, *Shoal of Time,* p. 269–70.

27. Daws, *Shoal of Time,* p. 284.

28. Daws, *Shoal of Time,* p. 282.

29. See references to this in the 31st Congressional Record, p. 6702 (1898). Cited in *Native Hawaiian Study Commission* Vol I, p. 307.

30. Daws, *Shoal of Time,* p. 289–90.

31. Daws, *Shoal of Time,* p. 291.

32. Congress could change the Organic Act at will. Gavan Daws, *Shoal of Time,* p. 382.

33. Congress passed Public Law 88-233 on December 23, 1963, under which approximately 227,972 acres of national parks became the fee simple property of the federal government. Melody Kapilialoha Mackenzie, ed., *Native Hawaiian Rights Handbook* (Honolulu: University of Hawaii Press, 1991). Linda Menton and Eileen Tamura, *A History of Hawai'i,* Honolulu: Curriculum Research and Development Group, Univeristy of Hawai'i, 1989, p. 317, give 143,700 acres of Ceded Lands as belonging to the military in Hawai'i.

34. *'Aina Ho'opulapula,* 1983–84 Annual Report Department of Hawaiian Home Lands, p. 5.

35. *'Aina Ho'opulapula,* 1983–84, p. 7.

36. Fuchs, *Hawaii Pono,* p. 255.

37. Fuchs, *Hawaii Pono,* p. 173.

38. Fuchs, *Hawaii Pono,* pp. 252–3.

39. Fuchs, *Hawaii Pono,* p.253.

40. *Hawaiian Homes Commission Act,* Sixty-Seventh Congress. Session I, Chapter 42. 1921. Sec. 213.

41. Daws, *Shoal of Time,* p. 298.

42. Testimony given before Senator Daniel K. Inouye on August 21, 1988 by Ms. Julie Cachola. This figure was included in an earlier draft of this section, which was reviewed by Kenneth Toguchi, news spokesperson for the Department of Hawaiian Home Lands. Asked for comments and corrections, he left this figure alone.

43. Figures copied from speeches at the Native Hawaiian Rights Conference, August 5–7, 1988, at Kamehameha Schools. Not challenged by Kenneth Toguchi of the DHHL during the discussion mentioned in footnote 42 above.

44. *Hawaiian Homes Commission Act,* Sec. 302.

45. Fuchs, *Hawaii Pono,* pp. 256–7.

46. Daws, *Shoal of Time,* p. 312–313.

47. Laenui, Pōkā (Hayden Burgess), *A Thief in Judgement of Itself,* mms., p. 22. We have edited this paragraph from the original.

48. Laenui, Pōkā (Hayden Burgess), *A Thief in Judgement of Itself,* mms., p. 22.

CHAPTER 5

COLONIZING KNOWLEDGES

Linda Tuhiwai Smith

We have a history of people putting Maori under a microscope in the same way a scientist looks at an insect. The ones doing the looking are giving themselves the power to define.

MERATA MITA[1]

THIS ARTICLE ARGUES THAT THE FORM of imperialism that indigenous peoples are now confronting emerged from that period of European history known as the Enlightenment. The Enlightenment provided the spirit, the impetus, the confidence, and the political and economic structures that facilitated the search for new knowledges. The project of the Enlightenment is often referred to as "modernity," and it is that project which is claimed to have provided the stimulus for the industrial revolution, the philosophy of liberalism, the development of disciplines in the sciences and the development of public education. Imperialism underpinned and was critical to these developments. While imperialism is often thought of as a system that drew everything back into the centre, it was also a system which distributed materials and ideas outwards. Said's notion of "positional superiority" is useful here for conceptualizing the ways in which knowledge and culture were as much part of imperialism as raw materials and military strength. Knowledge was also there to be discovered, extracted, appropriated, and distributed. Processes for enabling these things to occur became organized and systematic. They informed not only the field of study referred to by Said as "Orientalism," but also other disciplines of knowledge and "regimes of truth." It is through these disciplines that the indigenous world has been represented to the West and it is through these disciplines that indigenous peoples often search for the fragments of ourselves which were taken, catalogued, studied, and stored. It is not the intention of this article to tell the history of Western knowledge, but rather to draw that history down into the colonized world, to show the relationship between knowledge, research, and imperialism, and then to discuss the ways in which it has come to structure our own ways of knowing, through the development of academic disciplines and through the education of colonial elites and indigenous or "native" intellectuals. Western knowledge and science are "beneficiaries" of the colonization of indigenous peoples. The knowledge gained through our colonization has been used, in turn, to create in us what Ngugi wa Thiong'o calls the colonization "of the mind."[2]

ESTABLISHING THE POSITIONAL SUPERIORITY OF WESTERN KNOWLEDGE

The project of modernity signalled the end of feudalism and absolutist authority, legitimated by divine rule, and announced the beginning of the modern state. The new state formation had to meet the requirements of an expanding economy based on major improvements in production. The industrial revolution changed and made new demands upon the individual and the political system. The modern state was wrested from the old regime of absolutist monarchs by the articulation of liberal political and economic theories.[3] As a system of ideas, liberalism focuses on the individual, who has the capacity to reason; on a society which promotes individual autonomy and self-interest; and on a state which has a rational rule of law which regulates a public sphere of life, but which allows individuals to pursue their economic self-interest. Once it was accepted that humans had the capacity to reason and to attain this potential through education, through a systematic form of organizing knowledge, then it became possible to debate these ideas in rational and "scientific" ways.

The development of scientific thought, the exploration and "discovery" by Europeans of other worlds, the expansion of trade, the establishment of colonies, and the systematic colonization of indigenous peoples in the 18th and 19th centuries are all facets of the modernist project. Modernism is more than a re-presentation of fragments from the cultural archive in new contexts. "Discoveries" about and from the "new" world expanded and challenged ideas the West held about itself.[4] The production of knowledge, new knowledge and transformed "old" knowledge, ideas about the nature of knowledge and the validity of specific forms of knowledge, became as much commodities of colonial exploitation as other natural resources.[5] Indigenous peoples were classified alongside the flora and fauna; hierarchical typologies of humanity and systems of representation were fuelled by new discoveries; cultural maps were charted and territories claimed and contested by the major European powers. Hence some indigenous peoples were ranked above others in terms of such things as the belief that they were "nearly human," "almost human," or "sub-human." This often depended on whether it was thought that the peoples concerned possessed a "soul" and could therefore be "offered" salvation, and whether or not they were educable and could be offered schooling. These systems for organizing, classifying and storing new knowledge, and for theorizing the meanings of such discoveries, constituted research. In a colonial context, however, this research was undeniably also about power and domination. The instruments or technologies of research were also instruments of knowledge and instruments for legitimating various colonial practices.

The imaginary line between "east" and "west," drawn in 1493 by a Papal Bull, allowed for the political division of the world and the struggle by competing Western states to establish what Said has referred to as a "flexible positional superiority" over the known, and yet to become known, world.[6] This positional superiority was contested at several levels by European powers. These imaginary boundaries were drawn again in Berlin in 1934 when European powers sat around the table once more to carve up Africa and other parts of "their" empires. They continue to be redrawn. Imperialism and colonialism are the specific formations through which the West came to "see," to "name," and to "know" indigenous communities. The cultural archive with its systems of representation, codes for unlocking systems of classification, and fragmented artefacts of knowledge enabled travellers and observers to make sense of what they saw and to represent their new-found knowledge to the West through the authorship and authority of their representations.

While colonialism at an economic level, including its ultimate expression through slavery, opened up new materials for exploitation and new markets for trade, at a cultural level, ideas, images, and experiences about the Other helped to shape and delineate the essential differences between Europe and the rest. Notions about the Other, which already existed in the European imagination, were recast within the framework of Enlightenment philosophies, the industrial revolution, and the scientific "discoveries" of the 18th and 19th centuries. When the scientific foundations of Western research are discussed, the indigenous contribution to these foundations is rarely mentioned. To have acknowledged their contribution would, in terms of the rules of research practice, be as legitimate as acknowledging the contribution of a variety of plant, a shard of pottery, or a "preserved head of a native" to research. Furthermore, according to Bazin, "Europeans could not even imagine that other people could ever have done things before or better than themselves."[7] The objects of research do not have a voice and do not contribute to research or science. In fact, the logic of the argument would suggest that it is simply impossible, ridiculous even, to suggest that the object of research can contribute to anything. An object has no life force, no humanity, no spirit of its own, so therefore "it" cannot make an active contribution. This perspective is not deliberately insensitive; it is simply that the rules did not allow such a thought to enter the scene. Thus, indigenous Asian, American, Pacific, and African forms of knowledge, systems of classification, technologies, and codes of social life, which began to be recorded in some detail by the 17th century, were regarded as "new discoveries" by Western science.[8] These discoveries were commodified as property belonging to the cultural archive and body of knowledge of the West.[9]

The 18th and 19th centuries also constituted an era of highly competitive "collecting." Many indigenous people might call this "stealing" rather than "collecting." This included the collecting of territories, of new species of flora and fauna, of mineral resources, and of cultures. James Clifford, for example, refers to ethnography as a science which was

> [a] form of culture collecting ... [which] highlights the ways that diverse experiences and facts are selected, gathered, detached from their original temporal occasions, and given enduring value in a new arrangement. Collecting—at least in the West, where time is generally thought to be linear and irreversible—implies a rescue of phenomena from inevitable historical decay or loss.[10]

The idea that collectors were actually rescuing artefacts from decay and destruction, and from indigenous peoples themselves, legitimated practices which also included commercial trade and plain and simple theft. Clearly, in terms of trade indigenous peoples were often active participants, in some cases delivering "made-to-order" goods. The different agendas and rivalries of indigenous groups were also known to have been incorporated into the commercial activities of Europeans. Hence, muskets could be traded and then used to pursue traditional enemies, or one group of people could be used to capture and assist in the enslavement of another group who were also their traditional rivals. Indigenous property is still said to be housed in "collections," which in turn are housed either in museums or private galleries, and art and artefacts are often grouped and classified in the name of their "collector." These collections have become the focus of indigenous peoples' attempts to reclaim ancestral remains and other cultural items (known in the West as "artefacts") belonging to their people.

It is important to remember, however, that colonialism was not just about collection. It was also about re-arrangement, re-presentation and re-distribution. For example, plant species were taken by Joseph Banks for the Royal Botanic Gardens at Kew. Here they could be "grown, studied, and disbursed to the colonial stations, a centre of plant transfers on the scientific level, and of the generation and publication of knowledge about plants." [11] The British Empire became a global laboratory for research and development. New species of plants and animals were introduced to the colonies to facilitate development and to "strengthen" indigenous species. This point is worth remembering as it contrasts with the view, sometimes referred to as a diffusionist explanation, that knowledge, people, flora, and fauna simply dispersed themselves around the world. This botanical colonization had already been successfully carried out in other places: for example, maize, sweet potatoes, and tobacco from South America had been widely distributed. In the centre of this collection and distribution network was the imperial "home" country. The colonies were peripheral satellites which gained access to these new knowledges and technologies through "recourse to the writings of authors in the centre."[12] One effect of this system of redistribution was the interference caused by new species to the ecologies of their new environments and the eventual extinction of several species of bird and animal life.[13] In the case of New Zealand, Cherryl Smith argues that, ecologically, the indigenous world was colonized by weeds.[14]

Among the other significant consequences of ecological imperialism—carried by humans, as well as by plants and animals—were the viral and bacterial diseases which devastated indigenous populations. This devastation or genocide was, in the accounts of many indigenous peoples, used deliberately as a weapon of war. Stories are told in Canada, for example, of blankets used by smallpox victims being sent into First Nation communities while the soldiers and settlers camped outside waiting for the people to die. There were several ideologies which legitimated the Western impact on indigenous health and well-being. These supported racial views already in place, but which in the later 19th century became increasingly legitimated by the "scientific" views of social Darwinism. The concept of the "survival of the fittest," used to explain the evolution of species in the natural world, was applied enthusiastically to the human world. It became a very powerful belief that indigenous peoples were inherently weak and therefore, at some point, would die out. There were debates about how this could be prevented, for example through miscegenation and cultural assimilation, and whether this, in fact, was "desirable." Judgments on these issues circled back or depended upon prior considerations as to whether the indigenous group concerned had souls, could be saved, and also could be redeemed culturally. Influential debates on these matters by Catholic scholars such as Bartolomé de Las Casas took place during the 16th century. In 19th-century New Zealand, some of the debates delved right down into the supposed fecundity rates of indigenous women and the better prospects for racial survival if miscegenation occurred. There were very serious scientific views put forward to account for the demise of the indigenous populations. Some views included sterility caused by the "licentiousness" of the women, a vegetable diet, infanticide, and abortion. Other causes were put down to a sense of "hopelessness" and lack of spirit, which came about through contact with "civilization."[15]

But there were also state policies (federal, provincial, and local) of "benign neglect" which involved minimal intervention (the "infected blanket" strategy) while people suffered and died. There were also more proactive policies based around such ideas as "Manifest Destiny," which sanctioned the taking of indigenous lands by any means.[16] Ward Churchill and other indigenous writers classify these actions as part of the Columbian legacy of genocide.[17] In relation to the diseases and disease that the West is said to have introduced to indigenous peoples, the bigger question has always been the extent to which the impact of disease is an inevitable consequence of contact with the West. Currently, indigenous populations are undertaking a worldwide search for genetic solutions to Western diseases. Aborigine activist Bobbi Sykes has an "acid test" for the Western impact on indigenous health which consists of two lists: one a list of diseases introduced by Europeans to Aboriginal people, the other a list of diseases introduced by Aboriginal people to Europeans. There are no items on the second list. That empty space tells a very potent story.[18]

The globalization of knowledge and Western culture constantly reaffirms the West's view of itself as the centre of legitimate knowledge, the arbiter of what counts as knowledge and the source of "civilized" knowledge. This form of global knowledge is generally referred to as "universal" knowledge, available to all and not really "owned" by anyone—that is, until non-Western scholars make claims to it. When claims like that are made, history is revised (again) so that the story of civilization remains the story of the West. For this purpose, the Mediterranean world, the basin of Arabic culture and the lands east of Constantinople are conveniently appropriated as part of the story of Western civilization, Western philosophy, and Western knowledge.[19] Through imperialism, however, these cultures, peoples, and their nation-states were re-positioned as "oriental," or "outsider," in order to legitimate the imposition of colonial rule. For indigenous peoples from other places, the real lesson to be learned is that we have no claim whatsoever to civilization. It is something which has been introduced from the West, by the West, to indigenous peoples, for our benefit and for which we should be duly grateful.

The nexus between cultural ways of knowing, scientific discoveries, economic impulses and imperial power enabled the West to make ideological claims to having a superior civilization. The "idea" of the West became a reality when it was represented back to indigenous nations through colonialism. By the 19th century, colonialism not only meant the imposition of Western authority over indigenous lands, indigenous modes of production, and indigenous law and government, but also the imposition of Western authority over all aspects of indigenous knowledges, languages, and cultures. This authority incorporated what Said refers to as alliances between the ideologies, "clichés," general beliefs, and understandings held about the Orient, and the views of "science" and philosophical theories.[20]

For many indigenous peoples the major agency for imposing this positional superiority over knowledge, language, and culture was colonial education. Colonial education came in two basic forms: missionary or religious schooling (which was often residential), followed later by public and secular schooling. Numerous accounts across nations now attest to the critical role played by schools in assimilating colonized peoples, and in the systematic, frequently brutal, forms of denial of indigenous languages, knowledges, and cultures. Not all groups of indigenous peoples, however, were permitted to attend school—some groups being already defined in some way as "ineducable" or just plain troublesome and delinquent. Furthermore, in many examples the indigenous language was used as the medium of instruction, and access to the colonizing language was denied specifically. This policy was designed to deny opportunities to participate as citizens.

Colonial education was also used as a mechanism for creating new indigenous elites. It was not the only mechanism for producing elite groups, as the traditional hierarchies within an indigenous society that converted to the colonial ideology also formed part of the elite group. Schooling helped identify talented students who were then groomed for more advanced education. Many of these students were sent away to boarding schools, while others were sent to the metropolitan centre in Europe for their university studies. In these settings, and through their learning, students acquired the tastes, and sampled some of the benefits and privileges, of living within the metropolitan culture. Their elite status came about through the alignment of their cultural and economic interests with those of the colonizing group rather than with those of their own society.

School knowledge systems, however, were informed by a much more comprehensive system of knowledge which linked universities, scholarly societies, and imperial views of culture. Hierarchies of knowledge and theories that had rapidly developed to account for the discoveries of the new world were legitimated at the centre. Schools simply reproduced domesticated versions of that knowledge for uncritical consumption. Although colonial universities saw themselves as being part of an international community and inheritors of a legacy of Western knowledge, they were also part of the historical processes of imperialism. They were established as an essential part of the colonizing process, a bastion of civilization and a sign that a colony and its settlers had "grown up." Attempts to "indigenize" colonial academic institutions and/or individual disciplines within them have been fraught with major struggles over what counts as knowledge, as language, as literature, as curriculum, and as the role of intellectuals, and over the critical function of the concept of academic freedom.[21]

COLONIZING THE DISCIPLINES

Academic knowledges are organized around the idea of disciplines and fields of knowledge. These are deeply implicated in each other and share genealogical foundations in various classical and Enlightenment philosophies. Most of the "traditional" disciplines are grounded in cultural world views which are either antagonistic to other belief systems or have no methodology for dealing with other knowledge systems. Underpinning all of what is taught at universities is the belief in the concept of science as the all-embracing method for gaining an understanding of the world. Some of these disciplines, however, are more directly implicated in colonialism in that either they have derived their methods and understandings from the colonized world or they have tested their ideas in the colonies. How the colonized were governed, for example, was determined by previous experiences in other colonies and by the prevailing theories about race, gender, climate, and other factors generated by "scientific" methods. Classification systems were developed specifically to cope with the mass of new knowledge generated by the discoveries of the "new world." New colonies were the laboratories of Western science. Theories generated from the exploration and exploitation of colonies, and of the people who had prior ownership of these lands, formed the totalizing appropriation of the Other.

Robert Young argues that Hegel

articulates a philosophical structure of the appropriation of the other as a form of knowledge which uncannily simulates the project of nineteenth century imperialism; the construction of knowledges which all operate through forms of expropriation and incorporation of the other mimics at a conceptual level the geographical and economic absorption of the non-European world by the West.[22]

David Goldberg claims that notions of the Other are more deeply embedded in classical philosophy, but became racialized within the framework of liberalism and the ideas about people and society which developed as disciplines through liberalism.[23] In an interesting discussion on the discourses which employ the word "civilization," John Laffey suggests that the word "civilization" entered Anglo-French usage in the second part of the 18th century, enabling the distinction to be drawn between those who saw themselves as civilized and those whom they then regarded as the "savages" abroad and at home.[24] As a standard of judgement, according to Laffey, the word "civilized" became more defined with the help of Freud and more specialized in the way different disciplines employed the concept. One such use was comparative, allowing for comparisons between children and savages or children and women, for example. This way of thinking was elaborated further into psychological justifications for the distinctions between the civilized and the uncivilized. Freud's influence on the way disciplines developed in relation to colonialism is further explored by Marianna Torgovnick, who examines the links between Freud and anthropology in her analysis of Malinowski's book *The Sexual Life of Savages*.[25] According to Turgovnick,

Freud's explanation of the human psyche in terms of sexuality undergirded their endeavors and influenced the structure of many ethnographic enquiries at this stage of the discipline's development even when those enquiries suggested (as they often did) modifications of Freudian paradigms, such as the Oedipus complex.[26]

Other key intellectuals have also been referred to as not-so-innocent philosophers of the truth. Henry Louis Gates Jr. names Kant, Bacon, Hume, Jefferson, and Hegel as "great intellectual racialists" who have been influential in defining the role of literature and its relationship to humanity: "The salient sign of the black person's humanity ... would be the mastering of the very essence of Western civilization, the very foundation of the complex fiction upon which white Western culture has been constructed...."[27]

Of all the disciplines, anthropology is the one most closely associated with the study of the Other and with the defining of primitivism.[28] As Adam Kuper argued, "The anthropologists took this primitive society as their special subject, but in practice primitive society proved to be their own society (as they understood it) seen in a distorting mirror."[29] The ethnographic "gaze" of anthropology has collected, classified and represented other cultures to the extent that anthropologists are often the academics popularly perceived by the indigenous world as the epitome of all that it is bad with academics. Haunani Kay Trask accuses anthropologists of being "takers and users" who "exploit the hospitality and generosity of native people."[30] Trinh T. Minh-ha makes similar references to anthropology and anthropologists, including those whose intent now is to train Third World anthropologists. "Gone out of date," she says, "then revitalised, the mission of civilizing savages mutates into the imperative of 'making equal.'"[31] In writing a history of geography, Livingstone refers to this discipline as the "science of imperialism par excellence." [32] His comment relates to geographical studies into such things as the mapping of racial difference, the links which were drawn between climate and mental abilities, the use of map makers in French colonies for military intelligence, and the development of acclimatization societies.[33]

History is also implicated in the construction of totalizing master discourses which control the Other. The history of the colonies, from the perspective of the colonizers, has effectively denied other views of what happened and what the significance of historical "facts" may be to the colonized. "If history is written by the victor," argues Janet Abu-Lughod, "then it must, almost by definition, 'deform' the history of the others."[34] Donna Awatere claims that "The process of recording what happened automatically favours the white occupiers because they won. In such a way a whole past is 'created' and then given the authority of truth."[35] These comments have been echoed wherever indigenous peoples have had the opportunity to "talk back" to the academic world.

While disciplines are implicated in each other, particularly in their shared philosophical foundations, they are also insulated from each other through the maintenance of what are known as disciplinary boundaries. Basil Bernstein has shown how this works in his paper on the "classification and framing of knowledge." [36] Insulation enables disciplines to develop independently. Their histories are kept separate and "pure." Concepts of "academic freedom," the "search for truth" and "democracy" underpin the notion of independence and are vigorously defended by intellectuals. Insularity protects a discipline from the "outside," enabling communities of scholars to distance themselves from others and, in the more extreme forms, to absolve themselves of responsibility for what occurs in other branches of their discipline, in the academy, and in the world.

In the context of research and at a very pragmatic level, researchers from different projects and different research teams can be in and out of the same community (much in the way many government social services are in and out of family homes), showing "as a collective" little responsibility for the overall impact of their activities. At other levels criticism of individual researchers and their projects is deflected by the argument that those researchers are different in some really significant "scientific" way from others. How indigenous communities are supposed to work this out is a mystery. There are formal organizations of disciplines, researchers, and communities of scholars, many of which have ethical guidelines. These organizations are based on the idea that scholars consent to participate within them as scholars, as professionals, or as ethical human beings. Not all who carry out research in indigenous communities belong to, or are bound by, such collegial self-discipline.

DISCIPLINING THE COLONIZED

The concept of discipline is even more interesting when we think about it not simply as a way of organizing systems of knowledge, but also as a way of organizing people or bodies. Foucault has argued that discipline in the 18th century became "formulas of domination" which were at work in schools, hospitals, and military organizations. [37] Techniques of detail were developed to maintain discipline over the body. The colonizing of the Other through discipline has a number of different meanings. Knowledge was used to discipline the colonized in a variety of ways. The most obvious forms of discipline were through exclusion, marginalization, and denial. Indigenous ways of knowing were excluded and marginalized. This happened to indigenous views about land, for example, through the imposition of individualized title, through taking land away for "acts of rebellion," and through redefining land as "waste land" or "empty land," and then taking it away. Foucault suggests that one way discipline was distributed was through enclosure. This is the other side of exclusion in that the margins are enclosures: reserved lands are enclosures, schools enclose, but in order to enclose they also exclude, for there is something on the outside. Discipline is also partitioned, individuals separated, and space compartmentalized. This allowed for efficient supervision and for simultaneous distinctions to be made between individuals. This form of discipline worked at the curriculum level, for example, as a mechanism for selecting out "native" children and girls for domestic and manual work. It worked also at the assessment level, with normative tests designed around the language and cultural capital of the white middle classes.

The deepest memory of discipline, however, is of the sheer brutality meted out to generations of indigenous communities. Aborigine parents in Australia had their children forcibly removed, sent away beyond reach, and "adopted." [38] Native children in Canada were sent to residential schools at an age designed to systematically destroy their language and memories of home. There is a growing body of testimony from First Nations people in Canada which tells of years of abuse, neglect, and viciousness meted out to young children by teachers and staff in schools run by various religious denominations. [39] These forms of discipline were supported by paternalistic and racist policies and legislation; they were accepted by white communities as necessary conditions which had to be met if indigenous people wanted to become citizens (of their own lands). These forms of discipline affected people physically, emotionally, linguistically, and culturally. They were designed to destroy every last remnant of alternative ways of knowing and living, to obliterate collective identities and memories, and to impose a new order. Even after the Second World War, when the post-colonial period was beginning according to some cultural studies theorists, many indigenous peoples around the world were still not recognized as humans, let alone citizens. The effect of such discipline was to silence (forever, in some cases) or to suppress the ways of knowing, and the languages for knowing, of many different indigenous peoples. Reclaiming a voice in this context has also been about reclaiming, reconnecting, and reordering those ways of knowing which were submerged, hidden, or driven underground.

COLONIALISM AND "NATIVE" INTELLECTUALS

The position within their own societies of "native" intellectuals who have been trained in the West has been regarded by those involved in nationalist movements as very problematic. Much of the discussion about intellectuals in social and cultural life, and their participation in anti-colonial struggles, is heavily influenced by Marxist revolutionary thought, is framed in the language of oppositional discourse, and was written during the post-war period when struggles for independence were underway. [40] Included within the rubric of "intellectual" by liberation writers such as Frantz Fanon are also artists, writers, poets, teachers, clerks, officials, the petite bourgeoisie, and other professionals engaged in producing "culture." Their importance in nationalist movements is related to their abilities to reclaim, rehabilitate, and articulate indigenous cultures, and to their implicit ability to lead "the people" as voices which can legitimate a new nationalist consciousness.

At the same time, however, these same producers and legitimators of culture are the group most closely aligned with the colonizers in terms of their class interests, their values, and their ways of thinking. This view was restated in 1984 by Donna Awatere, who wrote that Colonial Maori "are noticeable because they have succeeded as white in some section of white culture; economically, through the arts, at sport, through religion, the universities, the professions."[41] There were concerns that native intellectuals may have become estranged from their own cultural values to the point of being embarrassed by, and hostile towards, all that those values represented. In his introduction to Cesaire's *Return to My Native Land,* Mazisi Kunene wrote that "those [students] who returned despised and felt ashamed of their semi-literate or illiterate parents who spoke inelegant patois." [42] In New Zealand, the few Maori who were trained at universities in the last part of the 19th century are generally viewed positively as individuals who retained a love for their culture and language and who were committed in the context of the times to the survival of indigenous people. What is problematic is that this group of men have been named by the dominant non-indigenous population as individuals who represent "real" leadership. They have been idealized as the "saviours of the people," and their example remains as a "measure" of real leadership.

As Fanon has argued, the problem of creating and legitimating a national culture "represents a special battlefield,"[43] and intellectuals are important to this battle in a number of different ways. In recognizing that intellectuals were trained and encul-turated in the West, Fanon identifies three levels through which "native" intellec-tuals can progress in their journey "back over the line." [44] First is a phase of proving that intellectuals have been assimilated into the culture of the occupying power. Second comes a period of disturbance and the need for the intellectuals to remem-ber who they actually are, a time for remembering the past. In the third phase, the intellectuals seek to awaken the people, to realign themselves with the people, and to produce a revolutionary and national literature.[45] In this phase the "native writer progressively takes on the habit of addressing his [sic] own people".[46]

Fanon was writing about Algeria and the structure of French colonialism in Africa. He himself was trained in France as a psychiatrist and was influenced by European philosophies. One of the problems of connecting colonialism in New Zealand with its formations elsewhere is that New Zealand, like Canada and Australia, was already privileged as a white dominion within the British Empire and Commonwealth, with the indigenous populations being minorities. While geographically on the margins of Europe, New Zealanders were economically and culturally closely attached to Britain. Within these states the indigenous people were absolute minorities. The settlers who came arrived as permanent migrants. For indigenous peoples in these places this meant a different kind of experience with colonialism and different possibilities for decolonization. What it also points to is that indigenous intellectuals have emerged from different colonial and indigenous systems. In the Pacific Islands, for example, scholars come from majority cultures and independent island nations, but they have also been incorporated at a regional level into the metropolitan cultures of Australia and New Zealand.[47] Hau'ofa argues that "the ruling classes of the South Pacific are increasingly culturally homogeneous. They speak the same language, which is English; they share the same ideologies and the same material life styles...."[48]

Currently the role of the "native" intellectual has been reformulated not in relation to nationalist or liberationary discourses, but in relation to the "post-colonial" intellectual. Many intellectuals who position themselves as "post-colonial" move across the boundaries of indigenous and metropolitan, institution and community, politics and scholarship. Their place in the academy is still highly problematic. Gayatri Spivak, who writes as a post-colonial Asian/Indian intellectual working in the United States, argues that Third World intellectuals have to position themselves strategically as intellectuals within the academy, within the Third World or indigenous world, and within the Western world in which many intellectuals actually work. The problem for Third World intellectuals, she argues, remains the problem of being taken seriously.

> For me, the question "Who should speak?" is less crucial than "Who will listen?" "I will speak for myself as a Third World person" is an important position for political mobilisation today. But the real demand is that, when I speak from that position, I should be listened to seriously; not with that kind of benevolent imperialism....[49]

Spivak acknowledges that the task of changing the academy is difficult: "I would say that if one begins to take a whack at shaking the structure up, one sees how much more consolidated the opposition is."[50]

The role of intellectuals, teachers, artists, and writers in relation to indigenous communities is still problematic, and the rhetoric of liberation still forms part of indigenous discourses. Indigenous communities continue to view education in its Western, modern, sense as being critical to development and self-determination. While on the one hand criticizing indigenous people who have been educated at universities, many indigenous communities will on the other hand struggle and save to send their children to university. There is a very real ambivalence in indigenous communities towards the role of Western education and towards those who have been educated in universities. This is reflected in many contexts in struggles over leadership, representation, and voice between those perceived as "traditional" and those seen either as "radical" or simply as having Western credentials. In Australia, the term "flash blacks" encompasses both those who are well educated and those who have high-flying jobs. In New Zealand, one struggle over the value of Western education was played out in the 1980s through a process of reprivileging of "elders" and a reification of elders as the holders of all traditional knowledge, and a parallel depriviliging of the younger, frequently much better-educated (in a Western sense) members of an *iwi* (tribe). Maori academics who work away from their tribal territories can easily be criticized because they live away from home, and are therefore perceived as being distanced from the people. At the same time they are drawn into tribal life whenever a crisis occurs or there are additional demands for specialist knowledge and skills. The bottom line, however, is that in very fundamental ways they still remain members of an *iwi* with close relations to families and other community ties.

THE "AUTHENTIC, ESSENTIALIST, DEEPLY SPIRITUAL" OTHER

At a recent international conference held in New Zealand to discuss issues related to indigenous intellectual and cultural property rights, the local newspapers were informed and invited to interview some of the delegates. One news reporter thought it would be a good idea to have a group photograph, suggesting that it would be a very colourful feature for the newspaper to highlight. When she and the photographer turned up at the local *marae* (cultural centre), they were visibly disappointed at the motley display of track suits, jeans and other items of "modern" dress, and chose not to take a photograph. "Oh, I forgot to come as a native," joked one of the delegates. "My feathers got confiscated at the airport when I arrived." "I suppose my eyes are too blue." "Are we supposed to dress naked?" As we have seen, the notion of "authentic" is highly contested when applied to, or by, indigenous peoples. "Authorities" and outside experts are often called in to verify, comment upon, and give judgements about the validity of indigenous claims to cultural beliefs, values, ways of knowing, and historical accounts. Such issues are often debated vigorously by the "public," (a category which usually means the dominant group), leading to an endless parading of "19th century" views of race and racial difference. Questions of who is a "real indigenous" person, what counts as a "real indigenous leader," which person displays "real cultural values," and what criteria are used to assess the characteristics of authenticity are frequent topics of conversation and political debate. These debates are designed to fragment and marginalize those who speak for, or in support of, indigenous issues. They frequently also have the effect of silencing and making invisible the presence of other groups within the indigenous society, like women, the urban non-status tribal person, and those whose ancestry or "blood quantam" is "too white."[51] In Tasmania, where experts had already determined that Aborigines were "extinct", the voices of those who still speak as Aboriginal Tasmanians are interpreted thepolitical invention of a people who no longer exist and who therefore no longer have claims.

Recent post-structural and psychoanalytical feminist theorists have argued against the claims made by earlier generations of feminists that women as a group were different, because their essence as women was fundamentally, undeniably different, and that therefore their "sisterhood" would be a natural meeting place for all women. Pedagogically, essentialism was attacked because of its assumption that, because of this essence, it was necessary to be a woman and to experience life as a woman before one could analyze or understand women's oppression. Third World women and women of colour also attacked this assumption because it denied the impact of imperialisms, racism, and local histories of women, who were different from white women who lived in First World nations. The concept of "authenticity," which is related to essentialism, was also deconstructed, but more so from psychoanalytic perspectives because the concept assumed that if we strip away the oppressions and psychological consequences of oppression we would find a "pure" and authentic "self." One of the major problems with the way words are defined is that these debates are often held by academics in one context, within a specific intellectual discourse, and then appropriated by the media and popular press to serve a more blatant ideological and racist agenda.[52] As Trinh T. Minh-ha put it when writing of anthropologists in particular, "But once more *they* spoke. *They* decide who is "racism-free or anti-colonial," and they seriously think they can go on formulating criteria for us ...."[53]

In the colonized world, however, these terms are not necessarily employed in the same way that First World academics may have used them. The term *authentic*, for example, was an oppositional term used in at least two different ways. First, it was used as a form of articulating what it meant to be dehumanized by colonization; and, second, for reorganizing "national consciousness" in the struggles for decolonization. The belief in an authentic self is framed within humanism, but has been politicized by the colonized world in ways which invoke simultaneous meanings; it does appeal to an idealized past when there was no colonizer, to our strengths in surviving thus far, to our language as an uninterrupted link to our histories, to the ownership of our lands, to our abilities to create and control our own life and death, to a sense of balance among ourselves and with the environment, to our authentic selves as a people. Although this may seem overly idealized, these symbolic appeals remain strategically important in political struggles. Furthermore, the imputing of a Western psychological "self," which is a highly individualized notion, to group consciousness as it is centred in many colonized societies, is not a straightforward translation of the individual to the group, although this is often the only way that Westerners can come to understand what may constitute a group. The purpose of commenting on such a concept is that what counts as "authentic" is used by the West as one of the criteria to determine who really is indigenous, who is worth saving, who is still innocent and free from Western contamination. There is a very powerful tendency in research to take this argument back to a biological "essentialism" related to race, because the idea of culture is much more difficult to control. At the heart of such a view of authenticity is a belief that indigenous cultures cannot change, cannot recreate themselves and still claim to be indigenous. Nor can they be complicated, internally diverse or contradictory. Only the West has that privilege.

The concept of essentialism is also discussed in different ways within the indigenous world. It is accepted as a term which is related to humanism and is therefore seen in the same way as the idea of authenticity. In this use of the word, claiming essential characteristics is as much strategic as anything else, because it has been about claiming human rights and indigenous rights. But the essence of a person is also discussed in relation to indigenous concepts of spirituality. In these views, the essence of a person has a genealogy which can be traced back to an earth parent, usually glossed as an Earth Mother. A human person does not stand alone, but shares with other animate and, in the Western sense, "inanimate" beings, a relationship based on a shared "essence" of life. The significance of place, of land, of landscape, of other things in the universe, in defining the very essence of a people, makes for a very different rendering of the term "essentialism" as used by indigenous peoples. The arguments of different indigenous peoples based on spiritual relationships to the universe, to the landscape and to stones, rocks, insects and other things, seen and unseen, have been difficult for Western systems of knowledge to deal with or accept. These arguments give a partial indication of the different world views and alternative ways of coming to know, and of being, which still endure within the indigenous world. Concepts of spirituality which Christianity attempted to destroy, then to appropriate, and then to claim, are critical sites of resistance for indigenous peoples. The values, attitudes, concepts, and language embedded in beliefs about spirituality represent, in many cases, the clearest contrast and mark of difference between indigenous peoples and the West. It is one of the few parts of ourselves which the West cannot decipher, cannot understand and cannot control ... yet.

NOTES

1. Mita, M. (1989), "Merata Mita On...," in the *New Zealand Listener,* 14 October, p. 30.
2. Ngugi wa Thiong'o. (1986), *Decolonizing the Mind: the Politics of Language in African Literature,* James Currey, London.
3. Jaggar, A. (1983), *Feminist Politics and Human Nature,* Harvester Press, Sussex.
4. Hall, S. (1992), "The West and the Rest: Discourse and Power," Chapter 6 of *Formations of Modernity,* eds S. Hall and B. Gielben, Polity Press and Open University, Cambridge, pp. 276–320.

5. Goonatilake, S. (1982), "Colonies: Scientific Expansion (and Contraction)," in *Review*, Vol. 5, No. 3, Winter, pp. 413–36.
6. Said, E. (1978), *Orientalism*, Vintage Books, New York, p. 7.
7. Bazin, M. (1993), "Our Sciences, Their Science," in *Race and Class*, Vol. 34, No. 2, pp. 35–6.
8. Goonatilake, "Colonies."
9. Adas, M. (1989), *Machines as the Measure of Man. Science, Technology and Ideologies of Western Dominance*, Cornell University Press, Ithaca.
10. Clifford, J. (1988), *The Predicament of Culture, Twentieth Century Ethnography, Literature, and Art*, Harvard University Press, Cambridge, p. 231. See also on the topic of collection, Ames, M. (1986), *Museums, The Public and Anthropology*, University of Columbia Press, London.
11. Brockway, L. H. (1979), *Science and Colonial Expansion. The Role of the British Royal Botanical Gardens*, Academic Press, New York, p. 187.
12. Goonatilake, "Colonies," p. 432.
13. Crosby, A. W. (1986), "Biotic Change in Nineteenth Century New Zealand," in *Review*, Vol. 9, No. 3, Winter, pp. 325–37.
14. Smith, C. W. (1994), "Kimihia te Matauranga, Colonization and Iwi Development," MA thesis, University of Auckland, p. 23.
15. Pool, D. L. (1977), *The Maori Population of New Zealand 1769–1971*, Auckland University Press and Oxford University Press, Auckland, pp. 75–105.
16. Churchill, W. (1994), *Indians Are Us? Culture and Genocide in Native North America*, Common Courage Press, Maine.
17. *Ibid.*, pp. 28–42.
18. Sykes, R. B. (1989), *Black Majority*, Hudson Hawthorn, Victoria, p. 185.
19. Bernal, M. (1991), *Black Athena, The Afroasiatic Roots of Classical Civilisation*, Vintage, London.
20. Said, E. *Orientalism*, pp. 205–6.
21. See, for examples of these debates in relation to indigenous issues, Ngugi wa Thiong'o (1986), *Decolonizing the Mind: The Politics of Language in African Literature*, James Currey, London, and Haunani Kay Trask (1993), *From a Native Daughter*, Common Courage Press, Maine.
22. Young, R. (1990), *White Mythologies, Writing, History and the West*, Routledge, London, p. 3.
23. Goldberg, D. T. (1993), *Racist Culture: Philosophy and the Politics of Meaning*, Blackwell, Oxford.
24. Laffey, J. F. (1993), *Civilization and its Discontented*, Black Rose Books, New York.
25. Torgovnick, M. (1990), *Gone Primitive: Savage Intellects, Modern Lives*, University of Chicago Press, Chicago.
26. *Ibid.*, p. 7.
27. Gates, H. L. (1994), "Authority (White) Power and the (Black) Critic: It's All Greek to Me," in *Culture/Power/History*, eds N. Dirks, G. Eley and S. B. Ortner, Princeton University Press, New Jersey.
28. Stocking, G. Jr (1987), *Victorian Anthropology*, The Free Press, London.
29. Kuper, A. (1988), *The Invention of Primitive Society*, Routledge, London, p. 5.
30. Trask, H. K. (1993), *From a Native Daughter*, Common Courage Press, Maine.
31. Minh-ha, Trinh T. (1989), *Woman, Native, Other*, Indiana University Press, Bloomington, p. 59.
32. Livingstone, D. (1992), *The Geographical Tradition*, Blackwell, Oxford.
33. *Ibid.*, p. 216.
34. Abu-Lughod, J. (1989), "On the Remaking of History: How to Reinvent the Past," in *Remaking History*, Dia Art Foundation, Bay Press, Seattle, p. 118.
35. Awatere, D. (1983), "Awatere on Intellectuals: Academic Fragmentation or Visionary Unity," article in *Craccum*, Auckland University Students' Association, 3 May, Auckland, pp. 6–7.
36. Bernstein, B. (1971), "On the Classification and Framing of Knowledge" in *Knowledge and Control: New Directions for the Sociology of Education*, ed. M. F. D. Young, Collier Macmillan, London, pp. 47–69.
37. Foucault, M. (1977), *Discipline and Punish: The Birth of the Prison*, trans. A. Sheridan, Penguin, London, p. 137.

38. This practice is known popularly as the "stolen children" policy but an official inquiry was conducted by the Australian government called "A National Inquiry into the Separation of Aboriginal and Torres Strait Islander Children from Their Families." This was completed in 1997.

39. A government commission to investigate the abuses in the residential school system for Indian children was recently completed by the Canadian government. For further background read Furness, E. (1995), *Victims of Benevolence: The Dark Legacy of the Williams Lake Residential School,* Arsenal Pulp Press, Vancouver; Haig-Brown, C. (1988), *Resistance and Renewal: Surviving the Indian Residential School,* Tillacum Library, Vancouver in L. Taine, ed. (1993), *Residential Schools: the Stolen Years,* University of Saskatchewan Press, Saskatoon.

40. Gramsci's views on the intellectual have been influential, among other Marxist views. So too have the existentialist views of Jean-Paul Sartre, who wrote the Introduction to Fanon's book, *The Wretched of the Earth.* A critique of these influences on Fanon, in particular, can be read in Young, *White Mythologies.*

41. Awatere, D. (1984), Maori Sovereignty, Broadsheet, Auckland, p. 83.

42. Cesaire, A. (1969), *Return to My Native Land,* translated by John Berger and Ana Bostock, Introduction by Mazisi Kunene, Penguin Books, Harmondsworth, p. 24.

43. Fanon, F. (1990), *The Wretched of the Earth,* Penguin, London, p. 193.

44. *Ibid.,* pp. 178–9.

45. *Ibid.,* p. 179.

46. *Ibid.,* p. 193.

47. Hau'ofa, E. (1987), "The New South Pacific Society: Integration and Independence," in *Class and Culture in the South Pacific,* eds A. Hooper, S. Britton, R. Crocombe, J. Huntsman and C. Macpherson, Centre for Pacific Studies, University of Auckland, Institute for Pacific Studies, University of the South Pacific, pp. 1–15.

48. *Ibid.,* p. 3.

49. Spivak, G. (1990), "Questions of Multiculturalism," in *The Post-Colonial Critic: Interviews, Strategies, Dialogues,* ed. S. Harasayam, Routledge, New York, pp. 59–60.

50. Spivak, G. (1990), "Criticism, Feminism and the Institution," in *The Post-Colonial Critic,* p. 6.

51. "Blood quantum" refers to the "amount" of native blood one has and is used in places such as Hawai'i to determine eligibility access to Hawaiian lands and identity. It is based on racial beliefs that the more indigenous peoples intermarried the more assimilated or "watered down" they became. Conversely if they did not inter-marry they remained "pure."

52. Similar debates occur over a word such as "invention," where anthropologists may talk to each other about the invention of culture; the media can then accuse indigenous people of inventing culture to serve their own interests *at the expense of the dominant group.* This occurred in New Zealand over an article written by A. Hanson (1991), "The Making of the Maori: Culture Invention and its Logic," in *American Anthropologist,* pp. 890–902. One of the larger daily newspapers took the article and turned it into the following headline: "US EXPERT SAYS MAORI CULTURE INVENTED," *Dominion,* Saturday 24 February.

53. Minh-ha, Trin T., *Woman, Native, Other,* p. 59.

CRITICAL-THINKING QUESTIONS

CHAPTER 1 *by David Maybury-Lewis*

1. What role do you consider that the theoretical concept of "Darwinism" played in the colonization of Indigenous Peoples?
2. Why is it difficult to give a precise definition of indigenous people?
3. According to the author, why is there widespread prejudice against Indigenous Peoples?

CHAPTER 2 *by Grant McCall*

1. Why do think that this remote island with few natural resources was worth the attention of European colonial powers?
2. What role did the missionaries play in the colonization of Rapanui?
3. Why do you think the Rapanui leader, Torometi, aligned himself with the Frenchman, Bornier, in fighting other Rapanui? Do you know of other examples, from other countries, of indigenous people siding with "outsiders" against people of their own kind?

CHAPTER 3 *by Brett L. Walker*

1. What was the effect of the market economy on Ainu autonomy?
2. In what ways did environmental degradation through mining in the 16th century affect Ainu subsistence living patterns? Are there any contemporary examples of this happening in Canada?
3. Explain why creating a dependence on trade goods among Indigenous Peoples is a colonizing strategy.

CHAPTER 4 *by Michael Kioni Dudley and Keoni Kealoha Agard*

1. Why was Hawai'i part of the United States of America's expansionist agenda?
2. When Hawai'i was annexed by the United States of America in 1897, Hawai'i had its own monarchy and an indigenous queen. How did the USA justify the annexation of this independent kingdom?
3. Why have the homestead rights negotiated by Prince Kuhio for his people not benefited Native Hawaiians?

CHAPTER 5 *by Linda Tuhiwai Smith*

1. In what way have schools been used in the colonization of indigenous people?
2. Why is the position of Western-educated indigenous academics in their home communities problematic?
3. How did colonization result in Western knowledge becoming regarded as superior to indigenous knowledge systems?

FURTHER READING

Blaut, J. M. 1993. *The Colonizer's Model of the World: Geographic Diffusion and Eurocentric History*. New York: The Guilford Press.

Blaut challenges the notion that the West has intellectual superiority over others and argues that this represents an ideology of colonialism.

Bodley, John H. 1999. *Victims of Progress*. 4th ed. London: Mayfield Publishing Company.

In this publication, the author positions indigenous societies in dichotomy with large-scale industrialized societies and argues that development policies continue to expand at the expense of the environment and Indigenous Peoples.

Burns, Bradford. 1994. *Latin America: A Concise Interpretive History*. New Jersey: Prentice Hall.

This book offers a comprehensive overview of the Portuguese and Spanish colonization of the Americas as well as the subsequent formation of the countries that now make up Latin America. Of particular interest to Indigenous Studies students is the imposition of Iberian notions of land tenure, which continue to privilege powerful landowners and act against the interests of Indigenous Peoples. Popular movements for land reforms are branded communist, and are very quickly and brutally suppressed, often with the assistance of other Western powers.

Wolf, Eric. 1997. *Europe and People Without History*. Berkley: University of California Press.

Using anthropology, history, and the social sciences, the author presents a Marxian analysis of the imperial expansion of Western Europe and the incorporation of indigenous societies into capitalism.

Stewart-Harawira, Makere. 2005. *The New Imperial Order: Indigenous Responses to Globalization*. Wellington, Huia Publishing.

A recent publication that brings forward many of the arguments of Wolf and other writers into the 21st century, in which historical colonization is supplanted by globalization.

PART II:

COLONIALISM, GENOCIDE, AND

THE PROBLEM OF INTENTION

ᕤ

THE TERM GENOCIDE IS ALMOST EXCLUSIVELY associated with deliberate Nazi attempts to obliterate Jews during World War II. Part of the reason why the association between genocide and the Nazis is so common is because it has been well-documented both by the Nazis themselves and by scholarly analysis. Additionally, however, in contemporary Canada we tend to place a great deal of importance on the role of *intention* in action; therefore, the fact that the Nazis *intended* to obliterate Jewish peoples renders their actions especially heinous. If we suspend our preoccupation with intention, however, and attempt to understand colonialism from the standpoint of its *effects*, we can explore the heterogeneity of genocidal effects on indigenous societies without getting caught up in arguments about whether colonial projects were intended to have these effects. Likewise, examining the effects of colonial intrusion highlights the falsity of creating a division between geno- and ethno-cide. Indeed, the following readings show that whether physical or cultural, intentional or not, the varied contexts and circumstances of colonialism often had devastatingly similar effects. These readings trace several contexts and effects through the impact of disease in South America, the complex politics through which nation-states (in this case Australia) attempt to mitigate or disavow altogether earlier genocidal activities, the devastating impact of past cultural-modification experiments on indigenous societies in Canada, and the impact of colonially based economics on the sustainability of indigenous societies in the contemporary era of globalization.

Taken from a speech by American Indian Movement leader Russell Means, the strongly worded first reading leaves no doubt as to the United States' role in the tacit approval or outright involvement in various genocidal moments that have occurred across the globe over the past century. The point of presenting this reading isn't to establish its true or falsity, but rather to demonstrate the *politics of memory* which have become central to any contemporary discussions about what genocide is and where it occurred. The extract from Noble David Cook's *Born to Die* provides a sobering account of the genocidal impact of various diseases on Indigenous Peoples in the first century after contact with South America and the Caribbean. Cook's reading makes clear that the conquering of indigenous societies did not result simply from explicit colonial strategies. Instead, Cook carefully notes the devastating impact of compound epidemics—different diseases which followed closely on the heels of one another—on the peoples of South America. Those who were resistant or lucky enough to survive the first wave of disease often fell prey to the second, third, or fourth. Cook's basic point is that colonial societies achieved the subjugation of indigenous ones not because of superior technology or more advanced civilizations, but because they carried with them various pathogens unknown to indigenous populations, who thus had no immunity to them. Cook shows how these pathogens devastated indigenous populations after even short periods of contact and transmission.

Although one might argue that the impact of pathogens on indigenous societies in central and South America was unintentional, many nation-states bearing the legacy of British colonialism like to believe that no systematic genocide of any kind occurred within their borders. In his article "Confronting Australian Genocide," Colin Tatz provides striking evidence that, though on a smaller scale, the Australian nation-state engaged in precisely the kind of genocidal activities (against the Indigenous Peoples of Australia) found so morally reprehensible in World War II Nazi Germany. More importantly, however, Tatz explores the ways that supposedly liberal nation-states like Australia attempt to come to terms—partly by denying or downplaying historical incidents—with their pasts. In particular, he demonstrates the central role played by denial in either refusing the terms of the debate altogether, or in dissociating the contemporary nation-state from past activities by virtue of the fact that they are just that—in the past.

Though in a different way, Canada also experimented with the cultural "modification" of Indigenous Peoples. In concert with various Churches, Canada set up a large number of residential schools which operated throughout the end of the 19th and a large part of the 20th centuries. Recently, several lawsuits have been launched by national Aboriginal political organizations to shed light on and seek redress for the physical and emotional trauma experienced by Aboriginal children who attended these residential schools. In their article "Killing the Indian in the Child," Suzanne Fournier and Ernie Crey recount the survival stories of these students as well as the racist social context within which these institutions were created. The authors note the operating procedures that saw Aboriginal children forced to leave their families and communities for years at a time, and the wide discretion given to priests and nuns that resulted in the physical and sexual abuse of Aboriginal children. The authors leave little doubt that residential schools were intentionally created in an attempt to erase all traces of indigeneity from the children who were unfortunate enough to attend them.

Sometimes, however, understanding the decline of indigenous societies—however we define them—is not so easy. In a subsection of a larger chapter on indigenous people and the nation-state entitled "The Guaraní: The Economics of Ethnocide," Richard H. Robbins examines the case of an indigenous society in eastern Paraguay. He explains how the Guaraní of this area had, in the centuries after contact with European traders and colonialists, managed to carve out an economically and culturally sustainable niche for themselves within the larger context of colonial economic relations. However, Robbins demonstrates how this relationship has in recent decades been threatened by the growing needs of economic globalization, in particular by the destruction of rainforests in pursuit of less ecologically sustainable but more profitable commodity crops. He shows how, in destroying their land base, these largely imposed economic structures forced the Guaraní into either growing their own cash crops or selling their labour to others who did.

EXTRACT FROM *A LITTLE MATTER OF GENOCIDE:*

HOLOCAUST AND DENIAL IN THE AMERICAS 1492 TO THE PRESENT

Russell Means

ALL MY LIFE, I've had to listen to rhetoric about the United States being a model of freedom and democracy, the most uniquely enlightened and humanitarian country in history, a "nation of laws" which, unlike others, has never pursued policies of conquest and aggression. I'm sure you've heard it before. It's official "truth" in the United States. It's what is taught to school children, and it's the line peddled to the general public. Well, I've got a hot news flash for everybody here. It's a lie. The whole thing's a lie, and it always has been. Leaving aside the obvious points which could be raised to disprove it by Blacks and Chicanos and Asian immigrants right here in North America—not to mention the Mexicans, the Nicaraguans, the Guatemalans, the Puerto Ricans, the Hawaiians, the Filipinos, the Samoans, the Tamarros of Guam, the Marshall Islanders, the Koreans, the Vietnamese, the Cubans, the Dominicans, the Grenadans, the Libyans, the Panamanians, the Iraqis, and a few dozen other peoples out there who've suffered American invasions and occupations first hand—there's *a little matter of genocide* that's got to be taken into account right here at home. I'm talking about the genocide which has been perpetrated against American Indians, a genocide that began the instant the first of Europe's boat people washed up on the beach of Turtle Island, a genocide that's continuing right now, at this moment. Against Indians, there's not a law the United States hasn't broken, not a Crime Against Humanity it hasn't committed, and it's still going on.

Russell Means

American Indian Movement

October 12, 1992

SETTLING IN: EPIDEMICS AND CONQUEST TO THE END OF THE FIRST CENTURY

Noble David Cook

The following extract explores the impact of various diseases on Indigenous Peoples in South America and the Caribbean in the first century after contact with the colonizers.

COMPOUND EPIDEMICS OF 1576–1591

EPIDEMICS THAT CLOSELY FOLLOWED earlier ones appear to have done the most severe damage, and the 1576 to 1591 series was one of the deadliest. People already weakened by a bout with the first sicknesses were swept away quickly when they came down with a subsequent malady. As one approaches the end of the century, the documentary record improves. Indeed, the epidemic series of 1576–80 is one of the best documented for Mexico, in part because of the efforts of Spanish royal officials to comply with Philip II's order to compile the geographical descriptions *(relaciones geográficas)* for each province. According to Borah and Cook, the agricultural year 1575–76 had been marked by drought, crop failure, and famine.[1] The epidemic first appeared in August 1576, according to the Chimalpahin source, and by October the number of cases was declining. It appeared again early in 1577 and continued to April. The following year seemed to be free of disease, but illness resurfaced in 1579 in conjunction with other sicknesses.[2] Other similar patterns of flare-ups followed by abatements characterize the epidemic in central Mexico, with some areas being spared during one passage only to be hit in a subsequent onslaught. Such a pattern could easily be a consequence of the existence of two, even three or more different disease factors, thus complicating analysis of the series. Observers note that by the end of the half decade, most regions of Mexico and Guatemala had come under the influence of these deadly infections.

Disease was also a factor in reducing the number of Amerindian peoples to the south in Nicaragua during the same period. The best modern study of the situation in the region is by Newson, who found evidence that *romadizo*, or catarrh, hit Nicaragua in 1578. Both native Americans and Europeans were infected, but mortality was generally low for both groups. Pneumonic plague may have been present in Guatemala at the time, and a Honduran epidemic may have been a minor localized outbreak of the same disease. Newson also found documentation for an unidentified epidemic reported to have taken 300 lives in Nicaragua (1573) in only 20 days.[3]

In the Andes the 1570s were not as deadly for Amerindians as in Mesoamerica, but the following decade was. Speed of disease dissemination depends on a number of factors, of which population density is one important component. The higher the population density, the more rapid the spread of infectious community diseases. Native American depopulation in the years immediately after contact, and the dispersed settlement pattern found throughout most of the central Andes, led Spanish officials to attempt to congregate the Indians into villages. Clerics and bureaucrats had advocated concentration of people earlier, and Francisco Pizarro had even made a half-hearted attempt in the late 1530s. But instability and civil wars had prevented systematic application of the process through the mid-1550s. Beginning in the early 1570s, Viceroy Francisco de Toledo's resettlement program *(reducciones)* in the viceroyalty of Peru was designed to create a Christian Utopia in the New World. Where earlier Andean residents had lived scattered in small communities of a few families, spread across the landscape, Toledo brought them together into villages of several thousand inhabitants, where they could be more closely watched, indoctrinated, and taxed. It was one of the most successful urban planning efforts in the Americas, and many of the towns established by the viceroy continue into the 20th century. But unwittingly, the viceroy established the conditions necessary for a new epidemic crisis by sharply increasing population density in an urban context. Quickly, Toledo's living Utopia turned into a death trap for the Amerindian peoples of the Andes.

Within a decade after the *reducciones* had been established, a devastating series of epidemics passed through the Andes; it proved to be one of the most severe to hit the west coast of South America in the era and was just as disastrous as the one in central Mexico in the early 1550s. The duration and sharp impact of the 1585–91 crisis indicates that two, perhaps three or more, disease factors were operating. Indeed, sifting through the extensive evidence exposes the difficulty in dating the termination of one epidemic and the inception of another. The first seems to have afflicted Peru in 1585. According to Montesinos, smallpox and measles reached Cuzco in the form of a *peste universal* in 1585.[4] One city resident described the ailment as "high fevers with mumps" and claimed that thousands died in the city. The council of Huamanga (modern Ayacucho) closed the road with Cuzco to prevent the spread of the contagion, suggesting that the epidemic was moving westward.[5] What was described as *dolor de costado,* or pleurisy, was present at the same time, and the illness came with such force that those who were stricken suffered intensely. The epidemic recurred in Cuzco in 1590, with many Indian and creole victims. Father Barrasa in 1586 wrote about a smallpox epidemic in which young people were attacked with a merciless fury that reaped numerous victims. Native

Americans were especially hard hit in this sweeping pandemic that stretched from Cartagena on the Gulf Coast of New Granada to Chile.[6] About 3,000 perished in Lima from the epidemic in 1586, mostly Indians, but many Blacks died too. As the rash healed, victims fell to "catarrh and cough," likely influenza or pneumonia, with the children and elderly the principal victims. Lima, with its population of approximately 14,262 in 1600, lost about 20 percent of its inhabitants to the 1586 onslaught. The city's Jesuits mourned six out of 60 of their own who died in the Lima house, so the death rate for the Jesuits was about half that of the population at large. In the Indian Hospital of Santa Ana, 14 to 16 died each day for a period of two months; the consequence was that "an innumerable quantity of Indians died."[7]

Andean South America was probably infected through the port and slave center of Cartagena de Indias, just as had happened in the 1558 Colombian epidemic outbreak. Old World disease could have been introduced in the normal course of the human trade, or might have been the result of infections carried by the crew of the expedition of Sir Francis Drake. Drake had departed from Plymouth, England, on 14 September 1585, with about 2,300 men. The fleet stopped on 17 November at the port of Santiago in the Portuguese Cape Verde Islands. The residents of the town fled, and the English stole anything of value they could lay hands on. Unfortunately, they carried away far more than they realized: "There was adjoining to their greatest church an hospital, with as brave rooms in it, and in as goodly order as any man can devise; we found about 20 sick persons, all negroes, lying of very foul and frightful diseases. In the hospital we took all the bells out of the steeple and brought them away with us." They took more than church bells; they took the peal of death, for on 1 December, two days after leaving the islands, disease flared among the crew with a vengeance. Victims broke out with a "rash of small spots" and suffered high fever. Drake stopped at Dominica, traded with Indians, sailed on and attacked the Spanish city of Santo Domingo, then continued and took the port of Cartagena, occupying it for six weeks in early 1586. The attacking force in mid-March 1586 consisted of about 1,000 men. Continuing to be plagued by disease, Drake's forces passed sickness on to the permanent residents, who suffered greatly from its effects. Weakened by the disease, the English gave up and headed home, but may have also transferred disease to St. Augustine. By the time the fleet set sail for the return to England, 750 men had perished, three-quarters of them from the fever taken in the Cape Verde Islands. Dobyns believes that the Drake group suffered from a vectored disease; because Europeans suffered too, it was not measles or smallpox but more likely typhus. Had it been bubonic plague, it would have probably been diagnosed accurately, for Spanish physicians had seen the plague all too frequently in Europe in the 16th century and could easily identify it.[8]

Alchon records the initial appearance of disease in Quito in or following 1585, and then chronicles the 1587 Quito outbreak in detail. In February 1587, the native American confraternity of the Holy Cross was so destitute that it was forced to petition the Audiencia to provide funds to help cure and bury those stricken by the disease. First noticed in July 1587, the epidemic continued for nine seemingly interminable months. A contemporary reported that 4,000 died during a brief three months; many victims were children.[9] According to the geographical report, the elements were "typhus, smallpox and measles … innumerable people, Creoles, men and women, children and Indians" died.[10] The epidemic lingered in the Ecuadorian highlands well into 1590. Before the series of diseases subsided in 1591, "they left behind a trail of death and destruction unsurpassed by even the 1558 outbreak. In fact, the sharpest drop in Quito's native American population during the 16th century, at least as far as is presently known, occurred between 1560 and 1590; the epidemics of 1585–91 were primarily responsible."[11]

The Colombian disease experience of 1588 is also well documented. Castellanos noted that the epidemic came by way of an infected female slave who had been brought from Mariguita on the coast.[12] The infection was present in Cartagena in 1588 and spread quickly throughout Colombia. Castellanos reported especially high mortality for "boys, girls, youth." Almost all informants from Colombia indicate smallpox as the principal component. One contemporary said that the 1553 bout was "one of the most unfortunate that the natives have experienced." It took more than a third of the population, striking Spaniards as well as Indians.[13]

Bernabé Cobo, who was an eyewitness, reported that the 1588 series covered Popayan and Quito and entered Peru. He traced the source of infection to trade goods imported on ships. It afflicted the black population and caused a "monstrous ugliness in the faces and bodies." Women were especially vulnerable; spontaneous abortions were commonplace in those who were infected: "The fetuses were not expelled from the womb, and they died from the force and the rigor of the fire and torment." Purges and bloodlettings, among the most common cures at the time, were used to combat the contagion, and, if we are to believe Cobo, the condition of many Indians improved with the bleedings.[14]

On 21 March 1589, Peruvian Viceroy Fernando de Torres y Portugal, the Conde de Villar, wrote to Philip II that the epidemic of "smallpox and measles" had reached coastal Trujillo. He had established a commission to block, by quarantine, the southward drift of contagion and to assist those who fell ill. On April 19, he wrote that in

the epidemic of smallpox and measles that began to hit the province of Quito, and from which some people have begun to die, the natives are receiving particular injury … following it is a pestilential typhus.… In the highland provinces there has arrived, at almost the same time, another sickness of cough and *romadizo* with fevers, from which in Potosí more than ten thousand Indians have sickened, as well as some Spaniards. Up until now there has not been noticeable harm either in Cuzco or Huancavelica.

Physicians Hierónymo Enriquez and Francisco Franco Mendoza advised the viceroy to recommend the use of sugar, oil, honey, raisins, and meat to help block infection. The all-too-common practice of bleeding was also cited as a useful tool to save those who were sick. The viceregal recommendation to burn the clothing of those who died was an important positive step to slow the contagion. It was precisely what the Conde de Villar had ordered in Seville at the beginning of the 1580s as an effort to block passage of the plague. Nonetheless, also on 19 April, the viceroy wrote that smallpox and measles already had done their damage in Quito, where they had "destroyed and killed a great number of Indians." It had reached Cuenca, Paitá, and finally Trujillo. In spite of the best efforts of the medical commission, the sickness reached Lima in June 1589, and by the end of the year it struck Cuzco.[15]

The Jesuit Provincial in Lima described victims in frightful detail: "Virulent pustules broke out on the entire body that deformed the miserable sick persons to the point that they could not be recognized except by name." Dobyns found that "the pustules obstructed nasal passages and throats, impeding respiration and food ingestion, occasioning some deaths from these complications. Many survivors lost one or both eyes."[16] The symptoms described in Cuzco parallel those of Lima. The epidemic arrived around mid-September, in spite of cutting transportation across the Apurimac bridge, halting the flow of wine into the city, and conducting many religious celebrations to ward off the approaching pestilence. The author of a Cuzco annal reported ulcerated lips, eyes, and throats, with "tumors, callous excrescences or itchy scabs or very nasty pustules." It was virtually impossible to prevent those afflicted from scratching themselves, and Cuzco's small-pox victims were marked with "monstrous ugliness in faces and bodies." It is little wonder that most of those with the disease fell into profound depression.[17]

The epidemic series greatly devastated Arequipa, where it erupted in 1589. Joralemon identifies the Arequipa outbreak as "a combination of fulminating and malignant confluent (variola major) smallpox." He noted that typical mortality in this combination is 30 percent. Infants tended to be affected most by the disease: "as recently as 1885 the case mortality for ages 0–4 was 60 percent."[18] The symptoms in adult cases in general were described in detail by Dobyns:

The onset of the disease brought severe headaches and kidney pains. A few days later, patients became stupefied, then delirious, and ran naked through the streets shouting. Patients who broke out in a rash had a good chance to recover, reportedly, while those who did not break out seemed to have little chance. Ulcerated throat extinguished the lives of many patients. Fetuses died in the uterus. Even patients who broke out in a rash might lose chunks of flesh by too sudden movement.[19]

Viceroy Villar on 11 May 1589 wrote Philip II that the illness was becoming less virulent in Peru's north and apologized that he had been unable to send more reports on local conditions "because everyone is ill and those who are well are very busy curing them." The sickness was spreading and recently had reached Lima, but at the time the viceroy reported to the monarch there were still few deaths, and most of those who did succumb were Blacks and native Americans. "But the illness is so general that there is scarcely a person in the place who is not touched with it." By the middle of June, epidemic-related deaths in Lima had soared. On 13 June, the viceroy wrote the king that "catarrhal smallpox and measles" were worse in the capital. His description of disease susceptibility is informative: "People have died in this city, among them natives and Blacks and mulattos and Spaniards born here, and now it has spread to those from Castile." All became sick, and mortality affected all ages in this compound series. On 16 June, the viceroy lamented that disease had again hit Trujillo with renewed fury and that many natives and "even Creoles and Spaniards died" from "catarrh and pleurisy."[20] Dobyns believes that influenza moved from Lima into Peru's north, following the disease that produced the symptoms of a rash. But in Lima the rash bearing the sickness followed influenza. By 28 June, Viceroy Conde de Villar sent an inspector to the communities of Surco, Lati, and Luringancho to set up hospitals supplied with beds and well stocked with medicines; on 12 July, he named a surgeon for a tenure of six months to cure the ill in San Juan de Matocana, San Gerónimo de Surco, and San Mateo de Guanchor.[21]

Mortality levels from the compound epidemics were as high as any previous ones, perhaps even higher, because during these years, not one epidemic but two or three coincided. If one suffered from one disease and survived, then was infected by a subsequent disease, the body's forces were incapable of fighting the second infection successfully. In the border districts between the Audiencias of Lima and Quito, deaths were exceptionally high. Native chiefs of the Jaén and Yaguarsongo districts reported in 1591 that, especially in the smallpox series, it was well known that in the valley of Jaén and province only 1,000 of an original 30,000 Indians remained.[22]

The epidemic series afflicted highland Charcas, too. Thanks to some exceptionally well-preserved records, Evans was able to study in derail one native-American community, Aymaya, from 1583 to 1623, and estimate mortality levels. The normal number of annual burials among the Aymaya in the 1580s was in the twenties. In 1590 the number exploded to 194, slightly over 10 percent of the community's population, based on Evans's estimate of about 1,800 as the total population of the

Aymaya on the eve of the epidemic. Of these deaths, 147 were listed in the registers as having been precipitated by smallpox. About 45 percent of deaths were of children under 10, again a reflection of the terrible impact of smallpox on the young. There were very few deaths among males over 40 during the 1590 smallpox epidemic. This suggests that the cohort above the age of 40 had experienced, or had at least been exposed to, one or more smallpox epidemics that had extended through the region in the decades before 1550.[23]

Most components of the series assailed the entire Andean region, ultimately flowing into Chile, where both Spaniards and Araucanian Indians were infected.[24] The 1585–91 epidemic series also invaded the upper Amazon basin and may have drifted downstream. We have noted the impact on Jaen, where the native population of 30,000 dropped to 1,000. Yaguarsongo and Pacamoros were hit hard. Between 1585 and 1586, "pestilence" and *"enfermedades"* were reported in Loyola and Santiago de las Montañas. In Cangasa the population fell by more than a third. All these population centers have relatively easy access to the lower stretches of the montaña and the Amazon basin beyond. Unfortunately, measurement of the impact of disease in the Amazon basin is difficult, the consequence of inadequate documentation. The early descriptions of the expeditions of Francisco de Orellana (1541–42) and Pedro de Ursúa, and Lope de Aguirre (1560–61) make no comment regarding poor health conditions in the places the explorers visited.

Foreign disease was inadvertently introduced to the peoples of the southeastern part of what became the United States, La Florida, many times during the course of the 16th century. The ill members of Sir Francis Drake's English fleet, as we have seen, carried sickness to Florida in 1586 on their way home from Cartagena in the Indies. Though much weakened by disease, the English stopped briefly, from 27 May to 2 June, and sacked the fortified port of St. Augustine on the Florida coast. According to the log of the *Primrose,* "The wilde people at first comminge of our men died verie fast and said amongst themselues, It was the Englisshe God that made them die so faste."[25] Four years later, another epidemic seemed to carry native victims to the grave. Royal accountant Bartolomé de Argüelles wrote to the Crown on 12 May 1591 that "this last year there was among them a mortality and many died, and also part of this cabildo and fortress was affected."[26] This epidemic, perhaps linked to the series that so seriously afflicted Mesoamerica and the Andean region, was probably separate from any sickness introduced by Drake.

Furthermore, epidemic disease struck Amerindians near the Raleigh colony on the coast of the Carolinas in 1587. Thomas Harriot reported that after the English had toured hostile native-American settlements, "people began to die very fast, and in many in short space; in some townes about twentie, in some fourtie, in some sixtie, and in one six score." As Harriot said, this, in proportion to the size of the town, was substantial. "The disease also was so strange that they neither knew what it was, nor how to cure it; the like by report of the oldest men in the countrey never happened before, time out of mind."[27] Apparently no serious ill effects were experienced by the approximately 100 Englishmen there at the time.

During the 16th century, the native peoples of the Americas experienced one disaster after another. The Europeans brought not only their arms for conquest but also their plants and animals and their pathogens. It was not a single infection that came, but one, then another, a third, a fourth, and more. Just as the outsiders settled and became colonists, Old World diseases settled in, and some gradually became endemic. Taken together, the various epidemics resulted in a huge loss of life and led to relatively easy subjugation of an entire hemisphere. Of the several pandemics to sweep the Americas in the 16th century, three series stood out in the popular mind as watersheds. In Mesoamerica, Juan Bautista Pomar, who compiled the history of Tetzcoco, emphasized the three major killers: those in 1520, 1545, and 1576. For him the first plague was the most deadly. In the same vein, Diego Muñoz Camargo wrote in the1580s of the impact of disease on Tlaxcala: "I say that the first [1520] ought to be the greatest because there were more people, and the second [1545] was also very great because the land was very full [of people], and this last one [1576] was not as great as the first two.[28] The sequence was similar in Andean America, although the third pandemic wave was especially devastating there because of the quick succession of highly mortal pathogens. Debilitated and convalescing peoples easily fell victim to fresh new infections.

NOTES

1. Borah and Cook, *Essays in Population History,* 2:115.
2. Prem, "Disease Outbreaks in Central Mexico," p. 42.
3. Newson, *Indian Survival in Nicaragua,* p. 247.
4. Lastres, *Historia de la medicina peruana,* 2:76–77.
5. Dobyns, "Andean Epidemic History," p. 501.
6. Lastres, *Historia de la medicina peruana,* 2:77.
7. Dobyns, "Andean Epidemic History," pp. 501–502; José Toribio Polo, "Apuntes sobre las epidemias del Perú," *Revista Histórica* 5(1913):50–109; Lastres, *Historia de la medicina peruana,* 2:77.
8. Dobyns, "Andean Epidemic History," p. 505; Alfred Crosby, *The Columbian Exchange. Biological and Cultural Consequences of 1492* (Westport, CT: Greenwood Press. 1972); David Beers Quinn, ed., *The Roanoke Voyages, 1584–1590,* 2 vols. (London: Hakluyt Society, 1955), 1:378.
9. Alchon. *Native Society and Disease,* p. 40.
10. Jiménez de la Espada, *Relaciones geográficas,* 3:70.
11. Suzanne Austin Browne, "Effects of Epidemic Disease," p. 56.
12. Villamarín and Villamarín, "Sabana de Bogotá," pp. 119–21.
13. María del Carmen Borrego Plá, *Cartagena de Indias en el siglo XVI* (Seville: Escuela de Estudios Hispano-americanos, 1983), p. 406; Villamarín and Villamarín, "Sabana de Bogotá," pp. 119–122.
14. Lastres, *Historia de la medicina peruana,* 2:77.
15. Dobyns, "Andean Epidemic History," p. 505; Alchon, *Native Society and Disease,* pp. 41-43; Roberto Levillier, ed., *Gobernantes del Perú. Cartas y papeles, siglo XVI,* 14 vols. (Madrid: Sucesores de Rivadeneyra, 1925), 11:207–208.

16. Dobyns, "Andean Epidemic History," p. 507; and Polo, "Apuntes," p. 56.

17. Dobyns, "Andean Epidemic History," p. 508; Polo, "Apuntes," pp. 16–17.

18. Donald Joralemon, "New World Depopulation and the Case of Disease," *Journal of Anthropological Research* 38(1982):121.

19. Dobyns, "Andean Epidemic History," p. 507; Jiménez de la Espada, *Relaciones geográficas.* 3:70; Archivo General de Indias, Lima 32.

20. Levillier, *Gobernantes del Perú,* 11:221, 284, 285–86.

21. Dobyns, "Andean Epidemic History," p. 506; Polo. "Apuntes," pp. 58–62.

22. Alchon, *Native Society and Disease,* p. 42; Archivo General de Indias, Seville, Quito 23.

23. Brian Evans, "Death in Aymaya of Upper Peru," in *Secret Judgments,* ed. Cook and Lovell, pp. 142–58.

24. Dobyns, "Andean Epidemic History," p. 508.

25. Quinn, *Roanoke Voyages,* 1:306.

26. University of Florida, P. K. Yonge Collection, 33; Archivo General de Indias, Santo Domingo 229.

27. Quinn, *Roanoke Voyages,* 1:378.

28. McCaa, "Spanish and Nahuatl Views," p. 428.

CHAPTER 8

CONFRONTING

AUSTRALIAN GENOCIDE

Colin Tatz

AUSTRALIA AND ARTICLE II

MY TWO RECENT PAPERS ON GENOCIDE can be read rather than be re-stated here. The 1997 chapter[1] reflects on the politics of remembering and forgetting in the Jewish, Armenian, and Aboriginal contexts. The 1999 research essay[2] addresses images of genocide, the physical and social attacks on Aboriginal society, disease as genocide, and examines how each of the clauses in Article II [of the United Nations Convention on the Prevention and Punishment of the Crime of Genocide of 1948] may or may not apply to Australia. However, several aspects of genocide and of the Convention need comment here.

The disease-as-genocide thesis is common in many texts. Butlin was its chief proponent: "it is possible and, in 1789, likely that infection [smallpox] of the Aborigines was a deliberate exterminating act."[3] Accident is not genocide and genocide is never accident. It isn't feasible that a fleet of soldiers and settlers, themselves suffering huge losses from a disease they didn't understand, ignorant of the germ theory that would explain such diseases nearly 100 years later, could conceive of extermination by deliberately inflicting "variolous matter" on the native peoples. This by-product of colonial invasion was catastrophic, but not intentional.[4]

The massacres and the organized killings, two of which were as recent as 1926 and 1928, were killings of Aborigines because they were Aborigines. White settlers, according to Evans et al, killed some 10,000 blacks in Queensland between 1824 and 1908.[5] Considered to be wild animals, vermin, scarcely human, hideous to humanity, loathsome, and a nuisance, they were fair game for white "sportsmen." In 1883, the British High Commissioner, Arthur Hamilton Gordon, wrote privately to his friend William Gladstone, Prime Minister of England:

> The habit of regarding the natives as vermin, to be cleared off the face of the earth, has given the average Queenslander a tone of brutality and cruelty in dealing with "blacks" which it is very difficult to anyone who does not know it, as I do, to realise. I have heard men of culture and refinement... talk, not only of the

wholesale butchery ... but of the individual murder of natives, exactly as they would talk of a day's sport, or having to kill some troublesome animal.

In 1896, Archibald Meston was appointed Royal Commissioner to investigate the slaughter. In his Report on the Aborigines of North Queensland,[6] he wrote that the treatment of the Cape York people was "a shame to our common humanity"; their "manifest joy at assurances of safety and protection is pathetic beyond expression. God knows they were in need of it." Aboriginal people met him "like hunted wild beasts, having lived for years in a state of absolute terror." He was convinced their only salvation lay in strict and absolute isolation from all whites, from predators who, in no particular order, wanted to kill them, take their women, sell them grog or opium. The world's first anti-genocide statute—the *Aboriginals Protection and Restriction of the Sale of Opium Act 1897*—followed.

The more loosely worded clauses in Article II bear examination. II(b)—"causing serious bodily or mental harm"—has never, to my knowledge, been used or invoked anywhere to bring, or sustain, an allegation of genocide. Nor has II(c)—deliberately inflicting destructive conditions of life. The latter has strong echoes of the forced labour and slave camps under the Nazis, but the former is a generalized and a less contextualized act, one which is, I believe, sustainable in our context.

Ironically, or perversely perhaps, protection-segregation practices, operative for more than half of the 20th century, amounted to both bodily and mental harm. Within the ambit of II(b) are the following "protections": draconian laws in all States and the Northern Territory; a separate legal status for Aborigines—as perpetual minors and wards; incarceration on reserves, settlements and missions in every jurisdiction; destruction of hunter-gatherer systems by such confinement in these penitentiary-like institutions; unappealable and unsupervised powers of officials and missionaries to imprison for offences which only Aborigines could commit, especially in Queensland; powers to exile Aborigines, without families, often for life, to remote and inaccessible penal colonies like Palm Island, Yarrabah, and Woorabinda; compulsory communal kitchens, further breaking down familial patterns in the Territory; removal of children across the nation, in Victoria as early as the 1840s; removal of women and boys to segregated dormitories; removals of whole clans and societies to new "lands," sometimes at gunpoint in Queensland; work for rations only, and then later for rations and a pocket-money component in northern Australia; imprisonment for refusing to work in Queensland; abolition of ceremonies that offended white officialdom, especially in Queensland; outlawing of Aboriginal painting at Elcho Island mission; control and guardianship of all children, even while natural parents were present in most jurisdictions; official control over marital and sexual relationships in the Territory; denial of access to alcohol, gambling, reading, and film material in most of the country; apprenticeships and indentures without payment to the individual but, instead, to the Welfare Board in New South Wales; prohibitions on trade-union membership and ineligibility to vote at elections for much of the last century. Some of these practices—often administered beyond the letter of the law[7]—could well fit within Article II(c).

From time to time allegations surface that State medical services engaged or engage in administering contraceptive "therapy" without informing the women of its purpose: in Western Australia, the use of Depo-Provera, producing three-to-six month infertility. Depo-Provera, by injection, has alarming side effects, necessitating dire warnings about contraindications and the need for stringent physical examination before administration. Another allegation is the permanent sterilization of Aboriginal women: in Queensland, a series of "non-explained" tubal ligations.[8] These birth prevention issues need careful research.

There is another, paradoxical sense in which we should pay more attention to II(d), preventing "births within the group." Attempts were first made by Victoria in the 1860s and 1880s, then later by senior bureaucrats in the 1930s and 1940s, to ensure births outside rather than within the group. C.F. Gale and later O.A. Neville in the West, Dr W.E. Roth and later J.W. Bleakley in Queensland and Dr Cecil Cook in the Northern Territory actively sought every form of separation possible between "half-castes" and "full-bloods." Their collective efforts bore fruit at the meeting of Commonwealth and State administrations in Canberra in 1937: "The destiny of the natives of Aboriginal origin, but not of full blood, lies in their ultimate absorption by the people of the Commonwealth, and it therefore recommends that all efforts shall be directed to this end." This meant child removal, "breeding them white," and "dismantling" everyone who was regarded as less than "full-blood." The Administrator's report for the Northern Territory in 1933 had this to say:

> In the Territory the mating of an Aboriginal with any person other than an Aboriginal is prohibited. The mating of coloured aliens with any female of part-Aboriginal blood is also forbidden. Every endeavour is being made to breed out the colour by elevating female half-castes to the white standard with a view to their absorption by mating into the white population.[9]

Neville had a three-point plan: first, the full-bloods would die out; second, he would take half-castes away from their mothers; third, he would control marriages among half-castes and so encourage intermarriage with the white community. The "young half-blood maiden is a pleasant, placid, complacent person as a rule, while the quadroon [one-quarter Aboriginal] is often strikingly attractive, with her oftimes auburn hair, rosy freckled colouring, and good figure..." These were the sort of people who should be elevated "to our own plane." In this way, it would be possible to "eventually forget that there were ever any Aborigines in Australia." In this way, too, births would be prevented within the half-caste, quadroon and octoroon societies because their offspring would henceforth be non-Aboriginal.

Eugenics, as a science of animal pedigree, can only work in controlled stud and stock farms. Fortunately, societies can't be regulated in the veterinary sense, but Neville, Bleakley, and Cook certainly intended the disappearance of the "part-Aboriginal" population by "eugenicizing" many of them. This was a clearly articulated intent to commit what would come to be called genocide. The Convention talks about the "intent to destroy, in whole or in part": it doesn't say that the crime requires successful completion.

We need careful examination of the applicability of the word *destroy* in the definition. "Destroy" was clearly used in the immediate aftermath of World War II with its tally of 50 million dead across the globe. Destroy is a negative, pejorative verb, resonant of evil, wantonness, violence. With hindsight and lapse of time, that is what can now be read into it. But, as with all statutes, we are obliged to look at the ordinary or plain meaning of the word(s), not at what we think the framers intended, or felt, at the time.

"Destroy" brings to light an issue current in the debate about the Stolen Generations, namely, that whatever was done in this country was done with good intent, and therefore could not, by definition, be genocidal. In 1997, *Bringing Them Home: The report of the National Inquiry into the Separation of Aboriginal and Torres Strait Islander Children from their Families*, concluded that child removal was an act of genocide. The essence of the crime, it said, was acting with the intention of destroying the group, not the extent to which that outcome resulted. The forcible removals were intended to "absorb," "merge," "assimilate" the children "so that Aborigines as a distinct group would disappear." That such actions by perpetrators were in their eyes "in the best interests" of the children is irrelevant to a finding that their actions were genocidal.[10]

We always assume that "with intent to destroy" means intent with *male fides*, bad faith, with evil intent. Nowhere does the Convention implicitly or explicitly rule out intent with *bona fides*, good faith, "for their own good" or "in their best interests." Starkman's is but one of several opinions that the reasons for the crime, or the ultimate purpose of the deeds, are irrelevant: "the crime of genocide is committed whenever the intentional destruction of a protected group takes place."[11] Storey points out that "genocide does not require malice; it can be (misguidedly) committed 'in the interests' of a protected population."[12] Elazar Barkan[13] asks whether there can be genocide "despite ostensibly good intentions": "The illegitimacy of the white man's burden may suggest that indeed the answer is affirmative." Gaita contends that "the concept of good intention cannot be relativised indefinitely to an agent's perception of it as good." If we could, he writes, then we must say that Nazi murderers had good, but radically benighted intentions, because most of them believed they had a sacred duty to the world to rid the planet of the "race" that polluted it.[14]

Larissa Behrendt discusses the nature and significance of two important legal cases— *Nulyarimma & Others* and *Kruger v Commonwealth*. The Peter Gunner and Lorna Cubillo cases[15] in the Northern Territory were also lost. My criticism of the plaintiffs' cases in Kruger, Gunner, and Cubillo is that they failed to confront the issue of whether any, or all, of the physical or social actions complained of fall within the ambit of Article II. In *Nulyarimma*, the statement of claim was that by securing the Wik 10-point plan legislation in 1998, senior Coalition ministers committed specified and unspecified acts of genocide. One has to say that, by any yardstick, the Wik judgment was hardly the worst experience to have befallen Aborigines since 1788.

Irrespective of these outcomes, I place great store in trials. They posit a *prima facie* case that "something happened." They usually establish the victims and perpetrators; certainly they establish the actors. Trials produce both historical and contemporaneous documents (of permanent record). They produce eyewitness accounts from all actors—victims, alleged perpetrators, and bystanders or observers. Trials are not undertaken in the pragmatic belief that every case will be won, that all charged in criminal court will be convicted, or that all plaintiffs will be awarded damages in civil suit. Trials are a contention, an articulation by the state, or by parties against the state, under strict rules of evidence, in a legal theatre. Trials are a public declaration that there are moral and ethical values which society should sustain. Trial records are infinitely more powerful educative tools about contemporary social and political history, and values, than the passive voice and the indirect speech of history texts, or of essays like this one.

ADMISSIONS AND DENIALS

The years 1997 to 2000 were crucial for both admissions and apologies about the past, and for vigorous denials that anything needed admission or apology.

Earlier, in 1990, the Secretariat of the National and Aboriginal and Islander Child Care organisation (SNAICC) demanded an inquiry "into how many of our children were taken away and how this occurred." It wanted to know whether these policies fell within the definition of Article II(e). Prime Minister Paul Keating was the first senior politician to acknowledge that we "took the traditional lands ... smashed the traditional way of life ... brought the diseases and the alcohol ... committed the murders ... took the children."[16]

The Australian Archives presented a national exhibition, *Between Two Worlds*, a study of the Federal government's removal of Aboriginal "half-caste" children in the Territory from 1918 to the 1960s.[17] It was a brilliant depiction of one facet of

genocide, without using the word. Throughout this entire history, there were exceptionally few men and women who heard whispers in their hearts that anything was
awry or amiss.[18] One who did was the late E.C. (Ted) Evans, then Chief Welfare
Officer, whose exhibited letters to the Administrator urged that removals cease:
because, he wrote, they were intrinsically evil and because the world would never
understand either the motives or the practices.

By 1994, Aborigines at the *Going Home* conference in Darwin felt sufficiently
confident to begin planning civil lawsuits against governments and missions for the
forcible removal of children and the break-up of family life.

Bringing Them Home became a bestseller when published in April 1997. Within a
month, some States were apologizing.[19] South Australia apologized for "the mistakes
of the past," including "any relevant actions of South Australia Police," and regretted
"the forced separation of some Aboriginal children." Western Australia apologized for
children removed, an act which "encompasses acknowledgment by the Western
Australian Police Service of its historical involvement in past policies and practices
of forcible removal." In June, New South Wales apologized unreservedly "for the
systematic separation of generations of Aboriginal children from their parents, families and communities," regretting parliament's passing of laws and endorsement of
policies which produced such grief. The NSW Police Commissioner offered an apology on behalf of his Service in May 1998. In June 1997, the ACT Legislative Assembly,
with no removals to apologize for, nevertheless did do so as a symbolic gesture.

The Tasmanian parliament, but not the police, regretted and apologized for "removed
children" in August 1997. A month later, Victoria apologized, expressing "deep regret
at the hurt and distress" caused. The police indicated that enforcing policies "that now
are acknowledged as racist" are a "significant cause of distrust of police."

Queensland, in May 1999, apologized for the "Indigenous children [who] were
forcibly separated," but the Police Service did not.

In 1998, the Northern Territory Legislative Assembly castigated the "empty-
apology option" taken by other parliaments. The Chief Minister had earlier told
the National Inquiry that the Territory, self-governing since 1978, wasn't party to
child removal (it wasn't) and that apology and compensation "are matters for
Commonwealth consideration."

In November 2000, a Senate committee reported on the Federal government's
implementation of the recommendations made in *Bringing Them Home*. Their document, *Healing: A legacy of generations,* recommended a "Motion of national apology
and reconciliation ... gesture of good faith" by the Northern Territory parliament,
and the establishment of a Reparations Tribunal.[20] This Committee, with two
dissenters, interviewed over a hundred witnesses, and received numerous written
submissions from churches, government agencies and Aboriginal individuals and

organizations. It produced compelling evidence for the conservative Federal government to do what it has so steadfastly refused to do.

Initially, Howard's government refused to make a formal submission to the national inquiry chaired by Sir Ronald Wilson. Under pressure, it did so just short of the deadline, in October 1996. Written by unnamed bureaucrats, sourced as *Anonymous: Commonwealth Government,* it declared—in advance of the findings—that the government would not compensate for child removal. In judging these practices, it said, "it is appropriate to have regard to the standards and values prevailing at the time of their enactment and implementation, rather than to the standards and values prevailing today." It ended with a remarkable rationalization: "there is no existing objective methodology for attaching a monetary value to the loss suffered by victims."[21] Restitution, it argued, would cause intolerable inequities, but it didn't say to whom.

When *Bringing Them Home* was released, media attention focused heavily on acknowledgment and apology. When pressed, the Minister for Aboriginal Affairs (then) Senator John Herron and the Prime Minister—neither of whom, I believe, had any thoughts of their own on the matter—appropriated the exact wording of the bureaucracy's inquiry submission and locked themselves into these "principles": restitution was not possible, there was no methodology for it, it would create "new injustices," formal apology could open the way for lawsuits, all this happened yesteryear, and, in a new version of "for their own good," removal was akin to Anglo children being sent to boarding school. Furthermore, some very successful Aborigines had come through these assimilation homes. Finally, in words that echo popular misconceptions, Herron declared, "This practice could not be described as genocide as it did not involve an intentional elimination of a race."[22]

With a degree of reluctance, the Prime Minister offered his personal apology. A formal apology, he insisted, would set up a chain of claims for reparation. Further, "Australians of this generation should not be required to accept blame for past actions and policies." Howard, like so many, claims that the present generation is not responsible for the past: yet the present inherits the riches, the spoils, and the acquisitions of the past and, in so doing, it also inherits the historical debts. In August 1999, the Federal parliament shed its own minimalist tear, its "deep and sincere regret" for past injustices—but without apology.

The low-water mark of the government's intransigence was Senator Herron's support for, and endorsement of, a paper written by his bureaucrats to the Senate *Healing* inquiry in April 2000. It denigrated and diminished the Stolen Generations issue. Herron contended that since an entire generation was not removed but perhaps only one in 10 children, one could not use the phrase "Stolen Generation(s)." This sophistry produced a national outcry which further fuelled Aboriginal (and non-Aboriginal) determination.

An even lower point was reached when the esteemed Aboriginal elder, Lowitja O'Donoghue, told a Melbourne journalist, Andrew Bolt, that she preferred to describe herself as removed rather than stolen.[23] The talkback "stars," a few tabloids, and the Prime Minister rejoiced in the inference that if she, of all people, wasn't stolen, then no one was.

In October 1999, an Anti-Genocide Bill was introduced privately by West Australian Democrat Senator, Brian Greig. A Senate committee inquired into the Bill, examining, *inter alia,* the adequacy of Australia's implementation of the Genocide Convention, with particular attention to finding an appropriate definition of the crime, the status of the Convention in Australian law, and the appropriateness of retrospectivity of any such new law. In June 2000, the Committee's *Humanity Diminished* recommended "that the parliament formally recognise the need for anti-genocide laws." In April 2001 the debate on the Bill was adjourned indefinitely. If it is ever debated, I doubt it will be passed, irrespective of party in office: we persist in refusing to confront the genocide issue in this country.

Amid these State and church apologies, and despite the work of Raimond Gaita, Robert Marine, and Colin Tatz, the national and Senate inquiries, and the careful journalism of Debra Jopson and others, a denial industry was born.

Denialism takes several forms. First, the denial of any past genocidal behaviour, whether physical killing or child removal. Second, the somewhat bizarre counter-view that whites have been the victims. Third, the hypothesis that concentration on unmitigated gloom (Professor Kenneth Minogue's phrase), or on the black armband view of history (Professor Geoffrey Blainey's phrase), overwhelms the reality that there has been more good than bad in Australian race relations.

Denials are accompanied by, or based on, several strange moral equations. Thus, the Holocaust equals past bitternesses (Barwick); removal of children is good for them (Howard-Herron); Aboriginal pluses outweigh the minuses (Blainey-Minogue-Howard); and that, at most, Australian racism is no more than "a sentiment rather than a belief, involving rejection of, or contempt for, or simply unease in the presence of, people recognised as different" (Minogue).[24]

The Witnesses for the Defence, as Padraic McGuinness styles himself and his colleagues, are remarkable for their anorexic arguments and, at times, quite silly explanations. In concert with a few academics, a small coterie of journalists—lacking any academic or practical credentials in Aboriginal affairs—contrive to claim, *inter alia,* that the charge of genocide is either pedantry or mischief; that Australia didn't commit genocide by forced removal because, if we had, we would have prosecuted the crime (when committed by Federal and State bureaucrats?); that many or even most removals were with parental consent; that only a "small number" (12,500) were removed, citing an Australian Bureau of Statistics 1994 survey to support the mini-removal thesis; that removal was akin to white kids at boarding school; that many benefited from removal; that Aboriginal leaders were assimilationists; that since earlier anthropologists didn't find genocide, it couldn't have occurred; and, finally, some—but unspecific as to number—who assert genocide "are of Jewish background and have an interest in the Holocaust."

Ron Brunton attacked the National Inquiry because, as an anthropologist, he wished to protect the standards of science—and he strongly believed the inquiry to be deeply flawed.[25] He is concerned at the "role of suggestion in creating false memories of events that never really happened." He castigates the failure to distinguish "truly voluntary" and "coerced" removals. He asserts that my "silence" on genocide over the years makes it look suspicious that I—"the doyen of genocide studies"—"suddenly" use the word now. Had I spoken out earlier, this "certainly would have brought a very rapid end to the supposedly genocidal practices." He is aware of the Genocide Convention but rails against the "elasticity" of the crime, at being asked to equate "misguided child welfare" with the skeletons hanging off the wire at Auschwitz.

Kenneth Maddock, reviewing Colin Macleod's patrol officer memoir,[26] suggested that two noted anthropologists thought well of the assimilation homes where "half-caste girls" could find haven from sexual predation and depravity. He pointed to the "significant silence" of anthropologists Marie Reay and (the late) Diane Barwick, neither of whom ever mentioned genocide. Later, he pointed to the silence of all anthropologists.[27] He quotes the Australian Law Reform Commission report on customary law as saying something it should never have said—that "genocide is restricted to forms of physical destruction." He talks of the "absurdity" of imputing evil to the Aboriginal authorities in Darwin. Besides which, his three academic acquaintances who worked with these authorities—Tatz, "the outspoken political scientist"; the pre-historian Carmel White; and the anthropologist John Bern—"were of Jewish background and interested in Israel." Even they, with Zionistically-attuned antennae, "caught not a whiff of genocide."

An array of conservative critics now refute genocide and/or the gloom and mourning pervading Aboriginal colonial history. Some are reputable academics like historian Geoffrey Blainey, British political scientist Ken Minogue, anthropologist Ken Maddock, and Keith Windschuttle, a former lecturer in social policy and media studies. Some are senior politicians—John Howard, John Herron, Bill Hayden, and former premiers Wayne Goss and Ray Groom. Goss, when Queensland Premier, insisted on the removal of such "offending" words as "invasion" and "resistance" from Queensland school texts. Former Tasmanian Premier Ray Groom contended that there have been no killings in the Island State—making him, in effect, Australia's foremost genocide denialist in the 1990s.[28]

There is a journalistic group vehement about the *Bringing Them Home* material:

between them, Piers Akerman, Andrew Bolt, Frank Devine, Michael Duffy, Padraic McGuinness, Christopher Pearson, and Bill Hayden, who now serves on the board of *Quadrant,* have described the entirety of *Bringing Them Home* as a hoax, a monument to false memory syndrome. Hayden sees the "use of victimhood as some sort of heavy waddy for punishing the guilty mass." Furthermore, the inquiry exercise showed "the extraordinary display of legal gullibility by Sir Ronald Wilson."[29] Devine talks of "frail wisps of evidence" and "manufactured" case studies.[30] McGuinness considers "truth, sentiment and genocide as a fashion statement," and the "whole Wilsonian edifice" of *Bringing Them Home* as "built on sand."[31] In his attack on Reynolds, Keith Windschuttle, the latest defence witness, labels the "alleged" physical killing as the "myths of frontier massacres" and as "the fabrication of the Aboriginal death toll."[32]

Windschuttle is author, *inter alia,* of *The Killing of History.*[33] This 1996 book—a concerted attack on structuralism, post-structuralism, cultural relativism, postmodernism, and assorted other new theories—stoutly defends traditional history, especially that of Rowley and Reynolds. By 2000, he had experienced a conversion and joined the company of McGuinness, ex-Liberal cabinet minister Peter Howson, former Assistant Administrator of the Northern Territory Reg Marsh, barrister Douglas Meagher, Brunton and others. But in his case, he was refuting the history of killing, with blistering attacks on Reynolds, his historical veracity, his sources and, above all, his "numbers dead."

Geoffrey Blainey is not a denialist in this vein. But he has now backtracked on a phrase he claimed was never anti-Aboriginal in the first place, the phrase that so enamoured the Prime Minister—"the black armband view of history." In 1997, Blainey disparaged the way in which interpretations of Aboriginal issues had allowed "the minuses to virtually wipe out the pluses." The swing of the pendulum was "wild" and even the High Court was "that black armband tribunal."[34] He now claims he was referring to such matters as the environment, for which he was and is in mourning and, Australian football fan that he is, he insists his metaphor was born out of the practice of these footballers wearing a black arm stripe when someone connected with the game dies.[35]

There is also a netherworld of radio talkback "philosophers," Alan Jones, John Laws, Stan Zemanek, Howard Sattler.[36] What many of these self-confessed "entertainers" have in common—apart from a seeming antipathy to Aborigines generally and to the whole Aboriginal "thing"—is that they do neither fieldwork nor homework. Like so many genocide denialists, they assert but don't demonstrate, they disapprove but don't ever disprove. They won't take on the burden of proving that Hamilton Gordon was lying when he wrote to Gladstone in 1883, or that Meston fabricated his evidence for a protective statute in 1896, or that Lieutenant Wheeler perjured himself when he told an inquiry in 1861 that he shot Aborigines. They could hardly sustain their views if ever they were in a civil suit witness box (which is where, I suggest, they should be "coaxed" into being.) Rather, they rely on a new methodology: attacking the integrity of authors and witnesses. Reynolds, for example, now has "a tattered reputation," and I am a scaremonger seeking to impale Australia on exaggerated history. Besides which, I am Jewish, with an interest in the Holocaust.

Are these denialists merely protecting themselves, and us, from a massive scam, as former senior bureaucrat and Senator, John Stone, would have us believe? He talks about "the misplaced remorse" of the Australians and the "well-groomed pseudo Aborigines ... whose sole personal achievement has been to climb aboard the lushly furnished gravy-train while holding out their hands for even more gravy."[37]

These men behave in the manner of genocide denialists generally: either asserting that genocide never occurred here, couldn't have occurred here, could never occur here, or more commonly, they nibble at the edges, sniping at weaker points, in the hope (or belief) that if they can demonstrate one error of fact or figure, the central and essential "contention" of genocide will fall apart.

But why the denials? Robert Manne, who has devoted the past three years to a study of the Stolen Generations, published an essay in 2001 called "In denial: The Stolen Generations and the Right." A forensic counter to McGuinness and his team, he has meticulously and impeccably dissected their claims and assertions. In his final section, he asks "why?" Motives differ, he says: "some of the *anti-Bringing Them Home* campaigners are now too old or proud to reflect on the cruelty of practices in which they were personally involved." Others are "former leftists who are so obsessed by the conduct of ideological combat against their former friends that they have come to believe that truth is simply the opposite of what they once believed." "Some are general purpose right-wingers who hunt in packs and can be relied upon to agree with whatever their political friends believe."

Manne is less concerned with their motives than with what he calls the heart of the campaign, namely, "the meaning of Aboriginal dispossession." There is, he argues, "a right-wing and populist resistance to discussions of historical injustice and the Aborigines." Separation of mother and child "deeply captured the national imagination": that "story had the power to change forever the way they saw their country's history"—hence the imperative to destroy that story. This is an acute observation. However, this imperative doesn't explain their systematic attacks on the "falsity" and "fabrication" of the physical killing era.

We need to probe deeper than this. Are these men simply guilty officials, or just anti-leftists, or indiscriminate pack-hunting rightists? Are some amongst them—including a "humanist" prime minister, two democratic premiers, and a once-acclaimed politician turned Governor-General—not simply passionate defenders of national pride and achievement? Are they not just a collective St George slaying the author-dragons—black and white—who insist that we do, indeed, have a "racist, bigoted past," because they know the truth—that we have no such past?

There can be no doubt that reparation and restitution to Aborigines are anathemas to the majority of Australians. Admitting "past mistakes" is one thing; paying compensation for what was done is quite another. The Prime Minister and his servants have made this clear. Howard was willing to spend $300 million on a gun buy-back scheme, but any similar or much lower figure on Aboriginal reparation is considered "outrageous." That there is a money motive in denialism is certain. But it is not just the money or the quantum thereof: it has much more to do with the attitudes towards the intended recipients of such money, as for example, John Stone's "well-groomed pseudo-Aborigines" who pursue lush gravy-trains.

Consciously perhaps, Howard's refusal of a parliamentary apology has produced a separate politics of "sorry," one which deflects and relegates the original forcible removal of children, the continuing removal through mandatory sentencing, and several other denials of human rights. Sorry, at this late juncture, isn't enough[38]: the longer the gap between the need for the token and its delivery (by someone other than Howard), the greater the chances that removed Aborigines will seek much more than apology.

I have another suggestion: that denialism in Australia is centrally about the place of morality in Australian politics. It is either a promotion of an especial Anglocentric nationalism, a particular Australian moral virtue, in which there is, by definition, no place for genocidal thoughts or actions, or it is an attempt to excise morality from political considerations—to create an amoral, economically centred body politic. I'm not quite sure which it is, and it may turn out to be both.

Much of the denialism is, I believe, a propping up of this mythical national moral hygiene, of an idealized "down under" way of life that is simply beyond comparison, or analogy, with the barbarisms of the Balkans or the murderous mindsets of the Nazis. As we see in daily sport *ad nauseam*, it is the Indian sub-continent and other "foreign elements"—like East Germans and the Chinese—who cheat, throw matches, accept bribes, or take drugs. Australians don't, or can't, do these things because we're Australians. It has been suggested that these journalists and former bureaucrats, who met in enclave and began publishing voluminously and simultaneously in *Quadrant* and the major newspapers in September 2000, did so to "clean up" Australia's history of race relations before the Sydney 2000 Olympic Games. The timing was, indeed, a curious coincidence.[39]

Are they protecting the inherent "moral gene" that runs through white and naturalized Australian veins? Or is it rather a case of their attempting to ridicule anything that acknowledges an underlying morality in politics, a moral nihilism which "de-moralizes" us all and leaves no room for issues of shame, guilt, atonement of any kind? In this way, for example, one doesn't have to think, or feel, about the refugees, the boat people and other "illegals" imprisoned in camps in the deserts of South and Western Australia.

Australian denialists are not men with credentials in history, or in any other disciplines: they won't be writing the textbooks for our school and university curricula. They will hold their private and celebratory seminars—essentially to reinforce each other rather than to "re-educate" the public. They will produce *Quadrant* with an increase in *ad hominem* attacks, perhaps concentrating on those of Jewish "background." (If such were the case, I would prefer to be regarded as one of Jewish foreground, as someone morally bound to investigate all manners and matters of genocide.)

But whether they be senior political figures, once powerful bureaucrats, journalists, or talk-back radio "philosophers," they miss two essential by-products of their denialism: they keep otherwise potentially "fading" issues very much alive, and they provoke infinitely more interest amongst, and research by, those who have the real qualifications, skills and ethics to do such work. In a bizarre sense, denialists—who see themselves as prophylactics protecting our society from a moral reappraisal of past behaviours—are the fecund: they actually increase the fertility of research into those very behaviours. They can, however, take comfort in their one undisputed achievement—their ability to hurt the victim peoples.

NOTES

1. Tatz 1997:308–61.
2. Tatz 1999:15–52.
3. Butlin 1983, p.175 especially.
4. See Tatz 1999:11–13, for a fuller discussion of this point.
5. Evans et al 1975: 75–78.
6. Tatz 1999:15–16.
7. Tatz 1963:17.
8. Moody 1988:324–26.
9. Tatz 1999:27ff.
10. Human Rights and Equal Opportunity Commission 1997: 270–5.
11. Starkman 1984:1.
12. Storey 1997:11–14.
13. Barkan 2000:247.
14. Gaita 1997: 21.
15. *Lorna Cubillo & Peter Gunner v Commonwealth of Australia*, [1999] FCA 518.
16. The Redfern speech, December 1992, quoted in Tatz, 1999:41.
17. The exhibition was held in 1993–94. It is now in book form: see MacDonald 1997.
18. Henry Reynolds, 1998, has written elegantly about the people who couldn't satisfy their consciences, who worried about the Aboriginal-white relationship, who said so publicly and who attempted some kind of action to try to change the way things were.
19. Senate Legal and Constitutional Affairs Reference Committee 2000:129–38.
20. Senate Legal and Constitutional Affairs Reference Committee 2000: xvii–xviii.

21. Yet Germany has (twice) given us a reparations model, and at the end of 1998 found the will to compensate the surviving slave labourers of over half a century ago. The Swiss banks—"inheritors" of Jewish deposited money—have now given us another model.
22. Herron, ABC Radio, 27 May 1997, in *The Australian*, 27 May 1997.
23. *Herald Sun*, 23 February 2001.
24. Minogue 1998:11–20.
25. Brunton 1998:19–24
26. Maddock 1998. 347–53.
27. Maddock 2000: 11–16.
28. *Australian*, 25 October 1994.
29. *Sydney Morning Herald*, 12 October 2000.
30. *Australian*, 14 September 2000.
31. *Sydney Morning Herald*, 14 September 2000.
32. See footnote 15.
33. Windschuttle 1996.
34. "Black Future," *The Bulletin*, 8 April 1997; see also *Sydney Morning Herald* editorial, 18 November 1996.
35. *Australian*, 13 November 2000.
36. Mickler 1998, chapters 3 and 8; Adams and Burton 1997.
37. *Australian Financial Review*, 2 February 1995.
38. Roy Brooks's book on the controversy over apologies and reparations, *When Sorry Isn't Enough*, was published in 1999. It dealt with seven major case studies: the Jewish victims of Nazism, Japanese "comfort women," Japanese-Americans, Native Americans, the slavery issue, the Jim Crow laws, and South Africa. Australia didn't rate a mention.
39. Windschuttle 2000, *Quadrant*, October: 8–21; Quadrant, November: 17–24 ; see also McGuinness *Sydney Morning Herald*, 14 September, 2000.

REFERENCES

Aarons, Mark. 2001. *War Criminals Welcome: Australia, a Sanctuary for Fugitive War Criminals since 1945*. Melbourne: Black Inc.

Adams, Phillip & Lee Burton. 1997. *Talkback: Emperors of the Air*. Sydney: Allen & Unwin.

Barkan, Elazar. 2000. *The Guilt of Nations: Restitution and Negotiating Historical Injustices*. New York: W.W. Norton & Co.

Barta, Tony. 1985. *Australian Journal of Politics and History*. 31(1), (special issue edited by Konrad Kwiet and John A. Moses: "On being a German-Jewish refugee in Australia.")

Brooks, Roy, ed. 1999. *When Sorry Isn't Enough: The Controversy over Apologies and Reparations for Human Injustice*. NY: New York University Press.

Brunton, Ronald. 1998. "Genocide, the 'Stolen Generations,' and the 'Unconceived Generations,'" *Quadrant*, May.

Button, Noel. 1983. *Our Original Aggression: Aboriginal Populations of Southeastern Australia 1788–1850*. Sydney: Allen & Unwin.

Cannon, Michael. 1990. *Who Killed the Koories?* Melbourne: William Heinemann.

Chisholm, Richard. 1985. *Black Children: White Welfare? Aboriginal Child Welfare Law and Policy in New South Wales*. SWRC Reports and Proceedings 52, Social Welfare Research Centre, University of New South Wales, Kensington.

Evans, Raymond, Kay Saunders and Kathryn Cronin. 1975. *Exclusion, Exploitation and Extermination: Race Relations in Colonial Queensland*. Sydney, Australia and New Zealand Book Company.

Gaita, Raimond. 1997. "Genocide: the Holocaust and the Aborigines," *Quadrant*, November: 17–22.

Hancock, W. K. 1961. *Australia*, Brisbane, Jacaranda Press.

Hansard. 1949. House of Representatives. 203(30): 1871, June. National Inquiry into the Separation of Aboriginal and Torres Strait Islander Children from their Families (Australia), 1997, *Bringing Them Home: Report of the National Inquiry into the Separation of Aboriginal and Torres Strait Islander Children from Their Families* [Commissioner: Ronald Wilson], Human Rights and Equal Opportunity Commission, Sydney.

Kimber, Richard. 1997. "Genocide or Not? The Situation in Central Australia, 1860–1895." in Tatz, Colin (ed.). *Genocide Perspectives I: Essays in Comparative Genocide*. Centre for Comparative Genocide Studies, Macquarie University, Sydney: 33–65.

Kuper, Leo. 1981. *Genocide*, Penguin.

Loos, Noel. 1981. *Invasion and Resistance: Aboriginal-European Relations in the North Queensland Frontier, 1861–1897*. Canberra: ANU Press.

MacDonald, Rowena. 1997. *Between Two Worlds: The Commonwealth Government and the Removal of Aboriginal Children of Part Descent in the Northern Territory*. Alice Springs: Australian Archives, IAD Press.

Maddock, Kenneth. 1998. "'The Stolen Generations': A Report from Experience." *Agenda*, 5(3): 347–53.

Maddock, Kenneth. 2000. "Genocide: the silence of the anthropologists." *Quadrant*. November: 11–16.

Manne, Robert. 2001. "In Denial: the Stolen Generations and the Right." *Quarterly Essay*, Melbourne, Black Inc.

Margossian, Ara. 2001. "The Anti-Genocide Bill: Our Submission." *International Network on Holocaust and Genocide*, 14(2–3): 21–39.

Markus, Andrew. 1990. *Governing Savages*. Sydney: Allen & Unwin.

McGrath, Ann, ed. 1995. *Contested Ground: Australian Aborigines under the British Crown*. Sydney: Allen & Unwin.

Mickler, Stephen. 1998. *The Myth of Privilege*. Fremantle: Fremantle Arts Centre Press.

Minogue, Kenneth. 1998. "Aborigines and Australian Apologetics." *Quadrant*, September: 11–20.

Moody, Roger, ed. 1988. *The Indigenous Voice, Visions and Realities*, vol. 1. London: Zed Books.

Read, Peter. 1983. *The Stolen Generations: The Removal of Aboriginal Children in New South Wales 1883 to 1969*. NSW Ministry of Aboriginal Affairs, Occasional Paper (1).

Reynolds, Henry. 1981. *The Other Side of the Frontier: Aboriginal Resistance to the European Invasion of Australia*. Ringwood: Penguin Books.

———. 1998. *The Whispering in our Hearts*. Sydney: Allen & Unwin.

Rowley, Charles. 1970. *The Destruction of Aboriginal Society: Aboriginal Policy and Practice*, (1). Canberra: ANU Press.

Ryan, Lyndall. 1981. *The Aboriginal Tasmanians.* St Lucia: University of Queensland Press.

Senate Legal and Constitutional Affairs Reference Committee. 2000. *Healing: A Legacy of Generations.* The report of the inquiry into the Federal government's implementation of recommendations made by the Human Rights and Equal Opportunity Commission in *Bringing Them Home.*

———. 2000. "Reference: Anti-Genocide Bill 1999." *Hansard,* 12 May, transcript of evidence by Colin Tatz and Ara Margossian: 11–23.

———. 2000. "Humanity Diminished: The Crime of Genocide." *Inquiry into the Anti-Genocide Bill 1999.* June: 60.

Starkman, P. 1984. "Genocide and International Law: Is There a Cause of Action?" *Association of Students' International Law Society International Law Journal* 8(1): 19.

Storey, Matthew. 1997. "*Kruger v The Commonwealth:* Does Genocide Require Malice?" *University of New South Wales Law Journal Forum,* Stolen children: from removal to reconciliation, December: 11–14.

Tatz, Colin. 1963. "Queensland's Aborigines: Natural Justice and the Rule of Law." *The Australian Quarterly,* XXXV(3): 17.

———. 1985. "Racism, Responsibility and Reparation: South Africa, Germany, and Australia." *Australian Journal of Politics and History* 31(1): 162–72.

———. 1997. "Genocide and the Politics of Memory," in Tatz, Colin, ed. *Genocide Perspectives I: Essays in Comparative Genocide.* Centre for Comparative Genocide Studies, Macquarie University, Sydney.

———. 1999. "Genocide in Australia." Research Discussion Paper No 8, Australian Institute of Aboriginal and Torres Strait Islander Studies, Canberra; reprinted under the same title in *Journal of Genocide Research,* 1999, 1 (3): 315–52.

Windschuttle, Keith. 1996. *The Killing of History: How Literary Critics and Social Theorists are Murdering our Past.* San Francisco: Encounter Books.

———. 2000. "The Myths of Frontier Massacres." *Quadrant,* October: 8–21.

———. 2000. "The Fabrication of the Aboriginal Death Toll." *Quadrant,* November: 17–24.

———. 2000. "The Enemies of Assimilation." *Quadrant,* December: 6–20.

CHAPTER 9

"KILLING THE INDIAN IN THE CHILD":

FOUR CENTURIES OF CHURCH-RUN SCHOOLS

Suzanne Fournier and Ernie Crey

EMILY RICE'S INTRODUCTION to residential school will be etched on her soul for the rest of her life. Raised on a lush British Columbia Gulf Island replete with wild deer, gardens, and orchards and surrounded by straits that ran silver with salmon and herring, Rice spoke little English at the age of eight when she was told the priest was coming to take her to boarding school. The nightmare began as soon as Emily and her sister Rose, then 11 years old, stepped on the small boat that would bear them away. "I clung to Rose until Father Jackson wrenched her out of my arms," Rice remembers. "I searched all over the boat for Rose. Finally I climbed up to the wheelhouse and opened the door and there was Father Jackson, on top of my sister. My sister's dress was pulled up and his pants were down. I was too little to know about sex; but I know now he was raping her. He cursed and came after me, picked up his big black Bible and slapped me across the face and on the top of the head. I started crying hysterically and he threw me out onto the deck. When we got to Kuper Island, my sister and I were separated. They wouldn't let me comfort her. Even today, all my sisters are strangers to me." [Father Jackson's name has been changed here since he has never been criminally charged, only named in a civil lawsuit.]

"Our Alcatraz," as survivors would later call the Kuper Island residential school, was just across the channel from the Vancouver Island town of Chemainus. The huge brick building, which towered over the island's only wharf, was operated from 1906 to 1978 by two Catholic orders, first the Montfort Fathers and then the Oblates of Mary Immaculate. (The school was built in 1890 by the Canadian government, which hired Father Donckele from the Diocese of Victoria as principal. The Montforts took over in 1906.) The school's most notorious principal, who presided throughout the 1930s, was Father Kurtz, known in Straits Halq'emeylem as *a:yex,* the crab, for the cruel, pincerlike fingers he used to pull a boy's ear until it bled or to grope a girl's private parts until she wept with pain and fear.

By the time Emily Rice left Kuper Island in 1959, at the age of 11, she had been repeatedly assaulted and sexually abused by Father Jackson and three other priests, one of whom plied her with alcohol before raping her. A nun, Sister Mary Margaret, known for peeping at the girls in the shower and grabbing their breasts, was infuriated when Emily resisted her advances. "She took a big stick with bark on it, and rammed it right inside my vagina," recalls Rice. "She told me to say I'd fallen on the stick and that she was just trying to get it out." The girl crawled into the infirmary the next day, too afraid to name the perpetrator. Nevertheless, when Emily returned to the dorm a few days later, the beatings by Sister Mary Margaret and the other nuns resumed without pause. In the years that followed, Emily would have to twice undergo reconstructive vaginal surgery, and she suffered permanent hearing loss. Father Jackson also wanted to make sure no one would talk. On the sisters' first trip home at Christmas, he suspended Rose by her feet over the side of the boat, threatening to release her into the freezing waves unless she promised to stay silent.

The stories of residential school survivors like Emily Rice began to slowly make their way into mainstream Canadian consciousness in the early 1980s. The schools' destruction of the lives of Indian children, in stark contrast to their supposed purpose of "saving" pagan youth from their parents' uncivilized fate, was known before that time to many Canadians who could have stopped it. The federal government—which by express legislation funded and guided the schools—amassed mountains of internal files over the years that documented not only the cruelties to which Aboriginal children were subjected but also the shoddy education they received and the shockingly high rates of illness and death, often the direct result of federal shortfalls in funding and supervision. Despite this evidence, some 60,000 files finally handed off to the Royal Commission on Aboriginal Peoples in 1993, the schools persisted as "internment camps for Indian children" for well over a century, ultimately affecting virtually every Aboriginal community in Canada. The death toll, excessive discipline and overall educational failure of the schools—well-known to any Indian Affairs bureaucrat who possessed a critical mind or a conscience—also leaked out frequently into the public eye, through the news media of the day or in the House of Commons. Aboriginal parents sometimes contacted journalists or politicians when their pleas to have their children better treated or returned home fell on deaf ears. In 1907, both the *Montreal Star* and *Saturday Night* reported on a medical inspection of the schools that found Aboriginal children were dying in astonishing numbers. The magazine called the 24 percent national death rate of Aboriginal children in the schools (42 per cent counting the children who died at home, where many were sent when they became critically ill), "a situation disgraceful to the country," and concluded, "Even war seldom shows as large a percentage of fatalities as does the educational system we have imposed upon our Indian wards." But Indian Affairs lawyer S. H. Blake Q.C. advised that since the department had done little to prevent the deaths, it could "bring itself within unpleasant nearness to the charge of manslaughter" should it entertain the reforms being pressed for by some politicians. Indian Affairs quickly moved to silence the furore by promising improvements to the schools, but over the next half-century, any thoroughgoing examination discovered the same scandals locked within their walls. The cumulative onslaught of criticism did little to deter Canada's complicity with the churches in obscuring the schools' failures until well into the 1960s.

Residential schooling reached its peak in 1931 with over 80 schools across Canada. From the mid-1800s to the 1970s, up to a third of all Aboriginal children were confined to the schools, many for the majority of their childhoods. The explicit mandate of the residential schools, throughout the lengthy partnership between the Canadian government and the churches who were responsible for operating them, was described succinctly by one federal bureaucrat: "To obtain entire possession of all Indian children after they attain to the age of seven or eight years and keep them at the schools."

Nowhere in Canada was the instrument of the residential school used more brutally and thoroughly than in British Columbia, where despite relatively late settlement by Europeans, the schools endured longer than anywhere else. The Anglican and United Churches, along with several Roman Catholic orders, divided up the province, which contained the largest population of Aboriginal people in Canada, into small religious fiefdoms. There, as they had elsewhere, clerics mounted a concerted assault on the spiritual and cultural practices of the First Nations by taking away their most vulnerable and precious resource, their children.

The seeds of a national system of institutions for Indian children were sown at the earliest contact between white Europeans and Aboriginal people in North America. In 17th-century New France, in what are now the provinces of Ontario and Quebec, the first clerics focussed their missionary zeal on the children. Their religious ideal was to create a class of "civilized" young Indians who would return to proselytize among their own people. In 1620, the Recollets, a Franciscan order, opened the first boarding school for Aboriginal boys, but by 1629, the friars had given up and abandoned New France. The Recollets were replaced by the Jesuits, the intellectual elite of European religious orders, who were better educated, more numerous and eager to try their hand with the "savages" of the New World.

After decades of unrewarding toil with the downtrodden European underclasses, the Jesuits were entranced by the prospect of converting robust young Aboriginal children into francized Christians who might, through intermarriage, improve the class of French settlers in the new country. The Jesuit missions Father Superior Paul Lejeune observed in the early 1630s in the *Jesuit Relations,* an exhaustive diary—kept primarily by Lejeune—that was printed and forwarded to France and Rome, that the Aboriginal people "are more intelligent than our ordinary peasants." Adult Indians were deemed unteachable, entrenched in their dying culture. As Father Lejeune remarked, "When we first came into these countries, as we hoped for scarcely anything from the old trees, we employed all our focus in cultivating the young plants."

When the practice of removing Aboriginal children to France proved to be an abject failure—those children who did not die became neither miniature Frenchmen nor Christian proselytizers—the Jesuits moved to establish boarding schools in the new colony. They attempted at first to separate the children from their parents, so as not to be "annoyed and distracted by the fathers while instructing the children." But as their boarding schools stood empty, the priests tried siting schools closer to Aboriginal villages. They soon found, however, as Father Lejeune reported, that the influence of the priests paled beside that of the children's families: "We could not retain the little Savages, if they be not removed from their native country, or if they have not some companions who help them to remain of their own free will ... when the savages were encamped near us, our [sic] children no longer belonged to us."

By 1668, the Ursuline order of nuns had arrived in Quebec from France and established a boarding school for Aboriginal girls, but soon they too were discouraged at their progress. "Out of a hundred that have passed through our hands scarcely have we civilized one," admitted the Ursuline Mother de l'Incarnation. "We find docility and intelligence in them, but when we are least expecting it they climb over our enclosure and go to run the woods with their relatives, where they find more pleasure than in all the amenities of our French houses. Savage nature is made that way; they cannot be constrained and if they are they become melancholy, and their melancholy makes them sick. Besides, the Savages love their children extraordinarily and when they know that they are sad they will do everything to get them back."

It was their powerful cultural and spiritual traditions, founded on seemingly immutable bonds between children and extended families, that enabled Aboriginal nations to hold their ground in these early encounters with Europeans. The initial period of contact represented a profound clash of cultures, and nowhere can that conflict be seen more starkly than in the radically opposed attitudes towards childhood.

Aboriginal children, regarded as the very future of their societies, were considered integral members of the family who learned by listening, watching, and carrying out tasks suited to their age, sex, and social standing. While diverse in language as well as cultural and spiritual practices, First Nations across North America shared a remarkable commonality in their approaches to child-rearing. Invariably they placed their children at the heart of a belief system closely aligned with the natural world. The economic and social survival of indigenous societies depended on the transmission of a vast amount of spiritual and practical knowledge from elders to the young, through an exclusively oral tradition.

By contrast, European society in the 1600s was evolving from a rigidly stratified feudal system, with monarchs at the apex and a powerful nobility sustained by the labour of a class of serfs, to "a new order in which trade and impersonal market-based relationships were becoming increasingly important," as author Margaret Conrad writes in her *History of the Canadian Peoples*. Political and financial alliances created competing nation-states in Europe, and the desire for overseas expansion was fuelled as much by population pressure and the need for trade and resources as by intellectual curiosity and religious zeal. The European cultural inverted pyramid, in direct contrast to Aboriginal cultures, was based on "the profound oppression of women in society at large," Conrad points out. As women were devalued, so were children; they were the chattels of a patriarch. Child labour and the consignment of a vast number of children and their families to grinding poverty were not questioned. Even the children of European aristocrats were to be seen and not heard. Across all classes, Europeans believed children required strict discipline underscored by physical punishment.

Although European religious orders were concerned with converting the "pagans" right from the time of their arrival, direct intervention by colonial governments in the lives of Aboriginal people did not begin in earnest until British hegemony was established in 1812. Until then, the various tribes had been needed as military allies by the French and the British, and both European powers recognized that meddling with the traditional Indian way of life would halt the valuable flow of furs. But just as the native peoples' military usefulness ebbed, so did their commercial value. By 1821, the two giant fur trade companies in Canada had merged and begun to directly employ their own people, including Europeans and an increasing number of Metis, who were able to range far and wide for furs, rendering Aboriginal tribes no longer essential trade partners.

By the 1820s, the new government of early Canada found itself pressured by a flood of British homesteaders who demanded the Indians be somehow neutralized or removed from the land. This political and economic imperative was a direct motivation for the colonial government's support of religious-run boarding schools for Indian children. In 1830, jurisdiction over the management of Indian affairs, which the European newcomers by then had firmly appropriated, became civil rather than military. The government of Upper Canada perceived its new charges as burdensome responsibilities, a people in transition from a dying culture represented by the adults, "the old unimprovable ones," to the children, who were destined for complete assimilation. In 1846, the government resolved at a meeting in Orillia, Ontario, to fully commit itself to Indian residential schools. Thus the interests of church and state merged in a marriage of convenience that was to endure more than a century: the churches could harvest souls at government-funded schools while meeting the shared mandate to eradicate all that was Indian in the children. The "Indian problem" would cease to exist.

The major denominations had already carved up the country among themselves, with Catholics, Anglicans, and Methodists launching schools for Indian children as far west as Manitoba and Alberta. In British Columbia, the earliest Indian boarding schools were established by rival Protestant and Catholic "missions," at Metlakatla in northern B.C. in 1857 and St. Mary's Mission in the Fraser Valley in 1861.

The churches soon received even more official support. With Confederation in 1867, the new national government was charged under the British North America Act with constitutional responsibility for Indian education. Limited experience had already indicated that day schools could not accomplish the government's goal of fully severing ties between Aboriginal parent and child. In 1876, the federal Indian Act effectively rendered all Aboriginal people children before the law, legal wards of the Crown. An Indian Affairs department was created in 1889, and Indian agents duly dispatched across the country. As the local hand controlling the government purse strings, the Indian agent could threaten to withhold money from increasingly destitute Aboriginal parents if they did not send their children away to school; he could even throw them in jail.

Aboriginal leaders were not uninterested in educating their children for the emerging white man's world. They could see their destiny as a subjugated people if they did not adjust. Chief Paulus Claus of the Bay of Quinte Mohawks had told the government in 1846 that he viewed the supposed "great cause of Indian improvement" as "our only hope to prevent our race from perishing and to enable us to stand on the same ground as the white man." Other leaders, weary of being displaced and dispossessed of their land, also regarded the education of their young as inevitable, and even desirable. Treaties signed with Aboriginal people, which covered virtually all of southern Ontario by the mid-1850s, even provided for schools on Indian land, funded by the government. But the apparently generous treaties were the harbinger of more sweeping provisions in the draconian Indian Act, which gave rise to the reserve system, under which Aboriginal tribes would be rigidly confined to small tracts of mostly unproductive lands. Day schools near Aboriginal children's homes were eliminated once it was determined they were unsuited to the primary *raison d'etre* of Indian education. Institutions far from the reserves could completely remove Indian children from their "evil surroundings" in favour of having them "kept constantly within the circle of civilized conditions," as Regina MP Nicholas Flood Davin urged in a report to the federal government in 1879.

For a model of institutional care for Indians, the fledgling Canadian government looked with interest to the south, where the United States was establishing a system of industrial boarding schools in the wake of a long and bloody conquest of American Indian tribes by the US Army. The prototype of an Indian school there actually had its origins in a prison for "pacified" Indians commanded by Lt. Richard Henry

Pratt. The US government embraced Pratt's methods and endorsed the evolution of American Indian policy from its guiding principle, "The only good Indian is a dead Indian," to Pratt's watchword: "Kill the Indian in him and save the man." Pratt established the Carlisle Indian School in Pennsylvania in 1878 with backing from the federal Bureau of Indian Affairs, which swiftly set up more "industrial" schools offering meagre academics augmented by agriculture and trades instruction for the boys and domestic training for the girls, sufficient to equip a servant class.

The American system was heartily recommended to the government of John A. Macdonald by backbencher Nicholas Flood Davin in the 1879 report. It was accepted that the Christian obligation to Indians could be discharged "only through the medium of children." The well-being of First Nations left bereft of their children was not addressed. Adults could not be rescued from "their present state of ignorance, superstition and helplessness," as they were "physically, mentally and morally ... unfitted to bear such a complete metamorphosis." Pragmatically, Indian Affairs bureaucrats advised Macdonald, the schools were "a good investment" to prevent Indian children from becoming "an undesirable and often dangerous element in society."

By 1896, the Canadian government was funding 45 church-run residential schools across Canada. Almost a quarter of these were located in British Columbia. In any given year, as many as 1,500 children from virtually every one of B.C.'s First Nations were interned in these schools. In addition to St. Mary's Mission, the Roman Catholic Church operated schools at Kuper Island, North Vancouver, Lower Post on the B.C.-Yukon border, Kamloops, Christie on northern Vancouver Island, Sechelt, Lejac in northern B.C., Cranbrook and Williams Lake. The Church of England, later the Anglican Church, operated three schools, the first in the model Indian village at Metlakatla, then St. George's at Lytton and one at Alert Bay, while the Methodist Church, later the United Church, ran schools in northwest B.C. at Port Simpson and Kitimat, Coqualeetza school in the Fraser Valley, and two schools in Nuu-chah-nulth territory on Vancouver Island: the Alberni Indian Residential School and another further north at Ahousaht.

In persuading Indian parents to send their children to these schools, authorities were assisted by a growing famine in Indian villages in western Canada. In this environment of hunger, amid recurring outbreaks of smallpox and influenza, the government withheld food rations from parents who resisted the removal of their children. Indian agents marched in lockstep with the religious orders, preparing lists of children to be taken from the reserves and then organizing the fall round-up. Strapping young farm boys, aided by R.C.M.P. officers, herded the children onto buckboard trucks or trains like cattle.

Official policy called for children to be isolated not only from their family and homelands but also, once at school, from their friends and siblings. Isolation made children more vulnerable to the massive brainwashing that was undertaken to replace their "pagan superstitions" with Christianity, and their "free and easy mode of life" with relentless labour and routine. "There should be an object for the employment of every moment," an 1891 federal report urged. Girls were taught domestic duties such as sewing, laundry, cooking, and cleaning, while boys were employed in agriculture, carpentry, shoemaking, and blacksmithing. Studies were confined to only half a day until well after the Second World War. Religion dominated every waking moment. Even recreation was controlled by European rules to teach "obedience to discipline." Expressions of Aboriginal culture and individuality were harshly punished. As soon as children entered school, their traditional long hair was shorn or shaved off; they were assigned a number and an English name and warned not to let a word of their language pass their lips.

Aboriginal parents were not complacent once their children were installed in the schools, even though their letters were censored and their visits, even by the few who could afford to make them, were discouraged. As early as 1889, the people of St. Peter's Reserve in Manitoba complained officially to Indian Commissioner David Laird about the principal of Rupert's Land Industrial School near Selkirk, Manitoba. Young girls of eight or nine still bore bruises on their bodies several weeks after being strapped, they said. During an investigation, the Anglican principal admitted he fed the children rancid butter and crept into the dormitories at night to kiss little girls, but he was reprimanded, not removed. Resistance among Indian parents manifested itself all across Canada and took many forms, from the withholding of children despite threatened sanctions to petitions, visits, and outright threats of violence. But despite these and other early signs of trouble, the Department of Indian Affairs continued to defend the boarding schools, declaring they were succeeding in "the emancipation of the Indian from his inherent superstition and gross ignorance."

REFERENCES

Out of the Depths: The Experiences of Mi'kmaw Children at the Indian Residential School in Shubenacadie, Nova Scotia, by Isabelle Knockwood (Lockport, N.S.: Roseway Publishing, 1992).

Breaking the Silence: An Interpretive Study of Residential School Impact and Healing as Illustrated by the Stories of First Nations Individuals, Assembly of First Nations (Ottawa: 1994).

Victims of Benevolence: The Dark Legacy of the Williams Lake Residential School, by Elizabeth Furniss (Vancouver: Arsenal Pulp Press, 1992).

Residential Schools: The Stolen Years, edited by Linda Jaine (Saskatoon: University Extension Press, 1993).

No End of Grief: Indian Residential Schools in Canada, by Agnes Grant (Winnipeg: Pemmican Publications Inc., 1996).

Indian Residential Schools: The Nuu-chah-nulth Experience (Port Alberni, B.C.: Nuu-chah-nulth Tribal Council, 1996).

Shingwauk's Vision: A History of Native Residential Schools, by J. R. Miller (Toronto: University of Toronto Press, 1996).

The Oblate Assault on Canada's Northwest, by Robert Choquette (Ottawa: University of Ottawa Press, 1995).

Chain Her by One Foot: The Subjugation of Native Women in Seventeenth-Century New France, by Karen Anderson (New York: Routledge, Inc., 1991).

The West Beyond the West: A History of British Columbia, by Jean Barman (Toronto: University of Toronto Press, 1991).

Indian Education in Canada: Vol. 1, *The Legacy,* and Vol. 2, *The Challenge,* edited by Jean Barman, Yvonne Hebert and Don McCaskill (Vancouver: University of British Columbia Press, 1986 and 1987).

A Narrow Vision: Duncan Campbell Scott and the Administration of Indian Affairs in Canada, by E. Brian Titley (Vancouver: University of British Columbia Press, 1986).

A Long and Terrible Shadow: White Values, Native Rights in the Americas 1492–1992, by Thomas R. Berger (Vancouver: Douglas & McIntyre, 1991).

Contact & Conflict: Indian-European Relations in British Columbia, 1774–1890, by Robin Fisher (Vancouver: University of British Columbia Press, 1977).

Reading, Writing and the Hickory Stick: The Appalling Story of Physical and Psychological Abuse in American Schools, by Irwin A. Hyman (Lexington, Mass.: Lexington Books, 1990).

Education for Extinction: American Indians and the Boarding School Experience 1873–1928, by David Wallace Adams (Lawrence, Kans.: University Press of Kansas, 1995).

"Champlain Judged by His Indian Policy: A Different View of Early Canadian History," by Bruce G. Trigger, in *The Native Imprint: The Contribution of First Peoples to Canada's Character,* edited by Olive P. Dickason (Athabasca: Athabasca University Educational Enterprises, 1995).

Looking Forward, Looking Back, Vol. 1, *Report of the Royal Commission on Aboriginal Peoples* (Ottawa: Canada Communication Group, 1996).

Kuper Island Industrial School: Conduct Books, Daily Diaries, Attendance Records (Victoria, B.C. Provincial Archives, Dept. of Indian Affairs and Northern Development: 1891–1907).

CHAPTER 10

THE GUARANÍ:

THE ECONOMICS OF ETHNOCIDE

Richard H. Robbins

IT IS DIFFICULT FOR ANY MEMBER of the culture of capitalism to take an unbiased view of indigenous peoples, that is not to view such groups as backward, undeveloped, economically depressed, and in need of civilizing. This, of course, is the way indigenous peoples have been portrayed for centuries. Theodore Roosevelt (cited Maybury-Lewis 1997:4), famous for his campaign to conserve nature, said "The settler and pioneer have at bottom had justice on their side; this great continent could not have been kept as nothing but a game preserve for squalid savages."

In the 19th century, "scientific" theories of evolution and racial superiority allowed people to rationalize the enslavement, confinement, or destruction of indigenous peoples. As late as the 1940s, British anthropologist Lord Fitzroy Raglan (cited Bodley 1990:11), who was to become president of the Royal Anthropological Institute, said that tribal beliefs in magic were a chief cause of folly and unhappiness. Existing tribes were plague spots: "We should bring to them our justice, our education, and our science. Few will deny that these are better than anything which savages have got." While many of these attitudes have changed, indigenous peoples still tend to be seen as needy dependents or victims, largely incapable of helping themselves. We tend to see their destruction as a consequence of their weakness, rather than of patterns of behavior and exploitation built into the culture of capitalism.

It may help to change that view if instead of seeing indigenous peoples as needy dependents living largely outmoded ways of life, we consider the resemblance between indigenous societies and a modern, socially responsible corporation that carefully manages its resources, provides well for its workers, and plans for the long term rather than the short term. Looking at indigenous societies in this way may help us better appreciate why they don't survive. The fact is that environmentally and socially responsible corporations do not fare well in the capitalist world; they fail not because of any inherent weakness but because they become targets for takeovers by individuals or groups who, after taking the corporation over, quickly sell off the carefully managed resources solely to make a quick profit, leaving the corporation in ruin and its workers unemployed.

Take the fate of the Pacific Lumber Company. The family-owned company was known as one of the most environmentally and economically sound companies in the United States. It pioneered the practice of sustainable logging on its large holdings of redwoods and was generous to its employees, even overfunding its pension plan to ensure that it could meet its commitments. Furthermore, to ensure the security of its employees, it had a no-layoff policy. Unfortunately, the very features that made the company a model of environmental and social responsibility also made it a prime target for corporate raiders. After they took control of the company in the late 1980s, they doubled the cutting rate on company lands, drained $55 million of the $93 million pension plan, and invested the remaining $38 million in a life insurance company that ultimately failed (Korten 1995:210). And the fate of Pacific Lumber is not unique.

Indigenous peoples possess all the characteristics that make them prime targets for takeovers. Like responsible corporations, they have managed their resources so well that those same resources (e.g. lumber, animals, farmlands) become targets for those who have used up theirs or who wish to make a quick profit. The indigenous peoples themselves become expendable, or themselves become resources to be exploited. To illustrate, let's look at the case of the Guaraní as described by Richard Reed (1997).

HISTORY AND BACKGROUND

Most of the 15,000 Guaraní are settled in the rainforests of eastern Paraguay; they live in 114 communities ranging from three to four houses to over 100 families. They are a minority population in a country in which most citizens are *mestizo* or *criollos,* descendants of Europeans who married Guaraní.

When Europeans arrived, over 1,000,000 Guaraní and related groups lived in the area stretching from the Andes to the Atlantic Ocean. The Guaraní welcomed the first conquistadors, joining them in carving out trade routes to the Andes. The earliest reports of travellers indicate that the Guaraní system of production and standard of living were successful. In 1541 the region's first governor, Cabeza de Vaca (cited Reed 1997:8), noted that the Guaraní

[a]re the richest people of all the land and province both for agriculture and stock raising. They rear plenty of fowl and geese and other birds, and have an abundance of game, such as boar, deer, and dantes (anta), partridge, quail and pheasants; and they have great fisheries in the river. They grow plenty of maize, potatoes, cassava, peanuts and many other fruits; and from the trees they collect a great deal of honey.

In addition to their economic success, the Guaraní were a relatively egalitarian society in which a person's place in society was determined by kinship. Leadership was usually determined by age, although political leaders had little or no power of coercion over others.

The Guaraní engaged European markets soon after contact, managing to combine their traditional subsistence activities of swidden agriculture and hunting and gathering with the collection of commercial products from the forests such as yerba mate, a naturally growing tea, animal skins, and honey. Anthropologists call this combination of productive activities *agroforestry*, the active management of forest resources for long-term production.

To understand agroforestry as practiced by the Guaraní, we need to understand a little about the nature of tropical rainforests. They are the most diverse biosystems on Earth, containing half the recorded species in the world, although only about 15 percent of these species have even been discovered. They are also among the most fragile ecosystems. A rainforest is a layered system. The top layer, or canopy, is provided by large trees protecting the layers underneath it, with each species of plant or animal in lower layers dependent on the others, and all surviving on a very thin layer of soil.

Guaraní agroforestry focuses on three activities: horticulture, hunting, and gathering, and commercial tree cropping. The agriculture is shifting or swidden agriculture, in which small areas of the forests are cut and burned, the ash providing a thin layer of nutrients for the soil. These areas are planted until spreading weeds and decreased yields force the farmer to move to a new plot. The old plot is not abandoned but planted with banana trees and manioc, crops that need little care and which produce for up to four years. In this way land is gradually recycled back into tropical forest. Furthermore, these plots provide forage for deer, peccary, and other animals, which the Guaraní trap or shoot.

Fishing is another source of protein. Usually the Guaraní fish with poison. They crush the bark of the timbo tree and wash it through the water, leaving a thin seal on top of the water. They wait for the water to be depleted of oxygen and the stunned fish float to the surface. The Guaraní also fish with hook and lines. Other food sources include honey, fruit, the hearts of palm trees, and roots gathered from the forest floor.

Finally, to earn cash, the Guaraní collect yerba mate leaves, animal skins, oils, and food. In these activities the Guaraní use the forest extensively but not intensively. For example, they will cut leaves from all yerba trees but take only the mature leaves from each tree every three years, thus promoting the plants' survival. In addition, since the Guaraní harvest from a number of ecological niches and since their consumption needs are modest, they never overexploit a commodity to earn cash.

Thus the Guaraní use the forest to supplement their other subsistence activities, integrating this resource into their production system. It is a production system that is modeled after that of the rainforest itself; by incorporating trees, the system preserves or recreates the forest canopy necessary for the survival of plants and animals below it. The surviving diversity of crops and animals ensures the recycling of nutrients necessary for their maintenance. In fact, as Richard Reed (1997:15) noted, "agroforestry often increases ecological diversity."

Agroforestry differs markedly from the typical exploitive forest activities in the culture of capitalism, such as intensive agriculture, lumbering, and cattle raising, activities modeled after factory production. First, indigenous production systems are diverse, allowing forest residents to exploit various niches in the forest without overexploiting any one niche. Second, unlike intensive agriculture, lumbering, or cattle raising, the Guaraní production system depends on the resources of plants and animals themselves rather than on the nutrients of the forest soils. Thus by moderate use of the soils, water, canopy, and fauna of the forest the Guaraní ensure that the whole system continues to flourish. Third, Guaraní production techniques lend themselves to a pattern of social relations in which individual autonomy is respected and in which activities do not lend themselves to a division of labour that lends itself to status hierarchy. The basic work unit is the family, with both men and women involved in productive labour—farming, gathering food, and collecting commercial products—and reproductive labour—child care, food preparation, and the construction and maintenance of shelters.

Fourth, unlike the activities of the culture of capitalism, the Guaraní mode of production is neither technology- nor labour-intensive. The Guaraní spend about 18 percent of their time in productive activities; one-third of that is devoted to horticulture, slightly less to forest subsistence activities, and about 40 percent to commercial activities. Another 27 percent of their time is devoted to household labour. In all, about half their daylight time is spent working; the rest is devoted to leisure and socializing. Reed said that the Guaraní workday is approximately half that of a typical European worker.

Finally, unlike capitalist production, which is tightly integrated into the global system, Guaraní production allows them a great deal of autonomy from the larger society. When prices for their products are too low, the Guaraní stop selling; if prices on store goods are too high, the Guaraní stop buying. Thus they do not have to rely on commercial markets; their stability is in their gardens, not their labour.

This autonomy can be attributed in part to the Guaraní's modest consumption needs. Food accounts for about 40 percent of the average family's monthly market basket—about two kilograms of rice, pasta, and flour; one kilogram of meat, a half liter of cooking oil, and a little salt. Cloth and clothing is the next most important purchase, perhaps a new shirt or pants (but not both) each year. Another one-fifth of the budget is spent on tools, such as machetes and axes, and an occasional luxury, such as tobacco, alcohol, or a tape recorder. Thus, as Reed (1997:75) noted, the Guaraní engage the global economic system without becoming dependent on it.

CONTEMPORARY DEVELOPMENT AND GUARANÍ COMMUNITIES

Guaraní culture and their system of adaptation are, however, being threatened. Since the 1970s, the rate of forest destruction in Paraguay has increased dramatically as forests are cleared to make way for monocultural agriculture and cattle ranching. As a result, Guaraní house lots stand exposed on open landscapes and families are being forced to settle on the fringes of mestizo towns. Reed made the point that it is not market contact or interethnic relations that are destroying the Guaraní; they have participated in the market and interacted with mestizo townspeople for centuries. Rather, it is a new kind of economic development spawned by the needs of the global economy.

After decades of little economic growth, in the 1970s the Paraguayan economy began to grow at the rate of 10 percent per year. This growth was fueled by enormous expansion of agricultural production, particularly cotton, soy, and wheat. Most of this growth came at the expense of huge tracts of rainforest felled to make way for the new cultivation. As Reed said, since 1970 every effort has been made to convert the land of eastern Paraguay into fields for commodity production. A number of things contributed to rainforest destruction.

First, roads built into the forests for military defense against Brazil contributed to the influx of settlers into the rainforest. Second, large-scale, energy-intensive agriculture displaced small farmers, who flooded to the cities in search of work.

This created pressures on these populations to find work or land, but rather than redistribute the vast tracts of cleared land held by wealthy cattle ranchers to peasants, the government chose to entice poor peasants into the forests with land-distribution programs. Between 1963 and 1973, 42,000 families had been given land; between 1973 and 1976, 48,000 families were given a total of 4,000,000 hectares of land.

A third factor was international finance. The oil boom of the 1970s, along with changes in currency, allowed core institutions to go on a lending spree as people sought ways to reinvest their profits. Like most other peripheral countries, Paraguay borrowed heavily in the 1970s to build roads, hydroelectric projects, and other things they believed necessary to build an industrial economy. The money that came into the country from the World Bank and other financial institutions needed to be reinvested by Paraguayan financiers, and some invested in farms and cattle ranches in the forests. Finally, to repay the loans, the country needed to raise funds, which it did by expanding agricultural growth in export crops, putting further demands on the rainforest.

The process of environmental destruction soon followed. For example, the Guaraní group Reed worked with (the Itanaramí) suffered their first major incursion in 1972, when the government cut a road into their forest. It was built partly to control the border with Brazil, but it also allowed logging in what had been impenetrable forests. Loggers brought in bulldozers to cut road directly to the hardwood trees. Lumber mills were positioned along the roads and the cut lumber was trucked to the capital city, where it was shipped to the United States, Argentina, and Japan. As Reed (1997:85) said, the forests that had provided the Guaraní with shelter and subsistence were cut down so that consumers in the United States, Europe, and Japan could enjoy furniture and parquet floors.

The roads also brought into the Guaraní forest impoverished Paraguayan families in search of land that they illegally cut to create fields in the forests, fields that will bear crops only for a short time before losing their fragile fertility. To complicate matters, Brazilian peasants, many displaced by large-scale agricultural projects in their own country, crossed the border seeking land on which to survive. The area even became home to a Mennonite community seeking to escape the pressures and problems of the larger world.

On the heels of these colonists came agribusiness concerns clearing more forest on which to raise soy and cotton. Within months of their arrival, thousands of hectares of forest were cut down and replaced by fields of cash crops. The road that had brought in the military, loggers, and peasant colonists was now used to haul out produce for foreign markets and for cattle drives to deliver meat to consumers across South and North America.

Thus in the same way that corporate raiders seize responsible corporations to turn a quick profit, often destroying them in the process, people seeking a profit from the lands of the Guaraní quickly destroyed the forest. The logging companies cut the trees that provided the canopy for the forests as well as the trunks on which vines such as orchids and philodendron climbed. Without the protective cover of the large trees, the enormous diversity of life that thrived beneath the canopy, was no longer viable. Faunal populations declined immediately because their habitat was being destroyed and because they were being hunted to extinction by the new settlers. With the flora and fauna decimated, all that remained was a fragile layer of topsoil, which the harsh sunlight and rains quickly reduced to its clay base.

The rate of forest destruction was enormous. From 1970 to 1976, Paraguayan forests were reduced from 6.8 million to 4.2 million hectares. Half of the remaining forest was cut by 1984, and each year thereafter another 150,000–200,000 hectares has fallen to axes and bulldozers. At this rate, the Paraguayan forests will be gone by the year 2025.

More to the point for this discussion, with the rainforest went the way of life of the Guaraní. When Reed first began working with the Itanaramí in 1981, they were isolated in the forest, living largely as they had for centuries. By 1995 they were on a small island of forest in an "ocean of agricultural fields."

The Guaraní had no legal title to the land they have inhabited for centuries, such title being claimed by the nation-state; those who bought the land from the government assume they have both a legal and moral right to remove any people occupying the land. Even when Guaraní were allowed to retain their houseplots, their traditional system of agroforestry was impossible because their forest was being destroyed and they were forced to seek new and smaller plots. Furthermore, the settlers destroyed their hunting stock, so the Guaraní quickly came to depend for meat on the occasional steer slaughtered by ranchers in the towns, for which the Guaraní had to pay cash. But the ranchers destroyed the stands of yerba mate, a source of cash for the Guaraní, that they had cultivated for centuries.

Gradually, with their traditional production system destroyed, the Guaraní were forced to enter the market economy as cotton or tobacco growers or as wage labourers on the lands they had sustained for centuries. Those who entered the agricultural sector found that the new system of farming was capital-intensive and required inputs of fertilizers, herbicides, and insecticides. Families went into debt, becoming dependent on mestizo merchants and lenders. Those who chose to work found that wages were often too low to support a family, forcing several or all family members to work. Furthermore, labour required people to travel outside their communities so that even those families who managed to gain access to land on which to garden had little time for it. Since wage labour demands the strongest workers, it is often the youngest and strongest who must leave their communities.

There are other effects. Illness and disease became more prevalent. Suicide, virtually unknown previously in Guaraní communities, increased from a total of six in 1989 to three suicides per month in the first half of 1995. The leadership system collapsed, as religious leaders who earned their authority through their ability to mediate disputes found themselves helpless to mediate the new problems that arose between Guaraní and mestizo or government bureaucrats. Today the government appoints community leaders, to make it easier for them to control and negotiate with Guaraní communities. These new leaders derive their power from assistance programs that funnel resources to the Guaraní, but which many leaders use to reward friends and relatives, and punish non-kin and enemies.

In sum, the debt assumed by the Paraguayan government to foster economic expansion and the resulting expansion of capital-intensive farming and cattle ranching in the 1980s disrupted Guaraní society more than had four centuries of contact; as a result its members are dispersing and assimilating into the larger society. It would be easy to condemn the Paraguayan government, and other governments whose indigenous peoples are being destroyed. Yet the nation-states are only doing what capital controllers are supposed to do: they are choosing modes of production and ways of life that will bring the greatest immediate monetary return.

REFERENCES

Bodley, John H. 1985. *Anthropology and Contemporary Human Problems,* 2nd ed. Mountain View: Mayfield Publishing.

Bodley, John H. 1990. *Victims of Progress,* 3rd ed. Mountain View: Mayfield Publishing.

Korten, David C. 1995. *When Corporations Rule the World.* Hartford: Kumarian Press.

Maybury-Lewis, David. 1997. *Indigenous Peoples, Ethnic Groups, and the State.* Boston: Allyn & Bacon.

Reed, Richard. 1997. *Forest Dwellers, Forest Protectors: Indigenous Models for International Development.* Boston: Allyn & Bacon.

CRITICAL-THINKING QUESTIONS

CHAPTER 6 *by Russell Means*

1. Why is Russell Means's discussion of "official truth" so important to his later discussion of genocide?

CHAPTER 7 *by Noble David Cook*

1. Why is it important to understand the devastating impact of disease on the "conquering" of indigenous societies?
2. What does Cook mean by the term "compound epidemics," and what is its importance?
3. According to Cook, how devastating were these compound diseases, and why?

CHAPTER 8 *by Colin Tatz*

1. According to Tatz, what role does intention play in current definitions of genocide?
2. How does Tatz suggest that Australia attempts to distance itself from any taint of genocide in its past?
3. Why does he suggest that Australia does this?

CHAPTER 9 *by Suzanne Fournier and Ernie Crey*

1. What do Fournier and Crey mean by the phrase "killing the Indian in the child"?
2. From where do Fournier and Crey suggest Canadian officials took their institutional models of residential schools?
3. According to the authors, what factors influenced parental decisions to send the children to these institutions?

CHAPTER 10 *by Richard H. Robbins*

1. What similarities does Robbins emphasize between Indigenous Peoples and socially responsible corporations?
2. What does Robbins mean when he suggests that the Guaraní were able to engage with the global economic system without becoming dependent on it?
3. What negative impacts on Guaraní ways of life do modern, more corporate models of economic development have?

FURTHER READING

Robbins, Richard. 2005. *Global Problems and the Culture of Capitalism*. 3rd edition. Allyn and Bacon.

This is an introductory text with a wide range of uses. It tackles the issue of capitalism head on, treating it as both an economic and a cultural system that has exerted an enormous and negative impact on indigenous societies.

Moses, D., ed. 2004. *Genocide and Settler Society: Frontier Violence and Stolen Indigenous Children in Australian History*. New York: Berghahn Books.

This collection of articles deals generally with the issue of genocide in an Australian context. In assessing the utility of the concept of genocide in explaining historical relations between indigenous and settler societies, some authors debate the role of intention in whether incidents may be termed *genocidal,* while others explore the conditions under which genocidal "incidents" are more or less likely to occur.

Alchon, Suzanne. 2003. *A Pest in the Land: New World Epidemics in a Global Perspective*. Albuquerque: University of New Mexico Press.

Tacitly critiquing romanticized notions of pre-colonial indigenous societies as Edens of health and prosperity, Alchon argues that the epidemics which followed colonial intrusions of "the new world" were nothing new—disease was an enduring feature of pre-colonial indigenous societies. What was new about post-contact diseases, she argues, was that for the first time, indigenous societies were unable to recover from them. She argues that this inability was exacerbated by new colonial contexts, including wars and forced slavery, and that these relations in particular were responsible for the high percentages of population loss.

Grant, Agnes, ed. 2005. *Finding My Talk: How Fourteen Native Women Reclaimed Their Lives After Residential School*. Calgary: Fifth House.

This text tells the stories of 14 Native women who endured the trauma of residential schools. The book relays their experiences and emphasizes their strength in surviving these institutions to lead productive lives. The book's real power lies in its first-person accounts and in the quiet dignity of the women who consented to relive these awful memories and let them stand in print.

PART III:

SOCIAL CONSTRUCTS

OF COLONIALISM

As SHOWN IN THE PREVIOUS SECTION, there is little doubt that much of the historical relationship between pre-existing indigenous societies and colonial state-building projects was built on, on the one hand, the use of brutality and physical violence; and on the other, the debilitating effects of compound disease epidemics. However, nation-states did not and do not rely only (or even mainly) on violence in their attempts to achieve success in cultural and economic projects. Instead, liberal nation-states operate on certain key social constructs whose historical importance serves to highlight certain differences (usually racial and cultural) between indigenous and non-indigenous communities and nations. Today, such social constructs, such *discourses*, assist in the production and maintenance of seemingly natural and logical ideas about who and what indigenous people are, and how they differ from settler citizens and societies. These "natural" differences are deeply embedded in the daily practices of citizens and operate at a largely "pre-reflective" level. In this light, rather than being understood as contingent social constructions they are instead seen as "just the way things are." Part of the power of such viewpoints is that they are often insulated from critical reflection; indeed, attaining the status of "truth," they are often used to explain other social phenomena.

Racialized discourses in liberal nation-states are, unquestionably, dominant ones, and as with any discourses, part of their power rests on us incorporating them, fairly unquestioningly, into our cultural imagination. They form the bedrock of myths and meanings upon which contemporary collective identities are situated, and they represent the categories we use to make our normative evaluations. Moreover, they provide a comforting simplicity which makes the world easier to understand. However, the world is a complex place, and simple arguments tend to fall apart when measured against the complexity of historical and contemporary social reality. The following readings attempt to map the ways in which some of the more powerful social constructs of the modern world collapse when juxtaposed with the messiness of empirical evidence.

The readings which follow represent various parts of the theme of social constructs. The first author, Stuart Hall, examines perhaps one of the most hallowed social constructs in the western world: the idea of "the west," and in particular how a discourse of "the west" established itself in a seemingly natural differentiation against "the other." Hall's article begins by positioning the importance of "discourse" as a crucial link between the creation of meaning and the representation of reality. That is to say, he makes the important argument that the very act of talking about a particular subject shapes the ways we understand it. Different discourses use different categories of thought and observation, and tend to create different forms of understanding. For example, western bio-medical models of medicine represent a very different discourse from indigenous healing methods. Importantly, Hall traces the ways in which dominant discourses (in his case "the west") draw on earlier discourses and sublimate them into new systems of meaning. He also demonstrates the practical ways in which we bring knowledge about a particular subject into being through such forms as archives, myth, folklore, and travellers' tales, each of which had an enormous impact on how the idea of "the west" was created and sustained. Finally, Hall points out that with sufficient time and effort, certain ways of understanding and talking about the world can become so powerful that they come to be seen as "true"—in these instances, these "regimes of truth" are able to marginalize other ways of understanding and talking about the world (think here about the power of scientific observation for explaining phenomena versus the power of, for example, magic).

Hall provides us with a tool box for thinking about our reality as something other than "just there," and lays out the ways in which "the west" attempted to differentiate itself from the rest of the world. In her beautifully written study on "ground up" Mohawk notions of citizenship, indigenous scholar Audra Simpson demonstrates the ways in which members of the Mohawk nation have created and maintained notions of collective indigenous identity which disturb the most powerful of social constructs in western societies—namely, the geo-political boundaries of Canada and the United States. Through an in-depth examination of the daily activities of an indigenous community (the Kahnawake Mohawk nation), Simpson articulates the ways in which members of the Mohawk nation actually *live* that nationalism on a daily basis, and how nationhood is consciously and unconsciously negotiated as it both colludes with and clashes against the legacies of colonialism in both Canada and the US.

The third reading ("The Criminalization of Indigenous People") examines the over-representation of indigenous people in the Australian criminal justices system. Conventional discussions about this topic often begin with the seemingly logical idea that, for a variety of reasons, indigenous people tend to commit more crimes and more serious crimes, which in turn leads to higher rates of arrest, conviction, and incarceration. In his study of contemporary Australia, Chris Cunneen paints a far more complex picture of the social relations within which this over-representation is situated. He argues that the specific ways in which criminal-justice officials police indigenous communities, and the wide power of discretion held by police officers, judges, and other criminal justice officials, conspire to exert an enormous impact on how particular incidents are framed. In this context, he presents evidence that police and other criminal-justice officials use their discretion in ways that increase the likelihood of indigenous people being charged, arrested, and imprisoned. Likewise, Cunneen emphasizes the importance of situating the criminal-justice relationship between Australian indigenous communities and policing agencies within the larger socio-economic and cultural context of Australia's colonialism, and its past and contemporary treatment of these indigenous communities.

The fourth reading examines a fable familiar to Indigenous Peoples around the world, that of their supposed "extinction" as a result of the impact of conquest and colonialism. In his reading "The Indians Are Coming to an End," Matthew Restall maps the ways in which a certainty about the extinction of the Andean peoples of Peru was used to buttress elementally powerful social constructs about the character and ethical justification of conquest, native reaction to conquest, and its longer-term effects on indigenous societies. Restall argues that in order to hold water, these arguments needed either to romanticize Native communities as paradises or denigrate them as primitive and barbaric. Both representations hinged on the assumption that this character rendered indigenous communities unable to bear the strain of conquest/civilization. Arguing that indigenous collectivities were every bit as complicated and imperfect as those of their supposed conquerors, Restall traces this "myth of extinction" from its inception with Columbus to European understandings of the after-effects of his travels. Restall critiques these simplistic writings by presenting the complex and heterogeneous responses of indigenous collectivities to such colonization projects, emphasizing the sophisticated reactions and adaptations by which indigenous collectivities attempted to ride out the storm of colonization.

The fifth and final reading in this section examines the work of Sarah A. Carter, a Canadian historian who critiques the seemingly logical idea that the Cree of western Canada made poor farmers because the sedentary lifestyle associated with agriculture represented too radical a change from their previous nomadic lifestyle as buffalo hunters. Carter argues that despite the fact that the Cree showed a lot of promise as farmers, government officials' perception of Cree as "primitive" led to the creation and enforcement of racist policies which harmed Cree farmers' ability to compete with non-Native farmers and to engage in the kinds of farming required to reap profits from the endeavour. Carter shows how early successes in

Cree farming were hampered by government policies that failed to provide Cree farmers with proper farming implements and that interfered with their ability to sell the product of their labours.

CHAPTER II

THE WEST AND THE REST:

DISCOURSE AND POWER

Stuart Hall

DISCOURSE AND POWER

THIS ARTICLE WILL EXAMINE the formation of the languages or "discourses" in which Europe began to describe and represent the *difference* between itself and the "others" it encountered in the course of its expansion. We are now beginning to sketch the formation of the "discourse" of "the West and the Rest." However, we need first to understand what we mean by the term "discourse."

WHAT IS A "DISCOURSE"?

In commonsense language, a discourse is simply "a coherent or rational body of speech or writing; a speech, or a sermon." But here the term is being used in a more specialized way. By "discourse," we mean a particular way of *representing* "the West," "the Rest," and the relations between them. A discourse is a group of statements which provide a language for talking about—i.e. a way of representing—a particular kind of knowledge about a topic. When statements about a topic are made within a particular discourse, the discourse makes it possible to construct the topic in a certain way. It also limits the other ways in which the topic can be constructed.

A discourse does not consist of one statement, but of several statements working together to form what the French social theorist Michel Foucault (1926–84) calls a "discursive formation." The statements fit together because any one statement implies a relation to all the others: "They refer to the same object, share the same style and support 'a strategy ... a common institutional ... or political drift or pattern'" (Cousins and Hussain, 1984, pp. 84–5).

One important point about this notion of discourse is that it is not based on the conventional distinction between thought and action, language and practice. Discourse is about the production of knowledge through language. But it is itself produced by a practice: "discursive practice"—the practice of producing meaning. Since all social practices entail *meaning,* all practices have a discursive aspect. So discourse enters into and influences all social practices. Foucault would argue that the discourse of the West about the Rest was deeply implicated in practice—i.e. in how the West behaved towards the Rest.

To get a fuller sense of Foucault's theory of discourse, we must bear the follow-ing points in mind.

1. A discourse can be produced by many individuals in different institutional settings (like families, prisons, hospitals, and asylums). Its integrity or "coherence" does not depend on whether or not it issues from one place or from a single speaker or "subject." Nevertheless, every discourse constructs positions from which alone it makes sense. Anyone deploying a discourse must position themselves *as if* they were the subject of the discourse. For example, we may not ourselves believe in the natural superiority of the West. But if we use the discourse of "the West and the Rest," we will necessarily find ourselves speaking from a position that holds that the West is a superior civilization. As Foucault puts it, "To describe a ... statement does not consist in analyzing the relations between the author and what he *[sic]* says ... ; but in determining what position can and must be occu-pied by any individual if he is to be the subject of it [the statement]" (Foucault, 1972, pp. 95–6).

2. Discourses are not closed systems. A discourse draws on elements in other discourses, binding them into its own network of meanings. Thus, as we saw in the preceding section, the discourse of "Europe" drew on the earlier discourse of "Christendom," altering or translating its meaning. Traces of past discourses remain embedded in more recent discourses of "the West."

3. The statements within a discursive formation need not all be the same. But the relationships and differences between them must be regular and systematic, not random. Foucault calls this a "system of dispersion": "Whenever one can describe, between a number of statements, such a system of dispersion, whenever ... one can define a regularity ... [then] we will say ... that we are dealing with a *discursive forma-tion*" (Foucault, 1972, p. 38).

These points will become clearer when we apply them to particular examples, as we do later in this article.

DISCOURSE AND IDEOLOGY

A discourse is similar to what sociologists call an "ideology": a set of statements or beliefs which produce knowledge that serves the interests of a particular group or class. Why, then, use "discourse" rather than "ideology"?

One reason which Foucault gives is that ideology is based on a distinction between *true* statements about the world (science) and *false* statements (ideology), and the belief that the facts about the world help us to decide between true and false state-ments. But Foucault argues that statements about the social, political, or moral world are rarely ever simply true or false; and "the facts" do not enable us to decide defin-itively about their truth or falsehood, partly because "facts" can be construed in different ways. The very language we use to describe the so-called facts interferes in this process of finally deciding what is true and what is false.

For example, Palestinians fighting to regain land on the West Bank from Israel may be described either as "freedom fighters" or as "terrorists." It is a fact that they are fighting; but what does the fighting *mean*. The facts alone cannot decide. And the very language we use—"freedom fighters/terrorists"—is part of the difficulty. Moreover, certain descriptions, even if they appear false to us, can be *made* "true" because people act on them believing that they are true, and so their actions have real consequences. Whether the Palestinians are terrorists or not, if we think they are, and act on that "knowledge," they in effect become terrorists because we treat them as such. The language (discourse) has real effects in practice: the description becomes "true."

Foucault's use of "discourse," then, is an attempt to sidestep what seems an unresolvable dilemma—deciding which social discourses are true or scientific, and which false or ideological. Most social scientists now accept that our values enter into all our descriptions of the social world, and therefore most of our statements, however factual, have an ideological dimension. What Foucault would say is that knowledge of the Palestinian problem is produced by competing discourses—those of "freedom-fighter" and "terrorist"—and that each is linked to a contestation over power. It is the outcome of *this* struggle which will decide the "truth" of the situation.

You can see, then, that although the concept of "discourse" sidesteps the problem of truth/falsehood in ideology, it does *not* evade the issue of power. Indeed, it gives considerable weight to questions of power since it is power, rather than the facts about reality, which makes things "true": "We should admit that power produces knowledge ...That power and knowledge directly imply one another; that there is no power relation without the correlative constitution of a field of knowledge, nor any knowledge that does not presuppose and constitute ... power relations" (Foucault, 1980, p. 27).

CAN A DISCOURSE BE "INNOCENT"?

Could the discourse which developed in the West for talking about the Rest operate outside power? Could it be, in that sense, purely scientific—i.e. ideologically innocent? Or was it influenced by particular class interests?

Foucault is very reluctant to *reduce* discourse to statements that simply mirror the interests of a particular class. The same discourse can be used by groups with different, even contradictory, class interests. But this does *not* mean that discourse is ideologically neutral or "innocent." Take, for example, the encounter between the West and the New World. There are several reasons why this encounter could not be innocent, and therefore why the discourse which emerged in the Old World about the Rest could not be innocent either.

First, Europe brought its own cultural categories, languages, images, and ideas to the New World in order to describe and represent it. It tried to fit the New World into existing conceptual frameworks, classifying it according to its own norms, and absorbing it into western traditions of representation. This is hardly surprising: we often draw on what we already know about the world in order to explain and describe something novel. It was never a simple matter of the West just looking, seeing, and describing the New World/the Rest without preconceptions.

Secondly, Europe had certain definite purposes, aims, objectives, motives, interests, and strategies in setting out to discover what lay across the "Green Sea of Darkness." These motives and interests were mixed. The Spanish, for example, wanted to

1. get their hands on gold and silver;
2. claim the land for Their Catholic Majesties; and
3. convert the heathen to Christianity.

These interests often contradicted one another. But we must not suppose that what Europeans said about the New World was simply a cynical mask for their own self-interest. When King Manuel of Portugal wrote to Ferdinand and Isabella of Spain that "the principal motive of this enterprise [da Gama's voyage to India] has been ... the service of God our Lord, and our own advantage" (quoted in Hale, 1966, p. 38)—thereby neatly and conveniently bringing God and Mammon together into the same sentence—he probably saw no obvious contradiction between them. These fervently religious Catholic rulers fully believed what they were saying. To them, serving God and pursuing "our advantage" were not necessarily at odds. They lived and fully believed their own ideology.

So, while it would be wrong to attempt to reduce their statements to naked self-interest, it is clear that their discourse was molded and influenced by the play of motives and interests across their language. Of course, motives and interests are almost never wholly conscious or rational. The desires which drove the Europeans were powerful; but their power was not always subject to rational calculation. Marco Polo's "treasures of the East" were tangible enough. But the seductive power which they exerted over generations of Europeans transformed them more and more into a myth. Similarly, the gold that Columbus kept asking the natives for very soon acquired a mystical, quasi-religious significance.

Finally, the discourse of "the West and the Rest" could not be innocent because it did not represent an encounter between equals. The Europeans had outsailed, outshot, and outwitted peoples who had no wish to be "explored," no need to be "discovered," and no desire to be "exploited." The Europeans stood, vis-à-vis the Others, in positions of dominant power. This influenced what they saw and how they saw it, as well as what they did not see.

Foucault sums up these arguments as follows. Not only is discourse always implicated in *power,* discourse is one of the "systems" through which power circulates. The knowledge which a discourse produces constitutes a kind of power, exercised over those who are "known." When that knowledge is exercised in practice, those who are "known" in a particular way will be subject (i.e. subjected) to it. This is always a power-relation. (See Foucault, 1980, p. 201.) Those who produce the discourse also have the power to *make it true*—i.e. to enforce its validity, its scientific status.

This leaves Foucault in a highly relativistic position with respect to questions of truth because his notion of discourse undermines the distinction between true and false statements—between science and ideology—to which many sociologists have subscribed. These epistemological issues (about the status of knowledge, truth, and relativism) are too complex to take further here. However, the important idea to grasp now is the deep and intimate relationship which Foucault establishes between discourse, knowledge, and power. According to Foucault, when power operates so as to enforce the "truth" of any set of statements, then such a discursive formation produces a "regime of truth."

Let us summarize the main points of this argument. Discourses are ways of talking, thinking, or representing a particular subject or topic. They produce meaningful knowledge about that subject. This knowledge influences social practices, and so has real consequences and effects. Discourses are not reducible to class-interests, but always operate in relation to power—they are part of the way power circulates and is contested. The question of whether a discourse is true or false is less important than whether it is effective in practice. When it is effective—organizing and regulating relations of power (say, between the West and the Rest)—it is called a "regime of truth."

REPRESENTING "THE OTHER"

So far, the discussion of discourse has been rather abstract and conceptual. The concept may be easier to understand in relation to an example. One of the best examples of what Foucault means by a "regime of truth" is provided by Edward Said's study of Orientalism. In this section, I want to look briefly at this example and then see how far we can use the theory of discourse and the example of Orientalism to analyze the discourse of "the West and the Rest."

ORIENTALISM

In his book *Orientalism,* Edward Said analyzes the various discourses and institutions which constructed and produced, as an object of knowledge, that entity called "the Orient." Said calls this discourse "Orientalism." Note that, though we tend to include the Far East (including China) in our use of the word "Orient," Said refers mainly to the Middle East—the territory occupied principally by Islamic peoples.

Also, his main focus is French writing about the Middle East. Here is Said's own summary of the project of his book:

> My contention is that, without examining Orientalism as a discourse, one cannot possibly understand the enormously systematic discipline by which European culture was able to manage—and even produce—the Orient politically, sociologically, militarily, ideologically, scientifically and imaginatively during the post-Enlightenment period. Moreover, so authoritative a position did Orientalism have that I believe no one writing, thinking, or acting on the Orient could do so without taking account of the limitations on thought and action imposed by Orientalism. In brief, because of Orientalism, the Orient was not (and is not) a free subject of thought and action. This is not to say that Orientalism unilaterally determines what can be said about the Orient, but that it is the whole network of interests inevitably brought to bear on (and therefore always involved in) any occasion when that peculiar entity "the Orient" is in question .... This book also tries to show that European culture gained in strength and identity by setting itself off against the Orient as a sort of surrogate and even underground self. (Said, 1985, p. 3)

We will now analyze the discourse of "the West and the Rest," as it emerged between the end of the 15th and 18th centuries, using Foucault's ideas about "discourse" and Said's example of "Orientalism." How was this discourse formed? What were its main themes—its "strategies" of representation?

THE "ARCHIVE"

Said argues that "In a sense Orientalism was a library or archive of information commonly ... held. What bound the archive together was a family of ideas and a unifying set of values proven in various ways to be effective. These ideas explained the behaviour of Orientals; they supplied Orientals with a mentality, a genealogy, an atmosphere; most important, they allowed Europeans to deal with and even to see Orientals as a phenomenon possessing regular characteristics" (Said, 1985, pp. 41–2). What sources of common knowledge, what "archive" of other discourses, did the discourse of "the West and the Rest" draw on? We can identify four main sources:

1. **Classical knowledge:** This was a major source of information and images about "other worlds." Plato (c. 427–347 B.C.) described a string of legendary islands, among them Atlantis which many early explorers set out to find. Aristotle (384–322 B.C.) and Eratosthenes (c. 276–194 B.C.) both made remarkably accurate estimates of the circumference of the globe which were consulted by Columbus. Ptolemy's *Geographia* (2nd century A.D.) provided a model for map-makers more than a thou-

sand years after it had been produced. Sixteenth-century explorers believed that in the outer world lay, not only Paradise, but that "Golden Age," place of perfect happiness and "springtime of the human race," of which the classical poets, including Horace (65–8 B.C.) and Ovid (43 B.C.–A.D. 17), had written.

The 18th century was still debating whether what they had discovered in the South Pacific was Paradise. In 1768 the French Pacific explorer Bougainville renamed Tahiti "The New Cythera" after the island where, according to classical myth, Venus first appeared from the sea. At the opposite extreme, the descriptions by Herodotus (484–425 B.C.) and Pliny (A.D. 23–79) of the barbarous peoples who bordered Greece left many grotesque images of "other" races which served as self-fulfilling prophecies for later explorers who found what legend said they would find. Paradoxically, much of this classical knowledge was lost in the Dark Ages and only later became available to the West via Islamic scholars, themselves part of that "other" world.

2. **Religious and biblical sources:** These were another source of knowledge. The Middle Ages reinterpreted geography in terms of the Bible. Jerusalem was the center of the earth because it was the Holy City. Asia was the home of the Three Wise Kings; Africa, that of King Solomon. Columbus believed the Orinoco (in Venezuela) to be a sacred river flowing out of the Garden of Eden.

3. **Mythology:** It was difficult to tell where religious and classical discourses ended and those of myth and legend began. Mythology transformed the outer world into an enchanted garden, alive with misshapen peoples and monstrous oddities. In the 16th century, Sir Walter Raleigh still believed he would find, in the Amazon rainforests, the king "El Dorado" ("The Gilded One") whose people were alleged to roll him in gold which they would then wash off in a sacred lake.

4. **Travellers' tales:** Perhaps the most fertile source of information was travellers' tales—a discourse where description faded imperceptibly into legend. The following 15th century German text summarizes more than a thousand years of travellers' tales, which themselves often drew on religious and classical authority:

> In the land of Indian there are men with dogs' heads who talk by barking [and] ... feed by catching birds.... Others again have only one eye in the forehead.... In Libya many are born without heads and have a mouth and eyes. Many are of both sexes.... Close to Paradise on the River Ganges live men who eat nothing. For ... they absorb liquid nourishment through a straw [and] ... live on the juice of flowers.... Many have such large underlips that they can cover their whole faces with them.... In the land of Ethiopia many people walk bent down like cattle, and many live four hundred years. Many have horns, long noses and goats' feet.... In Ethiopia towards the west many have four eyes ... [and] in Eripia there live beautiful people with the necks and bills of cranes ... (quoted in Newby, 1975, p. 17)

A particularly rich repository was Sir John Mandeville's *Travels*—in fact, a compendium of fanciful stories by different hands. Marco Polo's *Travels* was generally more sober and factual, but nevertheless achieved mythological status. His text (embellished by Rusticello, a romance writer) was the most widely read of the travellers' accounts and was instrumental in creating the myth of "Cathay" ("China," or the East generally), a dream that inspired Columbus and many others.

The point of recounting this astonishing mixture of fact and fantasy which constituted late medieval "knowledge" of other worlds is not to poke fun at the ignorance of the Middle Ages. The point is (a) to bring home how these very different discourses, with variable statuses as "evidence," provided the cultural framework through which the peoples, places, and things of the New World were seen, described, and represented; and (b) to underline the conflation of fact and fantasy that constituted "knowledge." This can be seen especially in the use of analogy to describe first encounters with strange animals. Penguins and seals were described as being like geese and wolves respectively; the tapir as a bull with a trunk like an elephant, the opossum as half-fox, half-monkey.

A "REGIME OF TRUTH"

Gradually, observation and description vastly improved in accuracy. The medieval habit of thinking in terms of analogies gave way to a more sober type of description of the fauna and flora, ways of life, customs, physical characteristics, and social organization of native peoples. We can here begin to see the outlines of an early ethnography or anthropology.

But the shift into a more descriptive, factual discourse, with its claims to truth and scientific objectivity, provided no guarantees. A telling example of this is the case of the "Patagonians." Many myths and legends told of a race of giant people. And in the 1520s, Magellan's crew brought back stories of having encountered, in South America, such a race of giants whom they dubbed *patagones* (literally, "big feet"). The area of the supposed encounter became known as "Patagonia," and the notion became fixed in the popular imagination, even though two Englishmen who visited Patagonia in 1741 described its people as being of average size.

When Commodore John Byron landed in Patagonia in 1764, he encountered a formidable group of natives, broad-shouldered, stocky, and inches taller than the average European. They proved quite docile and friendly. However, the newspaper reports of his encounter wildly exaggerated the story, and Patagonians took on an even greater stature and more ferocious aspect. One engraving showed a sailor reaching only as high as the waist of a Patagonian giant, and The Royal Society elevated the topic to serious scientific status. "The engravings took the explorers' raw material and shaped them into images familiar to Europeans" (Withey, 1987, pp. 1175-6). Legend had taken a late revenge on science.

This is where the notion of "discourse" came in. A discourse is a way of talking about or representing something. It produces knowledge that shapes perceptions and practice. It is part of the way in which power operates. Therefore, it has consequences for both those who employ it and those who are "subjected" to it. The West produced many different ways of talking about itself and "the Others." But what we have called the discourse of "the West and the Rest" became one of the most powerful and formative of these discourses. It became the dominant way in which, for many decades, the West represented itself and its relation to "the Other." In this article, we have traced how this discourse was formed and how it worked. We analyzed it as a "system of representation"—a "regime of truth." It was as formative for the West and "modern societies" as were the secular state; capitalist economies; the modern class, race, and gender systems; and modern, individualist, secular culture—the four main "processes" of our formation story.

Finally, we suggest that, in transformed and reworked forms, this discourse continues to inflect the language of the West, its image of itself and "others," its sense of "us" and "them," its practices and relations of power towards the Rest. It is especially important for the languages of racial inferiority and ethnic superiority which still operate so powerfully across the globe today. So, far from being a "formation" of the past, and of only historical interest, the discourse of "the West and the Rest" is alive and well in the modern world. And one of the surprising places where its effects can still be seen is in the language, theoretical models, and hidden assumptions of modern sociology itself.

REFERENCES

Cousins, M. and Hussain, A. 1984. *Michel Foucault.* London: Macmillan.

Foucault, M. 1972. *The Archeology of Knowledge.* London: Tavistock.

Foucault, M. 1980. *Power/Knowledge.* Brighton: England, Harvester.

Hale, J.R. et al. 1966. *Age of Exploration.* The Netherlands: Time-Life International.

Mandeville, Sir J. 1964. *The Travels.* New York: Dover.

Newby, E. 1975. *The Mitchell Beazley World Atlas of Exploration.* London: Mitchell Beazley.

Said, E.W. 1985. *Orientalism: Western Concepts of the Orient.* Harmondsworth: England, Penguin.

Withey, L. 1987. *Voyages of Discovery: Captain Cook and the Exploration of the Pacific.* London: Hutchinson.

CHAPTER 12

PATHS TOWARD A MOHAWK NATION:

NARRATIVES OF CITIZENSHIP AND NATIONHOOD IN KAHNAWAKE

Audra Simpson

MOHAWK NATIONHOOD AND NARRATIVITY

MICHAEL JACKSON IS A CONTEMPORARY ANTHROPOLOGIST who disagrees with the "scientific" tradition in anthropology that purports to be objective and value-free, affording us the ultimate and absolute finalities of truth. This latter view of anthropology and its method has been critiqued heavily by native and non-native scholars alike for making objects of living people, their culture, their place, and their way in the world. Jackson's work offers some important channels for students of culture and others who desire a way into the world that is different and perhaps more just than it was in the past.

Rather than focus his efforts on the style of anthropological discourse, as some contemporary anthropologists have done (Crapanzano 1986; Clifford 1986), Jackson instead maps out a phenomenological approach to writing culture that abandons the precepts of objectivity entirely and engages instead the flux of lived experience. His way into experience is "radical empiricism," a methodology that has as its unit of study the "plenum of existence" in which all ideas and intellectual constructions are grounded (Jackson 1988: 3). For Jackson, radical empiricism will be a method with which one will experience, interpret, and write culture. As such, Jackson's anthropological practice conjoins the intellectual ancestry of the discipline to the discursive practice of the subject as well as the subjectivity of the analyst. In weaving these elements together in the writing of culture, the understanding and "way of being in the world" of the anthropologist count as much as that of the subject, as each shapes the other in the defining moments of their exchange. The result of such an exchange produces renderings of social experience that lodge "anthropological subjects" as active agents in the representation of their culture rather than static objects of scholarly contemplation.

There is much, then, in Jackson's work that Indians should be concerned with. In placing an overall premium on the dialectics of being—the currency of exchanges between people—Jackson, in his approach to culture and his methodological suggestions, may deliver us from the necessary essentialisms that beset Indian people (and perhaps all former subject-peoples) in the representation of their culture.[1] As well, by engaging the flux of lived life, and having as its premise the untidiness and flux-ist nature of culture, radical empiricism acknowledges the partiality and shifting nature of knowledge, a partiality that Abu-Lughod likens to "standing on shifting ground" (1991: 142)—a perspective that embraces the politics of honesty (and humil-ity). This promise offers cultural analysts and Indians a way out of the static and necessarily reified representations of identities and cultures that earlier approaches to cultural analysis demanded.

It is for that reason that I take radical empiricism toward the day-to-day politics of nationhood in Kahnawake. Although Jackson is not a Mohawk, nor is his work informed by the plenum of their existence within the nation-state of Canada, his particular attention to lived experience has much to offer contemporary studies of Mohawk nationhood. Jackson's arguments and suggestions bear on the particular concerns of contemporary anthropological practice—a practice beset by a "crisis in representation"—by placing *experience* at the very centre of his analysis. But more importantly, perhaps, his analysis bears on this other *crisis in conversation*—issues pertain-ing to native-state relations, where the premium is on reconciling various solitudes and ways of being. Thus we have an alternative to integrating, as Kymlicka would have it, a "minority nationalist" model of ethnic relations within a broader frame-work of the state, by listening in substantive ways to the voices and experiences within. Here is a philosophically and sensorially tuned encounter, one that attempts an understanding through listening, observing, entering into a conversation with one another through an attempt at engaging what was commonly misunderstood and misconstrued—*experience*. Jackson's centring of experience in analysis resonates with native claims for sovereignty (if we may talk about exercising control over repre-sentations of native culture as well as control over native land) as much of our lives are lived with the knowledge that our experiences have simply not mattered much. And other experiences clearly have mattered more—witness canonical notions of history, literature, and curricula. The marginalization of certain experiences and narratives over others alone "tells us" that there are some stories that simply matter more than others. If we were to argue, then, from a generic "native" perspective we might say (and rather simply, at that) that there are "facts" that we own, knowledge that we share and, among these facts, that the land that we live on now is ours because (some of us believe that) we come from the earth. Furthermore, this land, which gave us our life and our subsistence and brought us into being, belongs by the mirac-ulous interplay of history, luck, force, acquiescence, and in some cases, outright battle, to outside people who claim it now as their own. This is a fact to us and is fiction to far too many others. We live then in a tension that must be resolved. Our ques-tions are more immediate and more pressing perhaps than the philosophical and practice-oriented issues of Jackson, but there is resonance still.

It is because of these facts that we own, the history and knowledge that we share of this past, that *nationhood* is a terribly important concept for Indians and academics alike. It is the prism through which many Indians view their historical experiences, themselves, and their aspirations and thought—"nationhood" in the contemporary native landscape may be understood as a movement toward a clearing. It is a Herculean gesture away from the enframing efforts of the Canadian state, toward a place and a state of being that is our own. As with culture and the analytical approach that Jackson is arguing for, the culture and issues of native peoples can best be examined in terms of the lived experience of nationhood. In order to appreciate that experience, one must take account of the shared set of meanings that are negotiated through narrations—through the voices and structural conditions that constitute selfhood. In order to appreciate these representations, analysts must examine the words and stories that people share with each other; they must pay attention to the ways that Indians render their own experiences into being, the ways they represent themselves and their people *to each other.*

KAHNAWAKE

This chapter is concerned with narrations of nationhood among contemporary Indians in Canada. My research centred on the volatile question of citizenship or "membership" among Mohawks of Kahnawake. As a reserve community, Kahnawake rests on land that is held in trust for the members of the community by the Canadian state (what is known as "crown land"). It is through the provisions of the *Indian Act* that the Mohawks of Kahnawake, like those Indians belonging to other reserve communities in Canada, receive their right to reside on the 12,000 acres known as the Kahnawake Indian Reserve.[2] Their names appear on a federal registry of Indians in Canada as well as on a band-controlled registry that accords them the rights of status Indians in Canada.[3]

As a reserve community of indigenous people within a settler society, Kahnawake is surrounded symbolically and materially by the governmental structures and peoples that inhabit the political landscape of Canada. Situated in the southern part of the francophone province of Quebec, the community is surrounded by largely white and francophone municipalities: St. Constant, Delson, and Chateauguay. Montreal, a large multicultural city, is approximately 10 minutes away from the community by vehicle. The proximity of non-native people to the community exacerbates a sense of urgency about the community's sovereignty and identity. Although Kahnawake has its own police force made up of community members and native people from other parts of Canada, the issue of policing and jurisdiction is a constant source of concern, with community members adamant that neither the provincial police force nor police forces from the surrounding areas have a right to enter the boundaries of the community unless invited.[4]

Although surrounded by seemingly foreign peoples with governmental structures that have legal claim to their land and the operations of their community, Kahnawake behave as other nations do and attempt, at every turn, to exercise authority and control over the affairs of the reserve. "Behaving as other nations do" requires that *Kahnawakero:non* maintain a strong sense of themselves as a distinct people with rights and obligations that flow from their distinctiveness. To maintain a sense of themselves as a nation, *Kahnawakero:non* shape their historical and contemporary experiences through discursive practice—a practice that uses the key tropes of "being Indian" and having "rights." These tropes are tied to social and cultural praxis by working in the service of identity construction and maintenance for Mohawk individuals—a process that not only signals to individuals the social ideal, but also suffuses everyday life with a sense of nationhood.

"Talking" nationhood and being Indian are not recent predilections or cultural inventions for *Kahnawakero:non*. As part of the larger matrix of Iroquois experience in what is now the Northeastern US, the Mohawks of Kahnawake are splintered from one of the Six (formerly five) Nations Confederacy, the Iroquois or *Haudenosaunee* ("People of the Longhouse"). The *Haudenosaunee* are a confederated group of Indian nations that before contact militarily dominated what is now the Northeastern U.S. The people of Kahnawake, along with Mohawks in Akwesasne and Kanehsatake (two other Mohawk reserves in the Province of Quebec), share a history of participation in the Confederacy and use this experience to construct and maintain their collective identity as a distinct people within the larger political and social geographies of Canada and the US *Kahnawakero:non* also draw from the Confederacy of the past to recreate alternative forms of religion and government in the contemporary era (this structure is known today in the community as "the Longhouse").

Kahnawakero:non have a strong sense of themselves as a distinct nation which is based on their pre-contact political experience and their more recent interactions with the governments of settler societies in Canada and the US This has been documented in anthropological and historical research (Voget 1951; Hauptman 1986), and has recently been the explicit focus of a contemporary study in political science (Alfred 1995). Although each of these works has documented or focused on structural or institutional elements of Mohawk and Iroquois consciousness of self and society, analysis of Kahnawake's nationhood thus far has not examined the critical role of discursive or cultural practice of community members in constructing their identity and sense of being in the world.

I focus here on discursive practice, or "what people say" to each other. The focus on discursive practice flows from the different premise that Mohawk nationhood is built upon. Ethnicity and structural inequality are often the starting points in analyses that examine nationalism. Rather than use these as an entangled premise for all cultural activity, and arguing from there that ethnicity = ethnogenesis (and ethnogenesis = nationalism), I will examine Kahnawake nationalism through the words of those people who produce it. To this end I will not be focusing wholly upon interactions with external forces (a precondition for the creation of "ethnic consciousness"), or ignoring these interactions altogether. By privileging the inter-actions that Mohawks are having with each other, rather than those that they have with the "outside," I hope to return nationalism to the web of meanings that make up culture—the plenum of experience, rather than ethnicity.

CITIZENSHIP, BLOOD, AND BELONGING

Indian reserves in Canada have only had control over their membership lists since 1985, when the federal government returned the authority to determine band member-ship from Indian and Northern Affairs Canada to reserve communities. Membership in an Indian community carries rights within and obligations to that community. Band members have the right to build a home on the reserve, reside on the reserve, vote in band council elections and have their social welfare managed by the band. In order to maintain their membership on the band list *Kahnawakero:non* are required since 1981 to "marry in" (Alfred 1995: 163-77). "Marrying in" means that in order to maintain their place on the list of members in the community, individuals are required to marry another person who has at least 50 percent Indian blood.

The 50 percent blood quantum is replete with problems within Kahnawake. These are problems that revolve around the dual axes of "rights" and identity, and are manifest as disagreements over what criteria should be used for the granting of membership, over who an Indian is, and, more specifically, what a Mohawk is and should be. Questions that then confront *Kahnawakero:non* when contemplating membership include: what should be the criteria for determining membership? To whom should it be given? Should membership be given to the children of two Indian parents? To children with one parent? What if that parent had one white parent? Furthermore, how far in one's lineage should the Mohawk Council of Kahnawake go to calculate one's quantum? Why even use blood when there are traditional Iroquois practices and options such as adoption and the clan system reck-oning of descent? Should rights to membership be given to anyone who does not have a clan or a commitment to Mohawk culture and community?

These questions and the resulting discussions around membership speak from and to the historical experiences that shape Kahnawake's collective sense of self. Here we will find interactions with the Canadian state that provided *Kahnawakero:non* with an enduring sense of mistrust and concomitant enclosure. At the same time *Kahnawakero:non* have had friendships, marriages, and alliances with non-natives;

this makes the matter of membership a politically and an emotionally loaded matter to contemplate, let alone adjudicate.

From here, both self and nation are braided into past experiences and stories of those experiences (Kerby 1991: 1; Bhabha 1990: 1-7; 1994: 7; Connerton 1989: 16-17). This past is tied to ways of seeing and being in the world that are not "pure"—modes of being that enter both indigenous and "statist" notions of being into a dialogue, producing the ongoing, processual and syncretic culture that is used forcefully to construct and maintain one's self and nation.

Here I have the experience and narrations of *Kahnawakero:non* that speak directly and sometimes obliquely to the issue of membership, but most definitely to notions of "being Indian" and "having rights."[5] We will go first to a bingo hall, where one person's presence and identity was contested in an indirect but forceful way by another community member. As well, we will go to a band council meeting, one of the monthly meetings of the elected council and community, where the subject of membership was discussed. A text then from *Onkwarihwa'shon:'a,* a monthly newsletter that is distributed by the Mohawk Council of Kahnawake to update community members on internal matters, which will provide a direct linkage made by the elected council between law, membership, and Mohawk sovereignty. Finally, we will return to a meeting of the elected council as they share their platforms for the then-upcoming elections in July 1996. Using a radically empirical method, we have provided these narratives to "revalidate the everyday life of ordinary people, to tell their stories in their own words" (Jackson 1996: 36).

THE SUPER BINGO

It is the summer of 1993 and we are sitting at the end of a long table in the Super Bingo. The hall has yet to fill up. Daniel and Martha, who work at the bingo, are smoking cigarettes and we are talking. I am waiting to play and killing time with them. The bingo is divided into service and security employees. The service employees, with the exception of Robert and Daniel, are women. The security guards are all men and are mostly young. They carry walkie-talkies and look for cellular phones, food brought in against regulations, and other offences. They seem more interested, however, in checking out the young women who work there. Their furtive glances to one another and the purple bruises on their necks (which are also against employee regulations) attest to romance, and we are trying to figure out which security and which service staff are involved. We are watching for these signifiers while recalling the contours and the taste of "zeppoles" in Brooklyn and the future of David Dinkins after the upcoming mayoral elections in New York City. Our conversation is redirected, however, to one service employee (in her thirties) who has just walked in wearing an almost-against-regulations white leotard. We joke about the "crack" security team and whether they will be able to concentrate on their work.

A man came near our table and Daniel knew he was close by. He didn't want to turn his head, so he asked Martha: "Is that 135?" (the man's name, as far as I know).

Martha exclaimed: "Oh yes, it's that dirty, skinny son of a bitch—30 per cent!"

Now we are looking at her, trying not to laugh, listening, stealing glances at each other—where did that come from?

"His mother wasn't Indian and his father was barely Indian, he is lucky if he is even 30 per cent! Look at him in that "Warriors" jacket—who the hell does he think he is?! He's not even an Indian and he's got his jacket on, walking around here like that."

Daniel and I are laughing out loud now, oblivious to the hickeys, David Dinkins, and 135 himself. We are "rolling," so to speak, and Martha is just catching her breath; she is excited with her information and the effect it is having on us. She then pointed a jewelled finger at Daniel and then at me (now dabbing a mess of make-up from under my eyes) and said, "Don't worry, you two—I know your mother [points at Daniel] and I know your father [points at me]—and I know your halves are whole."

We suddenly stopped laughing and Martha continued, unfazed. She continued with the details of 135's allegedly dubious family tree. I don't think either of us started to worry until then.

BAND COUNCIL MEETING

The Knights of Columbus Hall is almost full. Families are positioned in their usual seats; men are standing by the entrance to the hall with their hands in their pockets. People are smoking and drinking coffee out of styrofoam cups. The meeting has been going on for about half an hour. The chiefs are answering questions about membership.

"What are we going to do," one woman asks, "with so and so? He is with that white woman and they have a child—aren't they supposed to leave? How come so and so had to leave and he gets to stay? They married after '81, he knew what he was getting in to; how come the Peacekeepers don't go to his house?"

One chief gets up and says, "I know who you are talking about and he has been told. He knows he is supposed to leave, he has been asked to leave but we have to as a community let him know the Law [Mohawk Law on Membership]."

There are more questions now, about individuals and who they are with, about the Law itself and how it is applied. Some people are standing when they ask their questions and voices are raised several times.

One community member says something about Council members and one of the Chiefs says, "I know that this affects each and every one of you, each of us has someone in their family ... me too, I have family in the States and they married out and they have children. I tell them you can't come back here, you have to know that ... so don't think I don't know."

He sits down and somebody brings up a *Kahnawakero:non* who married a non-native man in 1983. She has a legal case against the MCK. One of the chiefs stands up and elaborates on the case. A man standing at the back of the Knights says, "We don't have anything in place to take care of those people [C-31s].[6] Who is gonna take care of them? If we had a Traditional government in place they would be taken care of, if we base things here on anything else but the *Kaienerakowa* then we will be racist."[7]

A woman seated near the back of the hall reminded us, "There was a 1979 mandate towards Traditional government. What happened to that? You know, there is no stigma on half-breeds whose fathers are Indian, but if you are a C-31 in this community, you are stigmatized and nobody talks about that. Why don't you people [at the meeting] throw down *The National Enquirer* and read the *Indian Act*? It's all there, why we are in this mess. How can we deal with these contradictions?"

An older woman then stands up. She is sitting by the chiefs at the front of the Knights. She speaks in Mohawk. Her voice is loud and she seems angry. Her voice is rising and I ask my auntie what she is saying. She shushes me.

The woman says in English, wagging her finger around: "Did you ever see those white women come on the reserve and *ask* [her emphasis] if they could marry an Indian?! [The non-Indian women who married Indian men before 1981.] Should our women have to do that—have a paper saying if they are widowed or divorced?!" [In order to get rights to residency on the reserve C-31s have to prove to the MCK that they are widowed or divorced.]

The Grand Chief stands up and says that the Mohawk Law on Membership should be a *method* [his emphasis], not a code. He then says: "If a traditional system is appropriate, then so be it."

ONKWARIHWA'SHON:'A ("OUR AFFAIRS")

Racism. In recent times, we have been accused of outright racism whenever we made any attempt to deny certain rights to those who are simply not entitled to those rights in the first place. Here, it has to be very clearly stated that there is a big difference between being backed into a corner and being guilty of racism. However, the tricky part is that, despite any such difference, the question of who is entitled to what must still be answered in terms of who is actually Indian. The aspect of the debate on membership is fixated on the term "blood quantum" ... Yes, race is involved in the matter Native Rights [sic]. And yes, it becomes a matter of who is entitled to those rights, by virtue of the kind of blood running through their veins. However, it is NOT about who is the purer of the species. It is about wrongs done through five hundred years of history to an entire race of people. It is about not allowing this to go on any more, and it is about putting things right once and for all, before they get any worse and a whole race of people is eradicated. It is about justice, and if nothing else at all, it is about survival. Indeed, we have a long, long journey ahead of us, if we're ever going to get this mess cleaned up. At times, journeys can be agonising, and clean-ups can be as messy as the mess itself. In any case the Mohawk Council of Kahnawake and the Membership Committee are duty-bound to follow the wishes of the Mohawk People of Kahnawake, and no-one else. In this, I can only ask that our own people contribute in any way they can, to the setting straight of the membership issue, and that for once, non-Native powers honor their part of the Two Row Wampum Treaty and stop meddling in our affairs.[8] *Nia:wen* (thank you). (Chief Allen Paul 1995: 5–6)

CANDIDATES' NIGHT

It is Candidates' Night and I am sitting with my auntie, some cousins, and my cousin's wife in the Knights of Columbus. We are a little jittery because a family member is running for Council. We got to the Knights early and worked on his platform, feverishly jotting ideas on index cards while his wife scolded him for waiting until the last minute to prepare his speech. The meeting begins with all but four of the candidates present.

A name is randomly selected by the moderator of the evening and the platforms begin.

The first candidate is a man in his thirties. This is his second time running for Council and he is very prepared. He has a text that he reads from and an obviously rehearsed platform. He lost the last election by 40 votes and seems likely to win next week. He weaves the importance of education into his platform and shares his experience of having to borrow money and fundraise in order to go to school in the States. I make a note to myself to vote for him next week. The platforms continue, with most candidates going over their allotted 10 minutes. One talked about land, another talked about his past, another talked about reform and another talked about the curbs. I was tired, taking notes the whole time, my eyes bleary from cigarette smoke and I was losing the taste in my mouth because of too much coffee.

It was Sak's turn. He walked to the mike and raised his hand, "*Kwe Kwe,*" he bellowed, and smiled while waving to the audience. I jolted upright. Much to my surprise, he started to sing a song in Mohawk to the people. The words, although unknown to me, were sung to the *very* recognizable tune by Hank Williams, "Hey Good Looking, What'cha got Cooking?" Everybody started laughing, looking at him, glancing at each other—what was he doing, what was he saying? Without giving us time to talk to each other, he started his platform. He had no paper, no index cards, and no unifying thread that I could identify at the time. He was telling stories, talking about language and the need to speak Mohawk: "Why don't our people even try to speak their language, I mean, really try? It is not enough to tell your children *"satien"* [sit down!] or *"tohsa"* [stop it!]; *make full sentences,* for heaven's sake! I speak to young people and I say *"Kwe Kwe"* and you know what they say back to me? They say "Hi" [at this point he did an imitation of an uptight and affronted person, curled up his arms a little and screwed up his face in displeasure] and then they run away from me. Don't you want your children to be able to speak in *full sentences?* How come these Chinese who come here speak their language to their children and their children speak two languages? How come they can do it and we can't do it? They even come to Kahnawake and speak *our language."* He now starts speaking Mohawk with a Mandarin accent, maybe alluding to the co-owners of Way Ta Le, a Chinese restaurant and take-out that opened on the reserve. He milks it more because everyone is laughing. I am thinking he is like Charlie Chaplin and an ironworker all in one.

And then he said, out of the blue: "I don't like blood quantum, you could live on the Farm [farmland off Highway 120 going towards St. Constant, remote in relation to 'Town,' which is more central, where the main highway and two iron crosses are] your entire life and then come into Town and people say 'Kwa! Who's that?! I don't know him!'" He continues, "Then next thing you know, he is listed at 47 per cent because nobody knows his face ... Being an Indian isn't whose band number is lower [does an imitation of someone bragging in a whiny voice, 'My band number is lower than your band number'], or how many beads you put in your ears—it's your ancestry ... *I could tell you a story about membership that would break your heart,* but I won't."

Sak sings more songs, and speaks in Mohawk. People are laughing and I'm laughing too. I stop taking notes. I am listening to him and watching him. He is imitating us—he is making fun—and in doing so, he is teaching us what being Mohawk *is.* He is holding up a mirror to us and we are laughing at ourselves.

POST-CANDIDATES' NIGHT: THE PHONE CALL

My good friend is in Albany, New York, working at the Iroquois Indian Museum. He called me after the meeting and we are talking about the platforms. He wanted to know what they said. He wants to know who, if anybody, said anything about education. I tell him what he wants to know and we agree that it is a good thing that there are so many young people running.

"We need some young blood in there," he says, and I agree. I tell him about Sak's song and his platform. We are laughing at the platform and at me trying to imitate Sak imitating everyone else. My friend says that it's so good that he is running for Council because he will really push language. Sak was a Mohawk language teacher and we like him for this. I ask my friend why Sak said that there was a story about membership that would break our hearts. Does he know what Sak meant by that? Does he know that story?

He answered, "Don't you know about his family?" And then he told me the story. Now I know.

This article engages the question of how anthropologists are to speak *about* people without speaking *for* people—how the discipline is to manage its information and its identity in the face of movements for native sovereignty at the level of scholarly representation. The result of this dialectic between anthropology and local life has created an anthropological praxis that is punctuated by introspection, reflexivity, revision, creativity, nervousness, and, at times, reactionary discourses. The discussion of these issues brought us to Kahnawake and these stories—stories that are laced together with hopes and desires for control and authority over life—in a naming and management of the issues that are our colonial inheritance.

The point of sharing these narratives was to contribute something to this conversation, to press into play the usefulness of a radically empirical method when considering contemporary culture and nationhood. As well, to share the interior frontiers of Mohawk nationhood, to step upon the terrain of agreement, discord, and hopeful contemplation that unites *Kahnawakero:non* in their search for a way through the mass of contradictions that one interlocutor at a community meeting referred to. The intricacies of these stories—the names that *Kahnawakero:non* have for each other, the categories that they place on each other's being—may be lost on you, but that is fine. You have here a sense that rights and contemporary Indian identity are enmeshed—that they are tied to stories and these stories are tied to ourselves. These narratives illustrate that Mohawk nationhood is shaped through what people say to each other, by what they say about each other—they illustrate how "place" in the world is staked out and guarded through the defining moments of shared experience and the words that then give shape to this experience.

Leaving the Knights of Columbus again, and only for a moment, I want to return once again to political theory, to anthropology, to Jackson, and ask if this praxis that he talks about—the traffic from one concept to another, one emotion to another—can this ever be a directed, and yet miraculously neutral, innocent, and value-free process? Can we ever go into our own reserves and political meetings and report on these events? Can we take into account the multiplicity of intentions that inform individual and social action and our own experience of it all and then suddenly, by some miracle, disengage? Is it possible for us to move across the terrain of knowledge production free from the constraints of specificity, locality, and experience? And, is it possible to listen to each other in a substantive and meaningful way?

Can we liken the thinking and living of life mapped out by Jackson to the path of Kahnawake's debates over membership? Each is a process that tests individual knowledge, emotion and vocabulary against the exigencies of the present. Each is informed by the desire for a future that is in some ways better than the one we left behind. Indeed, I think that we can. Are Kahnawake's attempts at finding a way back into the world—to find a clearing— an objective and value-free affair? Can we liken their attempts to find this clearing, much like the social and cultural analysis of the past, to shots that are fired into a universe of abstractions by a remarkably dispassionate marksman? Occurring at the intersection of experience and cognition, *thought,* like nationhood, is a process, and as such is shaped from social interactions, sensorial deposits, as well as personal and collective desires. It is not objective, nor is it a random praxis. Like the marksman and the community members in Kahnawake, you too will take shots that are shaped by these lessons: memory, forgetting, the sense and specificity of life and those around you. In these ways the marksman and the Mohawk stand on common ground with us. He is like us—he squares himself on the ground that he stands on, he takes aim and he fires. We watch the shot cut through the sky until it fades into sudden dissolution—we listen for a response from somewhere out there. He looks to the ground. We wait together for an answer.

NOTES

This paper was presented at the Australian National University for the "Indigenous Rights, Political Theory and the Reshaping of Institutions" conference in 1997. While there, the work profited from the suggestions and queries of many. It has also benefited from comments in the Canadian Anthropology Society meetings in 1998 as well as the Organization of American Historians meetings and the American Studies Association meetings in 1999. I am especially grateful to Duncan Ivison, Julie Cruikshank, Jean-Guy Goulet, Klaus Neumann, an external reviewer for CUP, and others who engaged in substantial ways with the paper. Responsibility for the arguments and content therein resides with me.

1. The representational tensions of text have "real-life" equivalents in the living issues of native-State relations, tensions that are readable in the form of claims that are made upon the state. These claims—for land, for reparation and other forms of indemnity—refer to a *past* of native-settler regime interactions that are expressed in the *present* by the critical notion of "cultural difference." This difference is premised more often than not upon a baseline of cultural wholeness, continuity, and authenticity, of a static and deeply essentialist notion of identity and tradition. These claims, and the role that anthropologists occupy in their articulation and execution, illustrate both the anthropological and indigenous investment in "tradition" in "authenticity" and the power of these analytical concepts within the larger picture of justice and rights. It is in the convincing deployment of these concepts that may "take" or may "give" indigenous peoples their past and their rights that accrue to a particular past (Clifford 1988: 277–346; Campisi 1991; Whittaker 1994; Dominy 1995; Paine 1996; Mills 1994; Povinelli 1999).

2. The Mohawks of Kahnawake claim an additional 24,000 acres of land given to them in the form of a seignioral land grant in 1680. This grant is known as the "Seigniory de Sault St Louis."

3. "Band" is the terminology used in the *Indian Act* and is interchangeable with "reserve." In this context, "band list" should be understood as the community-controlled list of members, administered by the band council, or Mohawk Council of Kahnawake (MCK).

4. In 1995, the MCK signed a policing agreement with the provincial and federal governments that elicited two days of semi-violent protest within the community. The issues that energized the protest in 1995 trace back to the late 1970s. In 1979, the MCK fired their local police force, the Kahnawake Police, for failing to enforce their resolution to close two government-leased quarries on reserve. The Kahnawake Police refused to close the quarries for want of an outside court injunction. Once fired, another local police force, the Kahnawake Peacekeepers, was formed in its place. Later that year, two officers of the Quebec Police Force (QPF) came into the community and shot and killed David Cross in a botched arrest attempt (Beauvais 1985: 150–52). Coupled with the issues that surrounded the firing of the police force and the quarries, the racist hues to the Cross shooting strengthened the resolve of the *Kahnawakero:non* to have the Kahnawake Peacekeepers, and not outside governments, enforce the laws of the community. However, since 1979 the authority of the Peacekeepers has been limited by their refusal to swear an oath of allegiance to the province of Quebec. In order to give them the authority that is required to issue fines and tickets with the backing of Quebec law, the MCK negotiated a tripartite policing agreement. As part of this agreement, outside police were given limited jurisdiction in the community. Considering the difficult history just detailed, this was viewed as a concession to Quebec. Some community members, especially youth associated with the "207 Longhouse," found this an affront to Mohawk sovereignty. The two days of protest that followed the signing of the agreement involved young men defacing personal property of elected chiefs and councillors. I am grateful to Peter Thomas Sr for explaining the chronology of events in 1979.

5. These narratives cover the period of 1993 to 1996. They are direct reprints of notes taken at meetings or are textual reconstructions of certain moments that had passed without note-taking. All names have been changed to protect the identity and privacy of the speakers.

6. "C-31" is the label used to describe community members and their children who regained their Indian status when Bill C-31 was amended to the *Indian Act* in 1985. Aimed at redressing the patrilineal bias of the *Indian Act,* which retained the Indian status of Indian men who married non-Indian women (and passed on their status to children) and disenfranchised Indian women who married non-Indian men (and did not pass on their lost status to their children), Bill C-31 granted status to all those who had lost it due to out-marriage and previous enfranchisement to the Canadian state. Before 1951, Indians lost their status because of enfranchisement: this may have occurred because of service in the military, post-secondary education, voting or the individual sale of status for alcohol. At the same time as the federal government was enlarging the number of Indians on the federal registry, Bill C-31 expanded the power of band council governments to determine their own membership requirements for their communities. In the case of Kahnawake, the results have been a situation where rules were developed (such as *The Mohawk Law on Membership)* that appear to exclude specifically those people whom the federal government now recognized as status Indians. For a thorough discussion of the *Indian Act* and Bill C-31 from a political science perspective, see Cassidy and Bish 1989. For a perspective on Bill C-31 from those Indian women that fought at a grassroots level to have it passed into law, see Silman 1987. With the exception of those women who are widowed or divorced, Kahnawake has refused to grant automatic re-admittance to anyone on the federal registry of Indians to the band list.

7. "The Great Law of Peace," understood by some anthropologists as the "constitution" of the Iroquois. This is one basis for a traditional mode of governance for Iroquois people. The other is the *Gawi'io,* or "Good Message of Handsome Lake."

8. Or *Kaswentha,* a 1613 treaty between the Dutch and the Iroquois represented by a belt of purple and white wampum shells. There are rows of white wampum parallel to each other, with deep purple wampum between and around them. The purple represents the sea of life that each row

shares. One row represents the Iroquois vessel and the other the European vessel. Although they share the same sea and sail alongside each other, they are separate: they should not touch or disturb each other or try to steer the other's vessel even though they must share the same space. Between the vessels are chains that connect them to each other. These are occasionally shined and maintained by one or the other vessel. The *Kaswentha* has great meaning to traditional and elected Council chiefs in Kahnawake as an enduring model of Indian-white relations that comes directly from Iroquois experience and history. The Two Row Wampum has also been incorporated into the Final Report of the Royal Commission on Aboriginal Peoples as a possible model for government relations between Aboriginal people as self-governing nations and the Canadian state.

REFERENCES

Abu-Lughod, L. 1991. "Writing against culture" in R. G. Fox, ed. *Recapturing Anthropology: Working in the Present*. Santa Fe: School of American Studies Research Press.

Alfred, G. R. (Taiaiake). 1995. *Heeding the Voices of our Ancestors: Kahnawake Mohawk Politics and the Rise of Native Nationalism*. Toronto; New York: Oxford University Press.

Beauvais, J. 1985. *Kahnawake: A Mohawk Look at Canada and Adventures of Big John Canadian*. Kahnawake: Khanata Industries.

Bhabha, H. K. 1990. "Introduction: Narrating the Nation" in H. K. Bhabha, ed. *Nation and Narration*, London: Routledge.

———. 1994. "DissemiNation: Time, Narrative and the Margins of the Modern Nation"; "Signs Taken for Wonders: Questions of Ambivalence and Authority under a Tree outside Delhi, May 1817" in *The Location of Culture*. London: Routledge: pp. 102–22, 139–70.

Campisi, J. 1991. *The Mashpee Indians: Tribe on Trial*. Syracuse: Syracuse University Press.

Cassidy, F. and Bish, R. L. 1989. *Indian Government: Its Meaning in Practice*. Lantzville: Oolichan Books.

Clifford, J. 1986. "On Ethnographic Allegory" in J. Clifford and G. E. Marcus, eds. *Writing Culture: The Politics and Poetics of Ethnography*. Berkeley: University of California Press.

———. 1988. *The Predicament of Culture: Twentieth-century Ethnography, Literature and Art*. Cambridge, Mass.: Harvard University Press.

Connerton, P. 1989. *How Societies Remember*. Cambridge: Cambridge University Press.

Crapanzano, V. 1986 "Hermes Dilemma: The Masking of Subversion in Ethnographic Description" in J. Clifford and G. E. Marcus, eds. *Writing Culture: The Politics and Poetics of Ethnography*, Berkeley: University of California Press: pp. 51–76.

Dominy, M. D. 1995. "White Settler Assertions of Native Status," *American Ethnologist*, 22, 2: 358–74.

Hauptman, L. M. 1986. *The Iroquois Struggle for Survival: World War II to Red Power*, Syracuse: Syracuse University Press.

Jackson, M. 1988. *Paths Toward a Clearing: Radical Empiricism and Ethnographic Inquiry*. Bloomington: Indiana University Press.

Jackson, M. 1996. "Introduction: Phenomenology, Radical Empiricism and Anthropological Critique" in M. Jackson, ed. *Things as They Are: New Directions in Phenomenological Anthropology*. Bloomington: Indiana University Press: pp. 1–50.

Kerby, A. P. 1991. *Narrative and the Self*. Bloomington: Indiana University Press.

Mills, A. 1994. *Eagle Down is Our Law: Witsuwit'en Law, Feasts and Stand Claims.* Vancouver: University of British Columbia Press.

Paine, R. 1996. "In Chief Justice McEachern's Shoes: Anthropology's Ineffectiveness in Court." *POLAR,* 19, 2: 59–70.

Paul, A. (1995) "On Rights, Racism and Retribution: A Systematic Analysis of the Membership Issue." *Onkwarihwa'shon:'a,* 3 (15): 5–6.

Povinelli, E. 1999. "Settler Modernity and the Quest for an Indigenous Tradition." *Public Culture,* 11, 1: 19–48.

Silman, J. 1987. *Enough is Enough: Aboriginal Women Speak Out.* Toronto: Women's Press.

Voget, F. W. 1951. "Acculturation at Caughnawaga: A Note on the Native-modified Group." *American Anthropologist,* 53, 2: 220–31.

Whittaker, E. 1994. "Public Discourses of Sacredness: The Transfer of Ayers Rock to Aboriginal Ownership." *American Ethnologist,* 21, 3: 310–34.

CHAPTER 13

THE CRIMINALIZATION OF

INDIGENOUS PEOPLE

Chris Cunneen

THE IMPACT OF POLICING ON OFFENDING

THE POLICE ROLE IS THE ONE MOST DIRECTLY connected to the production of knowledge about offending patterns of individuals or groups. In most instances, Indigenous people would not be before the courts without having been previously charged by the police with an offence. Indeed, for public-order offences in particular, the police play a direct role in observing and defining the commission of an "offence" and apprehending the offender. In this sense, there is a symbiotic link between policing and offending. Such a link makes nonsense of the notion of discrete criminal behaviour separate from the criminal justice system itself.

For the purposes of the current argument it is important to consider in general terms the way policing interacts with, and shapes, the measures we use for understanding criminal behaviour among Indigenous people.

POLICING EFFECTS ON CRIMINAL CHARGES

One way in which police can influence official figures for offending is through over-policing, particularly in relation to public-order offences. The concept of over-policing has been used to describe how Indigenous individuals in particular, and Indigenous communities more generally, are policed in a way that is different from, and more intensive than, the policing of non–Indigenous communities. Over-policing can partly explain the over-representation of Indigenous people in the criminal justice system, particularly where offences like assault police, hinder police, resist arrest, offensive behaviour, or language and public drunkenness are involved. These charges are often representative of direct police intervention and potential adverse use of police discretion. Except for a notional "community," the victim of the offence is almost invariably the police officer, as shown by numerous studies in most Australian jurisdictions.[1]

Levels of police intervention can impact on offending figures, particularly where police are the victims of the offences. Thus, the greatest policing impact is likely with less serious offences such as "offensive language," and the impact will be less with the most serious offences such as homicide. Between these two extreme examples exists

a variety of policing practices which are likely to influence the extent to which official figures on offending represent the actual occurrence of crime. For example, with
property offences there are a range of factors which limit the extent to which we can
discuss the actual level of offending as measured by official statistics. In commenting
on the South Australian experience, Gale and her colleagues note, "it is not clear to
what extent Aborigines actually commit more serious property offences or whether
other factors and, in particular, police discretion in charging are at work" (Gale et al.
1990, p. 46). The authors cite examples of police discretion in charging where less
serious offences, such as being unlawfully on premises and larceny, could be substituted for the more serious charge of break, enter, and steal. Similarly, Cunneen and
Robb (1987, p. 96) found that of all property offences, it was arrests for "break and
enter with intent to steal" for which Aboriginal people were most over-represented.
In such circumstances there is a range of possible resolutions available to police officers, including the use of diversion or other less serious charges.

Similarly, quite basic issues, such as the extent to which offences are reported,
can be related to the level of policing and the perceived likelihood of a satisfactory
response on the part of the victim. The extent to which offences are reported impact
on how we might measure the level of their commission. In addition, there is the
question of what we might make of police clear-up rates.[2] Clear-up rates are notoriously low for offences like motor vehicle theft and break, enter and steal, often
little more than 5 percent (NSW Bureau of Crime Statistics and Research 1990,
pp. 19–20). The low clear-up rate means there is considerable room for speculation
about what type of crimes are solved and which offenders are caught. The information on the few offenders who are apprehended is particularly susceptible to
policing practices, reporting levels in particular areas, and the relative age and sophis-
tication of the offenders. The over-representation of Indigenous people in some
categories of offences may tell us as much about detection by police as about the
frequency with which crimes are committed.

THE USE OF POLICE DISCRETION

Policing is an activity characterized by high levels of "discretion," which is routinely
used even by the most junior members of the organization and often with little
supervision. There is considerable evidence from various inquiries and research
literature that demonstrates that police intervene in situations, particularly in relation to street offences involving Indigenous people, in ways that are unnecessary
and sometimes provocative (ADB 1982; ICJ 1990; HREOC 1991; Wootten 1991a;
Amnesty International 1993; Cunneen and McDonald 1997a). Beyond the available observational evidence, it is difficult to demonstrate that police routinely use
their discretion to intervene in situations involving Aboriginal people where the

same behaviour or situation would be ignored if it involved non-Aboriginal people. However, the substantial contemporary and historical accounts presented in a range of forums, as well as other documentation on adverse police decisions after intervention, lend substantial weight to the conclusion that discretion is adversely used in this regard.

After police intervene in a situation, a number of discretionary decisions are made depending on the age of the person and the reason for intervention. These include decisions about whether to place a person in custody, whether to deal with the situation informally or to arrest or summons the person for the alleged offence, whether to administer a caution rather than charge the person if they are a juvenile, whether to grant bail to the person, and what bail conditions should be imposed, and so on.

In relation to juveniles, police make "negative" decisions concerning Indigenous young people which, independent of the reason for apprehension, have the effect of harsher decisions being made at points where discretion is available (Gale et al. 1990; Luke and Cunneen 1995; Aboriginal Affairs Department and Crime Research Centre 1996). When dealing with both adults and juveniles, police have the discretion to proceed by either arrest and charge or the use of a summons. Summons is a less intrusive way of ensuring attendance at court and does not require being detained, brought to the police station to be fingerprinted, and having bail determined. All the available evidence indicates that Indigenous people are significantly less likely to be proceeded against by way of summons than non-Indigenous people. For instance, in the Northern Territory, 42 percent of non-Aboriginal people appeared in court by way of summons compared to 29 percent of Aboriginal people during 1996 (Luke and Cunneen 1998, p. 19).

After police have decided to intervene and charge a person with a criminal offence, discretion is applied to the number of charges which are laid. Over the years there have been many references to what appear to be unnecessary numbers of charges laid against Aboriginal defendants arising out of single incidents (Wootten 1991b; ICJ 1990; Amnesty International 1993). These complaints are often associated with public-order offences and the use of what has colloquially been referred to as the "trifecta": charges for offensive behaviour/language, resist arrest and assault police.

Police decision-making and the use of discretion can have an enormous impact on the number of Indigenous people appearing before the courts and the nature of the offences with which they are charged. The discretions available to police in terms of whether to charge a person with a criminal offence, which charge and how many charges should be laid, as well as subsequent procedural decisions in relation to arrest or summons, the use of custody and bail and so on, all fundamentally mould the apparent criminality of the person detained. The public expression of criminality confirmed in the courtroom occurs at the end of a long social process. In the case of Indigenous people, we know from the evidence that police decision-making invariably gives rise to the use of the more punitive options available.

THE LAW AND POLICING

Police intervention does not occur in a legal vacuum, and at least on the face of it police are there to enforce the law. For a significant part of the European history of Australia, police have been required to enforce legislation which denied basic rights and protections to Aboriginal and Torres Strait Islander people. Colonial legislation embodied in various Protection Acts was used to exert control over Aboriginal people and communities in a racially discriminatory manner.

While laws based on overt racial discrimination have been repealed, the impact of law and its interpretation by police as they conduct their routine activities may still lead to profound, even if indirect, discrimination. Legislation covering public order is one example. In relation to recent legislation covering public drunkenness, in both its criminalized form in Victoria, Queensland, and Tasmania, and its decriminalized form in South Australia, New South Wales, Western Australia, and the Northern Territory, there has been concern that the laws have been used to maintain high levels of police intervention and custody. Some criminal laws appear to be applied only to Indigenous people. For instance, in north-western New South Wales, offences of riot and affray and various local government ordinances were used exclusively in relation to Aboriginal people (Cunneen and Robb 1987, pp. 221-2). There is widespread concern over police use of charges under various Summary Offences or Police Offences Acts with provisions for offensive behaviour and language. This type of legislation has been strengthened in recent years with increased penalties and rising numbers of arrests (Cunneen and McDonald 1997a, pp. 114–16).

Police may also use alternatives to the criminal law, such as welfare provisions, in the policing of Indigenous young people. In Western Australia, for example, it has been claimed that provisions providing for the protection of children are routinely used to remove Indigenous voting people from the streets and to place them in custody (NISATSIC 1997, p. 511). Similar provisions exist in New South Wales in the *Children (Protection and Parental Responsibility) Act 1997*. Complaints about the abuse of police powers under existing legislation are frequent, particularly in areas such as stopping and questioning Indigenous adults and young people (NISATSIC 1997, p. 512) or in the abuse of both search warrants and commitment warrants as a way of harassing individuals (Cunneen and McDonald 1997a, p. 62), or in some cases whole communities (Cunneen 1990b; NSW Office of the Ombudsman 1991).

The legislation covering the right to bail for a person charged with a criminal offence varies between different Australian jurisdictions. However, police determine in the first instance whether a person will receive bail and what conditions might be attached to the granting of bail. This gives rise to a number of issues. First, are Aboriginal people more likely to be refused bail than non-Aboriginal people? Second, are the conditions attached to bail unnecessarily onerous for Aboriginal people? Third, the need for a bail determination demonstrates the interconnectedness between adverse decisions by police. The police preference for proceeding by way of arrest and charge rather than using summons creates the need for bail in the first place. The Royal Commission into Aboriginal Deaths in Custody noted that the available evidence shows that police are more likely to refuse bail to an Aboriginal person than to a non-Aboriginal person in similar circumstances (Wootten 1991a, p. 353). Recent research has indicated widespread concern within Indigenous organizations that bail is determined in a discriminatory manner. Some of the discrimination can arise indirectly: Aboriginal and Torres Strait Islander people are more likely to be unemployed and homeless, and as a consequence are considered to be at greater risk of failing to appear in court (Cunneen and McDonald 1997a, p. 122).

JUDICIAL DECISION-MAKING

Ultimately it is magistrates and judges who, within the constraints of sentencing legislation, impose sentences on Indigenous people who are brought before the courts. There has been considerable argument about whether those sentences are equitable in comparison to the sentences received by non-Indigenous people.

Indigenous people are more likely than others to be sentenced to imprisonment. For example, in Western Australia it was found that magistrates were six times more likely to sentence Aboriginal adults to imprisonment than non-Aboriginal people (Harding et al. 1995, p. 69). In the absence of further details on offence seriousness and prior record, the researchers felt constrained in drawing any conclusions from these figures. Some commentators have argued that there is no adverse discrimination by the courts against Aboriginal people, if prior record is taken into account.

Walker, for example, argues that "the Courts often refer explicitly to prior record as a reason for remanding in custody and for greater severity in sentencing" (1987, pp. 110-11). Although Indigenous prisoners were more likely to have been previously imprisoned, the average length of sentence for an Indigenous prisoner was 42.6 months compared to 74.9 months for a non-Aboriginal prisoner. Walker argues that the shorter average prison sentences for Aborigines "cannot be entirely attributed to different types of offences committed by Aboriginal people," nor to "the relative youthfulness of Aboriginal offenders or to any differences in sentencing practices between States" (1987, p. 111). He concluded "that the courts cannot be held to blame for the high rates of Aboriginal imprisonment. On the contrary, they appear to be particularly lenient to Aboriginal offenders, especially when one considers that prior imprisonment record is regarded as a key factor in sentencing, tending towards longer sentences" (1987, p. 114). More recently, Walker and McDonald (1995) have argued that the results of the 1992 prison census show that Aboriginal offenders generally serve shorter terms of imprisonment than non-Indigenous people for a range of offences. They suggest that "courts may have a lenient view of Indigenous offenders, biasing sentence lengths in their favour to avoid accusations of racial biases in sentencing" (1995, p. 4).

However, there are serious flaws in this argument. There is no analysis of why such disproportionate numbers of Indigenous people are brought before the courts in the first place, the extent to which alternatives to prison are used for Indigenous and non-Indigenous offenders compared to imprisonment, or the relative serious-ness of the offences beyond broad categories such as "fraud" or "drugs."[3] Much of the problem with this type of analysis derives from the methodology of using prison statistics to analyze comparative sentencing decisions. A simple comparison between the length of prison sentences for Indigenous and non-Indigenous people provides us with no comparative information on their passage through the criminal justice system, nor on the decisions that are made at each stage. In particular, the effect of police practices in relation to targeting, arrest, and bail all impact on the crucial question of why Aboriginal people appear before the courts in the first place and how they in fact obtain criminal records. The end result may be an "accumulation of disadvantage" in the system deriving from the original police decision to arrest (Gale et al. 1990; Luke and Cunneen 1995).

A recent study of sentencing in the Northern Territory found that courts were using jail sentences more frequently for Aboriginal people and at an earlier stage in their offending history, and that they were more likely to have a prior offending history than non-Aboriginal people. However, when Aboriginal and non-Aboriginal offenders were matched by prior record and offence, a greater proportion of Aboriginal people were sentenced to imprisonment—irrespective of the offence or the level of prior record. The study also found that while Aboriginal people received shorter imprisonment sentences than non-Aboriginal people, they were less likely to receive the benefit of non-custodial sentencing options (Luke and Cunneen 1998). Thus a picture emerges of Aboriginal people receiving fewer non-custodial sentenc-ing options and more frequent short-term jail sentences than non-Aboriginal people.

In regard to juvenile offenders, Aboriginal young people have a greater chance of being sent to an institution than do non-Aboriginal offenders (Gale et al. 1990, p. 107; Broadhurst, Ferrante and Susilo 1991, p. 74; Luke and Cunneen 1995). South Australian research showed that differences in penalties remained even when specific charges were analyzed. Thus, twice as many Aboriginal young people compared to non-Indigenous young people were sentenced to detention for break, enter, and steal or for assault, for example. It was not the specific offence which determined the penalty (Gale et al. 1990, p. 109). The major determinant influencing penalty was the young person's prior offending record. Unemployment and family structure were also relevant, with those who were unemployed and living in a non-nuclear family situation being more likely to receive a custodial sentence. Research in New South Wales has reached similar conclusions in relation to the importance of prior criminal record (Luke and Cunneen 1995). A New South Wales Judicial Commission report confirmed that Indigenous and non-Indigenous youth received the same number and length of detention orders when factors including offence, prior record, bail, employment, and family structure were accounted for (Gallagher and Poletti 1998, p. 17).

The major import of this discussion on sentencing in relation to the question of policing is that sentencing decisions cannot be seen as discrete from policing practices. Police decisions obviously affect the number and type of criminal charges on which the court makes a sentencing decision. Policing also impacts on whether the person arrives in court in custody, on bail or by way of summons. Besides the actual offence, a prime determinant of sentencing outcome is prior record, which itself is an outcome of the social and political processes which involve police decision-making.

Policing practices partly shape sentencing, particularly where prior record becomes a factor in imposing more punitive sentencing outcomes.

SPATIAL FACTORS: ENVIRONMENT AND LOCATION

The shape of criminal behaviour—its nature and size—is also influenced by a range of spatial factors which lie outside both individual influence and the immediate responses of the criminal justice system. Environmental opportunities can structure criminal activity. Environment and location can also impact on the response by the community and the police.

For example, Gale and her colleagues, in their study of Aboriginal young people and juvenile justice, argued that even if it could be shown that Aboriginal people do commit more serious property offences, this would not demonstrate any greater inherent "criminality" because environmental opportunities and pressures influence the nature of property crime. In particular, urban-rural differences structure opportunities and pressures differently (Gale et al. 1990). Simple theft and shoplifting are primarily urban offences, particularly associated with large shopping complexes. The opportunities for these types of offences are considerably constrained in the environment of small rural communities. Similarly, there is increased likelihood of being detected either breaking into or attempting to break into a dwelling in a small country town or remote community. In these locations offenders are often easily identified by the community and the police.

Location also has a bearing on the likelihood of coming into contact with the criminal justice system as well as possible responses. While the results of research are somewhat conflicting, a number of criminologists, geographers, and sociologists have considered the spatial dimension of Indigenous contact with the criminal justice system. Gale et al. have shown that there are "enormous geographical variations in the position of young Aboriginal people before the law" in South Australia (1990, p. 36). Broadhurst (1997) has argued that the highest rates of Indigenous imprisonment are in the "frontier" areas like the Northern Territory and Western Australia, and the lowest rates are in settled states such as Victoria and Tasmania. A recent study in the Northern Territory showed Aboriginal people living in major centres were four times more likely to appear in court than those living in remote areas (Luke and Cunneen 1998, p. 21).

The processes of colonization significantly impacted on the human geography of Aboriginal and Torres Strait Islander communities. It is worth noting that many Indigenous communities in Australia have arisen out of the forced relocation of Aboriginal and Torres Strait Islander people into specific areas during the period of "protection." This movement has given rise to its own set of problems, which may manifest themselves in social conflict and disagreements over access to scarce resources. Some of the recent literature in the area urges a consideration of the diverse experiences of Indigenous people, both in terms of understanding the nature of offending (Broadhurst 1997; LaPrairie 1997) and in terms of the development of policy (Cunneen 1997).

CULTURAL DIFFERENCE

Cultural difference can lead to criminalization for a number of reasons. First, Indigenous people may have difficulties based on language and culture during police interrogation and in courtroom procedures. Second, Aboriginal people's cultural practices may lead to criminalization. Third, the attacks on Aboriginal culture through various colonial policies over many decades have weakened certain social control mechanisms within some communities, causing problems of disruptive and criminal behaviour.

The vulnerability of Aboriginal people when faced with police interrogation techniques has been noted in several government inquiries.[4] Some of the disabilities Aboriginal people face in front of the courts as a result of language and cultural differences have been explored by Eades (1995a, 1995b). For instance, cultural difference expressed through body language can be falsely interpreted as implying guilt. Cross-examination and interrogation techniques can lead to gratuitous concurrence, which may be interpreted as admission of guilt (Eades 1995a). Failure to provide interpreters is still a major problem in many parts of Australia, and affects both police and court stages of intervention (Cunneen and McDonald 1997a).

There is now a significant body of literature which outlines the difficulties that face Indigenous people in the formal legal process (Eades 1995b; Criminal Justice Commission 1996; Mildren 1997), difficulties which derive from both cultural and communicative (verbal and non-verbal) differences and can also include medical conditions (such as middle-ear infection leading to hearing loss). They are part of the structural parameters which prevent Indigenous people receiving fair treatment in the non-Indigenous legal process, and at times can lead to significant miscarriages of justice (Criminal Justice Commission 1996).

Distinct cultural patterns may also lead to intervention and eventual criminalization. One example is the policing of activities which occur in public places. Cultural differences in this area arise where Aboriginal social activities are more likely to lead to visibility and surveillance by police. Cultural differences in child-rearing practices can also lead to the intervention of non-Indigenous welfare and juvenile justice agencies, including police. Indigenous societies in Australia had, and continue to have, very different cultural notions in relation to childhood and young people compared to non-Indigenous groups. Generally there is not the same separation or exclusion of children from the adult world. Responsibility for children and young people is allocated through the kinship system and the wider community (Sansom and Baines 1988; NISATSIC 1997; Watson 1989).

A critical question is whether non-Indigenous criminal justice institutions simply fail to recognize and value Indigenous methods of social organization, or whether they in effect treat cultural difference as a social pathology and criminalize it. For example, from the late 1970s there has been considerable criticism of the ethnocentric nature of social-background reports and of the psychological tests administered to Aboriginal young people coming under state supervision. The reports gave free rein to the expression of prejudices in relation to Aboriginal culture, family life and child-rearing practices through descriptions of "dysfunctional families" and "bad home environments" (Milne and Munro 1981; Gale et al. 1990, p. 102; Carrington 1993, p. 48). Apparently neutral means of assessment such as IQ and psychological testing can reflect the norms of the dominant culture and provide apparently "scientific" evidence of maladjusted individuals or families. There have been similar criticisms of the social assumptions which can underlie the reports of probation and parole officers which are presented to the courts (Ozols 1994, p. 3).

Colonization has also wrought changes in the social patterns of Aboriginal life by wholesale disruption to communities through expropriation of the land, concentration of differing kinship groups on reserves, and through specific policies such as the removal of Aboriginal children and young people. Colonial processes have attacked Indigenous mechanisms of governance and social control. For example, the Royal Commission into Aboriginal Deaths in Custody has noted in detail the extent to which disruption, intervention, and institutionalization have left Aboriginal and Torres Strait Islander families facing severe difficulties with their children and young people. The historical legacy of colonialism is that families and communities now cannot call on the social and economic resources necessary to resolve these problems. It is important to recognize that since much of colonial policy was about undermining Aboriginal authority and methods of social organization, it is hardly surprising that now, in some communities, parental authority and traditional responsibilities have been rendered less effective.

Finally, it is important to recognize the cultural differences between Indigenous communities in Australia. While the most obvious are the significant cultural differences between Aboriginal people and Torres Strait Islanders, there are obvious cultural and linguistic differences between Indigenous peoples throughout Australia. Some of these differences derive from pre-colonial Australia, while others have arisen as a result of the colonial experience. These differences are often poorly understood and can lead to a simplistic approach to criminal justice policies (Cunneen 1997; NISATSIC 1997).

SOCIO-ECONOMIC FACTORS

A person's position in the social and economic class structure of society has a direct impact on their likelihood of ending up in the criminal justice system. The disadvantaged position of Aboriginal people in Australia has been well documented, not least by the Royal Commission into Aboriginal Deaths in Custody, the National Inquiry into the Separation of Aboriginal and Torres Strait Islander Children from Their Families, and various ATSIC reports (1995a, 1997).

Numerous studies have indicated the links between the socio-economic position of Aboriginal people and their level of offending, including Cunneen and Robb (1987), Devery (1991) and Beresford and Omaji (1996). A recent Australian Institute of Criminology study has also noted the importance of considering the links between offending levels (as measured by imprisonment figures) and employment and educational disadvantage (Walker and McDonald 1995). The authors identify the association of social problems such as crime with unemployment and income inequalities. They suggest that the reason crime is so problematic in Aboriginal communities is due to the lack of employment, educational and other opportunities, and argue that social policies aimed at improving these conditions are likely to have a significant effect on the reduction of imprisonment rates (p. 6). More recently, Hunter and Borland (1999) found that the high rate of arrest of Aboriginal people, often for non-violent alcohol-related offences, is one of the major factors behind low rates of employment.

MARGINALIZATION

Another way of considering socio-economic disadvantage and some offending patterns by Aboriginal people is through the notion of marginalization. Marginalization in this context is taken to mean separation and alienation from work relations, family, and other social relations which bind young people and adults to communities and give value and esteem to people's lives. The results of marginalization include self-destructive behaviour (including substance abuse), increased likelihood of violence among family members, and the development of strategies for survival, which include crime.

Marginalization and its relationship to crime are clearly not a phenomenon particular to Aboriginal people. However, because of the history of dispossession, colonial policy, and racism in Australia, it can be argued that marginalization impacts greatly on Aboriginal and Torres Strait Islander people, who show very poorly on all social indicator scales in terms of health, housing, education, unemployment, and welfare dependency. There have been many studies that show that poverty is associated with detected crime and police intervention. In South Australia, it was found that, of young people who had left school and were apprehended by police, some 91 percent of Aboriginal young people, compared to 61 percent of non-Aboriginal young people, were unemployed (Gale et al. 1990, p. 56).

Other social factors which correlate with poverty, such as single-parent families and residential location, were also more prevalent among Aboriginal young people who were apprehended by police (Gale et al. 1990, pp. 57–8; see also Devery 1991). The Royal Commission into Aboriginal Deaths in Custody argued that part of the high level of property offences committed by Aboriginal youth is indicative of the extent of poverty. At the most basic level, some offences are committed by young people because of their need for food (Johnston 1991a, p. 287).

Marginalization is also important in understanding the extent of self-destructive behaviour and its relationship to offending. Some Aboriginal communities have problems with substance abuse by young people and adults, including alcohol abuse and petrol sniffing. Substance abuse can be associated with offending in many ways, from the commission of break and enters to obtain alcohol or petrol to the association of alcohol abuse with violence. The Royal Commission into Aboriginal Deaths in Custody has also noted the effect peer group pressure and boredom have on offending. This would appear to be a particular problem in remote communities and is clearly related to marginalization, where juvenile and young adults have no opportunity for employment, for formal education in the community beyond junior high school, or for extended social activities (Johnston 1991a, pp. 289–90).

The notion of marginalization and economic disadvantage must always be seen within the context of colonialism, dispossession, and the destruction of an Aboriginal economic base. As many Indigenous people have stated, their people are not simply a disadvantaged minority group in Australia: their current socio-economic status derives from a specific history of colonization. In other words, an overly simplistic application of socio-economic (or class) analysis prevents an understanding of the distinct historical formation of Indigenous people within a dominant (and colonizing) society.[5]

RESISTANCE

The concept of resistance may also play some role in explaining the patterns of Aboriginal over-representation in crime figures. Some of the offences committed by Aboriginal people are specifically aimed at non-Indigenous targets or as responses and resistances to non-Indigenous institutions and authorities. A number of researchers have commented upon the fact that some property offences, vandalism, assaults, or behaviour classified offensive can be understood as a form of resistance (Brady 1985; Cunneen and Robb 1987; Cowlishaw 1988; Hutchings 1995). Brady notes that in the Aboriginal community where she did her research, the break-ins, by young people in particular, were directed at school buildings, non-Aboriginal staff houses, and the store (Brady 1985, p. 116). Aboriginal organizations have also noted that resistance has become part of Aboriginal culture, with a particular effect on juveniles. "What has been described as [juvenile] delinquency could also be regarded as acts of individual defiance. The scale and nature of Aboriginal children's conflict with "authority" is reflective of a historical defiance" (D'Souza 1990, p. 5). In some cases, public disorder may erupt in anti-police riots as a direct response to harassment (Cunneen and Robb 1987; Goodall 1990b).

Other patterns of offending which might be considered under the notion of resistance relate to defiance of court orders. Goodall has noted that, historically, the tactics which were used against welfare and protection board intervention included passive resistance, non-cooperation and absconding (cited in Johnston 1991a, p. 77). Today these types of offences are typically grouped under the category of "justice" offences. It is important to consider the extent to which breaches of court orders might reflect a refusal to comply with what are considered to be unjust levels of intervention and control. Similarly, high levels of fine default may reflect not just poverty (the inability to pay a fine), but also resistance to the idea of paying a fine deriving from an unjust conviction.

THEORIZING THE IMPACT OF POLICING ON CRIME FIGURES

The role of police specifically in implementing colonial policy is a large topic. It is important to note in the present context, however, that the colonial project involved a diverse range of strategies, including the murder of Indigenous people, dispersal away from traditionally owned lands, and the destruction of an economic base in many parts of Australia, concentration of diverse groups in government and mission-run reserves, and the removal of Aboriginal children from communities. The manifold effects of these policies were well documented by the Royal Commission into Aboriginal Deaths in Custody. The impact of policies such as child removal was noted in the investigations into various deaths, as well as other tangible outcomes of colonial policy, such as the enforced "invisibility" of Aboriginal people moved away from white communities, and the policing tactics that were employed to achieve those ends.

. More recently the National Inquiry into the Separation of Aboriginal and Torres Strait Islander Children from Their Families (1997) examined the effects of forced removals. It is worth clarifying the criminogenic effects generated by this particular colonial policy. It led to the destabilization and/or destruction of kinship networks, and the destabilization of protective and caring mechanisms within Indigenous culture. It led to the social and legal construction of Aboriginal child-rearing as socially incompetent and of Aboriginal culture as worthless. It led to a legal regime without procedural justice, which has been defined as genocide within international law. It led to the economic and sexual exploitation of Aboriginal children. It has contributed to a culture of resistance within Indigenous communities to welfare and criminal justice authorities. It has contributed to the generation of higher levels of mental illness, psychiatric disorders, and alcohol and substance abuse among those removed. It has contributed to the creation of a new generation of Aboriginal adults ill-equipped for parenting.

It would of course be an impossible task to "measure" the impact of a particular colonial policy such as child removal on contemporary Indigenous crime figures. Yet we know through the traumatic effects of such policies on individuals, families, and communities that the impact has indeed been great. We gain some glimpse of this in data that consistently show the greater numbers of the stolen generation among Indigenous arrests and deaths in custody. At one level, the concept of "colonialism" provides a highly generalized level of explanation for understanding Indigenous criminal offending, but as the example of the impact of the forced removal of Indigenous children shows, colonial policy can be contextualized with concrete examples and specific criminogenic effects.

A sophisticated approach to explaining the level of over-representation of Indigenous people in official criminal statistics is needed. It is not accurate to suggest that Indigenous people do not commit offences and are merely imprisoned as the result of a racist criminal justice system. Nor is it the case that the criminal justice system is simply a neutral institution enforcing an impartial legal system. At the broadest level, the legal system has been informed by a colonial project with a specific regime for Indigenous people. In more prosaic terms, the police (as part of the legal system) utilise their discretion in ways which have a negative impact on Indigenous people. The level of policing and the nature of police intervention impact directly on the extent to which Aboriginal and Torres Strait Islander people appear in the criminal justice system. In addition, the economic and social conditions under which Indigenous people have been forced to live as a result of dispossession and marginalization are criminogenic.

These explanations are not mutually exclusive and, if framed in either/or categorizations, fail to capture the complexities of social reality. For example, if we consider the comparatively large number of motor vehicle registration and licence offences for which Aboriginal people are imprisoned, we might consider the complex interaction of environmental considerations, the effects of unemployment and poverty, and the extent of discriminatory policing practices. Environmental considerations are important, because Aboriginal people often live in rural and remote areas poorly serviced by public transport and are therefore dependent on a motor vehicle in a way that the "average" non-Aboriginal person is not. Unemployment and low income affect the ability both to pay for registration and to own vehicles more likely to be classified roadworthy, and negatively impact on the ability to pay for any traffic fines. Failure to pay traffic fines results in licence cancellation. Discriminatory police practices may increase the likelihood of detection of unlicensed drivers through selective procedures of stopping Aboriginal drivers.

A similar explanation could be utilised for the comparatively large number of break and enters for which Aboriginal young people appear in court. When a small group of Aboriginal children is apprehended and appears in court in Brewarrina, New South Wales, say, for breaking into a house and stealing food, a satisfactory explanation for that event must be one that recognizes the economic and social outcomes of colonization and marginalization, the role of environmental opportunities for crime, the increased likelihood of detection as a result of police numbers and surveillance in small and predominantly Aboriginal communities, and the increased likelihood of an adverse police discretional decision to charge (rather than caution) an Aboriginal young person in the first instance.

In the end, measures of "crime" need to be understood as social, political, and historical artefacts. Their "truth" is certainly dependent on the regimes of which they are a product. In the case of Indigenous people, the regime has been particularly harsh, the empirical measures showing the deep levels of their criminalization in contemporary Australian society. Yet to see that as merely a reflection of offending levels in Indigenous communities would indeed be to mistake the outcome of social processes for a simple and unambiguous "fact." Crime as a social artefact needs to be continually deconstructed—it has no essential inner core other than the purely formal requirement of legal transgression.

There is little doubt that policing shapes the measuring of crime, and police decision-making can significantly impact on what we "know" as offenders and offences. In the specific case of Indigenous people in Australia, we can expect an even greater shaping of offending levels through police practices, given their contemporary role in Indigenous communities and their historic role in colonial policy.

NOTES

1. See, for example, ADB (1982); Cunneen and Robb (1987); Gale et al. (1990); Luke and Cunneen (1995); Mackay (1995) Allas and James (1996); Cunneen and McDonald (1997a); Luke and Cunneen (1998).
2. Clear-up rate: the percentage of recorded offences cleared by police.
3. For instance, it is not surprising that Indigenous people receive shorter sentences for drug offences given their lack of involvement in more serious trafficking offences.
4. For an examination of these issues two decades ago, see the House of Representatives Standing Committee on Aboriginal and Torres Strait Islander Affairs' Report on Aboriginal Legal Aid (Ruddock 1980). The courts have also expressed concern in this regard in *R v Williams* (1976) 14 SASR 1 and *Collins v R* (1980) 31 ALR 257. For an early summary of these issues, see Rees (1982). More recent reports drawing attention to the same issues include the Royal Commission into Aboriginal Deaths in Custody (Johnston 1991a) and CJC (1996).
5. See Brennan (1991) for a succinct discussion of why Indigenous people are not simply an oppressed minority group within Australia.

REFERENCES

Aboriginal Affairs Department and Crime Research Centre. 1996. *Aboriginal Young People and Contact with the Juvenile Justice System in Western Australia. Royal Commission into Aboriginal Deaths in Custody Vol. 3.* Perth: University of Western Australia, Crime Research Centre.

Aboriginal and Torres Strait Islander Social Justice Commission. 1995. *Indigenous Social Justice, Submission to the Parliament of the Commonwealth of Australia on the Social Justice Package.* Aboriginal and Torres Strait Islander Social Justice Commission, Sydney.

Allas, R. and James, S. 1996. *A Study of Victorian Aboriginal Offending 1989–90 to 1993–94,* A report to the Criminology Research Council, Canberra.

Amnesty International. 1993. *A Criminal Justice System Weighted Against Aboriginal People.* London: International Secretariat.

Anti-Discrimination Board. 1982. *Study of Street Offences by Aborigines.* Sydney: NSW Anti-Discrimination Board.

Beresford, Q. and Omaji, P. 1996. *Rites of Passage. Aboriginal Youth, Crime and Justice.* South Fremantle: Fremantle Art Centre Press.

Brady, M. 1985. *"Aboriginal Youth and the Juvenile Justice System,"* in A. Borowski and J. Murray, eds. *Juvenile Delinquency in Australia.* Sydney: Methuen.

Brennan, F. 1991. *Sharing the Country.* Ringwood: Penguin.

Broadhurst, R. 1997. "Aborigines and Crime in Australia," in M. Tonry, ed. *Ethnicity, Crime and Immigration: Comparative and Cross-National Perspectives, Crime and Justice.* vol. 21. Chicago: University of Chicago.

Broadhurst, R., Ferrante, A. and Susilo, N. 1991. *Crime and Justice Statistics for Western Australia. 1990.* Perth: Crime Research Centre, University of Western Australia.

Carrington, K. 1993. *Offending Girls.* Sydney: Allen & Unwin.

Cowlishaw, G. 1988. *Black, White or Brindle.* Cambridge: Cambridge University Press.

Criminal Justice Commission. 1996. *Aboriginal Witnesses in Queensland Criminal Courts.* Brisbane: Goprint.

Cunneen, C. 1990. "The Detention of Aborigines in Police Cells: Wilcannia." *Aboriginal Law Bulletin,* vol. 2, no. 45, pp. 8–10.

Cunneen, C. 1997. "Community Conferencing and the Fiction of Indigenous Control." *Australian and New Zealand Journal of Criminology,* vol. 30, no. 3, pp. 292–311.

Cunneen, C. and Robb, T. 1987. *Criminal Justice in North-West NSW,* Sydney: NSW Bureau of Crime Statistics and Research, Attorney-General's Department.

Cunneen, C. and McDonald, D. 1997. *Keeping Aboriginal and Torres Strait Islander People Out of Custody.* Canberra: ATSIC.

D'Souza, N. 1990. "Aboriginal Children and the Juvenile Justice System." *Aboriginal Law Bulletin,* vol. 2, no. 44, pp. 4–5.

Devery, C. 1991. *Disadvantage and Crime in New South Wales.* Sydney: New South Wales Bureau of Crime Statistics and Research.

Eades, D. 1995a. "Cross Examination of Aboriginal Children: The Pinkenba Case." *Aboriginal Law Bulletin,* vol. 3, no. 75, pp. 10–11.

Eades, D. 1995b. *Language in Evidence.* Sydney: University of New South Wales Press.

Gale, R., Bailey-Harris, R. and Wundersitz, J. 1990. *Aboriginal Youth and the Criminal Justice System.* Melbourne: Cambridge University Press.

Gallagher, P. and Poletti, P. 1998. *Sentencing Disparity and the Ethnicity of Juvenile Offenders.* Sydney: Judicial Commission of New South Wales.

Goodall, H. 1990. "Policing In Whose Interest?" *Journal For Social Justice Studies,* vol. 3, pp. 19–36.

Harding, R., Broadhurst, R., Ferrante, A. and Loh, N. 1995. *Aboriginal Contact with the Criminal Justice System and the Impact of the Royal Commission into Aboriginal Deaths in Custody.* Sydney: The Hawkins Press.

House of Representatives Standing Committee on Aboriginal and Torres Strait Islander Affairs. 1990. *Our Future, Our Selves.* Canberra: AGPS.

Human Rights and Equal Opportunity Commission. 1991. *Racist Violence.* Report of the National Inquiry into Racist Violence. Canberra: AGPS.

Hunter, B. and Borland, J. 1999. "The Effect of Arrest on Indigenous Employment Prospects." *Crime and Justice Bulletin, No. 45.* Sydney: New South Wales Bureau of Crime Statistics and Research.

Hutchings, S. 1995. "The Great Shoe Store Robbery," in G. Cowlishaw and B. Morris, eds. *Racism Today.* Canberra: AIATSIS Press.

International Commission of Jurists. 1990. *Report of the Aboriginals and Law Mission.* Sydney: Australian Section.

Johnston, E. 1991. *National Report, 5 Vols.* Royal Commission into Aboriginal Deaths in Custody. Canberra: AGPS.

LaPrairie, C. 1997. "Reconstructing Theory: Explaining Aboriginal Over-Representation in the Criminal Justice System in Canada." *The Australian and New Zealand Journal of Criminology*, vol. 30, no.1 March 1997, pp.39–54.

Luke, G. and Cunneen, C. 1995. *Aboriginal Over-Representation and Discretionary Decisions in the NSW Juvenile Justice System*. Sydney: Juvenile Justice Advisory Council of NSW.

Luke, G. and Cunneen, C. 1998. *Sentencing Aboriginal People in the Northern Territory: A Statistical Analysis*. Darwin: NAALAS.

Mackay, M. 1995. "Law, Space and Justice: A Geography of Aboriginal Arrests in Victoria." *People and Place*, vol. 4, no. 1.

Mildren, D. 1997. "Redressing the Imbalance Against Aboriginals in the Criminal Justice System." *Criminal Law Journal*, vol. 21, pp. 7–22.

Milne, C. and Munro, L. Jnr. 1981. "Who is Unresponsive: Negative Assessments of Aboriginal Children." Discussion Paper No. 1, Aboriginal Children's Research Project, Family and Children's Services Agency, Sydney.

NISATSIC. 1997. *Bringing Them Home: Report of the National Inquiry into the Separation of Aboriginal and Torres Strait Islander Children from Their Families*. Sydney: HREOC.

NSW Bureau of Crime Statistics and Research. 1990. *NSW Recorded Crime Statistics 1989/90*. Sydney.

NSW Office of the Ombudsman. 1991. *Operation Sue: Report to Parliament under Section 26 of the Ombudsman Act,* NSW Office of the Ombudsman, Sydney.

Ozols, E. 1994. "Pre-Sentence Reports on Aboriginal and Islander People: Overcoming the Myths and Providing Culturally Appropriate Information." Paper presented to the Australian Institute of Criminology, Aboriginal Justice Issues II Conference, Townsville, 14–17 June 1994.

Rees, S. 1982. "Police Interrogation of Aborigines," in J. Basten, et al., eds. *The Criminal Injustice System*. Sydney and Melbourne: Australian Legal Workers Group and Legal Service Bulletin.

Royal Commission into Aboriginal Deaths in Custody. 1990. *Transcript of Hearing into Juvenile Justice Issues*. Perth, 29 May 1990.

Sansom, B. and Baines, P. 1988. "Aboriginal child placement in the urban context," in B. Morse and G. Woodman, eds. *Indigenous Law and the State*. Dordrecht: Foris Publications.

Walker, J. 1987. "Prison Cells with Revolving Doors: A Judicial or Societal Problem," in K. Hazlehurst, ed. *Ivory Scales*. Sydney: University of New South Wales Press.

Walker, J. and McDonald, D. 1995. "The Over-Representation of Indigenous People in Custody in Australia," *Trends and Issues in Crime and Criminal Justice*, no. 47. Canberra: Australian Institute of Criminology.

Watson, L. 1989. "Our Children: Part of the Past, Present, and Providing a Vision for the Future: A Murri Perspective." *Australian Child and Family Welfare*, August 1989.

Wootten, H. 1991a. *Regional Report of Inquiry in New South Wales, Victoria and Tasmania*. Royal Commission into Aboriginal Deaths in Custody. Canberra: AGPS.

Wootten, H. 1991b. *Report of Inquiry into the Death of David John Gundy*. Royal Commission into Aboriginal Deaths in Custody. Canberra: AGPS.

CHAPTER 14

THE INDIANS ARE COMING TO AN END:

THE MYTH OF NATIVE DESOLATION

Matthew Restall

In 1539, Jerusalem was attacked by three Christian armies at once. One was an imperial force led by Charles V, Holy Roman Emperor and king of Spain, accompanied by his brother, the king of Hungary, and French king Francis I. This army had come as reinforcements for a separate Spanish army led by the Count of Benavente. The third attacking force was the army of New Spain, led by Viceroy Mendoza. The battle raged for hours, until the Muslim defenders of Jerusalem finally capitulated. Their leader, "the Great Sultan of Babylon and Tetrarch of Jerusalem," was none other than "the Marqués del Valle, Hernando Cortés."

This battle did not actually take place in the Middle East, but in the vast central plaza of Tlaxcala, the Nahua city-state whose alliance with Cortés had proved crucial to his defeat of the Mexica empire almost two decades earlier. The mock battle, part of a day-long series of plays and battles, was staged on Corpus Christi day by the Tlaxcalans, with the possible assistance of Franciscan friars. One of the friars witnessed the spectacle and wrote an account of it, published soon after in Motolinía's *History of the Indians of New Spain*.[1]

While a mock battle in which the victorious armies are led by the Spanish king, the colonial Mexican viceroy, and a Spanish count prominent in colonial Mexican affairs might seem to be a celebration of the Spanish Conquest of Mexico, Tlaxcala's theatrical "Conquest of Jerusalem" was hardly that. Cortés (played by a native Tlaxcalan actor) was not the victor in the drama, but the Sultan, doomed to defeat—and the captain general of the Moors was Pedro de Alvarado, the second most prominent Spaniard in the fall of Tenochtitlan and the subsequent conqueror of highland Guatemala. As the losers, Cortés and Alvarado requested mercy and baptism, and admitted that they were the "natural vassals" of the Tlaxcalan—played by Charles V—an interesting inversion of the conquistadors' claim that natives were naturally subject to Spaniards.[2] As possible insurance against Cortés's reacting negatively to his role in the play, the Tlaxcalans had the army of New Spain led by a Tlaxcalan playing the viceroy, don Antonio de Mendoza, with whom Cortés was in dispute in 1539 (resulting in Cortés's sailing to Spain later that year).[3]

The parts in the play were all played by Tlaxcalans. It was Tlaxcalan warriors, in their thousands, who took Jerusalem, just as 18 years earlier thousands of them had taken Tenochtitlán. And whereas the Tlaxcalans playing soldiers in the European armies all wore the same bland uniforms, the Tlaxcalans of the army of New Spain dressed as themselves—in the traditional multicolored costumes of the city-state's warriors, complete with feathered headdresses, "their richest plumage, emblems, and shields" (in the words of the Franciscan observer). The setting for the play was Tlaxcala's impressive new plaza, the size of four football fields, whose buildings, still under construction, became part of the elaborate scenery. An important aspect of the festival's political context was Tlaxcala's age-old rivalry with the Mexica, as the play was put on in part to trump a similar spectacle staged four months earlier in Mexico City and centered on an imaginary Spanish "Conquest of Rhodes" that was a thinly disguised Mexica reconquest of Mexico.[4] The "Conquest of Jerusalem" was thus a Tlaxcalan creation intended to glorify Tlaxcala's recent triumphs and current status as an important, if not the most important, *altepetl* or central Mexican city-state.

Called "the most spectacular and intellectually sophisticated theatrical event" of its time, Tlaxcala's 1539 Corpus Christi celebration is an especially rich illustration of the genre.[5] But it was by no means the only such festival in 16th-century Mexico, or indeed in colonial Spanish America. Throughout the colonies in Mesoamerica and the Andes, plays, dances, and mock battles were staged by native communities. Many persist to this day. All placed complex local spins on a mix of traditional native ritual performance and various elements of Spanish theatrical tradition. The effect, if not the purpose, of such festivals was to reconstruct the Conquest not as a historical moment of defeat and trauma, but as a phenomenon that transcended any particular historical moment and was transcended in turn by that local native community. These festivals were not commemorations of something lost, but celebrations of community survival, micropatriotic integrity, and cultural vitality.[6] Festivals of reconquest therefore represent the first of the seven indicators of Conquest-era and post-Conquest native vitality.

The second such indicator consists of other expressions of native denial or inversion of defeat. An extraordinarily rich body of sources illustrating this phenomenon with respect to Mesoamerica is contained within the genre referred to by scholars as the primordial title, or *título*. The *título* was a community history that promoted local interests, particularly related to land ownership, often those of the local dynasty or dominant noble families. Such documents were written down alphabetically, in native languages, all over Mesoamerica during the colonial period—but especially in the 18th century when land pressures mounted due to population growth among Spaniards and natives alike. Late-colonial *títulos* drew upon earlier sources, both written and oral, representing continuities from pre-Conquest histories and often including accounts of the Spanish invasion.[7] Maya accounts of the Conquest contained in *títu-los* from Yucatan reveal that there was no single, homogeneous native view; perspectives were determined largely by differences of class, family, and region. Most of the Maya elite, however, tended to downplay the significance of the Conquest by emphasizing continuities of status, residency, and occupation from pre-Conquest times. Mayas placed the Spanish invasion, and the violence and epidemics it brought, within the larger context of history's cycles of calamity and recovery, relegating the Conquest to a mere blip in their long-term local experience.[8]

Another example of the localized nature of native responses to the Conquest came from the Valley of Oaxaca, in southern Mexico. In the 1690s, a legal dispute over land erupted between two native communities in the valley, one Nahua, the other Mixtec. In court, both submitted *títulos* to prove their cases, each complete with a brief Conquest account. The Nahua version of events of the 1520s asserted that Nahua warriors had come down to Oaxaca from central Mexico in response to a plea from the Zapotecs, who needed help defending themselves from the cannibalistic Mixtecs. Cortés approved the mission, but when he came to Oaxaca in the wake of Nahua victory, he and the Nahuas fell out and fought. The Nahuas won this battle too, and after this, the "original conquest," they settled in the valley on land granted to them.

In contrast, the Mixtec version claimed that Cortés came to the valley first, where he was welcomed by the Mixtecs, who gave Spaniards some land on which to settle. The trouble began when Cortés returned with a group of Nahuas, who started a fight and were soundly defeated by the Mixtecs. With Cortés as peace broker, the Mixtecs graciously allowed the Nahuas to settle in the valley. The boundaries of the land they were given were, not surprisingly, less generous in the Mixtec *título* than in the Nahua version.

In both versions, local community—or micropatriotic—identities remain paramount. There is no acceptance of the colonial division of peoples into Spaniards and "Indians," nor is there an acceptance of the Conquest as either a Spanish initiative or a primarily Spanish triumph. Native defeat is not only denied, but inverted. Even the phrase "native defeat" is meaningless from a community perspective that views all outsiders in more or less the same way, whether they be Spaniards, Mixtecs, Nahuas, or Zapotecs—or even people of the same language group who live in a separate town.[9]

The third indicator of native vitality during the Conquest was the role played by natives as allies in the campaigns that followed the major wars of invasion. Although in the long run these campaigns usually (but not always) resulted in the spread of Spanish colonial rule, in the short run they often constituted local native exploitation of the Spanish presence to advance regional interests. For example, the armies of Nahua warriors who waged campaigns in what is now northern Mexico, southern Mexico, Yucatan, Guatemala, and Honduras helped create the colonial kingdom of New Spain and were led by Spanish captains. But the vast majority of those who fought were Nahuatl-speakers under their own officers. Many of them remained as colonists in new colonial towns such as Oaxaca, Santiago (Guatemala), Merida, and Campeche, and their culture and language made a permanent mark on these regions. As symbolized by place-names in highland Guatemala to this day, Nahuatl became a lingua franca in New Spain. In many ways, these campaigns were a continuation of the Mexica expansionism that had gone almost unchecked for a century before the Spanish invasion.[10]

A slightly different type of example is that of the Chontal Maya expansion of the late 16th century under their king, Paxbolonacha. His simultaneous colonial identity was as don Pablo Paxbolon, the region's governor. Although the Chontal Mayas's first major contact with Spaniards was as early as 1525, not until the 1550s did the region become fully incorporated into the nearest Spanish colony, Yucatan. Beginning in the 1560s, and running continuously until his death in 1614, Paxbolon engaged in campaigns against neighbouring Maya communities that had yet to be incorporated into the colony or that had slipped out of colonial control. The Spanish presence on most of these expeditions was minimal or nonexistent. Although Paxbolon had a license from Merida permitting him to round up refugees and "idolaters," a Chontal Maya *título* written during his rule recorded such campaigns before and after the Spanish invasion, revealing the colonial ones to be little more than continuations of age-old slaving raids.[11]

Paxbolon's expansionism was a localized phenomenon, but so were all cases of native military activity after the Spanish invasion—from Nahua campaigns after the fall of the Mexica empire to campaigns by Andean warriors for decades after the capture and execution of Atahuallpa. Local circumstances produced regional variations, but the general pattern reveals considerable native military activity during the Conquest and after it was supposedly over, not always directed against Spaniards but often pursued to advance local native interests.

The historian Charles Gibson, in his seminal study of colonial Tlaxcala, remarked that there were times when "Indians accepted one aspect of Spanish colonization in order to facilitate their rejection of another."[12] This situation is illustrated by the role often played by native elites, whose partial and complex collaboration in Conquest and colonial agendas represents the fourth anti-desolation indicator. At the highest level of native leadership, that of the Mexica and Inca emperors, such collaboration served only to buy time. But while Moctezuma and Atahuallpa lived, even as captives, their policies of collaboration and appeasement served to save native lives and prevent full-scale wars. The Moctezuma of myth—invented by Franciscans and Tlatelolcans and perpetuated by modern historians from Prescott to Tuchman—was no artful collaborator. But the real Moctezuma was the most successful ruler the Mexica empire had known; "the most dynamic, the most aggressive, the most triumphantly self-confident of all," in Fernández-Armesto's words, Moctezuma "outstripped all predecessors" with campaigns that ranged over some 150,000 square miles and continued even after Cortés had taken up residence in Tenochtitlán. Cortés later claimed to have captured Moctezuma soon after reaching the city, but it is clear from descriptions of the emperor's activities in other Spanish and native sources that his arrest did not take place for months. Meanwhile, the Mexica ruler spun a web of confusion around the Spaniards, who remained unsure right up to their disastrous and bloody escape from Tenochtitlán whether to expect submission, deadly duplicity, or open hostility.[13] Atahuallpa's capture was more immediate, but even as a captive he was able to plot and strategize, temporarily containing the Spaniards and using them to win his own war against his brother.

The high status of Moctezuma and Atahuallpa made them unsuited in the long run for the roles of puppet rulers and condemned them to death at the hands of Spaniards. Lesser native rulers, however, were able to negotiate their way out of captivity and execution, or avoid imprisonment altogether, and be confirmed in office by the colonial authorities. Don Pablo Paxbolon is a good example of such a ruler who was able to maintain this dual status throughout his long reign/rule, partly because his small kingdom was of relatively little interest to Spaniards. In contrast, Manco Inca Yupanqui's kingdom attracted so much Spanish attention that he soon rebelled against his dual status. As well as being Inca (meaning "emperor") by right of succession, Manco was confirmed in office as regent of Peru by the Spaniards in 1534 and was supposed to function as a puppet of the colonial regime (see Figure 14.1). But by 1536, the conditions of compromise had become too onerous, and the abuse of the Inca's family and retainers by the Pizarros and their associates had become intolerable. Manco fled the capital of Cuzco, raised an army, and laid siege to the city for a year before retreating into the Andes, where an independent Inca kingdom lasted until 1572. Meanwhile, in 1560, Manco's son Titu Cusi became Inca, later becoming baptized and negotiating a rapprochement with the Spanish. Although his brother, Tupac Amaru, and other family members were executed in 1572 as rebels, Titu Cusi, his descendents, and other members of the Inca nobility were able to maintain considerable economic and political status within colonial Peru for centuries.[14]

Inca survival paralleled in many ways the perpetuation of status by Moctezuma's relatives and descendents. While they lacked their pre-Conquest political clout, their local social and economic significance was underpinned by confirmation of titles and honours by the Spanish crown.[15] Likewise, most of the highest-ranking noble Maya families, as a result of protracted negotiations through a Conquest decades long, succeeded in preserving their local status as community rulers in

FIGURE 14.1

"Manco Inca, raised up as Inca king," in *Nueva corónica y buen gobierno*, by don Felipe Huaman Poma de Ayala (1615).

FIGURE 14.2

"The Xiu Family Tree," probably by Gaspar Antonio chi (c. 1557), updated by don Juan Xiu (c. 1685).

return for accepting Spanish political authority at a regional level. The Spanish governor of Yucatan became the *halach uinic* (provincial ruler), but the noblemen of dynasties such as the Cocom, Pech, and Xiu remained as *batabob* (local rulers or town governors) for the next three centuries.

The Xiu were among the most powerful noble families in Yucatan before and after the Conquest.[16] Figure 14.2 illustrates through the medium of a family tree the perpetuation of the Xiu dynasty's sense of historical legitimacy through the Conquest period. The semi-mythical founding couple are supposed to have lived centuries before the Conquest, while the named individuals run from the 15th to 17th centuries. Drawn in the 1550s by Gaspar Antonio Chi, and updated over a century later by a member of one branch of the family, the tree exhibits a complex mix of Maya, Nahua, and Spanish cultural elements. The image evocatively exhibits the blend of change and continuity, compromise and survival that underscored elite native adaptation to colonial rule.

Most of the Xiu noblemen named in Figure 14.2 served as *batabob*, illustrating the flourishing of the native municipal community from the 16th to 18th centuries—the fifth indicator of post-invasion native vitality. One of the native mechanisms of adaptation to colonial rule that fostered the golden age of the native town was the ready adoption of the Spanish *cabildo* (town council). Spaniards imposed the *cabildo's* election, offices, and functions on native towns early in the colonial period—or at least, Spaniards assumed they did. In fact, native elites only appeared to create Spanish-style *cabildos*. Their "elections," if held at all, were but a veneer covering traditional factional manoeuvers and cycles of power sharing. Spanish titles such as *alcalde* (judge) and *regidor* (councilman) were adopted, but the numbers, rankings, and functions of the officers followed local traditions, while many *cabildos* contained officers with pre-Conquest titles. In some cases, municipal governors were Spanish-appointed, but in many more instances native governors continued to function as they had before the Conquest, even keeping pre-colonial titles, ruling for life and passing the positions on to their sons.[17]

While Spaniards viewed native *cabildos* as products of colonialism, natives initially adopted the framework of the *cabildo* as a superficial change and then soon came to view it as a local institution rather than a colonial one. This double perception is another example of Double Mistaken Identity, whereby both Spaniards and natives viewed the same concept or way of doing something as rooted in their own culture. In this way, the native borrowing of Spanish cultural elements did not represent native culture loss or decline, but rather adaptability and vitality (the sixth indicator of post-Conquest native cultural vitality). Natives tended to view borrowings—be they Spanish words, concepts, ways of counting, of worship, of building houses, or of town planning—not as loans but as part of community practice and custom.

They viewed them not as Spanish, nor even as native, but as local. And they were able to do this because of the integrity and flourishing of semi-autonomous municipal communities. By the end of the colonial period, there was little about native culture in most of Spanish America that (in James Lockhart's words) "could safely be declared to have been entirely European or entirely indigenous in origin. The stable forms that emerged in the long run often owed so much to both antecedents, with many elements having been similar from the beginning and others now interwoven and integrated, that identifying what belonged to which antecedent becomes to a large extent impossible, and even beside the point."[18]

Just as the violence and drama of the Spanish invasion gave way to gradual cultural change, so did the immediate tragedy of native population decline give way in the long run to opportunities of various kinds. The Andean chronicler Huaman Poma warned in 1615 that the "Indians are coming to an end," and in demographic terms, a century after Spaniards began their conquests on the American mainland, this almost seemed a real possibility. The rapid decline in the Native American population, beginning in 1492 and continuing well into the 17th century, has been called a holocaust. In terms of absolute numbers and the speed of demographic collapse— a drop of as many as 40 million people in about a century—it is probably the greatest demographic disaster in human history.[19]

But the decline was not a holocaust in the sense of being the product of a genocide campaign or a deliberate attempt to exterminate a population. Spanish settlers depended upon native communities to build and sustain their colonies with tribute, produce, and labour. Colonial officials were extremely concerned by the demographic tragedy of Caribbean colonization, where the native peoples of most islands became extinct within a few decades. That concern mounted with evidence of massive mortality on the mainland during—and even preceding—Spanish invasions. What Spaniards did not fully understand was the degree to which disease caused this disaster. The arguments of a vocal minority—of whom Las Casas remains the best known—that colonial brutality was the principal cause of the natives seeming to "come to an end" were taken seriously by the crown. As a result, edicts were regularly passed that were designed to protect natives from colonial excesses. Their impact was limited, but they reflected the important fact that Spaniards needed Native Americans to survive and proliferate, even if this was only so they could be exploited.

The combination of population decline and Spanish colonial dependence upon a shrinking—and then very slow-growing—native population actually provided opportunities for the survivors. One type of opportunity was political. The relative stability of the ruling elite in Yucatan, and the few instances of upstart families acquiring power as a result, was not paralleled everywhere in Spanish America. In the Riobamba region of colonial Quito, for example, the pre-Inca elite and the surviving families among the local Inca nobility vied for power within the crucible of the Conquest and colonial rule. The situation was skillfully manipulated by the Duchiselas, a family that was prominent in the area before the Inca conquest, but not a ruling dynasty. The family welcomed the 1534 Spanish expedition under Sebastián de Benalcázar and as a result was granted a local lordship. By the 1570s, they had parlayed this into the governorship of the town of Yaruquies. Over the next two centuries, the Duchiselas consolidated considerable regional political power, established a land-based family fortune, and largely succeeded in inventing the dynasty's deep-rooted historical legitimacy.[20]

The Duchisela family fortune was land based, and by the early 17th century its patriarch, don Juan, and his wife, dona Isabel Carrillo, owned almost a thousand hectares of land. Indeed, land was another arena of native opportunity in the Conquest's wake. Contrary to common belief, Spaniards did not come to the Americas to acquire land. The goal of conquistadors was to receive an *encomienda*, a grant of native tribute and labour—not land. The Spanish pressure on native communities to give up or sell land was not serious until later in the colonial period. In the 16th century there was a great deal more land available to natives than before the Conquest. And with the advent of iron and steel tools and a new array of crops and domesticated animals, there were new opportunities for working that land.[21]

To be sure native peoples in 16th-century Spanish America faced epidemics of lethal disease and onerous colonial demands. But they did not sink into depression and inactivity because of the Conquest. Instead they tenaciously sought ways to continue local ways of life and improve the quality of life even in the face of colonial changes and challenges. Furthermore, the decline in population did not mean that native culture declined in some or any sense. Native cultures evolved more rapidly and radically in the colonial period as a result of exposure to Spanish culture and the need to adapt to new technologies, demands, and ways of doing things. But as historians of late-medieval Europe have observed, when populations were periodically decimated by plagues and epidemics, this did not result in culture loss.

All of this is ignored by the myth of native desolation, which subsumes into "nothingness" the complex vitality of native cultures and societies during and after the Conquest.[22] As Inga Clendinnen puts it, the mythic or "conventional story of returning gods and unmanned autocrats, of an exotic world paralyzed by its encounter with Europe, for all its coherence and its just-so inevitabilities, is in view of the evidence like Eliza's progression across the ice floes: a matter of momentary sinking balances linked by desperate forward leaps."[23]

NOTES

1. Motolinía, *Historia,* 1979 [1541]: *trat.* I, chap. 15; Harris, *Aztecs, Moors, and Christians,* 2000:132-47.

2. As Harris observes; *Aztecs, Moors, and Christians,* 2000:144.

3. Harris, *Aztecs, Moors, and Christians,* 2000:137. A further dimension to the slighting of Cortés in the drama is the fact that the governor of Tlaxcala in 1539 was don Luis Xicotencatl, nephew of the Axayacatzin Xicotencatl who had led Tlaxcalan resistance against Cortés in 1519, had reluctantly joined the allied cause in 1521 and then, when he seemed uncooperative, had been hanged by Cortés in Texcoco that year (Gómara, *Cortés,* 1964 [1552]: 100-16; Gibson, *Tlaxcala,* 1952: 98-100; Thomas, *Conquest,* 1995: 490-91; Harris, *Aztecs, Moors, and Christians,* 2000:139).

4. The exception to the actors being Tlaxcalans was a fictional Caribbean native army, defeated in the middle of the play in their attempt to take Jerusalem. These actors were Otomi natives—reflecting Tlaxcalan insight into colonial Caribbean history and their perception of Caribbean and Otomi natives in a different category from Tlaxcalans (a difference we would define as that between semi-sedentary and sedentary peoples). Harris, *Aztecs, Moors, and Christians,* 2000:140-41, 136, 135.

5. Harris, *Aztecs, Moors, and Christians,* 2000:134.

6. Bricker, *The Indian Christ,* 1981: 129-54; Hill, *Colonial Cakchiquels,* 1992: 1-8; Cohen, "Danza de la Pluma," 1993; Rappaport, *Cumbe Reborn,* 1994:145-66; Restall, *Maya Conquistador,* 1998: 46,193-94 n53; Harris, *Aztecs, Moors, and Christians,* 2000.

7. See Restall, "Heirs to the Hieroglyphs," 1997, which includes a fairly comprehensive bibliography of *título* studies. *Títulos* continue to be discovered and published, enriching our understanding of the native views of the Conquest described above; see Colom et al., *Testamento y Título,* 1999.

8. Restall, *Maya Conquistador,* 1998.

9. The only presentation and study of these *títulos* is Sousa and Terraciano, "Original Conquest," 2003; also see Terraciano, *The Mixtecs,* 2001: 336-38.

10. Fernández-Armesto in Prescott, *Conquest of Mexico,* 1994: xxx; Hassig, *Aztec Warfare,* 1988; Hill, *Colonial Cakchiquels,* 1992; Dakin and Lutz, *Nuestro Pesar,* 1996.

11. AGI, *Mexico* 97; 138; 2999; Restall, *Maya Conquistador,* 1998: 53-76; Scholes and Roys, *Maya-Chontal Indians,* 1948:142-290.

12. Gibson, *Tlaxcala,* 1952:191; also quoted by Harris, *Aztecs, Moors, and Christians,* 2000: 139.

13. Fernández-Armesto, "'Aztec' Auguries," 1992: 298; Prescott, *Conquest of Mexico,* 1994: xxix; Hassig, *Aztec Warfare,* 1988; Brooks, "Construction of an Arrest," 1995.

14. Cieza de León, *Peru,* 1998 [1550]: 447-66; Sarmiento, *History of the Incas,* 1907 [1572]: 258-61; Prescott, *Conquest of Peru,* 1847, II: chaps. 1-3; Wachtel, *Vision of the Vanquished,* 1977:169-84; Himmerich y Valencia, "Siege of Cuzco," 1998; Wood, *Conquistadors,* 2000: 155-85.

15. As illustrated in an important and fascinating series of documents of the 1530s to 1620s, most of them petitions to the king from Mexica royalty and other nobles, preserved in the AGI and recently published in Pérez-Rocha and Tena, *La nobleza indígena,* 2000. Complementary sources are the records of legal actions taken over lands and noble privileges by doña Isabel Moctezuma, the emperor's daughter, in the 1540s to 1560s, published in Pérez-Rocha, *Privilegios en Lucha,* 1998. Doña Isabel's descendants received government pensions until 1934, and in 2000 began a legal campaign to have the pensions reinstated (Lloyd, "The Scholar," 2002).

16. They were prominent members of what I have elsewhere termed Yucatan's "dynastic dozen"; Restall, "People of the Patio," 2001: 351-58, 366-68. The collection of documents known as the Xiu Papers, of which Figure 14.2 is a part, were recently published for the first time, as Quezada and Okoshi, *Papeles de los Xiu,* 2001.

17. For this argument laid out with Maya evidence, see Restall, *Maya World,* 1997:51-83; for treatments of native *cabildos* in other regions, see Spalding, *Huarochiri,* 1984: 216-26, Haskett, *Indigenous Rulers,* 1991, Stern, *Peru's Indian Peoples,* 1993:92-96, and Terraciano, *The Mixtecs,* 2001:182-97.

18. Lockhart, *Of Things,* 1999: 98. Also see Restall, "Interculturation," 1998:141-62.

19. Cook, *Born to Die,* 1998. Note that there is much disagreement on the size of native populations in the ancient Americas, with estimates on 16th-century losses varying above and below the middle-ground figure of 40 million. But even at, say, 25 million, the death toll was still greater than Europe's Black Death, for example.

20. See Powers, "Battle of Wills," 1998:183-213.

21. For readings on this issue with respect to central Mexico and Yucatan, for example, see Harvey, *Land and Politics,* 1991; Lockhart, *The Nahuas,* 1992:141-202; Horn, *Postconquest Coyoacan,* 1997:111-165; and Restall, *Maya World,* 1997:169-225.

22. "Nothingness" is Le Clézio's term *(Mexican Dream,* 1993: 5).

23. Clendinnen, "'Fierce and Unnatural Cruelty,'" 1991:19.

REFERENCES

PRIMARY ARCHIVAL SOURCE AND ITS ABBREVIATION

AGI   Archive General de las Indias, Seville, Spain

PRIMARY AND SECONDARY PUBLISHED SOURCES

Bricker, Victoria R. 1981. *The Indian Christ, the Indian King: The Historical Substrate of Maya Myth and Ritual.* Austin: University of Texas Press.

Brooks, Francis J. 1995. "Motecuzoma Xocoyotl, Hernán Cortés, and Bernal Díaz del Castillo: The Construction of an Arrest," in *Hispanic American Historical Review* 75:2: 149-83.

Cieza de León, Pedro de. 1998. *The Discovery and Conquest of Peru* [ca. 1550]. Alexandra Parma Cook and Noble David Cook, eds. Durham: Duke University Press.

Clendinnen, Inga. 1987. *Ambivalent Conquests: Maya and Spaniard in Yucatan, 1517-1570.* Cambridge: Cambridge University Press.

Clendinnen, Inga. 1991. "'Fierce and Unnatural Cruelty': Cortés and the Conquest of Mexico," in *Representations* 33, Winter. (Reprinted in *New World Encounters.* Stephen Greenblatt, ed., 12-47. Berkeley: University of California Press, 1993).

Clendinnen, Inga. 1991. *Aztecs: An Interpretation.* Cambridge: Cambridge University Press.

Cohen, Jeffrey H. 1993. "Danza de la Pluma: Symbols of Submission and Separation in a Mexican Fiesta," in *Anthropological Quarterly* 66: 149-58.

Colom, Alejandra, et al., eds. 1999. *Testamento y Título de los Antecesores de los Señores de Cagcoh (San Cristóbal Verapaz).* Guatemala City: Universidad del Valle de Guatemala.

Cook, Noble David. 1998. *Born to Die: Disease and the New World Conquest, 1492-1650.* Cambridge: Cambridge University Press.

Dakin, Karen, and Christopher H. Lutz. 1996. *Nuestro Pesar, Nuestra Aflicción: Memorias en Lengua Náhuatl Enviadas a Felipe II por Indigenas del Valle de Guatemala Hacia 1572.* Mexico City: Universidad Nacional Autónoma de Mexico and CIRMA.

Fernández-Armesto, Felipe. 1992. "'Aztec' Auguries and Memories of the Conquest of Mexico," in *Renaissance Studies* 6:3-4, 287-305.

Gibson, Charles. 1952. *Tlaxcala in the Sixteenth Century.* New Haven: Yale University Press.

Gómara, Francisco López de. 1964. *Cortés: The Life of the Conqueror by His Secretary.* Lesley Byrd Simpson, ed. (trans. of *Istoria de la conquista de Mexico* [1552]) Berkeley: University of California Press.

Harris, Max. 2000. *Aztecs, Moors, and Christians: Festivals of Reconquest in Mexico and Spain.* Austin: University of Texas Press.

Harvey, H. R., ed. 1991. *Land and Politics in the Valley of Mexico: A Two-Thousand Year Perspective.* Albuquerque: University of New Mexico Press,.

Haskett, Robert. 1991. *Indigenous Rulers: An Ethnohistory of Town Government in Colonial Cuernavaca.* Albuquerque: University of New Mexico Press.

Hassig, Ross. 1988. *Aztec Warfare: Imperial Expansion and Political Control.* Norman: University of Oklahoma Press.

Hill, Robert M., II. 1992. *Colonial Cakchiquels: Highland Maya Adaptation to Spanish Rule, 1600-1700.* Fort Worth: Harcourt Brace.

Himmerich y Valencia, Robert. 1998. "The 1536 Siege of Cuzco: An Analysis of Inca and Spanish Warfare," in *Colonial Latin American Historical Review* 7:4 (Fall): 387-418.

Horn, Rebecca. 1997. *Postconquest Coyoacan: Nahua-Spanish Relations in Central Mexico, 1519–1650.* Stanford: Stanford University Press.

Jones, Grant D. 1998. *The Conquest of the Last Maya Kingdom.* Stanford: Stanford University Press.

Le Clézio, J.M.G. 1993. *The Mexican Dream. Or, The Interrupted Thought of Amerindian Civilizations* [translation of *Le rêve mexicain*]. Chicago: University of Chicago Press.

Lloyd, Marion. "The Scholar as P.I.: A Historian Takes on the Case of Moctezuma's Heir," in *The Chronicle of Higher Education* (12 April 2002), p. A14 (accessed online).

Lockhart, James. 1992. *The Nahuas After the Conquest.* Stanford: Stanford University Press.

Lockhart, James. 1999. *Of Things of the Indies: Essays Old and New in Early Latin American History.* Stanford: Stanford University Press.

Motolinía, fray Toribio de. 1979. *Historia de los indios de la Nueva Espana* [1541]. Edmundo O'Gorman, ed. Mexico City: Pornia.

Pérez-Rocha, Emma. 1998. *Privilegios en Lucha: La información de Doña Isabel Moctezuma.* Mexico City: Instituto National de Antropologia e Historia (Colección científica).

Pérez-Rocha, Emma, and Rafael Tena. 2000. *La Nobleza Indígena del Centro de México Después de la Conquista.* Mexico City: Institute Nacional de Antropología e Historia (Colección obra diversa).

Powers, Karen Vieira. 1998. "A Battle of Wills: Inventing Chiefly Legitimacy in the Colonial North Andes," in *Dead Giveaways: Indigenous Testaments of Colonial Mesoamerica and the Andes.* Susan Kellogg and Matthew Restall, eds., 183-214. Salt Lake City: University of Utah Press.

Prescott, William H. 1847. *History of the Conquest of Peru.* 2 vols. Philadelphia: Lippincott & Co.

Prescott, William H. 1909. *The Conquest of Mexico* [1843]. London: Dent.

Prescott, William H. 1994. *History of the Conquest of Mexico* [1843]. Introduction by Felipe Fernandez-Armesto. London: The Folio Society.

Quezada, Sergio, and Tsubasa Okoshi Harada. 2001. *Papeles de los Xiu de Yaxá, Yucatán.* Mexico City: Universidad Nacional Autonóma de México.

Rappaport, Joanne. 1994. *Cumbe Reborn: An Andean Ethnography of History.* Chicago: Chicago University Press.

Restall, Matthew. 1997. *The Maya World: Yucatec Culture and Society, 1550-1850*. Stanford: Stanford University Press.

Restall, Matthew. 1997. "Heirs to the Hieroglyphs: Indigenous Writing in Colonial Mesoamerica," in *The Americas* 54:2 (October): 239-267.

Restall, Matthew. 1998. *Maya Conquistador*. Boston: Beacon Press.

Restall, Matthew. 1998. "Interculturation and the Indigenous Testament in Colonial Yucatán," in *Dead Giveaways: Indigenous Testaments of Colonial Mesoamerica and the Andes*. Susan Kellogg and Matthew Restall, eds., 141-62. Salt Lake City: University of Utah Press.

Restall, Matthew. 2001. "The People of the Patio: Ethnohistorical Evidence of Yucatec Maya Royal Courts, in *Royal Courts of the Ancient Maya, Volume 2: Data and Case Studies*. Takeshi Inomata and Stephen D. Houston, eds., 335-90. Boulder: Westview.

Sarmiento de Gamboa, Pedro. 1907. *History of the Incas* [1572]. Sir Clements Markham, ed. London: Hakluyt Society.

Scholes, France V., and Ralph L. Roys. 1948. *The Maya-Chontal Indians of Acalan-Tixchel: A Contribution to the History and Ethnography of the Yucatan Peninsula*. Washington: Carnegie Institution. (Reprinted by University of Oklahoma Press, 1968).

Sousa, Lisa M., and Kevin Terraciano. 2003. "The Original Conquest of Oaxaca: Nahua and Mixtec Accounts of the Spanish Conquest," in *Ethnohistory* 50: 2.

Spalding, Karen. 1984. *Huarochirí: An Andean Society Under Inca and Spanish Rule*. Stanford: Stanford University Press.

Stern, Steve J. 1993. *Peru's Indian Peoples and the Challenge of Spanish Conquest: Huamanga to 1640*. 2nd ed. Madison: University of Wisconsin Press.

Terraciano, Kevin. 2001. *The Mixtecs of Colonial Oaxaca: Ñudzahui History, Sixteenth through Eighteenth Centuries*. Stanford: Stanford University Press.

Thomas, Hugh. 1995. *Conquest: Montezuma, Cortés, and the Fall of Old Mexico*. New York: Simon and Schuster.

Wachtel, Nathan. 1977. *The Vision of the Vanquished: The Spanish Conquest of Peru through Indian Eyes, 1530-1570*. Hassocks, UK: Harvester Press. (Translation of *La vision des vaincus. Les Indiens du Pérou devant la conquête espagnol 1530-1570*. Paris: Gallimard, 1971.)

Wood, Michael. 2000. *Conquistadors*. Berkeley and London: University of California Press and the BBC.

CHAPTER 15

"WE MUST FARM TO ENABLE US TO LIVE":

THE PLAINS CREE AND AGRICULTURE TO 1900

Sarah A. Carter

INTRODUCTION

THIS ARTICLE EXPLORES THE TOPIC of agriculture on Plains Cree reserves in the late 19th century, addressing the question of why farming failed to form the basis of a viable economy in these communities by 1900. The answer to this question is complex, but has little to do with the prevailing explanation that Plains people had no inclination or ability to farm. The Plains Cree made sustained, determined efforts to establish an economy based on agriculture, but they faced many obstacles. There were environmental and technological challenges shared by all farmers at this time. Aboriginal farmers laboured under particular disadvantages because of their unique relationship with the federal government that ought to have assisted them in this enterprise, but ultimately functioned to undermine their efforts. A "peasant" farming policy imposed from 1889 to 1896 was especially damaging to Plains Cree agriculture. It is also argued in this chapter that non-Aboriginal people have persistently found it useful to insist that Aboriginal people and agriculture were incompatible, despite obvious evidence to the contrary. It was a convenient myth to sustain because it could be claimed that people who did not farm were not in need of much land, and that economic underdevelopment of the reserves was due to the indifference and neglect, not of the government, but of Aboriginal people.

Early in September 1879, at Fort Carlton, North-West Territories, Plains Cree chiefs Ahtahkakoop, Mistawasis, and Kitowehaw, with five councillors, met with Edgar Dewdney, the recently appointed Commissioner of Indian Affairs. The chiefs were frustrated that promises of agricultural assistance, made to them three years earlier in Treaty No. 6, were "not carried out in their spirit" (Anon., 1879: 26). They stated that they intended to live by the cultivation of the soil, as "the buffalo were our only dependence before the transfer of the country, and this and other wild animals are disappearing, and we must farm to enable us to live." They insisted that government had not fulfilled its part of the treaty in assisting them to make a living by agriculture and that what had been given them made a mockery of the promises made in 1876. This was by no means the first effort of these chiefs to place their concerns before government officials, and there were similar expressions of dissatisfaction and disappointment throughout Manitoba and the North-West Territories.[1]

Such evidence of the strong commitment of the Plains Cree to agriculture seemed startling to me when I set out to explore why agriculture failed to provide a living for residents of arable Indian reserves in western Canada. The standard explanation, one firmly embedded in the non-Aboriginal prairie mentality, seemed compelling: that Aboriginal people of the Plains never had any inclination to settle down and farm despite concerted government efforts and assistance. I originally approached the topic with the argument in mind that agriculture was the wrong policy, for the wrong people, at the wrong time. Before I was too far along in my research, however, I found that there was little evidence of agriculture floundering because of the apathy and indifference of Aboriginal people, although it was certainly the case that this view was consistently maintained and promoted by the Department of Indian Affairs and later by many historians. Yet from the time of the treaties of the 1870s and well before, Aboriginal people were anxious to explore agriculture as an alternate economy when they began to realize the buffalo were failing them. It was not government negotiators but the Aboriginal spokesmen who insisted that terms be included in the treaties that would permit agricultural development. Aboriginal people of the western Plains were among the earliest and largest groups to attempt agriculture west of the Red River Settlement. Like most other "sodbusters," Aboriginal farmers were inclined to become commercial farmers specializing in grain. The fact that they did not had to do with government policy and intent, not with Aboriginal choice and inability.

My topic and approach are the product of a number of influences, including the work of "new" social historians who, beginning in the 1960s, argued that history should be not only the study of elites but of ordinary people as well, and of the day-to-day as well as the dramatic events. The new social history stressed that non-elites—ethnic minorities, women, the working class, and non-literate peoples—sought in various ways to transcend the limitations placed on them and were not hopeless victims of forces beyond their control, but rather coped creatively with changing conditions. While Arthur J. Ray, Sylvia Van Kirk, and John Milloy cast Native people in a central role as active participants in the history of the pre-1870 West, the same could not be said of the more modern era. In the dominant narrative histories of the West in the post-1870 era, Aboriginal people all but disappeared after they made treaties and settled on reserves. The story of the establishment of the rural core of the prairie West was inevitably told from the point of view of the new arrivals, with little mention of the host society, and generally a record of positive achievement was stressed and the casualties of development were downplayed. Studies of late 19th-century imperialisms, which increasingly drew regions into a transcontinental network, provided context for understanding that what happened in western Canada was not unique, but was part of a global pattern of Western expansion.

ABORIGINAL ADAPTATIONS TO THE NORTHERN PLAINS

The Plains culture that evolved over centuries in western Canada seemed far removed from the sedentary lifestyle of farms, fields, and fences that began to alter forever the prairie landscape in the late 19th century. The Plains Cree, the northernmost people of the Great Plains of North America and one of the last Aboriginal groups to adopt Plains culture, developed a lifestyle that was well suited to the predominantly flat, treeless landscape and to the northern Plains climate of extremes and uncertainties. Particular habits of movement and dispersal suited the limited and specialized nature of the resources of the northern Plains. The Natives exploited the seasonal diversity of their environment by practising mobility. Plains people moved their settlements from habitat to habitat, depending on where they expected to find the greatest natural food supply. All aspects of life hinged on this mobility; their tepees, for example, were easily taken apart and moved, and their other property was kept to a strict minimum so that they would be unencumbered. As homesteaders were later to learn, basic necessities such as good soil, water, game, and fuel rarely came together in many Plains areas, and this combined with the great variability and uncertainty of the climate to make mobility central to the survival of the indigenous peoples of the Plains. Many of the earliest homesteaders on the Plains found that they could not stay put either, certainly not at first; they sought off-farm jobs, especially during the "start-up" years, or they were obliged to try several localities in their search for basic necessities. External inputs in the way of seed-grain relief, subsidies, or rations were often necessary as the resources of a fixed locality could not always sustain the inhabitants.

The buffalo was the foundation of the Plains economy, providing people not only with a crucial source of protein and vitamins, but also with many other necessities, including shelter, clothing, containers, and tools. Aboriginal life on the Plains followed a pattern of concentration and dispersal that to a great extent paralleled that of the buffalo. But Plains people were not solely hunters of buffalo. To rely on one staple resource alone was risky in the Plains environment, as there were periodic shortages of buffalo, and it was mainly the gathering and preserving work of women, based on their intimate understanding of the Plains environment, that varied the subsistence base and contributed to "risk reduction," a role the immigrant women to the Plains would also acquire. Midsummer camp movements were determined not only by the buffalo but also by considerations such as the ripeness and location of saskatoon berries, the prairie turnip, and other fruits and tubers. Many of the

FIGURE 15.1

Cree camp near Saskatoon, c. 1900. (Courtesy Saskatchewan Archives Board, R–B1016)

foodstuffs women gathered were dried, pounded, or otherwise preserved and stored for the scarce times of winter. Women fished, snared small game, caught prairie chickens and migratory birds, and gathered their eggs. A high degree of mobility was essential for people effectively to draw on the varied resources of the Plains.

Nineteenth-century European observers tended to see the Great Plains as a timeless land, as a place without history, its people unaffected by any outside forces and leaving no mark of their presence upon the land. Captain William Butler, who described the Plains in 1870 as a great ocean of grass, wrote that "This ocean has no past—time has been nought to it; and men have come and gone, leaving behind them no track, no vestige of their presence" (Butler, 1968: 317-18). European observers saw Plains people as living at the mercy of natural forces, and failed to appreciate the sophisticated adaptations to the environment and the many ways in which resources were altered, managed, and controlled. Methods such as the buffalo pound, like the Huron enclosures and Beothuk drivelines for capturing deer, have been described as a form of animal management. There is evidence that people of the northern Plains were concerned with keeping up buffalo herd numbers as they periodically burned the grasslands in the autumn to keep forage levels high. This burning increased yields, encouraged spring grass growth earlier, and induced buffalo into favoured areas of fresh, young grass. Fire was used to influence buffalo movement—to direct a herd to a kill site and to keep buffalo away from fur trade posts so that Europeans could not provision themselves. Fire was also used to protect valuable stands of timber.

Well before the treaties of the 1870s some Plains people, particularly the Cree and Saulteaux, had begun to raise small crops and to keep cattle to smooth out the seasonal scarcities that were increasing as the buffalo receded westward. As the home-steaders were later to learn, however, especially those who attempted farming before the development of dry-land farming techniques and early-maturing varieties of grain, yields from cultivated plants were highly unpredictable, and a more flexible economy that combined agriculture with hunting and gathering was the most feasi-ble until the disappearance of the buffalo in the late 1870s. Agriculture was a far more ancient and indigenous tradition on the Plains than the horse culture, which was a much more fleeting episode. Cree were acquainted with cultivated plant food and techniques of agriculture through several of their contacts, most notably the Mandan, Arikara, and Hidatsa, who maintained a flourishing agricultural economy on the upper Missouri. There is evidence of an agricultural village on the banks of the Red River near the present-day town of Lockport, Manitoba, that dates from between AD 1300 and AD 1500 (Putt, 1991: 64). Blackfoot were found by the earli-est of European fur traders to be growing tobacco.

Aboriginal people of the Plains were not as "passive" as the landscape; their world was not static and timeless. The archaeological and historical records suggest that on the Plains, learning new ways took place regularly, that there was much adap-tation and borrowing among people, and that changes occurred constantly. The Plains Cree, for example, had a history of making dramatic adjustments to new economic and ecological circumstances, modifying the ways in which they obtained their livelihood. With the establishment of fur trade posts on Hudson Bay after 1670, the Cree, along with their allies the Assiniboine, quickly seized the opportu-nity to function as middlemen to the trade. With the expansion of European fur trade posts inland in the late 18th century, the Cree took advantage of a new economic opportunity and worked as provisioners of buffalo meat to the trading companies. They showed themselves to be remarkably flexible in rapidly adjusting to the rewards and demands of different environments—the forest, parklands, and Plains. The branch that became the Plains Cree readily adopted many of the char-acteristics, techniques, and traits of Plains buffalo and horse culture. Aboriginal people such as the Cree were accustomed to making dramatic adjustments to new ecological and economic circumstances, and there is no inherent reason to believe that they could not have made adjustments to the new order of the post-1870 era by becoming full participants in the agricultural economy. The fact that they did not was due not to their own choice; rather, there was a refusal to let them do so as they were denied access to the opportunities and resources that would have allowed them a more independent existence.

While Aboriginal people of the Plains required assistance and instruction to establish a farming economy, they had certain advantages that new arrivals did not enjoy. They had an intimate knowledge of the resources and climate of the West. They were much better informed on rainfall and frost patterns, on the availability of water and timber, and on soil varieties. They had experience with locusts, fires, and droughts. Aboriginal farmers might have had a better chance than many of the settlers from the humid East. Many of these never could accept the discomforts and conditions, and they departed, and even for those who remained, acclimatization could take several years. Settlers from elsewhere might well have benefited from the knowledge Aboriginal people of the Plains had to offer. One settler in Saskatchewan, who had previously worked as a trader, consulted an Aboriginal friend named South Wind when he wanted to locate his homestead in the 1880s, and learned, for example, how to use fire to protect stands of timber and how to replenish the hay swamps. He later found local legislation regarding fire to be a "positive evil" and wrote that "our legislators should have had old South Wind at their Councils."[2] Accounts of such consultation are, however, very rare.

As early as the 1850s, European travellers to the Plains reported that the Cree were concerned about the scarcity of buffalo, that many were anxious to try agriculture and wanted assistance in the way of instruction and technology. They were well aware that the buffalo hunt was no longer going to sustain them. With the demise of the fur trade, agriculture appeared to be the only option. During the treaty negotiations of the 1870s, Plains people sought government aid to make the transition to an agricultural economy. In return for their offer of an opportunity for peaceful expansion, Aboriginal people asked that they be given the instruction and technology that would allow them to farm. Aboriginal spokesmen did not see any inherent conflict between their distinctive identity and active participation in an agricultural economy. Circumstances obliged them to cease living as their ancestors had done, but they did not therefore cease to be Aboriginals. Like the Natives of the older provinces of Canada, they were in favour of agriculture, resource development, and education that would assist them to survive, but they did not, for example, intend to abandon their religious ceremonies and beliefs. Euro-Canadian observers consistently insisted on seeing Plains people as hunters, gatherers, and warriors incapable of adopting agriculture.

A CROP OF BROKEN PROMISES: THE 1870s

The main focus of this study are those people of the Treaty No. 4 district of southeastern Saskatchewan who settled on reserves in the Touchwood Hills, File Hills, and along the Qu'Appelle River. Most were Plains Cree, collectively known as the *mamihkiyiniwak,* the Downstream People, although Assiniboine, mixed Cree-Assiniboine (Young Dogs), and Saulteaux also settled here and were intermingled with Plains Cree bands. Although these people form the main focus, evidence was also drawn from the Treaty No. 6 district, settled primarily by Plains Cree known as the Upstream People. In the later 1870s, the earliest years of Indian reserve settlement in present-day Saskatchewan, farming proved nearly impossible despite concerted efforts. For some bands, farming was never to be successful because of the nature of the reserve site itself. Other bands received high-quality agricultural land that was later to excite the envy of other settlers. The earliest instructions to surveyors were that care should be taken to ensure reserve lands "should not interfere with the possible requirements of future settlement, or of land for railway purposes." At that time, what was seen as the "fertile belt," and the proposed route for the Canadian Pacific Railway, ran northwest along the Assiniboine and North Saskatchewan rivers. Land further south was considered arid and unlikely ever to be wanted by settlers, so many reserves, such as those along the Qu'Appelle River, were surveyed there. But when the CPR route was changed in 1881 and rerouted through the south, many of these reserves were located near or on the railway route, in the midst of what was hoped would become the settlement belt and the heart of a prosperous agricultural economy.

Farming in the 1870s proved to be nearly impossible because the implements and livestock promised in the treaties were inadequate. Ten families, for example, were to share one plough. Bands varied in size, numbering between 17 and 50 families, but regardless of size, each was offered only one yoke of oxen, one bull, and four cows. To earn a living from the soil, a yoke of oxen was required by every farming family. As one Plains Cree chief pointed out in 1879, it was perfectly ridiculous to expect them to get on with so few oxen. He noted that every farmer in the Northwest, however poor, had his own yoke of oxen, that "We are new at this kind of work, but even white men cannot get on with so few oxen" (Anon., 1879: 28). In addition to the overall inadequacy of the agricultural assistance promised in the treaties, government officials were reluctant and tentative about distributing what was promised. The people prepared to farm expected their supply of implements, cattle, and seed immediately, but officials were determined to adhere strictly to the exact wording of the treaty, which stated that implements, cattle, and seed would be given to "any band ... now actually cultivating the soil, or who shall hereafter settle on these reserves and commence to break up the land." Aboriginal people could not settle until the surveys were complete, and in some cases this took many years. They could not cultivate until they had implements to break the land, yet these were not to be distributed until they were settled and cultivating. Government officials shared the belief that the distribution even of those items promised in the treaties could "encourage idleness," and there was concern that the implements and cattle would not be used for the purposes for which they were intended.

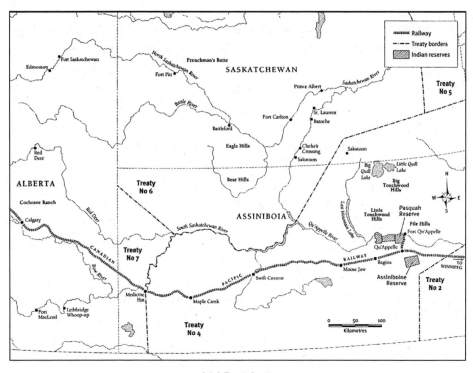

MAP 15.1

Saskatchewan and Assiniboia Districts, circa 1900

There were also problems with the quality and distribution of seed grain. In the earliest years the seed arrived in a damaged state and was received in midsummer when the season was far too advanced for planting. Acres sometimes lay idle because there was no seed available, and more land might have been broken had there been seed to sow. It was also learned after a number of years that people cultivating the reserves had to be supplied with some provisions in the spring during ploughing and sowing. The people of Treaty No. 6 had successfully bargained for this during their negotiations, but no such promise had been made to the people of Treaty No. 4. Although David Laird, Lieutenant-Governor and Indian superintendent for the North-West Superintendence, recommended in 1877 that some provisions be distributed in the spring to Treaty No. 4 bands, this request was struck from the estimates in Ottawa. It proved impossible for more than a few to remain on their reserves and cultivate as the others were obliged to hunt and gather provisions for the group to survive. Once seeding was finished, and sometimes even before, many residents of the reserves were out on the Plains, leaving behind only a few to tend the crops.

Aboriginal farmers were hampered in their earliest efforts by the kind of ploughs they were issued. By the late 1870s, Manitoba farmers had learned that American ploughs, especially the John Deere, with its chilled-steel mouldboard, were far superior for western conditions than the Ontario models. The Indian Department, however, continued until 1882 to purchase only Canadian-manufactured ploughs, which proved to be unsatisfactory. There were problems keeping in good repair the implements and wagons that were distributed, as they frequently broke down, crippling operations. Wooden parts were sometimes replaced by the farmer, but the breakage of metal parts was much more serious, as reserve farmers did not have access to blacksmiths, who were also required to point, or sharpen, ploughshares. Other equipment and livestock supplied by contractors under the terms of the treaties were clearly inferior, and Aboriginal people simply refused to accept some of it. An 1878 commission of investigation found Winnipeg Indian commissioner J.A.N. Provencher guilty of fraud in the awarding of contracts. It was discovered, among other things, that it was standard practice to furnish the Indian Department with "the most inferior articles" (Titley, 1997). In 1879 one observer described the carts and wagons supplied to but refused by Treaty No. 6 people near Fort Carlton as "the poorest description of Red River carts, which have been used by freighters up to this point, and are really unfit for further use; while the wagons are literally falling to pieces." The axes, "miserably small," were also refused (Anon., 1879: 29).

Perhaps the most scandalous example of corruption was in the cattle sent to a great many reserves in the late 1870s. They received wild Montana cattle, which were unaccustomed to work and could not be hitched to the plough. The milk cows given out were of the same description. The Fort Carlton bands were astounded when these cattle were brought to them from Montana, when tame cattle could have been purchased at Prince Albert or Red River. Most of them died over the first winter of 1878-9. Some choked themselves when tied in stables; others could not be fed because they did not take to the food. As one Plains Cree chief stated, "We know why these Montana cattle were given us; because they were cheaper, and the Government, thinking us a simple people, thought we would take them" (ibid., 28). He was correct. It became clear during the 1878 investigation that individuals in Winnipeg had profited by purchasing these creatures from Montana at about half the rate that they actually charged the Indian Department.

Aboriginal farmers laboured under other disadvantages as well. In these earliest years, there were no grist mills located near reserves, and the wheat they raised was of no use to them without milling facilities. With the disappearance of the buffalo, the main source for all their apparel also vanished. They lacked clothing and footwear, which one official described as the greatest drawback to their work. To cover their feet they cut up old leather lodges, but these too rapidly diminished. Often hungry, weak, and ill, people could not work, no matter how willing.

There was little progress in agriculture in the years immediately following the treaties of the 1870s. Early on, government officials insisted that this had to do with the indifference and apathy of Aboriginal people, who willfully rejected an agricultural way of life and inflexibly and stubbornly insisted on pursuing hunting and gathering. Through idleness they were creating their own problems. An explanation that belittled and deprecated the abilities of Aboriginal farmers absolved the government of any responsibility in the matter, and it was to be the favoured explanation of department officials well into the 20th century. During these initial years of government parsimony, indifference, and outright corruption, an opportunity was lost. Many of those who wished to farm found it impossible and became disheartened and discouraged. Had the government shown a genuine interest, some steps towards the creation of an agricultural economy might have been taken during the years before 1878-9, when the food crisis, brought on by the total disappearance of the buffalo, became severe. There was much distress, suffering, and death throughout the Northwest by 1878, although reports of starvation were systematically denied by government officials and the western press, as such news could damage the reputation of the region as a prospective home for thousands of immigrants. Once again, Aboriginal people were portrayed as chronic complainers with imaginary grievances, and they were blamed for having "not made the usual effort to help themselves."[3]

The other legacy of the years immediately following the treaties was the sense of betrayal felt by Aboriginal people who had expected government assistance in the difficult transition to an agricultural economy. As Chief Ahtahkakoop stated in 1879, "On the transfer of the country we were told that the Queen would do us all the good in the world, and that the Indians would see her bounty. With this message came presents of tobacco, and I took it at once; and I pray now that the bounty then promised may be extended to us." Three years after the treaty the chief was convinced that the "policy of the Government has been directed to its own advantage, and the Indians have not been considered so much." These chiefs had made several representations to government authorities, "but they were as if they were thrown into water" (ibid.).

Chief Pasquah, from the Pasquah Reserve in southeastern Saskatchewan, had presented Joseph Cauchon, Lieutenant-Governor of Manitoba, with similar grievances and concerns a year earlier.[4] His people, though willing to farm and diversify their subsistence base, had no cattle to break and work the land, no seed to sow, and no provisions to sustain them while at work. Aboriginal people had reason to feel that they had been deceived and led along a path that ended in betrayal, that their treatment constituted a breach of faith. They were getting the clear impression that the treaties were made simply as a means of getting peaceable possession of the country without any regard to their welfare. As Aboriginal spokesmen grasped every opportunity to implore the government to assist them to make a living by agriculture, department officials increasingly reacted by blaming the Natives for their misfortunes and portraying them as troublemakers and chronic complainers, incapable of telling the truth.

THE HOME FARM EXPERIMENT

In the wake of alarming reports from the Northwest of destitution and starvation, an ambitious plan to both feed and instruct Aboriginal people in farming was hastily contrived in Ottawa in the fall and winter of 1878-9. A squad of farm instructors, mainly from Ontario, was sent west in the summer of 1879. They were to establish "home farms" at 15 sites in the Northwest: six in the Treaty No. 4 district and nine in the Treaty No. 6 district. At these farms, located on or near the reserves, the instructors were to raise large quantities of provisions to support not only themselves, their families, and employees but also the neighbouring Aboriginal population. Their farms were to serve as "model farms" for Aboriginal observers, and in addition the instructors were to visit the reserve farmers from time to time to assist them in breaking, seeding, and harvesting, and in building their houses, barns, and root houses. At two "supply farms" in the Treaty No. 7 district, large quantities of produce were to be raised, but the farmers at these sites were not given the additional responsibility of instructing Aboriginal farmers.

The home farm plan was hastily and poorly conceived in Ottawa by people without any knowledge of Aboriginal people or of the region's soil and climate. The men chosen as instructors were unfamiliar with conditions of life in the West and knew nothing about Aboriginal people. They had to be provided with both guides and interpreters. As one Aboriginal spokesman stated, it only made sense that a farm instructor be a man "from the country, who understands the language, and with whom I could speak face to face, without an interpreter" (ibid., 29). The official rationale for not choosing local people was that "strangers" were likely to carry out their duties more efficiently, would not have their favourites, and would treat all fairly and alike. It is also clear, however, that the position of farm instructor was a patronage appointment, and all were chosen by Sir John A. Macdonald, the Canadian Prime Minister, from a list furnished by Laurence Vankoughnet, deputy superintendent-general of Indian Affairs. In addition, the tasks assigned the instructors were beyond the resources and capabilities of any individual, however well acquainted he might be with conditions in the Northwest. It soon proved that the instructors had great difficulty establishing even the most modest farms. The government found itself responsible for the support of instructors, their families, and employees, who ran farms with such dismal returns that they contributed almost nothing to the expense of running them. It was also soon discovered that the farmers simply could not attend both to their own farms and to assisting on reserve farms. The instructors seldom visited the reserves and lacked even basic knowledge about the people they were to instruct. The program turned out to be an administrative nightmare. Difficulties with personnel arose early, and the program was characterized by resignations and dismissals. The instructors were angered by government decisions to charge them for the board of themselves and family, and also to charge them for food they consumed that they had raised themselves.

AHTAHKAKOOP, MISTAWASIS, AND KITOWEHAW, 1879

On 2 September 1879 a meeting took place at Fort Carlton between Indian Commissioner Edgar Dewdney and Treaty No. 6 Plains Cree leaders Ahtahkakoop, Mistawasis, and Kitowehaw. A "special correspondent" from the *Montreal Gazette* also attended and reported on the meeting in an article published in that paper on 29 September. The Hudson's Bay Company interpreter translated the words of the Plains Cree leaders beginning with Ahtahkakoop:

> We waited for you, and we see you now; we wonder if our word met you. We have often been talking of the promises we got and when we saw that they were not carried out in their spirit, we made representations to the Minister, but they were as if they were thrown into the water. We are very glad to meet you now, as you come with full authority to act. We will not touch on anything, but the promises which have not been fulfilled.... The cattle we got from Government all died; they were brought from Montana, and we protested that they would not do.... They were like the wild fowl, we saw them here, and then they disappeared; some, when tied in stables, choked themselves; some could not be fed, and to catch them was a fight, so wild were they....

Mistawasis then came forward and said:

> I will tell you, as we understood the treaty made with Governor Morris. We understood from him that he was coming into the country to help us to live, and we were told how we were to get a living, and we put ourselves at work at once to settle down ... We expected that we would have had good cattle, but those brought were so poor that it was a mockery of the promises to give us cattle with little else than skin and bone.... Government is too slow in helping the Indians if they are going to help us at all. The fall before we saw [Lieutenant-] Governor [David] Laird, and wished him to give us more ample assistance in the way of farm implements and seeds. He said his powers were limited, but he would write to the Government, and let us know. To all these representations we received no answer. The country is getting so poor that it is for us either death by starvation, and such aid as will enable us to live. The buffalo was our only dependence

before the transfer of the country, and this and other wild animals are disappearing, and we must farm to enable us to live....

Ketawayo [Kitowehaw]:

Every farmer, however poor, at Prince Albert has his yoke of oxen and we have tried and find that we cannot do with so few. We are new at this kind of work, but even white men cannot get on with so few oxen.... We know why these Montana cattle were given us; because they were cheaper, and the Government, thinking us a simple people, thought we would take them. The cattle have all died.... Hitherto everything we have asked has been promised to be represented to the Government, but we have never got any answer, and we want now an answer....

—ANONYMOUS, 1879

Beset with all of these difficulties, the home farm program floundered. In the House of Commons, government critics hammered away at the plan. They claimed that the instructors were incompetent carpetbaggers, but the central criticism was that there should be no such expenditure on the Aboriginal people of the Northwest, as this was encouraging idleness when they should be made to rely solely on their own resources. One member of Parliament argued that the program was an enormous waste of money because efforts to "civilize Indians" were inevitably doomed to failure.[5] Government defenders of the program argued that the essential problem lay with Aboriginal people, who were "idlers by nature, and uncivilized." In the opinion of Prime Minister Macdonald, they were not suited to agriculture, as they "have not the ox-like quality of the Anglo-Saxon; they will not put their neck to the yoke."[6]

There were many vocal critics of the home farm program in the Northwest as well. Non-Aboriginal residents viewed the program as unfair, because too much was being done to equip Aboriginal people to farm, more than was available to the true "homesteaders," upon whom it was felt the prosperity of the region depended. The home farm program ingrained the idea that Aboriginal farmers were being lavishly provided with farm equipment and other assistance that was "conducive to the destruction of self-reliance, and calculated to give them a false impression of what the Government owed them." In the wake of the food crisis in the Northwest, the government had begun to provide modest rations to reserve residents. Indeed, some of the farm instructors found much of their time taken up issuing relief in the form of "musty and rusty" salt pork in exchange for assigned work. Many non-Native residents were critical of the distribution of rations, which they saw as a reward for idleness and as unfair because it gave Aboriginal farmers an advantage over other struggling farmers.

The home farm program had a very brief life in its original form. By 1884 the department had officially retired the policy, which had already undergone much modification. Farm instructors remained and their numbers increased, but their own farms were to consist of no more than a few acres and they were to concentrate on instruction. New recruits were no longer brought from Ontario at great expense, but were men from the Northwest.

THE PIONEER EXPERIENCE: AGRICULTURE IN THE 1880s

All who attempted farming on the Plains in the 1880s experienced frustration and failure. Crops during this decade were damaged year after year by drought and early frosts. Prairie fires became a serious hazard, consuming haystacks as well as houses, stables, and fences, and hampering the abilities of farmers not only to winter cattle, but also to carry out the whole cycle of farming operations. There was a high rate of homestead cancellation, and many of the community experiments of ethnic, religious, working-class, and aristocratic groups did not survive the decade.

A major difference between the Aboriginal farmer and his neighbours was that while newcomers had the option to leave and try their luck elsewhere, reserve residents had little choice but to persevere, as under the Indian Act they were excluded from taking homesteads. Aboriginal farmers could not obtain loans because they were not regarded as the actual owners of any property, however extensive and valuable their improvements might be, and they had difficulty obtaining credit from merchants. Because of many of the technicalities and prohibitions of the Indian Act, Natives were prevented from doing business or transacting even the most ordinary daily affair. They were deprived of the right to do what they chose with nearly everything they acquired by their own personal industry. People who came under the Indian Act were prevented by a permit system from selling, exchanging, bartering, or giving away any produce grown on their reserves without the permission of department officials. A pass system, imposed initially during the 1885 Rebellion but continued well into the 20th century, controlled and confined the movements of people off their reserves. Those who wished to leave the reserve were obliged to acquire a pass from the farm instructor or Indian agent declaring the length of and reason for absence. The most recent arrivals to the country had far more rights, privileges, and freedom than the original inhabitants.

Despite these restrictions and the drought, frost, and prairie fires of these years, reserve farmers in some localities made significant advances in the 1880s. Several of the problems that had hampered reserve farming in the past had to some extent been ameliorated. Through a "cattle on loan" policy, for example, many bands had considerably increased their numbers of work oxen, cows, steers, heifers, and bulls.

FIGURE 15.2

Native farmers, *c.* 1906–10. (Courtesy Archives of Manitoba, Edmund Morris Collection, GII-510)

Under this system the department "loaned" a cow to an individual who was to raise a heifer, either of which had to be returned to the Indian agent. The animal became the property of the individual, although the agent's permission was required to sell or slaughter. Reserve farmers also had increased access to grist mills in the 1880s as the department initiated a program of granting bonuses to individuals who would establish mills in the Northwest. Recipients of the bonus were obliged to charge Aboriginal customers a little less than ordinary customers for a 10-year period. The department also displayed greater concern to supply the services of blacksmiths, which bolstered agricultural operations.

Reserve farmers began to acquire some of the up-to-date machinery necessary to facilitate their operations. Mowers and rakes were the most common purchases. Some reserves were fortunate in their abundant hay supplies, and a number of bands sold hay on contract to other reserves, to settlers, and to the North-West Mounted Police. Selling hay was one of the very few opportunities for outside employment available to reserve residents. These machines were purchased with their own earnings or through pooled annuities. They were not purchased for them by the department. Agents and farm instructors in the 1880s felt that access to mowers and rakes was essential for all bands, not only those that sold hay. As stock increased on the reserves, mowers and rakes were necessary to provide enough hay. Reapers and self-binders were also acquired during this period. The self-binder lessened the danger of being caught by frost during a protracted harvest and it also reduced the waste experienced in binding with short straw. Such machinery permitted farmers to cultivate larger areas. By the late 1880s on some reserves in the districts of Treaty No. 4 and Treaty No. 6, farmers were beginning to see some significant results of their labour, and they had produce that they wished to sell: predominantly cattle, grain, and hay.

Like other prairie women of this period, Aboriginal women helped in the fields during peak seasons such as haying and harvest, but otherwise the business of grain farming was predominantly a male activity. Women continued to harvest wild resources such as berries, wild rhubarb, prairie turnip, and birch sap, and they hunted rabbits, gophers, and ducks. Because of increased settlement, the pass system, and calls for the restriction of Aboriginal hunting rights, these opportunities became increasingly constricted. Aboriginal women were eager to learn new skills and to adopt new technology By the late 1880s the wives of many farm instructors acquired the title of "instructress" and they, as well as the wives of missionaries, taught skills such as milking, butter-making, bread-making, and knitting. Women adapted readily to these activities, but a chronic shortage of raw materials made it difficult to apply what they had learned. While the women knew how to make loaf bread, for example, they did not have the proper ovens, yeast, or baking tins, so they continued to make bannock, despite government attempts to abolish it from the diet as it required more flour than loaf bread. They seldom had yarn with which to knit. There were no buttons for the dresses the women made. They were often short of milk pans, although they made their own using birchbark. One instructress reported in 1891 that the greatest drawback was "their extreme poverty, their lack of almost every article of domestic comfort in their houses, and no material to work upon."[7] They lacked basic necessities such as soap, towels, wash basins, and wash pails, and had no means with which to acquire these.

The log dwellings on reserves in this era and well into the 20th century were invariably described as "huts" or "shacks" that were one storey and one room. The roofs were constructed with logs or poles over which rows of straw or grass were laid. They were chinked inside and out with a mixture of mud and hay, and had clay stoves but no flooring, and tanned hide was used for window covering. It was impossible to apply lessons of "housewifery" in such shacks. In publications of the Department of Indian Affairs, however, Aboriginal women were often depicted as poor housekeepers who willfully ignored instruction in modern methods. They were blamed for the poor living and health conditions on the reserves. Explanations

that stressed the incapacity of Aboriginal women to change, like those that disparaged the farming abilities of the men, absolved the government of any responsibility for the poverty of the reserves.

THE PRESSURE OF COMPETITION

As Aboriginal farmers acquired the technology required by western conditions and
began to increase their acreages and their herds, they also began to pose a threat as
competitors in the marketplace. By the late 1880s, farmers in parts of the Northwest
were complaining loudly about "unfair" competition from Aboriginal people. It
was widely believed that government assistance gave Aboriginal farmers an unfair
advantage. Non-Aboriginal settlers had the misconception that reserve farmers
were lavishly provided with livestock, equipment, government labour, and rations,
and did not have to worry about the price at which their products were sold. There
was absolutely no appreciation of the disadvantages they laboured under, or of how
government regulation and Canadian laws acted to stymie their efforts. Editorials
in the *Fort Macleod Gazette* regularly lamented "Indian competition," which was
injuring the "true" settlers of the country. If the Siksika (Blackfoot), Kainai (Blood),
Pikuni (Peigan), and Tsuu T'ina (Sarcee) were "cut loose" from the treaty, support
could be given to their industries, according to the *Gazette,* but it was "pretty hard
to ask the people of the country to contribute toward the support of a lot of idle
paupers, and then allow them to use this very support for the purpose of taking
the bread out of the settlers month [sic]."[8]

It was argued in the *Gazette* throughout the 1880s and 1890s that Aboriginal
people should not be permitted to compete with the settlers in the sale of hay,
potatoes, or grain. Any evidence that they were successful in securing contracts was
used as proof that they had underbid non-Natives. There was no consideration that
their product might be superior, as was certainly the case with the hay purchased
by the North-West Mounted Police, who often noted in their reports that the best
hay was bought from reserve farmers.[9] In a letter to the editor in July 1895, one
local resident claimed that "it is altogether unfair to allow these Indians to enter
into competition with white men who, even with hard work, find it difficult to
make both ends meet and provide for their families." Evidence of unfair competition was used by the editors of the *Gazette* to bolster their larger campaign of the
later 1880s to have Aboriginal people moved to one big reserve, an "Indian territory" out of the way of the Euro-Canadian settlements. It was argued that Indian
policy had been a failure as Aboriginal people "had not made a single step toward
becoming self-supporting."[10] There was apparently no recognition of the fact that
it was impossible to become self-supporting to any degree unless they were allowed
to sell their products.

Concerns about unfair "Indian competition" were echoed in other parts of the Northwest as well. The residents of Battleford and district were particularly strident in their objections to the competition of the Plains Cree in the grain, hay, and wood markets. Here, as well as in the district of southern Alberta, there was concern that reserve residents not become successful stock-raisers as the supply of cattle to the Indian Department for rations was a vital source of revenue for many settlers. On 13 October, 1888, the editor of the *Saskatchewan Herald* of Battleford denounced any plan to "set the Indians up as cattle breeders, encouraging them to supply the beef that is now put in by white contractors."

Here, as in other districts, Aboriginal farmers were in competition with new settlers for hay land. Because of the predominantly dry years of the 1880s, hay was very scarce some seasons. Off-reserve areas where reserve farmers had customarily cut hay became the subject of heated disputes. Non-Aboriginal residents of the Battleford district successfully petitioned the Minister of the Interior in 1889 to limit the hay land available to Aboriginal farmers off the reserves, despite the fact that the Battleford agent had warned that there would be no alternative but to decrease stock on the reserves. Many influential people in the West had a direct interest in the continuation of rations and in seeing that Aboriginal people were not self-supporting. Large operations like the WE Cochrane Ranch in southern Alberta found a sizable market for their beef on the neighbouring reserves. In his correspondence to department officials he naturally objected to any reduction in rations, arguing that this meant that their lives, as well as their property and cattle operation, would be in danger.[11]

THE PEASANT FARMING POLICY, 1889-97

In 1889, Hayter Reed, Commissioner of Indian Affairs in Regina, announced that a new "approved system of farming" was to be applied to Indian reserves in western Canada. Reserve farmers were to reduce their area under cultivation to a single acre of wheat and a garden of roots and vegetables. Along with a cow or two, this would sufficiently provide for a farmer and his family. They were to use rudimentary implements alone: to broadcast seed by hand, harvest with scythes, bind by hand with straw, thresh with flails, and grind their grain with hand mills. They were to manufacture at home any items they required, such as harrows, hayforks, carts, and yokes. This policy complemented government intentions to subdivide the reserves into small holdings of 40 acres each. Publicly, the subdivision of the reserves and the peasant farming policy were justified as an approach intended to render reserve residents self-supporting. Individual tenure, it was claimed, would implant a spirit of self-reliance and individualism, thus eroding "tribalism." Hayter Reed argued that the use of labour-saving machinery might be necessary and suitable for settlers, but Indians first had to experience farming with crude and simple implements. To do otherwise defied immutable laws of evolution and would be an "unnatural leap." In Reed's view, Aboriginal people had not reached the stage at which they were in a position to compete with white settlers.[12] Another argument forwarded against the use of labour-saving machinery was that rudimentary implements afforded useful employment for all.

Clearly, however, there were other reasons for the peasant farming formula and for allotment in severalty, reasons that were understood and appreciated by non-Aboriginal settlers. The *Saskatchewan Herald* (20 August 1887) applauded the policy for the Aboriginal farmer:

> Thrown thus on himself and left to work his farm without the aid of expensive machinery, he will content himself with raising just what he needs himself, and thus, while meeting the Government's intention of becoming self-sustaining, they at the same time would come into competition with the white settler only to the extent of their own labour, and thus remove all grounds for the complaint being made in some quarters against Government aided Indians entering into competition with white settlers.

This was a policy of deliberate arrested development. The allotment of land in severalty was viewed by officials, as well as by Prime Minister Macdonald himself, as a means of defining surplus land that might be sold (Tyler, 1979: 114). Severalty would confine people within circumscribed boundaries, and their "surplus" land could be defined and sold. Arrested development was a certain means of ensuring that much reserve land would appear to be vacant and unused.

Despite the protests of Aboriginal farmers, Indian agents, farm instructors, and inspectors of the agencies, the peasant farming policy was implemented on Plains reserves beginning in 1889. Officials were not to authorize the purchase, hire, or use of any machinery. Even if people had purchased machinery before the policy was adopted, they were still to use hand implements. Farmers with larger holdings were to use the labour of others rather than revert to the use of machinery, or they were to restrict their acreages to what they could handle with hand implements alone. Officials in the field were dismayed by the policy that robbed the farmers of any potential source of revenue. They argued that the seasons in the Northwest were simply too short for the use of hand implements, which meant a loss in yield at harvest time and resulted in a much reduced supply of hay. Agent W.S. Grant of the Assiniboine Reserve protested that "the seasons in this country are too short to harvest any quantity of grain, without much waste, with only old fashioned, and hand implements to do the work with." In his view the amount of grain lost in his agency through harvesting with hand implements would be of sufficient quantity to pay for a binder in two years.[13]

Aboriginal farmers were profoundly discouraged by the new rules. It was widely reported that many refused to work with the hand implements and gave up farming altogether. One farmer from Moose Mountain declared he would let his grain stand and never plough another acre, while another gave up his oxen, his wheat, and the reserve.[14] Other aspects of the program, such as the home manufactures idea, were unrealistic and unworkable. Homemade wooden forks, for example, were simply not strong enough for loading hay, grain, or manure. Aboriginal farmers were to make their own lanterns, but agents protested that people could not look after their cattle at night without proper lanterns. At headquarters in Ottawa it proved impossible even to acquire some of the old-fashioned implements, such as hand mills, destined for the Aboriginal farmers. But Reed was not sympathetic to or moved by the objections and complaints, and he refused to give in to the "whims of Farmers and Indians." He advised that losing some of the crop or growing less grain was preferable to the use of machinery. If grain was being lost, the solution was for farmers to confine their acreage to what they could handle. Department employees were not to convene or be present at meetings with Aboriginal farmers, as this would give "an exaggerated importance" to their requests for machinery. They risked dismissal if they refused to comply with peasant farming policy.

EFFECTS OF THE RESTRICTIVE POLICY

The policy of deliberate discouragement of reserve agriculture worked well. By the mid-1890s, per capita acreage under cultivation had fallen to about half of the 1889 level, and many serious farmers had given up farming altogether. In 1899 a resident of Prince Albert, William Miller Sr., wrote to the Minister of the Interior that in passing through the Duck Lake and Carlton reserves, he noted "no less than five fields [which can] be seen from the trail now without a bushel of grain sown in them ... that previously used to be an example to the settlers around."[15] Peasant farming, severalty, and measures such as the permit system combined to undermine and atrophy agricultural development on reserves. The Canadian government acted not to promote the agriculture of the indigenous population, but to provide an optimum environment for the immigrant settler. Whatever Canada did for its "wards" was subordinate to the interests of the non-Aboriginal population. Government policy was determined by the need to maintain the viability of the immigrant community.

Aboriginal people protested policies that affected them adversely, as they had from the 1870s. They raised objections to government officials, petitioned the House of Commons, sent letters to newspapers, and visited Ottawa. But the outlets for protest were increasingly restricted. Grievances related to instructors and agents

THE PERMIT SYSTEM

Edward Ahenakew used a fictional character named "Old Keyam" to convey the Plains Cree experience of life on a prairie reserve in the early 20th century. In this passage, he describes the aggravations of the permit system that discouraged interest in farming and the cattle industry:

> This may be "kindly supervision" but it is most wretchedly humbling to many a worthy fellow to have to go, with assumed indifference, to ask or beg for a permit to sell one load of hay that he has cut himself, on his own reserve, with his own horses and implements. I say again, it may be right for some, but that is no reason why those who try to get on, and who do get on should have to undergo this humiliation....
>
> For myself, I think that I would rather starve than go to beg for such a trifling thing as a permit to sell one load of hay, while I am trying to make every hour of good weather count. To sell ten loads might be different. From the standpoint of the Government it may seem good, a kind of drill or discipline. But who on earth wants this when he is busy, in a hurry, and needs food for himself? I have seen with my own eyes, Indians wasting a day, even two days, trying to get a permit to sell, when they are short of food. The Agent cannot always be at home, the clerk may be away, or busy, and the Indian must wait though he may have to drive to the Agency from another reserve....
>
> As for our cattle—there again, they are not ours. A white man, owning cattle and having no ready money, draws up a plan for himself which includes selling. An Indian may have more cattle than that white man has, but do you think that he can plan in the same way? No. He is told that the commissioner has said that no cattle are to be sold until the fall. It is useless to plan under this system, yet planning is what successful work requires....
>
> Old Keyam paused to let his words sink in, and before he could continue, a young man spoke. "I have something to add to that. Sure, we all like the farm instructor. He's good-natured, teases us, doesn't mind when we tease him. Well, we were branding cattle last week, and he asked in his joking way what we thought ID [the brand of the Indian Department] meant. Old Knife was there, and he's smart. He gave quite a speech about it, said that it stood for our chief source of light in the darkness, a sort of half-moon—only the outward curve with its full true light shone towards Ottawa in the east, the other part to the west, and that it was hollow, not giving much light, and double barred at that. Whoever planned that brand, he said, knew the whole business well."
>
> —AHENAKEW (1973: 148–50)

rarely went further. Agency inspectors were, as mentioned, not allowed to hold audiences with reserve residents. The published reports of agents and inspectors were to divulge only that "which it was desired the public should believe."[16] Visiting officials such as the Governor-General, who were usually accompanied by journalists, were taken only to select agencies that would leave the best impression. Department officials, particularly those in the central office, shared the view that Aboriginal people were chronic complainers not to be believed and a people who would go to extraordinary lengths to avoid diligent work.

Hayter Reed and the peasant farming formula were disposed of the year after Wilfrid Laurier and the Liberals came to power in 1896, but the damaging legacy of the policy was to be felt for years to come. Laurier was fortunate in coming to power just at a time when a constellation of factors, including rising world wheat prices, increased rainfall on the Prairies, innovations in dry-land farming techniques, and massive immigration allowed a wheat economy to prosper in western Canada. Aboriginal farmers, however, had little place in this new age of prosperity. By the turn of the century, agriculture did not form the basis of a stable reserve economy, and after that date the likelihood faded even further as the new administrators of Indian Affairs promoted land surrenders that further limited the agricultural capacity of reserves. The fact that there was "vacant" and "idle" land on many reserves, to a great extent the result of the peasant farming years, conveniently played into the hands of those who argued that Aboriginal people had land far in excess of their needs and capabilities. Government policy was that it was in the best interests of all concerned to encourage reserve residents to divest themselves of land they held "beyond their possible requirements," and the policy received widespread support in the western press and from farmers and townspeople. Residents of towns near Indian reserves regularly submitted petitions claiming that these tracts retarded the development and progress of their districts. Such pressure resulted in the alienation of many thousands of acres of reserve land, often the best land, in the years shortly after the turn of the century. The economic viability of reserve communities was deliberately eroded by the dominant society, mainly through government policies.

CONCLUSION

In the post-treaty era to 1900, the Plains Cree were resolved to establish a new economy based on agriculture. They faced many impediments and frustrations in these efforts. Implements and livestock promised under treaty were inadequate, and government officials proved reluctant to distribute these. These officials insisted that people were to be settled on their reserves *and cultivating* in advance of their receiving the implements and cattle promised to them, although that which had been promised was necessary for cultivation. Seed grain arrived too late or in a damaged state, and wild Montana cattle were distributed instead of domestic oxen. Workers on reserves lacked proper clothing and footwear, and they were weak because of hunger and illness. Many reserves were distant from markets and transportation, and there were no milling facilities in the earliest years of reserve life.

The government attempted to address some of these problems and the food crisis in the Northwest through a "home farm" policy that was hastily devised and implemented in 1879. The plan was to have farm instructors establish model farms, raise large quantities of food for rations, and teach agriculture. It was a poorly conceived policy as these tasks were beyond the capabilities of the men appointed, most of whom had no acquaintance with Aboriginal people or with conditions in the Northwest. This policy was shelved by 1884, but farm instructors remained on many reserves, indicating an important measure of government commitment to the establishment of farming at that time, and some advances in agriculture were made in the mid- to late 1880s. But environmental conditions were grim for all farmers at that time. There were early frosts, and drought and prairie fires caused enormous damage. Aboriginal farmers laboured under particular disadvantages. Because of the prohibitions of the Indian Act, they could not expand their land base or try their luck elsewhere by taking out homesteads, and they could not take out loans or transact their own business affairs.

Despite all of the challenges of the 1880s, Plains Cree farmers in some localities made significant advances, raising a surplus for sale and acquiring necessary machinery by the end of that decade. Non-Aboriginal residents of the West expressed concern about this success and the threat of competition in the limited markets. In 1889, in response to these concerns, the government introduced a "peasant" farming policy. Reserve farmers were to cultivate no more than an acre or two using only rudimentary hand implements. The central argument of this chapter is that this policy, combined with the other disadvantages and conditions that beset Plains Cree farmers, impaired the establishment of a viable economy.

EPILOGUE

Aboriginal farmers, who lost the opportunity to participate in commercial agriculture in the 1890s, did not regain any ground in the early 20th century. Cree historians Edward Ahenakew and Joe Dion both describe a pattern in their communities of an initial interest in agriculture and stock-raising that was atrophied because of the weight of regulation and supervision. They fell further behind in technology as well as training, as they did not have access to either the formal or informal agricultural education programs of the wider farming community. The reserves remained pockets of rural poverty. Twentieth-century visitors to reserves often found Aboriginal people living in the midst of farmland that was not cultivated at all, was leased to non-Natives, or was worked with obsolete methods and technology. It was generally concluded that they were a people who had been unable to adapt to farming, who stubbornly clung to the past, and who were impervious to "progressive" influences despite years of government assistance and encouragement. The initial enthusiasm of many for agriculture and the policies of deliberate discouragement have been obscured and forgotten.

A 1966 survey of the social, educational, and economic conditions of the Aboriginal people of Canada, headed by anthropologist Harry B. Hawthorn, found that some of the most depressed reserve communities in the country were in agricultural districts of the Prairies where there appeared to be land for livestock or crops. Investigators described what few farms there were as marginal or sub-marginal, or the land was leased to neighbouring non-Aboriginal farmers, or farming had been abandoned altogether. Although in recent decades there has been some expansion of agricultural and livestock industries, many of the old obstacles remain, including some of the limitations of the Indian Act. The process of settling outstanding treaty land entitlements in Saskatchewan will eventually expand reserve holdings for economic development, but here, too, old obstacles remain. Members of the non-Aboriginal public continually question the Office of the Treaty Commissioner about the wisdom of such measures, insisting that "Prairie Indians were never farmers, only hunters and warriors. Why should they get land for farming now? They ... will only waste good farmland."[17] Such attitudes remain deeply embedded, and collective amnesia continues, as it remains important to deny that Aboriginal people could ever make proper use of such a valuable commodity as land.

NOTES

1. "North-West Territories" was the form used until 1912, when it became the present "Northwest Territories."
2. National Archives of Canada (NAC), Saskatchewan Homesteading Experiences, MG 30 C 16, vol. 3, 790.
3. *Saskatchewan Herald* (Battleford), 26 Apr. 1879.
4. NAC, RG 10, vol. 3665, file 10094, interpreter to Joseph Cauchon, 1 June 1878.
5. *House of Commons Debates,* 1884, 2: 1105 (Philipe Casgrain).
6. Ibid., 1107 (John A. Macdonald).
7. NAC, RG 10, vol. 3845, file 73406-7, T.P. Wadsworth to Hayter Reed, 17 Feb. 1891.
8. *Fort Macleod Gazette,* 16 Aug. 1887.
9. Annual Report of Commissioner L.W. Herchmer for 1889, in *The New West: Being the Official Reports to Parliament of the Activities of the Royal [sic] North-West Mounted Police Force from 1888–89* (Toronto: Coles Publishing Company, 1973), 6.
10. *Fort Macleod Gazette,* 7 Dec. 1886.
11. NAC, Hayter Reed Papers, W. F. Cochrane to L. Vankoughnet, 6 Sept. 1893, file W.F. Cochrane.
12. NAC, RG 10, vol. 3964, file 148285, Hayter Reed to A. Forget, 24 Aug. 1896.
13. Ibid., W.S. Grant to Reed, 1 Oct. 1896.
14. Ibid., J.J. Campbell to Reed, 8 Oct. 1896, and Grant to Reed, 1 Oct. 1896.
15. NAC, RG 10, vol. 3993, file 187812, William Miller Sr., to the Minister of the Interior, 21 July 1899.
16. NAC, RG 10, Deputy-Superintendent Letterbooks, vol. 1115, Reed to J. Wilson, 3 Aug. 1894.
17. Peggy Brezinski, Review of Carter, *Lost Harvests, Anthropologica* 34 (1992): 267.

REFERENCES AND RECOMMENDED READINGS

Ahenakew, Edward. 1973. *Voices of the Plains Cree,* ed. Ruth M. Buck. Toronto: McClelland & Stewart. Through his fictional character Old Keyam, Ahenakew (1885–1961) presents a vivid portrait of life on prairie reserves, especially of the crippling effects of government policies and regulations.

Anonymous. 1879. *Chronicles By the Way: A Series of Letters Addressed to the Montreal Gazette Descriptive of a Trip Through Manitoba and the North-West.* Montreal: Montreal Gazette Printing Co.

Butler, William F. 1968 [1872]. *The Great Lone Land.* Edmonton: Hurtig,

Carter, Sarah. 1999. *Aboriginal People and Colonizers of Western Canada to 1900.* Toronto: University of Toronto Press. A historiographical overview of the wealth of interdisciplinary scholarship of the last three decades on the history of the Canadian prairie West with an emphasis on the multiplicity of perspectives that exist.

———. 1990. *Lost Harvests: Prairie Indian Reserve Farmers and Government Policy.* Montreal and Kingston: McGill-Queen's University Press. An analysis of agriculture on prairie reserves from the treaties to World War I.

Christensen, Deanna. 2000. *Ahtahkakoop: The Epic Account of a Plains Cree Head Chief, His People, and Their Struggle for Survival 1816–1896.* Shell Lake, Sask.: Ahtahkakoop Publishing. A comprehensive biography of a prominent Plains Cree leader, as well as a rich account of the culture, society, and economy during an era of rapid change. There is a great deal of emphasis on reserve agriculture.

Dion, Joseph. 1979. *My Tribe the Crees,* ed. Hugh Dempsey, Calgary: Glenbow-Alberta Institute. An account of the early years of settlement at Onion Lake and Kehiwin.

Dyck, Noel. 1991. *What is the Indian 'Problem?': Tutelage and Resistance in Canadian Indian Administration.* St John's: Institute of Social and Economic Research, Social and Economic Studies No. 46. A critical examination of past and present relations between Aboriginal people and governments in Canada, with emphasis on prairie Canada.

Elias, Peter Douglas. 1988. *The Dakota of the Canadian Northwest: Lessons for Survival.* Winnipeg: University of Manitoba Press. A detailed analysis of the different economic strategies adopted by the Dakota, including the farming bands at Oak River, Birdtail, Oak Lake, Standing Buffalo, and White Cap.

Hawthorn, H.B., ed. 1966. A *Survey of Contemporary Indians of Canada: Economic, Political, Educational Needs and Policies.* Ottawa: Indian Affairs Branch.

Lux, Maureen. 2001. *Medicine That Walks: Disease, Medicine and Canadian Plains Native People, 1880–1940.* Toronto: University of Toronto Press. An account of the diseases that afflicted Aboriginal people, which along with poverty, malnutrition, and overcrowding, dramatically reduced their numbers. Lux analyzes how non-Aboriginal specialists theorized the impact of these diseases and also explores the persistence of Aboriginal healing practices.

Milloy, John S. 1988. *The Plains Cree: Trade, Diplomacy and War, 1790–1870.* Winnipeg: University of Manitoba Press. An analysis of the complex trade and military patterns of the branch of the Cree that became a Plains people. Milloy argues that the Plains Cree culture flourished in the era to 1870 and was not undermined by their contact with European fur traders.

Putt, Neal. 1991. *Place Where the Spirit Lives: Stories from the Archaeology and History of Manitoba.* Winnipeg: Pemmican.

Ray, Arthur J. 1974. *Indians in the Fur Trade: Their Role as Hunters, Trappers, and Middlemen in the Lands Southwest of Hudson Bay, 1660–1870.* Toronto: University of Toronto Press. The first and most significant revision of fur trade history, placing the emphasis on the role of Aboriginal people. Ray explored how the Cree and Assiniboine were involved, the extent to which they shaped the trade, and the effects of the fur trade on these societies.

Sluman, Norma, and Jean Goodwill. 1982. *John Tootoosis: Biography of a Cree Leader.* Ottawa: Golden Dog Press. Tootoosis, from Poundmaker Reserve in Saskatchewan, gives an account of the obstacles facing reserve farmers, of government efforts to effect land surrenders, and strategies adopted to circumvent them.

Titley, E. Brian. 1997. "Unsteady Debut: J.A.N. Provencher and the Beginnings of Indian Administration in Manitoba," *Prairie Forum* 22, 1: 21–46.

Tobias, John L. 1983. "Canada's Subjugation of the Plains Cree, 1879–1885," *Canadian Historical Review* 64, 3: 519–48. An important revisionist analysis of Plains Cree actions and strategies in the immediate post-treaty years.

Tyler, Kenneth J. 1979. "A Tax-Eating Proposition: The History of the Passpasschase Indian Reserve," MA thesis, University of Alberta.

Van Kirk, Sylvia. 1980. *"Many Tender Ties": Women in Fur Trade Society in Western Canada, 1670–1870.* Winnipeg: Watson and Dwyer.

SUGGESTED WEBSITES

Annual Reports of the Department of Indian Affairs
www.collectionscanada.ca/indianaffairs/index-e.html
The complete annual reports for the years 1864–1990.

National Aboriginal Document Database
http://collections.ic.gc.ca/aboriginaldocs/
A vast array of online documents including treaties, statutes, court decisions, and government policies.

CRITICAL-THINKING QUESTIONS

CHAPTER 11 *by Stuart Hall*

1. According to Hall, what is a discourse and what is its importance?
2. What does Hall mean by the phrase "a regime of truth"?
3. What, for Hall, is the relationship between discourse and power?

CHAPTER 12 *by Audra Simpson*

1. What does Simpson mean by the term "lived nationhood"?
2. How does indigenous nationhood differ from that practiced by settler society?
3. What does it mean to suggest that indigenous nationhood takes place in the "seams" of colonialism?

CHAPTER 13 *by Chris Cunneen*

1. According to Cunneen, what conventional explanations are used to make sense of the over-representation of indigenous people in the Australian criminal justice system?
2. Why does Cunneen suggest that these explanations are simplistic, and what explanation does he offer instead?
3. What evidence does Cunneen give to support his argument?

CHAPTER 14 *by Matthew Restall*

1. What is the "myth of extinction"?
2. According to Restall, why was the myth of extinction central to early writings on encounters between indigenous and settler societies?
3. What alternative explanation does Restall offer about what happened following these initial encounters?

CHAPTER 15 *by Sarah A. Carter*

1. What does Carter suggest is a dominant argument for explaining the agricultural failure of Cree farmers?
2. How do the policies that Carter examines complicate the story about this failure?
3. How were dominant racial discourses about the inherent inferiority of "Indians" encoded in government policy towards indigenous farmers?

FURTHER READING

Francis, Daniel. 1992. *The Imaginary Indian: The Image of the Indian in Canadian Culture.* Vancouver: Arsenal Pulp Press.

Using a wide array of popular cultural icons including paintings, travel writings and fictional accounts, Daniel Francis explores the ways in which the image of "the Indian" was constructed and entrenched in the consciousness of 19th-century Anglo-Canadians. Francis persuasively argues that much of 19th-century consciousness about "the Indian" was based in erroneous (though widely held) assumptions about the eventual extinction of the "Indian race."

Hall, Stuart. 1997. "The Spectacle of the 'Other.'" *Representations: Cultural Representations and Signifying Practices.* Thousand Oaks: SAGE.

In this lengthy but well-crafted article, Stuart Hall explores a number of issues related to the creation and maintenance of stereotypes in contemporary liberal democratic societies. Of particular interest is Hall's wide-ranging discussion of the ways stereotypes are created, the social conditions under which they are maintained, and their damaging effects.

Woodward, Karen, ed. 1997. *Identity and Difference.* Thousand Oaks: SAGE.

What are identities and how are they constructed? How stable are they and why do they remain (or not) in particular social contexts? The questions at the heart of this text are crucial for Indigenous Peoples across the globe, especially those who are now "integrated" into liberal nation-states. This text provides a strong theoretical background while discussing various social contexts within which identity politics and the contestation of identities take place.

Ray, Arthur. 2005. *I Have Lived Here Since the World Began: An Illustrated History of Canada's Native People.* Toronto: Key Porter Books.

In his elegantly written text on the Native history of Canada (and before), Arthur Ray exposes Canada's pretensions of benevolence and goodwill towards Aboriginal people for what they are—social constructs. He convincingly shows how the pace of Canadian colonial expansion was fitted into larger economic plans, and how these plans had a devastating impact on indigenous societies.

PART IV:

THE INDIGENOUS STRUGGLE

AND THE POLITICS OF INDIGENEITY

ℰ⅏

I F   T H E   "I N D I G E N O U S   E X P E R I E N C E" has been framed by colonization, Indigenous Peoples today devote much of their energy to the struggle to shake off the legacies of this social context. As quoted in the Introduction to this book, Jose Martinez Cobo states that indigenous communities, peoples, and nations "are determined to preserve, develop and transmit to future generations their ancestral territories, and their ethnic identity, as the basis of their continued existence as peoples, in accordance with their own cultural patterns, social institutions and legal systems."

Indigenous Peoples are determined not simply to survive, but also to prosper and to see their cultures and societies grow and flourish on their own terms. This political and social ideal is in tension with the ever-present alternative of assimilation posed by the forces of colonization and globalization. The core of the indigenous struggle is not simply freedom from oppression and poverty, but the right to progress as peoples on their own terms. The struggle focuses on land, political rights, economic parity, and the recognition and preservation of their cultural institutions. Indigenous struggles take many forms, and the focal point of each varies according to its circumstances.

The readings in this section demonstrate that indigenous resistance has many faces and many facets, as well as a number of common characteristics. One of the most common characteristics, brought to our attention by Trond Theun in his article on the Saami of Norway, is the obligation of indigenous people to continually explain themselves to outsiders. Be they sympathetic observers or opponents to the indigenous cause, outsiders feel the need to pose the "who," "how," and "why" questions. Before they can make any headway in their pursuit of justice and equity, Indigenous Peoples are obliged to explain who they are, and why their rights as distinctive peoples should be acknowledged . In addition, indigenous people must explain the politicization of their collective identity as peoples. Theun observes that the Saami had a clear sense of their peoplehood as far back as 1862, and Ronald Niezen takes this discussion further in his section on the difference between People and Peoples.

Another characteristic of the struggle that faces indigenous people is the tension between advancement as a pan-indigenous national group and advancement as separate regional, linguistic, or ethnic groups. This tension is illustrated in Theun's discussion on peoplehood for the Saami, and is implied in Joe Sawchuk's description of the complex Canadian constitutional system of categorizing their indigenous peoples. The Sawchuk reading also offers an important insight into the evolution of political organization and the politics of representation within an indigenous people. This evolution represents an ongoing challenge as indigenous people are obliged to deal with the apparatus of the state, while their traditional forms of political representation have been severely eroded, if not totally destroyed, by the ravages of colonization.

The themes of political representation and power carry through into the other readings. Offering a very indigenous perspective, Gerald Taiaiake Alfred argues that as sovereignty implies dominance over people and the environment, it is an inappropriate vehicle for indigenous advancement. He calls on Indigenous Peoples to seek solutions from within their own traditional structures and to find new and innovative expressions of indigenous self-determination, ways that respect the rights of individuals. Neizen also considers sovereignty, and finds a tension between social advancement as traditional collectivities and the rights of the individual. Like most of the other authors, he concludes that Indigenous Peoples are seeking not succession, but rather the right to self-determining autonomy within the state.

Using examples from a variety of Indigenous Peoples from Australia, Canada, Mexico, New Zealand and Nigeria, Anthony J. Hall addresses the indigenous struggle in global terms. This reading reminds us that the other part of the indigenous struggle is the actions and reactions of governments and of the general populations. People in liberal democracies are beginning to understand the need to face their colonial past and its impact on the indigenous citizens of their country. Having examined the situations in Canada and Aotearoa New Zealand, Roger Maaka and Augie Fleras take this line of thinking beyond simply recognizing the problems of the past; they promote a notion of "constructive engagement," which entails creating a new social contract between nation-states and their Indigenous Peoples.

The indigenous experience can be summarized as the struggle to have national societies decolonized so that indigenous people are able to come in from the periphery of national life, where they are most often considered social pariahs and a tax burden, in order to become fully functional and productive citizens without having to assimilate.

CHAPTER 16

IMAGINING CIVILIZATION ON THE FRONTIERS OF ABORIGINALITY

Anthony J. Hall

> In the world of the mighty only the great and their servants fit. In the world we want we all fit. The world we want is one where many worlds fit.
>
> FOURTH DECLARATION OF THE SOUTHERN LIBERATION ARMY,
> EMILIANO ZAPATA, 1996

INDIGENOUS PEOPLES ON THE GLOBAL FRONTIERS OF ACTIVISM AND IMAGINATION

IN THE SPRING OF 2000, about a quarter of a million Australians converged on Sydney to create the country's largest demonstration ever. At the symbolic heart of the event was the walk across the Harbour Bridge. There, at the mid-point, the Australian national flag flew alongside the black, red, and yellow Aboriginal flag. As the walkers passed by, they reflected on the goal of achieving reconciliation between the country's non-Aboriginal majority and the country's half-million Indigenous peoples. Overhead, a skywriter printed "SORRY" from the white vapour flowing from behind his small plane.[1]

The scope of the demonstration illustrated how the issues at its core had captured the attention and energies of a significant proportion of Australia's population. What had begun in 1991 with the establishment by the Australian parliament of the Council of Aboriginal Reconciliation had moved well beyond the confines of government and its attending academic and technocratic agencies. Instead, the challenge of reconciliation with Australia's First Nations has become a matter that has stimulated a diverse range of groups and individuals who have effectively begun to reinvent the Australian nation by grappling with its oldest, most profound, and most notoriously neglected human-rights issue.

As Australians addressed the current legacies of the crimes against humanity that were integral to the country's historical genesis, many fresh perspectives on the future presented themselves to Australia's national imagination. One of the key animators and chroniclers of this process has been Henry Reynolds, a historian whose treatises on the history of Aboriginal policy proved instrumental in persuading the High Court to recognize the existence of Aboriginal title in Australia's *Mabo* ruling of 1992.[2] In recounting his own experience in some of the hundreds of community meetings that led to the mass passage across the Sydney Harbour Bridge, Reynolds wrote,

> Almost everywhere I have been, no matter how large or small the community, whether the meeting was at lunchtime or at night, on almost every occasion I was impressed by the size of the audience. But there was something else about the audiences and that was their deep concern, their intensity, their obvious concentration on the subject, their clear sense that this was an important thing they were involved in. The significant thing is that the reconciliation process has spread right across Australia. It is no longer just a movement of educated middle-class people. It is no longer just an urban movement. There are reconciliation groups all across the country.
>
> These groups are doing many interesting things. They are meeting together with local Indigenous people. The degree of Indigenous participation varies widely, but in some places it is very substantial. In communities right across Australia, there are people meeting, thinking, researching, talking and coming up quite often with extremely interesting and creative proposals to try and reach reconciliation there in their own communities.[3]

The intensity of activism and debate on the place of the First Nations was an essential element of a many-faceted quest to fashion a decolonized identity for Australia that transcended the mean narrowness of its white supremist origins. This contemporary quest for a national identity has included intense contestation over the role of the monarchy in a revised constitution. The movement to transform the Australian Constitution and the movement aimed at reconciliation with Indigenous peoples were clearly approaching the same kind of convergence that made Aboriginal and treaty rights a major factor in the patriation of the Canadian Constitution in 1982.

The timing of the Harbour Bridge demonstration came on the eve of the Sydney Olympics and on the cusp of the country's centennial celebrations of the creation of the Australian federation in 1901. Clearly the mood was propitious for some kind of sweeping declaration of national purpose, looking both forward and backward at the country's defining and most fundamental relationships. The reconciliation movement presented an ideal opening to announce that Australia was entering the third millennium with the confidence to face even the darkest chapters of its own history as a necessary condition of genuine maturation and renewal. "If achieved," announced Senator Aden Ridgeway, a Gumbayyngirr Aboriginal from New South Wales, "reconciliation can become a crucial factor in giving the gift of national social cohesion."[4] Australia's quest for a more pluralistic form of self-determination through the elaboration of a more edifying range of relations with the country's First Nations gives recent expression to a very old process in the history of Western civilization.[5] Again and again, Indigenous peoples have figured prominently in the labours and imaginative endeavours of those whose goal has been to expand the frontiers of old civilizations or to invent new ones in the New World.

A key to understanding Australia's quest to grow out of the most racist aspects of its colonial heritage involves the legal and philosophical rejection of the doctrine of *terra nullius* as the basis of the country's system of apportioning land tenure and jurisdiction. Australia was not empty at the time of its incorporation into the British Empire, and the land was the home of an extremely diverse range of peoples. The pluralism of these peoples was reflected in the existence of approximately 600 dialects spread out over 270 languages at the time when European expansion drew Australia into the process of globalization at the end of the 18th century. The vast majority of Australia's Indigenous languages have gone silent in the course of colonization. Among those twenty or so languages that remain vital are Pitjantjatjari, Yolngu, Bundjalung, and Kaurna, all of which have been incorporated into the country's curricula of higher education.[6]

A strike in 1966 by Aboriginal workers in Australia's Northern Territory proved to be pivotal in casting the first rays of national doubt on the doctrine of *terra nullius*. That strike was led by the Gurindji sage Vincent Lingiari. With Lingiari as their spokesman, Gurindji workers in the expansive ranching operations owned by Lord Vestey withdrew their labour. While the dispute with the employer began over issues of pay and work conditions, Lingiari asserted the existence of an unceded Aboriginal title to the ancestral lands of the Gurindji people. This stand resonated with many groups and individuals throughout Australia. It does so still. The activism led to a referendum that theoretically opened the door of Australian citizenship for the first time to the country's Indigenous peoples.[7]

The idea of the existence of an Aboriginal title in the lands of Australia has slowly percolated into political and juridical thinking about the country's constitutional character.[8] In 1988, the year of Australia's Bicentennary, the Labor government of Prime Minister Bob Hawke broke what has sometimes been referred to as "the great Australian silence." He raised and quickly abandoned the idea of a new treaty with Indigenous peoples. This initiative followed a brief but intense effort on the part of the Labor Party to incorporate what it called "Aboriginal self-determination" into Australia's governmental system. Between 1983 and 1985, the National Aboriginal Conference, a body of elected Aboriginal representatives, was elevated to a more instrumental role in directing the process of policy formation in the Ministry of Aboriginal Affairs.[9]

The High Court of Australia dramatically increased the pressure for some kind of fundamental reckoning with the country's Indigenous peoples with two rulings in 1992 and 1996. Both unequivocally overturned the old doctrine of *terra nullius*. The *Mabo* decision and the more recent *Wik* decision rejected the principle that Australia was an empty land when Captain Cook first arrived. The *Mabo* ruling represented one of the most cathartic and powerful statements to emerge from the 500th anniversary of 1492. Much as in the Nisga'a ruling of Canada's Supreme Court in 1973, Australia's top judges essentially pointed the political wing of government at the need to initiate negotiations with Indigenous peoples on the issue of land title. In the *Mabo* ruling, this appeal was made in language that went beyond technicalities to identify the extent of the moral cancer that had gripped the soul of Australia from the time of its founding.

The High Court made it clear that it was dealing with nothing less than "the assessment of the legitimacy of the propositions that the continent was unoccupied for legal purposes and that the unqualified legal and beneficial ownership of all the lands of the continent were vested in the Crown." The magnitude of what was at stake justified them, the judges argued, in the use of "unrestrained language." The ruling described "the conflagration of oppression and conflict" that "spread across the continent to dispossess, degrade and devastate the Aboriginal peoples and leave a national legacy of unutterable shame." The exploitation of the doctrine of *terra nullius* to justify the unilateral dispossession of Indigenous peoples constituted "the darkest aspect of the history of this nation." And, the court judges added, "the nation as a whole must remain diminished unless and until there is an acknowledgement of and retreat from, those past injustices."[10]

The evocative court ruling made Aboriginal rights by far the most polarizing issue in the political culture of Australia. The decision of the High Court was initially embraced by the Labor government of Australian prime minister Paul Keating. In moving towards the enactment in 1993 of the Native Title Act to bring Australian legislation into more comfortable conformity with the High Court's jurisprudence, Keating characterized the *Mabo* ruling as a "practical building block of change." He added, "by doing away with the bizarre conceit that this continent had no owners prior to the settlement of Europeans, *Mabo* establishes a fundamental truth and lays the basis for justice."[11]

Those supporting some sort of fundamental reconciliation with Australia's First Nations organized themselves in groups such as Women for Wik or Wik Ed. By 1998, observers were noting that the debate in and around the work of the Council of Aboriginal Reconciliation had generated "the largest people's movement since the Vietnam War."[12] The mobilization of popular will in defence of Aboriginal rights drew particularly from the shocking details outlined in a report on *Stolen Generation Aborigines* released in 1997 by the Australian Human Rights and Equal Opportunity Commission. That report chronicled how, until the 1970s, many Aboriginal children were seized from their families and subjected to all kinds of abuse in the name of the country's assimilationist policies. Many young Aborigines were fostered out and used essentially as slave labour or even as sex slaves by their overseers.[13] Australia's governor-general, Sir William Deane, issued a formal apology to the country's Indigenous peoples for the wrongdoing exposed in *Stolen Generation*[14]—an apology backed by hundreds of thousands of Australian citizens' signatures in what were dubbed the "Sorry Books."

The movement to reshape Australia's identity through the embrace, rather than the negation, of Aboriginal rights drew vitality from many sources. First among these was the Koori Renaissance, led by a number of gifted Aboriginal artists, activists, and educators including Kevin Gilbert, Noel Pearson, Faith Bandler, Geraldine Briggs, Rob Riley, and Galarrway Yunupingu.[15] Their efforts were supported and complemented by a host of non-Aboriginal academics and journalists who added to the literary depth and scope of the reconciliation movement. For instance, John Pilger, an Australian filmmaker and investigative journalist based in London, did much to widen appreciation of the international implications of the struggle to realize the rights and titles of Aboriginal peoples in Australia.[16]

The proponents of reconciliation in Australia advanced contemporary variations on a number of themes that have long formed a significant, if subordinate, text in the saga of European colonization. This subtext was historically advanced by organizations such as the British-based Aborigines' Protection Society. The more recent interventions in Australia helped to energize the response of some whose position on Aboriginal rights lay squarely within the ongoing continuum of imperial expansion as it has dominated global history since at least 1492. The reactionary power of these unbroken imperial patterns was realized in the election in 1996 of the government of Prime Minister John Howard. That government represented the fullest application to Australia of the neo-liberal policies of Margaret Thatcher and Ronald Reagan.

One of the first acts of the new Howard regime was to cut $400 million from the Aboriginal Affairs budget. Condemning what he referred to as "the guilt industry," Howard dramatized the government's policy shift away from the Keating legacy by refusing to add his own initials to the hundreds of thousands of signatures collected in the Sorry Books.[17]

Howard's Aboriginal policies drew on the right-wing populism of Pauline Hanson and her One Nation Party as well as on the writings of historian Geoffrey Blainey. Hanson came to political prominence in the Australian state of Queensland by co-opting the language of individual equality to oppose what her campaign literature referred to as "immigrationism, multi-culturalism, Asianisation and Aboriginalism (romantic primitivism)." All these trends, Hanson alleged, "ultimately divided and weakened the unified cohesion of the Australian nation.[18] Social scientist Geoffrey

Blainey reinforced this perspective by referring derisively to the writings of Henry Reynolds and John Pilger, for instance, as "black armband history."[19]

Incorporating the provocative language of Hanson and Blainey in justifying government policy, the Howard government bent before the pressure exerted by several powerful lobbies, but especially that of the Australian mining industry. In 1998, the Howard government enacted a series of amendments to the Native Title Act of 1993. These amendments all had the effect of undermining the bargaining position of Aboriginal groups and strengthening the hand of all parties who derived many of their entitlements to the minerals, waters, and pastoral lands of Australia from the state governments. These controversial modifications of the country's fundamental laws attracted severe condemnations from a number of sources, including Australia's Law Reform Commission and the United Nations Committee on the Elimination of Racial Discrimination. These bodies were among the most prominent proponents of the position that the Howard government's amendments to the Native Title Act violated Australia's Racial Discrimination Act. The passing of the Racial Discrimination Act in 1975 signalled Australia's adhesion to the International Convention on the Elimination of All Forms of Racial Discrimination.

The rising influence in Australia of right-wing fringe groups such as Hanson's One Nation Party foreshadowed the growth of xenophobic nationalism throughout many countries in the West. In France, for instance, this phenomenon found expression in the ascent to political prominence of Jean-Marie Le Pen. In Canada this tendency was embodied in the mid-1990s in the emergence of the Reform Party from the resource-rich western provinces. The Reform Party was subsequently renamed the Alliance Party. Like their fellow right-wing populists in Australia, members of Canada's Reform Party advocated the invocation of parliamentary supremacy to negate judicial recognition of Aboriginal title.[20] In the spring of 2002, the Alliance party worked closely with the government of Canada's westernmost province to implement a modified application of the scheme to extinguish Aboriginal rights by mobilizing the electoral force of a non-Aboriginal majority. Citing the imperatives of "direct democracy," Canada's right-wing politicians collaborated in organizing a provincial referendum whose object was to create a legal and political mandate intended to narrow the jurisdictional scope of treaty negotiations with the Indigenous peoples in British Columbia.[21]

Most of the proponents of the referendum in British Columbia hoped to reverse the outcome of the Supreme Court of Canada's *Delgamuukw* ruling in 1997. That decision gave greater clarity to the Supreme Court's earlier ruling on the Nisga'a case in 1973, one that seminally identified the existence of an unextinguished Indian title in most of British Columbia. The *Mabo* and the *Delgamuukw* rulings can be conceptualized as two manifestations of the same inconsistencies in the application of crown law to the colonization of Indigenous peoples' lands in many regions of the British Commonwealth.

As I see it, the mass march in Sydney during the spring of 2000 represented one of many significant rituals in the worldwide movement emphasizing the need for major initiatives, both domestically and internationally, to reverse the destructive course of the ongoing Columbia conquests through various forms of reconciliation with Indigenous peoples. Another major ceremony in this same process took place in Mexico City a year later, as the leaders of the Zapatista Liberation Army left their strongholds in the Mayan highlands of Chiapas.

The Zapatistas had first gained international prominence when these Indian freedom fighters timed their initial brief assertion of armed control over several centres in Chiapas to coincide with the inauguration in 1994 of the North American Free Trade Agreement. With this founding act, one soon reinforced by a pioneering mobilization of the communications potential of the Internet and of home computers, the Zapatistas initiated an unorthodox campaign for political change that was simultaneously locally rooted and globally oriented.

In moving towards the centre of Mexico's political process in the spring of 2001, the Zapatistas renewed and elaborated in a different context many of the same themes of social justice publicized a year earlier by the quarter-million marchers on Sydney Harbour Bridge. The leaders of this procession sought to broaden the base of *Zapatismo* in Mexico and globally through a dramatic movement over a 3,500-kilometre route, culminating in a mass gathering at the Zócalo Plaza. This central ceremonial place can be envisaged as the site where the imperial regime of New Spain and the new Mexico meet the old capital of Mesoamerica—namely the Aztec metropolis of Tenochitlan, which lies beneath modern-day Mexico City. The Zapatistas characterized their triumphant arrival in Zócalo Plaza as the first entry of a rebel group onto this sacred site since Pancho Villa and Emiliano Zapata arrived in 1914 to participate in the revolutionary transformation of a Mexico traumatized by US military intervention at Veracruz earlier that year.

In claiming to represent the true heritage of Emiliano Zapata and the Mexican Revolution, the Zapatistas aroused a huge fascination over a surprisingly wide spectrum of world public opinion. As illustrated by the geographic distribution of over 45,000 Zapatista-related websites, Zapatista cells and support groups proliferated, especially in the urban centres of Europe and North America. The international celebrity of some of those who greeted the Zapatista leadership in their dramatic entry in Zócalo Plaza attests to the exuberant hopes attached to a movement that first caught root among the Mayan peasantry of southern Mexico. Among those in attendance were American film icons Robert Redford and Oliver Stone. Also present were Spain's most prominent writer, Manuel Vasquez Montalban, and Portugal's Nobel Prize-winning author, Jose Saramago.[22] "I have to be in Mexico City on March 11," declared Canada's Naomi Klein, author of a bestselling text condemning neo-liberal globalization.[23] "It's like Martin Luther King Jr.'s March on Washington."[24]

How did the Zapatistas transform their stand from an armed resistance in an obscure corner of Mexico into a genuinely transnational intellectual movement aimed at global transformation? Certainly timing was a key factor. Their uprising came at a moment when the globalization of a particularly unrestrained form of corporate capitalism seemed so invincible that Fukuyama and others were triumphantly proclaiming a virtual end to history. The Zapatistas provided intellectual asylum and a big, many-coloured ideological tent for a diverse array of thinkers and activists desperate to explore viable alternatives to a universal regime of unfettered corporate rule. This refuge for neo-liberalism's dissenters was placed squarely in the context of the world's oldest, most pervasive, and most multicultural resistance movement. The basis of this resistance is the ongoing struggle against the continuing conquest of Aboriginal lands and Indigenous peoples that began in 1492, when Europe first christened the Americas as a New World and as its primary frontier of colonial expansion.

In seeking to justify his own participation in the rise of *Zapatismo* in North America, the prominent Californian activist and politician Tom Hayden explained that the movement "suggested we could reclaim the indigenous roots that lie mangled beneath the architecture of our modern selves." He added, "We of the North were invited, challenged, to do our part in resisting a Conquest 500 years old."[25]

The attraction of the Zapatistas was closely connected to the mystique generated by the movement's main spokesperson, a masked figure identified to the world simply as Subcommandante Marcos. In the sketchy outlines of his publicized biography, the story is told of how he first came to the jungles and mountains of Chiapas to enlist the Indians in Marxist class struggle. Instead of indoctrinating the Mayans, it was Marcos who is said to have been assimilated into the decentralized democracy of Indian approaches to consensus building. The results of this transformation showed up following the Zapatista's initial successes in asserting their presence in Chiapas. Rather than making moves to insert their own representatives directly into Mexico's governing system, the Zapatistas, through Subcommandante Marcos's rhetorical interventions, embarked on a cultural campaign aimed at remaking the very framework of power politics. In this way, the Zapatistas were able to combine their pro-Indian stance with an agenda for change that transcended the limitations of ethnic fundamentalism and identity politics. In contributing to this feat, Marcos cunningly crafted a media image directed at knitting together a broad coalition of those shut out of neo-liberalism's narrow enclave of concentrated privilege. In elaborating this theme, the masked enigma is reported to have said,

Marcos is gay in San Francisco, black in South Africa, an Asian in Europe, a Chicano in San Ysidro, an anarchist in Spain, a Palestinian in Israel, a Mayan Indian in the streets of San Cristóbal, a Jew in Germany, a Gypsy in Poland, a Mohawk in Quebec, a pacifist in Bosnia, a single woman on the Metro at 10:00 p.m., a peasant without land, a gang member in the slums, an unemployed worker, an unhappy student, and, of course, a Zapatista in the mountains.[26]

The Zapatistas arrived in Zócalo Plaza just months after a new Mexican president, Vicente Fox, had taken office. With the election of Fox, the notoriously corrupt hold of the Party of the Institutionalized Revolution, which had monopolized the national government of Mexico for most of the 20th century, was finally broken. In his presidential campaign, Fox had vowed that he would be able to arrive at a peace settlement with the Zapatistas based on some accommodation of their assertions and claims concerning Aboriginal rights. When they entered Zócalo Plaza, Fox referred to their masked leader, saying, "Welcome Subcommandante Marcos, welcome to the Zapatistas, welcome to the political arena, the arena of the discussion of ideas." As a former president of the local branch plant of Coca-Cola, the company whose global expansion served over the course of the 20th century as an icon for the growth of the American empire as well as the export of the American way of life, President Fox embodied many of the attributes of neo-liberal globalization that had given the Zapatistas a worldwide platform to present their alternatives.

Marcos emphasized the ideological distance between the two main visions of the future that were struggling for the hearts and souls of humanity in the opening years of the 21st century. As he said of his group's governing philosophy, compared with that of Fox: "We are part of the world moving toward recognizing differences, and he [Fox] is working toward hegemony and homogenizing, not just the country, but the world."[27]

The Zapatistas sought entrenchment of major reforms in the laws, policies, and institutions of Mexico to facilitate more effective forms of Aboriginal self-governance for the Indians of Mexico. Building on significant reforms achieved by Mayan activists in Guatemala,[28] the Zapatistas made the renewal of Indian languages through pedagogical reform and ambitious schemes of Aboriginal broadcasting a priority. In an interview with Ignacio Ramonet of Le Monde, Marcos described the Zapatistas vision of Aboriginal rights:

Our principal object is that the Mexican Congress will recognize Indigenous peoples as collective subjects of law. The Constitution of Mexico doesn't now recognize Indianness. We want the state to admit that Mexico is composed of different peoples; that Indigenous people possess their own political, social and economic organizations. And that they retain a strong relationship with the land and with their community, their roots and their history ... We don't want to proclaim the birth of the Maya nation, or split up the country into a multiplicity of small Aboriginal countries. We want rather that the laws recognize an important part of Mexican society, which possesses its own form of organization and which demands that its Aboriginal characteristics be recognized.

Marcos moved easily between this agenda for Mexico and a larger critique of neo-liberal models of globalization. "To some degree," he maintained, "economic globalization signifies the globalization of the way of life in the United States." This approach to human organization, he asserted, is imposed on every facet of life. Even the proposal of an alternative is made to seem "utopian, unrealistic," and a denial of the "inevitable" course of history. Neo-liberal forms of globalization, he added, come to reign "not only in the functioning of government, but also in the media, in the school and in the family." They lead in particular to the elimination of those societies based not on mobility but on complex attachments to the local ecology of particular places. "And that concerns all the Indigenous peoples of Latin America," Marcos said. "Globalization demands their elimination."[29]

One of the explanations for the attractiveness of *Zapatismo* in Mexico lay in its renewal and elaboration of themes already well developed in nationalist discourse. The movement renewed ideals and concepts raised particularly in the 1920s by Manuel Gamio, Jose Vasconcelos, and others. Through *indigenismo* they sought to direct the course of the Mexican revolution towards the official embrace of Mexico's distinct Indian and mestizo personality in a country where a large majority of the country's citizens have some Indian ancestry.[30]

The Zapatista entry into Zócalo Plaza took place on the eve of the clash of hemispheric agendas that converged dramatically in Quebec City in April 2001. The meeting was planned to help initiate a Free Trade Area of the Americas (FTAA), which some saw as a vehicle for the entrenchment of the pan-American empire centred in the United States. In the early years of the 21st century, no less than in the 1920s, increased emphasis on Mexico's Indian character continued to represent an obvious strategy of resistance against the incursions, enticements, and absorptions of the "gringo" empire of the United States.

This pan-American empire had grown from the Old World empires of Spain, France, Holland, Russia, Portugal, and, in particular, Great Britain. The United States was the primary inheritor of the imperial missions of these powers to remake the Americas in the image of Europe and Western Civilization. The emergence of the American republic from the British Empire constituted the formation of the first and the most influential of the Creole nationalisms that had formed in the American colonies to replace European empires. The Columbian conquests found expression in these Creole nationalisms whose shared aim was to empower the transplanted European populations even as the Indian populations were, in varying degrees, shunned, persecuted, and pushed aside. They were seen as impediments to the progress of those new nation-states whose first prototype was the United States.

The secret negotiations aimed at establishing a Free Trade Area of the Americas seemingly continued a well-established pattern of New World imperialism, whose pan-American dimensions were first revealed in 1823 when the United States in its Monroe Doctrine laid claim to the entire Western Hemisphere as its exclusive domain of remote-control hegemony. While the United States embodied a potent blend of Creole decolonization and New World imperialism, the transplanted majority populations of Canada, Australia, and New Zealand gradually negotiated their transition to self-government and qualified independence within the constitutional framework of continuing crown sovereignty.

Australia has been one of the most tardy of the Commonwealth countries to address the deep legal and moral questions derived from the unextinguished existence of Aboriginal rights and titles in the ancestral lands of Indigenous peoples. New Zealand, however, evolved in a very different way.[31] For the Maori, the Indigenous peoples of that country, New Zealand has been Aotearoa since time immemmorial. In 1840 the British government sought to gain the sanction from the Maori for the transformation of New Zealand into a colony whose main role in the empire was to receive and host European settlers. These settlers would acquire the rights of local self-government in a jurisdiction that also afforded the rights and responsibilities of New Zealand citizenship to the Maori. The Treaty of Waitangi can be perceived as the founding charter on which the legal and moral legitimacy of New Zealand is ultimately grounded. This interpretation has broad implications. Like the ideas embodied in the Royal Proclamation of 1763, the role of the Waitangi Treaty in New Zealand's legal make-up raises the idea that Indigenous peoples throughout the planet have retained the constitutional power to give or withhold sanction to the empires and nation-states that have developed and evolved on their ancestral lands. A key feature of the Waitangi Treaty, which was viewed as being very enlightened in the era of its negotiation, was the extension to adult Maori males of New Zealand citizenship and, with it, the franchise in national elections. In later years this legal innovation was expressed by the creation of several seats in the New Zealand parliament specifically to represent Maori electors.[32]

In 1975 the Treaty of Waitangi Act established the Waitangi Treaty Tribunal as an intercultural institution for hearing and ruling on allegations that the terms of the original agreement between the crown and the Maori have not been fulfilled. Since 1975, the mandate and membership of the tribunal have been gradually expanded towards the evolution of a highly innovative diplomatic protocol for the unfolding negotiation of crown–Maori relations.[33] This process has made the Waitangi Treaty the most important founding agreement with an Aboriginal group in the construction, organization, and evolution of a modern–day nation-state. In 1987, Mr Justice Richardson ruled on the treaty's centrality in the legal and political culture of New Zealand. He said, "The Treaty must be viewed as a solemn compact between two identifiable parties, the Crown and the Maori, through which the colonization of New Zealand was to become possible. For its part the Crown sought legitimacy from indigenous people for its acquisition of sovereignty and in return it gave certain guarantees."[34]

The legal and political muscle the Maori retain in their own governments and in the government of New Zealand stems from their firm insistence on the constitutional pre-eminence of the Treaty of Waitangi. From this treaty flow the founding recognitions that have afforded Maori voters direct representation in the New Zealand parliament. From this political base, some Maori activists have questioned the New Zealand government's power to open the country's natural resources to yet further exploitation by foreign investors as long as these same resources remain the subject of unresolved negotiations with Indigenous peoples.

This Maori response came in reaction to those dramatic neo–liberal transformations in New Zealand that prompted some critics to compare the country's right-wing governors to the Pinochet regime: to them, New Zealand became "Chile without the gun." Beginning in the early 1980s, this bloodless coup saw the rapid slashing of social programs, quick government downsizing, and the elimination of almost all restrictions on foreign investment. As a result, between 1988 and 1993, New Zealand led the world in the sale of government-owned assets. These changes had dramatic implications for the Maori, who were deeply integrated into New Zealand's welfare state. The new investment regime affected the course of many disputes over title to extensive parts of the country's lands and fisheries. It biased the economy against broad interpretations of the Treaty of Waitangi. The active enticement of foreign investment into the disputed resources, therefore, seemed to prejudice the possibility of mutually satisfactory resolutions.

Maori participation in the mainstream of New Zealand's political culture resulted in some modest effort on the part of the government to consult with Native organizations in deliberations concerning the country's economic relations with the outside world. In 1997, for instance, the Ministry of Maori Development announced a process of talks to consider the significance for Maori people of New Zealand's participation in the controversial Multilateral Agreement on Investment (MAI). Maori resistance to the proposed global treaty was part of a larger wave of opposition that contributed to the temporary retreat of MAI's proponents.[35]

While some Maori activists have been prominent in the identification of neo-liberalism's dark side, they have tended to look with suspicion at certain varieties of *Pakeha,* or non-Indigenous, opposition to the new inroads and agencies of global corporatism. "It is not enough," Aziz Choudry observed, "to seek to nostalgically return to the golden age of the strong nation state." Moreover, said he, "a true peoples' sovereignty cannot be based on the denial of the sovereign rights of others." At the basis of the new coalition needed to promote viable alternatives to the kind of global corporate rule advanced through agencies like the World Trade Organization or the Asian-Pacific Economic Co-operation (APEC), Aziz envis-aged a regime that would take seriously "the work of women, the exploitation of workers, the lack of government accountability, and the enormous contributions made by Indigenous peoples and peoples of the South."[36]

The rise of Fourth World politics in Australia, New Zealand, Mexico, Canada, and many other parts of the Americas has been paralleled by the prominence of Indigenous peoples elsewhere as significant centres of resistance against the inte-gration of nation-states and global corporations in the privatized commodification of natural resources. This importance has grown as understanding has developed that the governments of many nation-states have become so subordinate to the power of global capital that the key levers of decision-making are less and less acces-sible to the democratic controls of ordinary men and women. As the democratic flexibility of national governments became progressively crippled through the hand-ing off of powers to the unaccountable private sector—and especially to the transna-tional private sector that operates increasingly through the instruments of supranational sovereignty such as the World Trade Organization[37]—Indigenous peoples have emerged as an older form of polity and as alternative centres of legal jurisdiction with long histories of resistance to assimilation into colonial structures not of their own making.

Hence, when the phenomenon of globalization is understood as a continuation of the major forces in history unleashed in 1492, the societies of Indigenous peoples emerge by virtue of the longevity of their struggles as key centres of activism in the arts and sciences of resistance. The continuity of their resistance represents a mirror image to the continuity of the forces of expansion whose instruments have been European empires, the successor states of European empires, and those corpo-rate conglomerates of capital and technology that have moved beyond the power and control of single national governments. From the Massachusetts Company to the East India Company to the Hudson's Bay Company, from the Ohio, Indiana, and other land speculation companies to the railway companies, from the ranch-ing enterprise of Lord Vestey, to the commercial activities of Hydro-Quebec, Shell Oil, Weyerhaeuser, Carghill, Monsanto, and Daishowa-Marubeni International, the expanding frontiers of corporate culture have often pushed at the imploding territorial and jurisdictional frontiers of Indigenous peoples.

The rising transnational influence of *Zapatismo* at the dawning of the 21st century has been especially influential in clarifying the continuities in a five-centuries-old cycle of colonialism whose present incarnation is most succinctly described as neoliberal globalization. With the growth of this understanding has come widening appreciation that the pre-Columbian sources of Aboriginality make the laws and institutions of Indigenous peoples the last line of defence against various forms of extinguishment, disempowerment, and dispossession which began with European imperialism and continued under the authority of new lawgivers whose primary fealty is to corporations rather than countries. These lawgivers often used the rhetoric of free trade even as the hidden agenda has been to bind both peoples and national governments to the higher authority of huge regional and global commercial regimes whose overwhelming tendency is to monopolize and centralize power in tighter and tighter circles of concentrated wealth.

When the issues are framed in this way, the struggle of Indigenous peoples to exercise self-determination and to defend their Aboriginal lands and resources takes on many larger meanings at the symbolic frontiers of a more inclusive, transcultural democratic movement. Activists in this movement may march under many banners, but they are inclined to find common cause in a shared commitment to defend the ecology of diversity among human beings and among our plant and animal relatives. This defence of biodiversity and cultural pluralism leads inevitably to various expressions of opposition to the inroads of monoculturalism through the standardization of property law and the unlimited commodification of nature.[38]

The opposition of Ogoni activists to the environmental desecration of their ancestral land in the Niger Delta region of West Africa constituted one of the clearest examples of an Aboriginal group on the cutting edge of protest against the more violent aggressions of global corporatism. Their resistance movement attracted international attention to the corporate tactics of the Shell Oil Company, whose operations in Nigeria depended on their close collaboration with that country's military dictatorship under General Sani Abacha. In 1995 this oil-rich regime executed author Ken Saro-Wiwa and eight other Ogoni activists in an effort to silence Ogoni criticism of Shell's exploitation and desecration of Ogoni lands.[39] Although the Nigerian government subsequently declared its intention to move away from the extremes of military dictatorship, these reforms had minimal effect on the plight of the Ogoni, whose ancestral lands were still exploited primarily for the benefit of foreign oil producers. Most of the pipelines, for instance, continued to be unburied, and health problems abounded from the open flaring of toxic chemical soups.

Similarly, the Ogoni lands were poisoned by oil spills, involving over 47,000 barrels from the operations of Shell alone over a six-month period in 1997.[40]

The Ogoni resistance movement inspired scores of Fourth World struggles on every continent, where various kinds of coalitions have protested and lobbied in a variety of ways to prevent Indigenous peoples from being further uprooted and rendered even more marginal and powerless in their Aboriginal lands. More often than not, a key dimension of the continuing struggle included new tensions created by growing class differences within many Aboriginal communities. This tension unfolded against a background where many of the old colonial policies of forced cultural assimilation—as implemented, for instance, by the work of Christian boarding schools—had been formally abandoned."[41] The new colonialism became manifest primarily in the pressures to assimilate Indigenous peoples into the economies, legal systems, and corporate structures that grew out of the old colonialism.

While the governments of many nation-states endeavoured to treat issues arising from their relations with Indigenous peoples as topics of domestic politics to be constrained as much as possible within the boundaries of domestic law, the international and global character of the questions involved came increasingly to the surface.[42] Local activism pushing for the recognition and implementation of Aboriginal and treaty rights was mirrored in various international forums, including the United Nations, the International Labour Organization, the European Parliament, and the World Bank. Within the United Nations since the early 1980s, a Working Group on Indigenous Populations has hosted an important annual forum in Geneva to bring forward new models of self-determination that might modify the monopolization of sovereign authority by nation-states and their corporate clients and patrons. The formal aim of this working group is to bring about UN ratification of an instrument establishing international standards for the protection of the rights and titles of Indigenous peoples.[43] In 2002 this working group was upgraded from a subcommittee of the UN Human Rights Commission to become a more self-contained agency, the Permanent Forum on Indigenous Issues.

George Manuel, an erudite and energetic Shuswap leader from British Columbia, did much of the essential groundwork in the 1970s to establish the intellectual and organizational framework for the globalization of Indigenous peoples' issues.[44] A contemporary of Vincent Lingiari, Manuel was part of that generation of First Nations leaders who threw off the verdict of Social Darwinism that had defined Indigenous peoples' societies as primitive, archaic, and dying forces without relevance to the future genesis of the world's economic, political, and cultural organization. As the primary founder of the World Council of Indigenous Peoples, Manuel had a clear vision of the threat posed by the unfettered dominion of global corporatism. In the years before his death in 1989, he foresaw the genesis of a great debate on globalization that was taking shape on the horizons of humanity's imagination. Manuel conceived of plans for fundamental reforms, beginning with his own peoples but extending beyond politics and economics towards the more all-encompassing field of global ecology.

He stands in the tradition of Tupac Amaru and Tecumseh, as a bridge-builder between peoples. His endeavours to advance the ideals of what he called the Fourth World amounted to a fundamental reckoning with basic definitions of progress. In bringing his perspectives from the frontiers of Aboriginality to the task of imagining what constitutes a truly civilized society, Manuel stood prominently within an old tradition of reflection. This tradition of thought has developed especially in that transition zone of ideas, law, geography, and politics where Indigenous peoples encountered, first, European imperialism and, then, the accelerated, New-World form of empire-building most dramatically illustrated by the westward expansion of the United States. The intellectual intensity of the thought to emerge from this frontier region of cross-cultural conflict and intercultural collaboration represents an ideological equivalent to the biodiversity that tends to flourish in zones of transition between significantly different ecological regions.

As a nation-state that came into colonial existence first as a fur-trade preserve of Indigenous peoples and then as a commercial hinterland of the American empire centred in the United States, Canada offers many examples of how those on both sides of the frontiers of Aboriginality, including George Manuel, used their vantage points to develop all sorts of visions of the way civilization should be imagined and organized.[45]

NOTES

1. *Edmonton Journal*, 29 May 2000, A3; Harvey Goldberg, "The Wisdom of Oz: Canada can learn from Australia's gestures of reconciliation to its First Nations," *Globe and Mail*, 1 June 2000, A17.
2. Henry Reynolds, *Aborigines and Settlers: The Australian Experience, 1788–1839* (Melbourne: Cassell Australia, 1972); Reynolds, *The Other Side of the Frontier: Aboriginal Resistance to the European Invasion of Australia* (Ringwood, Australia: Penguin, 1981); Reynolds, *Dispossession: Black Australians and White Invaders* (Sydney: Allen and Unwin, 1989).
3. Reynolds, "A Crossroads of Conscience," in Michelle Grattan, ed., *Reconciliation: Essays on Australian Reconciliation* (Melbourne: Black, 2000), 54.
4. Aden Ridgeway, "An Impasse or a Relationship in the Making," ibid., 16.
5. See Herbert Cole Coombs, *Aboriginal Autonomy: Issues and Strategies* (Cambridge: Cambridge University Press, 1994); Robert Tonkinson and Myrna Tonkinson, "Aborigines of Australia," *Cultural Survival Quarterly* 17, 3 (1993).
6. House of Representatives Standing Committee on Aboriginal and Torres Strait Islander Affairs, *Language and Culture: A Matter of Survival*. Report into Aboriginal and Torres Strait Islander Language Maintenance (Canberra: Australian Government Printing Service, 1992); Collin Yallop and Michael Walsh, *Language and Culture in Aboriginal Australia* (Canberra: Aboriginal Studies Press, 1993); Rob Amery and Colin Bourke, "Australian Languages: Our Heritage," in Colin Bourke, Eleanor Bourke, and Bill Edwards, eds., *Aboriginal Australia: An Introductory Reader in Aboriginal Studies*, 2nd ed. (St. Lucia: University of Queensland Press, 1998), 122–45.
7. Patrick Dodson, "Lingiari: Until the Chains Are Broken," in Grattan, ed., *Reconciliation*, 264–74.

8. G. Cowlishaw and V. Kondos, eds., *Mabo and Australia: On Recognizing Native Title After Two Hundred Years* (Sydney: Anthropological Society of New South Wales, 1995).

9. Sally Weaver, "Self-Determination, National Pressure Groups, and Australian Aborigines: The National Aboriginal Conference, 1983–1985," in Michael D. Levin, ed., *Ethnicity and Aboriginality: Case Studies in Ethnonationalism* (Toronto: University of Toronto Press, 1993), 53–74.

10. Cited in Raimond Gaitla, "Guilt, Shame and Collective Responsibility," in *Reconciliation*, 276. See P.J. Butt and R. Eagleson, *Mabo: What the High Court Said and What the Government Did*, 2nd ed. (Sydney: Federation Press, 1996); John Bastien, "Recent Developments in Native Title Law and Practice: Issues for the High Court," in *Land, Rights, Laws: Issues of Native Title*, Issues Paper 13 (Canberra, February 2002); Christine Choo and Margaret O'Connell, "Historical Narrative and Proof of Native Title," in *Land, Rights, Laws: Issues of Native Title*, Issues Paper 3 (Canberra, September 1999); Ian Keen, "Cultural Continuity and Native Title Claims," in *Land, Rights, Laws: Issues of Native Title*, Issues Paper 28 (Canberra, July 1999).

11. Speech by Prime Minister Paul Keating, December 1992, cited on the website of Oxfam, Community Aid Abroad, August 1993.

12. Michael Perry, "Public support for Aborigines booming in Australia," *Globe and Mail*, 10 June 1998, A5.

13. Human Rights and Equal Opportunity Commission, *Bringing Them Home: A Guide to the Findings of the National Inquiry into the Separation of the Aboriginal and Torres Strait Islander Children from Their Families* (Sydney: The Commission, 1997).

14. "An Open Letter to Her Majesty Queen Elizabeth II, Queen of Australia, from Australians for Native Title et al.," 23 June 1997.

15. Noel Pearson, "The Concept of Native Title in Common Law," in Galarrway Yunupingu, ed., *Our Land Is Our Life: Land Rights Past, Present, Future* (St. Lucia: University of Queensland Press, 1996); Kevin Gilbert, *Living Blacks: Blacks Talk to Kevin Gilbert* (Sydney: Penguin, 1984); Gilbert, *Because a White Man'll Never Do It* (Sydney: HarperCollins, 1994).

16. John Pilger, *A Secret Country* (London: Vintage, 1990); Pilger, "Secret Waters," in Pilger, *Hidden Agendas* (London: Vintage, 1999, 223–48).

17. Pilger, "Secret Waters," 232.

18. Cited in "Hansonism: We Are All Australians," www.gwb.com.au/onenation/truth/condus.html

19. Geoffrey Blainey, *A Shorter History of Australia* (Port Melbourne: William Heinemann, 1994); Blainey, *Blainey: Eye on Australia. Speeches and Essays of Geoffrey Blainey* (Melbourne: Schwartz Books, 1991).

20. Preston Manning, "Parliament, not judges, must make the laws of the land," *Globe and Mail*, 16 June 1998, A23.

21. Anthony J. Hall, "The Denigration of a Great National Question," *Windspeaker*, April 2002, 4–6.

22. Ignacio Ramonet, "Marcos Marches on Mexico City," in Tom Hayden, ed., *The Zapatista Reader* (New York: Thunder's Mouth Press/Nation Books, 2002), 133–41.

23. Naomi Klein, *No Logo: Taking Aim at the Brand Bullies* (Toronto: Alfred A. Knopf, 2000).

24. Naomi Klein, "The Unknown Icon," in Hayden, ed., *The Zapatista Reader*, 122.

25. Tom Hayden, "In Chiapas," ibid., 83, 78.

26. Subcommandante Marcos, cited in Naomi Klein, "The Unknown Icon," 118.

27. John Rice, "Zapatista Rebels Ride into Mexico City," *National Post*, 12 March 2001, A16.

28. Kay B. Warren, *Indigenous Movements and Their Critics: Pan-Mayan Activism in Guatemala* (Princeton: Princeton University Press, 1998).

29. Ignacio Ramonet, "Marcos marche sur Mexico," *Le Monde*, March 2001. See also Dan Tschirgi, "Des islamistes aux zapatistes, la révolte des 'marginaux de la terre,'" *Le Monde*, January 2000; Carlos Pardo, "Résistances zapatistes," *Le Monde*, August 1998.

30. Alan Knight, "Racism, Revolution, and *Indigenismo*: Mexico, 1910–1940," in Richard Graham, ed., *The Idea of Race in Latin America, 1870–1940* (Austin: University of Texas Press, 1990), 71–114.

31. Augie Fleras and Paul Spoonley, *Recalling Aotearoa: Ethnic Relations and Indigenous Politics in New Zealand* (Auckland: Oxford, 1999).

32. See Paul McHugh, *The Maori Magna Carta: New Zealand Law and the Treaty of Waitangi* (Auckland: Oxford University Press, 1991).

33. Alan Ward, *An Unsettled History: Treaty Claims in New Zealand Today* (Wellington: Bridget William, 1999); Paul Havemann and Kaye Turner, "The Waitangi Tribunal: Theorising Its Place in the Re-Design of the New Zealand State," *Australian Journal of Law and Society* 10 (1994): 165–94; Roger Maaka and Augie Fleras, "Treaty Settlements and Social Change: The Treaty of Waitangi, the Waitangi Tribunal, and the Re-scripting of Maori-Crown Relations in New Zealand," paper presented to the Canadian Indigenous/ Native Studies Association (CINSA) conference at the University of Alberta, 28–31 May 2000.

34. *New Zealand Law Reports* (1987): 673.

35. Ministry of Maori Development, Government of New Zealand, "New Zealand Government Consults with Maori on MAI," 5 November 1997, press release.

36. Aziz Choudry, "APEC, Free Trade and Economic Sovereignty," paper presented at a conference in Davao, the Philippines, before the Manila People's Forum on APEC, 14 November 1996.

37. See Anthony J. Hall, "Magazine Meglomania: Are World Trade Rulings the New Indian Act?" *Canadian Forum,* March 1997, 5–6 (Kumarian Press / San Francisco: Berrett-Koehler Publishers, 1995).

38. See David Korten, *When Corporations Rule the World* (West Hartford, Conn.: Kumarian Press/San Francisco: Berrett-Koehler Publishers, 1995)

39. Ken Saro-Wiwa, *Genocide in Nigeria: The Ogoni Tragedy* (Port Harcourt, 1992); "Testimony of Dr. Owens Wiwa before the Joint Briefing of the Congressional Human Rights Caucus and the Congressional Black Caucus," Washington, DC, 30 January 1996, published electronically by the Sierra Club; Ken Wiwa, *In the Shadow of a Saint* (Toronto: Knopf Canada, 2000).

40. Mark MacKinnon, "Saro-Wiwa's Battle Still Being Fought," *Globe and Mail,* 10 June 1999, A13.

41. See Andrew Armitage, *Comparing the Policy of Assimilation: Australia, Canada, and New Zealand* (Vancouver: UBC Press, 1995).

42. For different perspectives on Indigenous peoples' struggles around the world, see Roger Moody, ed., *The Indigenous Voice: Visions and Realities* (Utrecht: International Books, 1993); Patricia Morales, ed., *Indigenous Peoples, Human Rights and Global Interdependence* (Tilburg: International Centre for Human and Public Affairs, 1994); Julian Berger, *Report from the Frontier: The State of the World's Indigenous Peoples* (London: Zed Books, 1987); Independent Commission on International Humanitarian Issues, *Indigenous Peoples: A Global Quest for Justice* (London: Zed Books, 1987); Noel Dyck, *Indigenous People and the Nation State: Fourth World Politics in Canada, Australia and Norway* (St John's: Institute of Social and Economic Research, Memorial University of Newfoundland, 1985); Jens Brøsted et al., *Native Power: The Quest for Autonomy and Nationhood of Indigenous Peoples* (Gergen: Universitetforlaget AS, 1985); William Renwick, ed., *Sovereignty and Indigenous Rights: The Treaty of Waitangi in International Contexts* (Wellington: Victoria University Press, 1991); Augie Fleras and Jean Leonard Elliot, *The Nations Within: Aboriginal-State Relations in Canada, the United States and New Zealand* (Toronto: Oxford University Press, 1992).

43. See Dean B. Suagee, "Human Rights of Indigenous Peoples: Will the United States Rise to the Occasion?" *American Indian Law Review* 21.2 (1997): 365–90; Russel Lawrence Barsh, "Indigenous Peoples in the 1990s: From Object to Subject of International Law?" *Harvard Human Rights Journal* 7 (1994): 35–86

44. Jeff Sallot, "Indigenous Issues Topic of UN Forum," *Globe and Mail,* 13 May 2002, A8.

45. Peter McFarlane, *Brotherhood to Nationhood: George Manuel and the Making of the Modern Indian Movement* (Toronto: Between the Lines, 1993).

CHAPTER 17

SAAMI AND NORWEGIANS:

SYMBOLS OF PEOPLEHOOD AND NATIONHOOD

Trond Thuen

INTRODUCTION

EXCEPT FOR THE OUTBURST OF REBELLION against the state which occurred during the Alta conflict,[1] Saami political emancipation can hardly be conceived as a nationalist, that is a separatist, movement. Even on that occasion, those few who proposed that "Saami should be masters in their own house" never specified their aspirations beyond the level of political slogans; they were far from being representative. As Part Three will demonstrate, Saami ethnopolitical voices express diverging perspectives on the status of Saami culture, rights, and organizations within the Norwegian political system. The oppression of cultural distinctiveness, in particular the Saami language, with the aim of assimilating the Saami population between 1860 and 1960, produced a widespread ambivalence and even antagonism towards those who propagated Saami cultural and political interests, and thus confronted their Norwegian social environment as well as Norwegian governmental institutions. There has been, and still is, a scepticism concerning the politicization of Saami ethnic identity, which is intimately linked to ambivalences of identity management. The questions "who is Saami?" and "what does it mean to be a Saami?" are commonly conceived as being political, implicating the question "where do I belong in the ethnopolitical landscape?"

In an influential article, Eidheim (1971:68–82) presented a model comprising two basic aspects of the idiomatic recodification inherent in the Saami ethnic incorporation during the 1960s: *complementarization* and *dichotomization*. The first depicts interethnic (Saami-Norwegian) transactions serving "to facilitate the establishment of interethnic relations based on equality" (*op. cit.*:79), and the second emphasizes intraethnic (Saami-Saami) transactions engendering a dichotomization of the two groups "so that Lappish [i.e. Saami] ethnic designata can be shared and made objects of transactions of incorporation by Lappish people" (*ibid.*:79). These concepts emphasize aspects of ethnopolitical incorporation that are basic to the emancipatory efforts of ethnic minorities everywhere. Saami themselves recognize that their cultural manifestations contrast with those of the Norwegians on a comparable and even a complementary basis, and that their Norwegian counterparts increasingly have come to accept this self-ascription; this implies that they share a sense of peoplehood founded on this relationship. Their shared sense of distinctiveness is not, in other words, based on any set of "objective" criteria of cultural differences *per se,* but on their symbolic relevance in communicating ethnic belonging and dissimilarity.

Whether these qualities of peoplehood should also be extended to encompass a sense of nationhood is another question, however. If so, it would entail a recurring denial of any sharing of national symbols with the Norwegians as well as consistently evaluating pan-Saami relationships over and above relationships with Norwegians. As I will argue, this does not seem to be the case. There are allegiances and evaluations shared with the Norwegians which attest to the fact that Saami ethnopolitical aspirations do not encompass any purpose of separating from the Norwegian nation-state.

POLITICIZATION OF PEOPLEHOOD

Conventions about how ethnic identity is constituted and signalled may be regarded as manifest or latent communicative opportunities corresponding to idioms which may be adopted or rejected by individuals in their ongoing presentations of self. As demonstrated in the last chapter, their application is either mandatory or optional, largely dependent on how well the ascription of ethnic status from others corresponds to self-identification, how skilled one is in performances customarily associated with a specific ethnic identity, and how extensive and relevant is the public knowledge of a person's origin of descent. In this respect, Saami ethnic identity differs from Norwegian in that Saami-ness may be undercommunicated or even abandoned, whereas Norwegian identity derives from origin and does not command any specific performances other than language (which has to be idiomatically correct, not "broken"). Norwegian identity can hardly be substituted for any other ethnic identity. These considerations apply to individual challenges of identity management. However, we should also consider the differences between Norwegian-ness and Saami-ness, which concern their respective "national" symbols. What are the characteristics of Saami images of peoplehood that constitute their collective and encompass belonging? To what extent are they considered separate from, and complementary to, Norwegian nationhood, and to what extent do shared idioms of common nationhood exist?

The opening of the Saami Assembly in Karasjohka in October 1989 marked an important official upgrading of the status of the Saami as an Aboriginal people within the Norwegian society and state system. The opening was celebrated with greetings from Norwegian authorities, Saami organizations on a Nordic level, and first and foremost by the Norwegian king, King Olav V, who officially performed the solemn inauguration. The occasion visualized an important step in the evolution of a Saami peoplehood, and at the same time demonstrated a major change in the ethnopolitical relationship between the Saami people and the Norwegian nation-state. The institution is an innovation within the Norwegian polity inasmuch as the Norwegian Parliament has bestowed upon one segment of Norwegian citizens the opportunity to recruit a representative assembly through a general election organized and supervised by the government. In fact, Saami electoral boards authorized the elected representatives. The Saami Assembly has a consigned authority to voice its opinion on any issue that it deems relevant to its constituency, and may have its authority extended to include decisive control over issues later to be negotiated. During the first period (1989-1993), the government has transferred to it a number of specific administrative responsibilities, and the politicization of Saami people-hood has entered a new phase: it has reached a level of officially recognized comple-mentarity to the Norwegian peoplehood.

As one symbol of Saami peoplehood, the Saami Assembly may be compared to other symbols of this peoplehood as they relate to features of cultural diversities within the Saami population and to the varying identity ascriptions of Saami-ness relative to the Norwegian nationhood encompassing it. To corroborate my assump-tion that Saami political aspirations aim at some measure of self-determination within the Norwegian national system rather than separation from it, I will depict some images of the Saami-Norwegian relationship exposed at events prior to the establishment of the Saami Assembly.

Tensions between divergent conceptions of how the future relationship between these two peoples should be managed permeates Saami ethnopolitics, creating inter-nal political rivalry. However, none of the contesting factions within the Saami polity have adopted a one-sided ideology on the question of integration within Norwegian nationhood or separation from it. The issue seems too complex to invite a non-compromising stand, and its complexity reflects the long-lasting history of Saami-Norwegian relationships, which has been experienced differently by vari-ous categories of the ethnic minority. Like many other ethnic minorities, the Saami present images of peoplehood that differ markedly when notions on the grass-roots level are compared to those prevalent within the elite.

The very concept of "a Saami people" may have originated among intellectu-als early in this century, but the organization of collective movements has a longer history. There were protests against missionaries, priests, sheriffs, merchants, and farmers, caused by their encroachment on Saami territories, the eradication of their religious beliefs and symbols, the destructive effects of alcohol, and the closure of borders which excluded reindeer from their habitual pastures. Religious revivals occurred in the late 18th century and had a major outburst in the "Kautokeino rebellion" of 1852; this may have been more of a social protest than a "religious delusion" or "mental delirium," as it was explained by Norwegian authorities at the time. Since about 1860, protests were also launched against the school authorities which from that time ordered a complete eradication of the Saami language in the schools.[1]

In his history of the Saami coastal community of Kvænangen in Northern Troms, Bjørklund cites a local Saami protest against a Norwegian farmer's appropriation of a field of special grass used in footwear (*sennagras*), which they always considered as their common property:

> [We], the common people of Kvænangen, hereby authorize these men (two elected representatives] to do on our behalf anything that seems legal and necessary in this case, so that we may know how to behave, and, if necessary, even go to His Majesty the King of Norway to ask our gracious King to protect us, *who are the aboriginal inhabitants of this country,* against our oppressors, so that we may keep our use and rights in peace, like we used to do from ancient times in hundreds of years; or is it really so that we shall have to leave this country forced by the encroachments of our adversaries? Signed by 101 persons in 1862 (Bjørklund 1985:278-279, my translation).

The Saami lost their case, but irrespective of who formulated it, it is a remarkable testimony of a local Saami community's early self-conception as a people. It also alludes to a theme to which we shall return: the king as superimposed protector.

Around the turn of the last century, the national movement in Norway was paralleled by a Saami ethnopolitlcal mobilization. From 1906 to 1912, Isak Saba, a Saami teacher who also wrote the Saami national anthem, represented rural districts in Finnmark in the Norwegian Parliament. A Saami newspaper, edited by another Saami teacher, Anders Larsen, appeared from 1904 to 1911. Their demands were particularly directed at the abolishment of a clause in the law on the sale of state-owned land in Finnmark, which claimed that buyers commanded the Norwegian language, and they also protested against the "Norwegianization" of the school system. In principle, they argued a policy of ethnic equality. A second effort at parliamentary representation on a basis independent of Norwegian political parties was unsuccessfully made in 1921 (Finnmark) and 1924 (Nordland). Between 1905 and 1920, several Saami local and regional associations were founded, and in 1917 and 1921 national meetings held in Trondheim were also attended by Saami from Sweden. However, a national, permanent organization was not established (Otnes 1970). In 1948 the reindeer owners founded their own national organization, the NRL. But, as we have seen, the idea of a separate and general Saami national organization and a uniting program of Saami claims and interests does not surface again until the late 1950s.

How to relate to Norwegian political parties and organizations was a pervasive problem for the Saami movement. After Saba, their spokesmen opted to cooperate with the Labour movement but did not succeed even there in gaining acceptance for a Saami program (Minde 1984). As farmers' and fishermen's organizations developed and gained influence over governmental policies, Saami also joined and tried to make their voices heard. [2]

The political and economic climate did not encourage the development of a genuine Saami national movement, whether inside the Norwegian nation-state or on a Nordic basis. Instead, they sought protection of their cultural distinctiveness (language, reindeer breeding) within the Norwegian nationhood. It has only been since the 1970s that an image of an extended self-government has developed, starting with some unspecified declarations and developing into a more coherent claim of decisive power, which, according to some voices (Stordahl 1987a), went further than what the Saami Rights Committee proposed at the time.

Changing political aspirations are also revealed in a collective self-ascription. The application of terms denoting a group's cohesiveness and aspirations to advanced status within the political realm of the encompassing political system is of course itself a question of the symbolic presentation of self. The change in labels for Saami peoplehood illustrates this. Throughout the 1970s the NSR used the term "the Saami minority," but the tendency in later years has been to replace it with "the Saami people" and even "the Saami nation." The "minority" label suggested an acceptance of that status and did not just denote the existing asymmetrical relationship. The change corresponds to, and is probably inspired by, the adoption of "nation" by other Aboriginal peoples, such as the Assembly of First Nations in Canada, which strongly emphasizes the status of original (pre-colonial), self-governing entities as the justification for future legal and political independence. And not surprisingly, the term "nation" is dismissed by the integrationist ethnopolitical opposition to the NSR and the Saami Assembly since it implies a separatist stance.

The enrolment of the Saami for participation in an election of their own political organization could be seen as the first step towards building a nation. Their claim of land rights implying some control of resource management within a specified territory, and a measure of self-government implying the right to decide on their own public affairs, would be the minimum preconditions for the development of a Saami nation and nationhood. Aside from internal antagonism on these issues, which basically concerns the question of self-ascription of Saami versus Norwegian identity, the problem is also a practical one. Not only is the demarcation of their territory problematic, but as they are also the subjects of different state jurisdictions, this would make the creation of an encompassing Saami nation a rather distant aim, if politically accomplishable at all.

When conceptualized as an alternative to the nation-states in which they now live, the notion of a "pan-Saami" nationhood is hardly conceivable to Saami political leadership. Rather, their political task is conceptualized as the development of self-determination within the respective national state borders that intersect Saami settlement areas. Consequently, their efforts to determine their political space are aimed at demarcating it for the political and administrative authorities of governmental agencies on the central and lower levels of ministries, provinces, and municipalities. In these efforts they seek acceptance from the top level of the political system, notably from the national parliament.

State borders physically intersect the Saami society: they represent obstacles to traffic between communities that traditionally enjoyed close contact, and after 1917 completely prohibited interaction between Eastern Finnmark and the Kola peninsula. In other parts, traditional adaptations such as reindeer breeding are subject to agreements between the state governments, according to which pastures on the other side of the border have limited access for a limited number of animals. Equally important is the subdivision engendered among the Saami because they have to relate to different governments and are treated according to policies which are part of the general understanding and acceptance of their interests. The Saami, encapsulated within different state jurisdictions, are exposed to diverging administrative regimes and state policies, which halt the formation of an encompassing Saami political community. As a consequence, the achievements of their national organizations within the realms of a particular nation-state are considered important and attract the most interest and demand the most effort. It is within the nation-state that particular claims have an addressee and concrete amendments can be gained. Coordinated Nordic efforts are typically aimed at symbolic statements of unity of culture and peoplehood, and are rarely backed by concrete demands or strategies for specific pan-Saami achievements. The Nordic Saami Council (established 1956) is an umbrella organization for the national associations of the NSR and the NRL in Norway, the *Same Ätnam* and the Swedish Saami Association in Sweden, and the Saami Assembly in Finland, and arranges a Nordic Saami Conference every third year. In 1980, it adopted a program of basic principles for the definition of Saami political aims and interests; the first read: "We Saami are one people, and the national borders shall not break up the community of our people."

New perspectives on the prospects of pan-Saami unification were presented, derived from the ideology of regionalism emerging within the European Union (EU). However, following plebiscites in 1994, Sweden and Finland joined the EU while Norway stayed outside. The general idea was that the corrosion of state borders would vitalize cultural links across those borders and encourage the establishment of stronger organizational links between peoples who had hitherto been separated by them.

STRUCTURAL CHARACTERISTICS OF THE EXTRA-LOCAL SAAMI SOCIETY

The problems of developing a pan-Saami nationhood is of course a reflection of the historical state-building processes in Scandinavia. Traditionally, relationships between Saami communities have been stronger with other Saami to the east, on the other side of the Norwegian-Swedish border, than with adjacent communities on a north-south axis. This is reflected in the distribution of Saami dialects. Dialect differences between the northern and southern parts of their settlement area are greater, to the extent that they are not mutually comprehensible, whereas communities on a west-east line belong to the same dialect area. In a real sense, then, national borders cut across the Saami settlement area and reduce or prohibit east-west connections, for instance for cross-border reindeer nomadism, which can only be maintained by limited inter-state agreements.

The cohesiveness of Saami peoplehood is perhaps best conceptualized as a network of social relationships with zones of varying density. The extensive resource utilization by reindeer husbandry facilitates and encourages social interaction over vast areas; it has served to develop an extensive network of social exchange, which compensated for the isolation that geographical distance and topographical barriers would otherwise have engendered. In addition, individuals and families have to some extent traditionally switched between varying niche exploitations. Nomads have resorted to a sedentary adaptation when their reindeer husbandry failed, and sedentary individuals and families have become nomads when prospects invited them to do so (Paine 1964, 1981). Bilateral and affinal kinship relations have made the transitions easy. Demographic investigations reveal that the stability of the sedentary population has not usually been very strong. The roots of local populations in many communities usually do not extend over more than three or four generations. This is in marked contrast to the immigrant Norwegian farming population in inner Troms, where pioneers settled during a 40- to 50-year period starting just before the turn of the 18th century. For this population, the concept of an "organic" relationship between lineage of descent and the farm and its cultivated area is very solid (Bårnes 1991). This contrast between the extensive, combined, and mobile use of a number of resources on one hand and the permanent adaptation to a geographically limited area on the other articulates a difference in cultural preferences and skills. It should also be related to the problem of retaining land ownership and control among the Saami after the introduction of a state registration of farm plots and absentee land ownership in the 18th century. Whether Saami geographical mobility was enforced as a consequence of the loss of land or as a strategy for a varied and complex resource utilization, the existence of a large number of kin in close and distant localities was a major asset as well as an adaptational prerequisite.

Market relations and congregational gatherings at particular times of the year also cemented the linkages between partners within this extensive network.

The characteristics of a Saami traditional peoplehood may be visualized, then, as an informal network bound together by consanguine and affinal relations, trade and gift exchange, and religious faith. These fields of interaction partly overlapped, partly subdivided the population into entities with characteristic dialects, congregational divergences, and economic pursuits. But these variations were subcultural in character compared to the distinctiveness of their relationship to the Norwegian society. Although interethnic relations also developed, they were limited and constrained by the mutual perception of difference. As state authorities changed from a position of control and taxation to one of governmental responsibility for economic development and social welfare, Norwegians learned to enjoy their citizenship within a national realm sustained by an ideology of unity, whereas Saami cohesive networks were made obsolete by new forms of communication, trade, and production as well as by their emerging dependency on bureaucracies of an extra-local kind (Paine 1958, 1962, 1965).

SYMBOLS OF PEOPLEHOOD AND THEIR VARYING INTERPRETATIONS

The single event that most decisively engendered a change in the governmental apprehension of Saami ethnopolitical rights was the hunger strike of 1979. The Alta-Kautokeino project highlighted the question of Saami land claims and Aboriginal status on an unprecedented scale. The hunger strike was an unequalled demonstration of the power relationship prevailing between the Norwegian state and the Saami people, as interpreted by the public and the mass media. The significational impact was achieved by the juxtaposition of metonymic signs relating the two parties to the specific confrontational situation: the *lavvo* (reindeer herder's tent) erected in front of the *parliament building* in Oslo. The hunger strikers demonstrated a strong conviction in the legitimacy of their cause by their chosen form of action, *starvation,* while at the same time exhibiting their lack of power; state authorities demonstrated their power of jurisdiction and their physical strength by surrounding the hunger strikers with *police*. The *urban scene* contrasted with the *nature-dependent* and *exotic* Saami.

This juxtaposition aroused massive support from the Norwegian public in the South, but the reaction was considerably more varied among the Saami population. Although some applauded the hunger strikers for their perseverance and determination, a number of other voices disqualified them on the grounds that they were not at all representative of the Saami population, neither by their emphasis on reindeer nomadism nor by their political message. Some who disparaged them would agree with protesting against the damming, but disagree on the political means used;

some would accept the project since it had been decided by the Norwegian Parliament, following regular decision-making procedures within the Norwegian political system. A number of Saami condemned the hunger strike and the Alta road blockade as an illegitimate challenge of Norwegian democratic institutions, as a rejection of the political system to which every citizen owed allegiance, whereas for the majority of the general public the authorities lost their credibility by enforcing this unfair treatment of a tiny minority's legitimate claim to survive ethnically and culturally within the Norwegian society. Introducing the Saami on the Norwegian political agenda reopened a division among the Saami concerning their peoplehood as well as their relationship to the encompassing political system and its national symbols. In the way it challenged supreme Norwegian institutions, it was conceptualized as an act of separation from the Norwegian national community, which these Saami considered deserved their allegiance as well. In the short run, the Saami ethnopolitical offensive proved counterproductive in creating Saami unity.

Investigations which followed proposed recommendations that included a constitutional amendment: "It is incumbent on the government authorities to take the necessary steps to enable the Saami population to safeguard and develop their language, their culture and their societal life."[3] On the basis of its interpretation of international legal principles, the committee stated that "[t]here is no doubt that the Saami population comprises a people in a political and sociological sense." But concerning the implications of peoplehood, the committee had reservations:

> ... [the] Saami minority in Norway cannot invoke any of the principles of the right of self-determination of all peoples as they are formulated in current conventions. In this respect, the position of the Saami people is different from that of the Inuit population in Greenland—where the area and its population are distinctly separate, geographically, historically and culturally, from the "mother country," and where the area has, moreover, for many years had the explicit status of a colony— even though there are points of resemblance between the Saami and the Inuits [sic] in other respects (Kommunaldepartementet, n.d.:15).

However, the committee found support for the principle of positive discrimination, particularly in Article 27 of the UN International Covenant on Civil and Political Rights:

> The conclusion of our report is that Article 27 probably imposes an obligation on the various states to provide economic support to enable the minority groups virtually to use their own language and other aspects of their culture. As regards quantification of this obligation, it should be presumed that the states are under

an obligation to implement measures whereby a reasonable degree of equality is attained with regard to allowing a minority to enjoy its own culture in relation to the rest of society (*ibid.*: 16).

These considerations formed the basis for the committee's recommendation of the constitutional amendment cited above. Again, Saami committee representatives were divided on the issue of constitutional reference to the Saami, namely whether the continued existence of a Saami people and culture required an acknowledgement within a legislation codifying Norwegian nationhood.

Another event which signified divergences of Saami attitudes towards Norwegian national symbols occurred one year before the hunger strike. In 1978 the NSR, the main Saami organization at that time, was invited to send its chairman to the 75th anniversary of King Olav V. At the annual assembly, the NSR board announced that it had turned down the invitation, allegedly because the organization could not afford to send its chairman to Oslo when there was already a lack of funds for other urgent needs. However, a number of representatives at the annual assembly considered it an offensive act to challenge the king: he was a national symbol not only for Norwegians, but also for Saami. It was argued that the invitation was by itself a token of acknowledgement of the Saami as a people. The opposition signalled their discontent with the board's decision by exiting from the organization. They later joined with other Saami who had long considered the NSR to be too much of a "separatist" and "extremist" organization to be representative of the Saami, and founded a rival organization, the SLF (The Saami National Association) (Stordahl 1982), which explicitly stated that SLF should work on the basis of the principles of the Norwegian constitution and show deference and respect for the king and his government, Parliament, and other public authorities in a democratic fashion. This extraordinary avowal of Norwegian national and governmental allegiance should be interpreted as a distancing from the NSR, which, by implication, was accused of alienating the Saami from their nation-state membership.

Again, we can observe the symbolic prominence of certain national emblems, notably the king. The guiding principle of the SLF's policy has been to promote Saami interests from within established institutions, contending that they are Saami *and* Norwegians. This contention, whether implicitly or explicitly stated, should be interpreted in two interrelated ways: a) that the Saami are Norwegian citizens as well, and the ordinary institutions of the Norwegian political system guarantee their equal treatment and participation in the democratic process of government; and b) although they consider themselves Saami, many of them do not feel like having an exclusive Saami identity as opposed to a Norwegian. They argue that they are of "mixed" origin, and their culture is influenced by the Norwegian to the extent that they differ more from those who exhibit an obvious Saami identity (for instance, reindeer breeders) than from Norwegians in the North. Therefore, the ethnic border is not significant. Rather, Saami should be considered to be marginal in a geographical sense as are many Norwegians, and there is no need for an antagonistic relationship between Saami and Norwegians when regional development and a firmer basis for the existing settlement pattern are the main concerns for both parties. There is also a deeply felt fear among many Saami that the antagonism of the past should be reinvoked. To them, the notion of "positive discrimination" brings to mind a situation where Saami are given special access to resources which Norwegians equally evaluate and depend upon for their livelihood; they fear that this situation will provoke Norwegian resentment.[4]

As previously mentioned, the SLF members of the Saami Rights Committee opposed the idea of a directly elected Saami Assembly. However, when the institution was finally adopted by the Norwegian Parliament, and in particular when it was given symbolic value by the king's act of inauguration, the SLF chairman greeted the Saami Assembly by taking the king's presence to be a token of the future friendly relationship between the two categories of Norwegian citizens. The interpretation of the occasion may have differed among other Saami participants. What had started as a juxtaposition 10 years earlier in Oslo was now transformed into some kind of equivalence, even complementarity. It was no longer weakness confronting power in the Norwegian capital, but symbols of peoplehood displayed in Karasjohka, "capital of the Saami."[5] It could even be seen as the embryo of nationhood: an organizational tool had been created that could be developed further into an institution for the management of self-determination within those areas of public administration that most decisively concerned the Saami, which was obviously the aim of the majority of its representatives.

Still, some notion of Norwegian nationhood is retained. There seems to be no wish to disregard the legally and symbolically significant principle that states that the Saami Assembly derives its mandate from the Saami Act adopted by the Norwegian Parliament. A balance must be kept between Saami political aspirations and Norwegian nationhood, inspired by a deeply anchored allegiance towards Norwegian nationhood which many Saami do not feel is incompatible with their feeling of Saami peoplehood.

THE KING: EMBLEM OF JOINT NATIONHOOD?

The personification of Norwegian nationhood that the king represents is a master symbol which derives its importance from its quality of lending itself to different interpretations. As noted earlier, it is plausible that the effects of "Norwegianization" on a large proportion of the Saami led them to internalize a self-identification of

Saami-ness as being of a lesser value than Norwegianness. To them, its signification would mean an ultimate guarantee that Saami are fully accepted as Norwegian citizens while sustaining their identity as Saami. They would not demand any separate treatment by the state beyond that which pertains to subcultural variations within the Norwegian population as long as this acknowledgement of equivalence is sustained. The formal position of the king, above antagonism within the nation-state and independent of shifting governments, has a special significance: he is also above ethnic difference. He may even have his own political will and act as a corrective to government or to Norwegian condescension toward Saami. To others, and here those self-conscious Saami who have continuously demanded that the acknowledgement of Saami political rights be contingent upon their Aboriginal status are included, the king embodies a strong symbol of nationality, but without much political power of his own. His presence is a manifestation of the governmental acknowledgement of a complementary status for the Saami as a people in their own right. His performance of the inauguration was significant not only as an expression of governmental and parliamentary approval of the Saami Assembly as an exceptional institution, but also by the impression they knew that this act would have on the Saami and the Norwegian populations at large.

In the mind of Norwegians, the position of the late King Olav V can hardly be underestimated, and there is no reason to assume that as part of the Norwegian image of nationhood this was not equalled by the one held by Saami. In this respect, then, we envisage nationhood as encompassing the two peoplehoods. Since this leaves the Saami without any overarching symbol of their own nationhood, would it mean that they are inevitably bound to see their minority position confirmed? No one other than a Saami would recognize any particular symbolic relationship between the king and the category of Norwegian citizens, the Saami. As suspected by their opposition, it would not have been politically inconsistent for the NSR leadership to reject the invitation in 1978 on more than pragmatic grounds. It is perhaps more than a curiosity that the Saami newspaper *Ságat* argued, prior to the inauguration of the Saami Assembly in 1989, that the king should consider wearing a Saami costume (a *kofte*) on the occasion in order to symbolize his status as sovereign of the two peoples. It was further argued, obviously as a curiosity, that he even had the right to wear it in terms of ethnicity, since he had "Saami blood in his veins." The newspaper referred to the old Norse saga in which King Harald Fairhair, the founder of the Norwegian kingdom in the ninth century, had a number of sons with the daughter of a Saami "chief." Through one of these sons the Norwegian royal dynasty in the Middle Ages was infused with "Saami blood." An old Saami had compared the "strength" of Saami blood to the effect of a drop of ink in a glass of water: the water turns black, but a drop of water in a glass of ink has no effect.

Why do Saami, seemingly irrespective of political allegiance and conception of future prospects for their people, regard the King of Norway as "their" king as well? I suggest two explanations: first, to Norwegians the king-image is an image of their national belonging, whereas to the Saami it is, in addition, an image of a relationship between the two categories of citizens. Grammar is important here, and I propose the following distinctions:

"King of Norway"

Norwegian codification	Saami codification
King of the Norwegians	King of Norwegian citizens (Norwegians and Saami)
Norwegian king	King of the Saami, but not Saami king (but may be of "mixed" origin?)

Second, we should recognize in this overarching emblem something more than a metonym in its ordinary sense of a condensed symbol. In hereditary monarchies, sovereigns are not elected: they are not personally installed by the majority or the power elite to rule over the minority(ies), although historically that may have occurred. They are "above" ethnicity, although they belong culturally to one category (prior to the creation of the nation-state they belonged to an "international" aristocracy). They may even be accepted and venerated for using symbols that are considered exclusive to the other category, as when on special occasions members of the royal family (usually female) dress in native costume. Such mixing of ethnic signs would otherwise be considered as a kind of sacrilege, since they are used for constituting ethnicity: when the rule is that only Saami wear Saami costume, anyone in such costume signals that s/he wishes to be recognized as a Saami.[7] Royal persons seemingly do not blur the message; they are recognized as who and what they are anyhow, and their use of the costume might be considered a device for ceremonial definition of specific occasions, and, as *Ságat* argued, "It would represent an appraisal of the traditional Saami costume which might make it easier to restore it from oblivion in Norwegianized Saami areas."[8] The monarch is not merely a symbol rendered meaningful by "his" people, but an agent giving meaning to his "peoples." He can be a good or bad king, a failure or an inspiration. Although he has little formal political power, he may still be considered a supreme judge of politics, and on certain occasions may actually perform his role in a way that renders particular meaning to decisive events (as King Haakon VII did when he refused to abdicate after the German attack and occupation of Norway in 1940, although asked by the Parliament).

THE RELEVANCE OF ETHNICITY: PAROCHIAL OR PAN-SAAMI?

The challenge of any ethnopolitical movement is to translate the everyday experiences of an ethnically suppressed category into a common fate to be changed by their concerted efforts. Attention should be given to the range of interethnic experiences and their relationship to differences in the expression of Saami identity. Simplified, these differences may be conceptualized as

(i) those who identify as Saami as an obvious, unquestionable reality (reindeer breeders as the prototype);

(ii) those who identify as Saami because denying it would be unthinkable, despite experiencing stigmatization. A number of these Saami, particularly the younger generation, are converting their self-image from shame to pride, and joining the Saami ethnopolitical movement;

(iii) those who reckon themselves to be "both Saami and Norwegians" who may be on the way to an assimilated status, but may also find some advantage and future in cultivating their Saami relationship; and

(iv) those who do not identify as Saami anymore, who live in communities that for all practical purposes would seem to be assimilated, or have moved away from their Saami home community to a career leading them out of the Saami and into Norwegian society.

The Saami ethnopolitical movement, having regained its momentum in the 1960s after an impasse since the 1920s, had to face these varying identifications and try to translate them into an encompassing ethnopolitical perspective in which these inward-directed and parochial codifications of Saami-ness could merge. They were confronted with scepticism and rejection: Saami nationhood was a theoretical construction by academics who did not have a proper understanding of the grassroots problems and identity conceptions of the ordinary Saami (Eidhelm 1971, Ingold 1974). And in a sense, these allegations were real. Laestadian congregations have been and still are a central focus of Saami identification in many Saami communities, and there is little correspondence between their religious philosophy and the aspirations of the ethnopolitical movement (Torp 1986). The Laestadian confrontation with the majority society is based on a paradigm other than that of power and self-determination. It is a religious opposition: the state-operated Lutheran Church and its clergy have wrongly interpreted the holy message of salvation and taken control of the sinful individual's access to God. This access can only be obtained through confession and forgiveness by the congregation. A Laestadian meeting is a collective enactment of co-identity: "a congregational realization of self ... reached through ecstatic confession."[9] In "mixed" communities, the congregation may consist of individuals of both Saami and Norwegian origin who find in this community a sense of unity and equality against the valuational temptations and the administrative pressures of the outside world (Thuen 1987:80). Their ethos is strongly attached to a defence of their religious values, and if they are provoked to take political action, it will have to be in defence of their religious interests (Steinlien 1984). If connected to ethnopolitical alignments, some of these identifications are transformed into political allegiances such as the SLF and the NSR. But the Saami Assembly might evolve into an institution that will engender ethnopolitical commitments among Saami who do not feel engaged by what they presently consider to be a somewhat theoretical construction.

The identifications listed above do not parallel any divisions found within the Norwegian polity. Here we find political commitments on a scale from liberalist Thatcherism to socialism, with the Labour and Conservative parties as the dominant antagonists. Norwegian-ness is not an issue, but as we have seen, regionalism may be: whenever large investments are planned in one part of the country, some form of "compensation" is often due to another. Norwegian political representatives are accountable to their regional constituencies, and on some occasions their regional balance sheet counts more than their party's ideological responsibilities. Norwegian regionalism has never challenged nationhood, however strong might be the regional voices complaining of unequal distributions of public goods.

As I have argued, Norwegian nationhood (or peoplehood, as it were) depends on, or is expressed through, some regional guise. Spoken Norwegian always has its dialectal style from which natives can tell a person's geographical background, and regional characteristics abound with folk stereotypes. Northerners are traditionally debased, particularly by urbanites in the central eastern region, much as the Norwegian northerners used to debase Saami for their appearance and allegedly broken Norwegian.

In the present context, regional diversities and the parochial aspect of ethnic identification can be summed up: Norwegian nationhood encompasses a number of regional or subcultural variations. Inasmuch as the national "totality" is larger than the sum of these parts and has a quality of its own, this totality is the Norwegian nationhood. It is expressed at ritual occasions (the king's death, Independence Day) and as outbursts of patriotism at international athletics contests, and the monarchy serves to idiomatize it. Saami culture and society also exhibit parallel regional variations, or actually of a more divisive kind (for example, dialect differences of the Saami language). Until the present, however, the Saami "totality" has been more of a construction or a contention than a felt reality lacking those ritual and emblemic forms of expression characteristic of its Norwegian counterpart. And what is more,

Saami attitudinal divergences are related to identity management and ascription in a qualitatively different way than how Norwegians feel about their identity or nationhood. Politicization among the Saami concerns ethnic identity and self-iden-tification, which are questions related to nationhood and peoplehood, whereas for Norwegians it concerns more pragmatic interests, however ideologically flavoured.

CONCLUSION

Whereas for Norwegians, state borders correspond with national identity, state borders have split the Saami. Although linkages across the borders separating Norway, Sweden, and Finland have been firm between local Saami populations, and despite the fact that reindeer nomadism through its long-distance movements links otherwise sepa-rated Saami communities, the concept of Sapmi—Saamiland—is still very much a fiction. For the Saami, lack of traditional overarching institutions, language and adap-tive differences, and the long-lasting state jurisdiction over their territories have effec-tively prohibited the creation of encompassing national symbols and institutions. And naturally, pressures to assimilate have counteracted the evolution of a general concep-tion of Saami commonality. Common symbols such as a Saami flag have only recently been constructed. A Nordic Saami council has been in existence since 1953, but rela-tive to the Nordic countries its political role has not been substantial. NSR, in signalling its stand on SLF accusations of "separatism" and "extremism," has repeatedly denied that their policy includes a constitutionally independent Sápmi.

While most Saami interpret Norwegian nationhood as deserving their loyalty, the state has been blamed for being ethnically blind. As far as this blindness goes (the allegation might not be completely fair), it has confirmed what its majority inhab-itants perceived, that Saami had become so similar to Norwegians that special concerns were uncalled for, and even considered reactionary. Why should Saami be treated differently on ethnic grounds when class differentiation had been declared immoral? Through most of the post-war period, *marginality*, not ethnicity, was considered the main source of inequality. Accordingly, the ethnopolitical task of the Saami move-ment was to add *ethnic* disqualification to the majority's conceptualization of *economic* deprivation as an illegitimate social differentiation between Norway's citizens.

Saami and Norwegian regional diversities represent two contrasting series of differences, but in addition, as a minority the Saami are split among themselves as to how nationality should be conceptualized. Few, if any, demand separation from the Nordic nation-states. Many are concerned that the articulation of Saami inter-ests does not bring about antagonism on the community level between those Saami and Norwegians equally dependent on the resource base in the north.

Norwegian national symbols, in particular the king and the royal family, but also the Norwegian Parliament after almost unanimously adopting the constitutional amendment and Saami Act, are considered to be overarching and also embrace Saami. The Norwegian Parliament is seen as a watchdog and guarantor of Saami interests against the government. Images of nationhood and common ideals, such as that of the king depicted as a symbol of unity with his people, would be as dear to most Saami as to Norwegians. In fact, a lack of representative Saami national institutions made them seek an ultimate authority for their appeals when suffering ill-treatment from authorities on lower levels, much as ordinary people before representative democracy went to the king in Copenhagen with their complaints. The king could be accorded a position beyond ethnic differences as much as he was considered above other divisions of class and ideology within Norwegian society. The ultimate proof of political extremism within the Saami ethnopolitical movement has been the rejection of the royal family on the grounds that they idiomatized Norwegian-ness *par excellence*. Thus, the opposition within NSR exited and formed SLF in 1978, protesting against the alleged disrespect for the king expressed by NSR "extremists." On the same pretext, the SLF chairman in 1989 greeted the opening assembly of the Saami Assembly to which his organization had been so vehemently opposed, by taking the king's presence as a guarantee for a future harmonious relationship between "the two categories of Norwegians."

In this respect, then, certain prominent emblems of Norwegian nationhood are also venerated by Saami. The king is the symbolic personification of national coexistence, not of majority supremacy. Other experiences testify to this codification, primarily during the German occupation when the test of a good Norwegian was the closing of ranks against collaboration with the enemy. Saami did not score less than Norwegians in that test. The "scorched earth" strategy of the German occupation forces, who destroyed homesteads and production equipment as they retreated from the Soviet army, put Saami and Norwegians literally on the same level as they were evacuated to the south of Norway. The rebuilding during early post-war years added to this experience of sharing the same destiny across ethnic boundaries.

However, although sharing common experiences and evaluating identical national symbols, the Saami were never equivalent to the Norwegians within a plural cultural system. In this respect Saami have been excluded as a nation while being incorporated, on Norwegian terms, into the state. Accordingly, the king may be conceptualized as bringing citizens rather than nationalities together.[10] Saami nationhood may be considered to embrace all Saami living in the four nation-states, but this is an abstract notion as long as no institutional arrangements symbolize this nationhood. The development of an all-embracing political, cultural, and social Saami unity is a challenging image not yet fully introduced on the Saami agenda.

A model for Saami self-determination is still in the making. It seems easier for the government to transfer administrative responsibilities that concern Saami exclusively, such as the allocation of funding for Saami small enterprises and artistic activities, to the Saami Assembly, rather than on issues which concern non-Saami interests, such as resource management as well. But Saami will expectedly have divergent opinions among themselves when it comes to such issues.

In essence, the balance of powers between Saami and Norwegian authorities concerns the future distinction of Saami nationhood relative to the Norwegian: will the dimensions of nationhood that have been missing in the Saami vision of the future Sapmi—territorial demarcation and self-government—be added at some future point? For the moment, this vision is restrained by the Nordic nation-state borders. The Nordic states have made minimal efforts to coordinate their policies on Saami demands.

NOTES

1. Otnes (1970). See also Worsley (1957).
2. In 1989 and 1993 this relationship was turned around: Norwegian political parties formulated Saami programmes and participated in the Saami election. As mentioned, only the Labour Party won any seats.
3. Quotations are from Kommunaldepartementet (n.d.): "Summary of the First report of the Norwegian Saami Rights Committee," which is a translation of the summary of the Norwegian version of the report.
4. This is not without corroboration. In the fall of 1991, the Saami Assembly commented on a proposed amendment of the game act, advising that the management of wildlife and hunting licences should be transferred to Saami agencies in Saami settlement areas which should be given the mandate to rent out hunting permits to non-resident hunters. This proposal was immediately interpreted by the Norwegian Hunters' and Anglers' Association as a Saami effort to monopolize access to and utilization of traditionally "free" resources.
5. Karasjohka's status of capital may be disputed by the neighbouring community of Guovdagealdnu (Kautokelno). If it should deserve that status, it would be contingent upon the localization of the Saami Assembly itself, which was decided on the basis of a fair distribution of central Saami institutions between the two townships.
6. As it turned out, he was dressed in the uniform of the supreme commander of the military forces.
7. Paine (1985b: 175). See also Paine (1988a and 1988b).
8. Sågat. October 7, 1989.
9. Paine (1985b: 175). See also Paine (1988a and 1988b).
10. I owe this formulation to Robert Paine.

REFERENCES

Bårnes, Vibeke B. 1991. "Dølakultur som delkultur. Kontlnuitet og en-dring hos ei østnorsk innvandrerbefolkning i Indre Troms." Master's thesis, mimeographed. Tromso: University of Tromsa.

Bjørklund, Ivar. 1985. Fjordfolket t Kvænangen. Oslo: Universitetsforlaget.

Eidheim, Harald. 1971. Aspects of the Lappish Minority Situation. Oslo: Universltetsforlaget.

Ingold, Tim. 1974. "Entrepreneur and Protagonist: Two Faces of a Political Career." Journal of Peace Research, (11)3:179-88.

Kommunaldepartementet. n.d. "Summary of the First Report of the Norwegian Sami Rights Committee." Mimeographed. Oslo: Ministry of Municipal Affairs.

Otnes, Per. 1970. *Den samiske nasjon.* Oslo: Pax Forlag.

Paine, Robert. 1958. "Changes in the Ecological and Economic Bases in a Coast Lappish District." *Southwestern Journal of Anthropology,* 14(2):168–88.

Paine, Robert. 1962. "Innlemmelse av et utkantstrok i det nasjonale samfunn." *Tidsskrift for samfunnsforskning,* 3(3):65–82.

Paine, Robert. 1964. "Cultural Demography and Nomad/Sedentary Relations of Reindeer Lapp Groups in Norway and Sweden." Paper read at the VIIth International Congress of Anthropological and Ethnological Sciences, Moscow. Mimeographed.

Paine, Robert. 1965. *Coast Lapp Society II. A Study of Economic Development and Social Values.* Oslo: Universitetsforlaget.

Paine, Robert. 1981. "Til Norges Høyesterett. Uttalelse fra professor Robert Paine som oppnevnt sakkyndig i Samespørsmål og Altavassdraget." Mimeographed.

Paine, Robert. 1985b. "Ethnodrama and the "Fourth World": The Saami Action Group In Norway, 1979-81." In N. Dyck (ed), *Indigenous Peoples and the Nation-State.* St. John's, Newfoundland: Institute of Social and Economic Research, Memorial University.

Paine, Robert. 1988a. "The Persuasions of 'Being' and 'Doing': An Ethnographic Essay." *International Journal of Moral and Social Studies,* 3(1):17–40.

Paine, Robert. 1988b. "Grace out of Stigma: The Cultural Self-Management of a Saami Congregation." *Ethnologia Europeae,* 18:161–78.

Steinlien, Øystein 1984 "Kulturell endrlng og etnisk kontlnuitet. Lsestadianisme som politisk samlingsverdi i en samisk kystbygd." Master's thesis. University of Tromsø.

Stordahl, Vigdis. 1982. "Samer sier nel til Kongen.' En analyse av Norske Samers Rlksforbunds utvlkling og vilkar som etnopolitlsk organisasjon." Master's thesis, University of Tromsø.

Stordahl, Vigdis. 1987a. "Sámithing and Sámi Committees—a Useful Political and Administrative Solution for the Sámi In Norway?" In *Self Determination and Indigenous Peoples. Sami Rights and Northern Perspectives. IWGIA Document* no. 58. Copenhagen.

Thuen, Trond. 1987. "One Community—One People? Ethnicity and Demography In a North-Norwegian Community 1865-1930." *Acta Borealia,* 4(1-2):65–84.

Torp, Eivind. 1986. "Fra 'markaflnn' til same. Etnopolltisk mobilisering i en laestadiansk kontekst." Master's thesis. University of Tromsø.

Worsley, Peter. 1957. *The Trumpet Shall Sound: A Study of "Cargo" Cults in Melanesia.* London: MacGibbon and Kee.

THE NEW POLITICS

OF RESISTANCE

Ronald Niezen

THE SIGNIFICANCE OF SELF-DETERMINATION

THE ISSUES OF RELATIVISM and collective versus individual rights reveal the pervasiveness of sovereignty as a point of contestation between indigenous peoples and states. Antirelativism does not commonly consider parties other than states to be moral actors, at least not in the practice of human rights, and thus it unintentionally denies the self-determination claims of minority peoples through a limited vision of moral agency and responsibility. The individual-rights argument is similarly statist in orientation, reluctant to see beyond states as the parties responsible for respecting (or violating) individual human rights. Neither the antirelativist nor the individualist tendency in human rights is fully able to come to terms with indigenous peoples' claims of difference, especially of distinct rights, or, from another perspective, *equal* rights of self-determination.

In this article I consider some of the ways that self-determination has become a source of indigenous resistance to the centralizing tendencies of states, especially to prevailing notions and policy implications of individual rights, as affirmed and defended by states. Indigenous leaders often see sovereignty as a matter of immediate concern, upon which other rights—such as rights to land, subsistence, and health care—depend. It is a matter revealed in what people say to each other, in resistance through political uses of language, oral and written. The dialogue I have paraphrased in notes at international meetings is, unlike most contents of the recent anthropological literature, unashamedly and directly about power, expressed in an odd assortment of legal language and metaphor.[1]

The term "self-determination" encompasses every conceivable aspiration of politically organized societies. James Anaya (1996: ch. 4) finds various elements of self-determination elaborated in international instruments, including nondiscrimination, cultural integrity, control over lands and resources, social welfare and development, and self-government. The UN International Covenants alone articulate rights of peoples to self-determination in their political status, control of resources, practice of subsistence, and cultural development.

The ways that indigenous leaders envision self-determination reflect this variety of interconnected possibilities. In a paper entitled "The Right of Indigenous Peoples to Self-Determination," presented to the 1999 Midnight Sun Worship in Inari, Finland, Ted Moses (2000) stated, "[W]hen I think of self-determination, I think of hunting, fishing and trapping. I think of the land, of the water. I think of the land we have lost" (162). For Juan Leon of the Defensoría Maya of Guatemala, one of the most important aspects of his organization's work is the reconstruction of the Mayan legal system to make the administration of justice less punitive and corrupt, more consistent with what Francisco Raymundo (1997: 5-6), in a Defensoria Maya website, describes as the Maya's oral, preventive, conciliatory, restorative, and flexible approach to social conflict. There are nearly as many indigenous visions of self-determination as there are possibilities for economic, political, and cultural development.

The question arises of whether (and if so in what form) indigenous goals of self-determination are likely to include exercising the right of nationalist secession. But first it is necessary to draw out the implications of the significant fact that there is a consensus at work among internationally active indigenous leaders concerning the strategic approach to be taken in forwarding their claims of self-determination. Whether or not this consensus proves to be unshakable, the fact that it has influenced the work of the UN Commission on Human Rights for approximately a decade gives us leave to consider the development of human rights standards as an emerging form of indigenous political resistance. Unlike any other form of indigenous resistance, the pursuit of self-determination through human rights standards is global in its ambition; at the same time it aspires to effect reform at a variety of levels: in international organizations, the constitutions and laws of states, and the organization and values of indigenous polities themselves.

One of the concerns expressed by elders in attendance at international meetings is the erosion of their peoples' sovereignty by what they see as an alien and illegitimate state legal system. For example, Tony Black Feather, spokesman for the Tetuwan Oyate, Teton Sioux Nation Treaty Council, told his listeners in Geneva that "[a]s long as our people seek a solution in the American federal system, we will be subject to the corruption the system imposes" (Tetuwan Oyate 2000:1). This point of view is shared by the James Bay Crees: "Although we find ourselves in our own homelands, our own territories, living in the places we and our ancestors have never left, we are confronted by a legal system that is not ours. None of the indigenous peoples have any recollection that they have ever revoked or abrogated their own system of law, or that they have ever consented to have their rights determined by European or colonial legal systems" (Moses 1996:1). Such rejection of state legal systems does not imply a rejection of formal laws altogether. It is rather an indication of awareness that the formal system in the control of states cannot be relied upon as a mechanism to redress grievances. This rejection of state legal systems, while recognizing the usefulness of law, is what constitutes a new approach to indigenous resistance: there is no longer a clear contrast between formal redress of grievances and the informal "ordinary" politics of resistance. New opportunities have become available for indigenous peoples to use written laws for their own purposes. One of these is the international regime of human rights, which supersedes state laws internationally; another is the development of written indigenous constitutions and laws, which supersede state systems locally. There are thus two principal ways in which the indigenous peoples' movement challenges state sovereignty. One is at the international level, pressing for reforms within international law and eroding the statist orientation of the international system; the other is as a pluralistic force within states that presses for realization in practice of the notion, uncomfortable to many, of nations within nations, of peoples who have rights to self-determination nested within their rights as citizens of states.

Formalizing indigenous codes of behavior in the form of written laws and procedures is by no means the only option available in times of inevitable transition, but it certainly has its advantages over the alternatives. Maintaining oral traditions in the face of encroachments from state and industry has become increasingly untenable; time and again, contests between mores and law have been decided in favor of the latter. And acquiescing to all the political arrangements and codes of conduct imposed by the state has fragmented communities, led to crises of identity, and delegitimized local governance. Inherent law-making, on the other hand, has the advantage of connecting tradition with state constitutional and institutional arrangements, with many of the terms dictated by local practice. This does not arrest change, but controls it, gives it some shape and direction, keeps it from spinning out of control, holds it as much as possible within the orbit of legitimate and recognizable social arrangements.

This does not mean that indigenous nationalism is inherently or inevitably innocuous. If we have learned anything about nationalism since the French Revolution, it is that the development and reinforcement of loyalties based upon race, class, language, or religion are not without their costs. It is becoming ever more widely understood that indigenous societies—the victims of xenophobia, racism, and intolerance—are not immune to the risks of imitating the faults of their oppressors. "One of the unresolved dilemmas of basing indigenous claims on self-determination," Kingsbury (2000) writes, "is that in encouraging groups to mobilize as 'nations,' some groups or their leaders may take what to outsiders (and to some insiders) appears the path of nationalist excess, oppressing dissenters, mistreating and even creating minorities in order to create a clear majority and reinforce the dominant identity" (35). There is a small step between national restoration and nationalist retribution.

How, then, can we expect indigenous nationalism to be any different from other forms of nationalism, to be free of chauvinism and counter-hate, even if it develops within existing nation-states and is entirely or largely without secessionist ambitions? The answer to this question is not to be found in the centers of international politics, where displays of intolerant indigenous nationalism would be counterproductive, but in the local revival of self-determination, the untidy politics of micronationalism, and the use of self-determination as an instrument of indigenous resistance.

"PEOPLE" VS. "PEOPLES": THE BATTLE OF THE "S"

The "battle of the 'S'" has been fought in one form or another, and with varying degrees of intensity, at every gathering of indigenous peoples and states under the auspices of the United Nations. It continues to be one of the most important sources of disagreement between indigenous peoples and states, although, on the state side, the lines have shifted and only a minority remains entrenched against the forays of the "S." If the called-for use of the "S" is left out of any human rights standard-setting exercise, indigenous delegates immediately raise the issue, to which recalcitrant states reply from their trenches.

In fact, the "S" does not always stand alone but, written in possessive constructions, marches in unison with an apostrophe, the position of which is vitally significant: an apostrophe placed to the left of the "S" is fatal to its plurality. Only an apostrophe on the right affirms the collectivist authority, the inherent pluralism, of the "S."

On the surface, the controversy surrounding the "S" appears to be a mere product of the pedantry of jurists; but hanging upon the "S" is the question of whether indigenous peoples are the same "peoples"—with an "S"—so prominent in the Charter of the United Nations (the preamble of which is formulated in the name of "the Peoples of the United Nations"), and who therefore must be recognized as possessing all the rights that flow from that status, including the right to self-determination. So the "S" in "peoples" represents something quite important: the unfettered right of self-determination, as given pride of place in Article 1 of the Covenants and Article 3 of the Draft United Nations Declaration on the Rights of Indigenous Peoples.

A right to self-determination covers a spectrum of political choices, from assimilation into a dominant state to independent statehood (Nettheim 1988: 118). Between these poles is a range of options involving arrangements of self-government or regional autonomy with the state. If anything, the United Nations has exercised a bias in favour of independent statehood as a way of resolving conflicts stemming from colonial situations. This in itself has inclined states toward resisting the "S" favored by indigenous peoples because it raises the specter of uncontrollable indigenous secessionist claims and conflicts. The debate over the "S" has therefore led to an impasse at the Commission on Human Rights, one result of which has been little progress on the approval of the Draft United Nations Declaration on the Rights of Indigenous Peoples.

The "battle of the 'S'" also made an appearance at the International Labour Organization (ILO) during discussions leading up to final drafting and passage of the Indigenous and Tribal Peoples Convention of 1989 (No. 169). Here, the "S" emerged as part of a wider debate between those who favored a bold and comprehensive statement of rights and aspirations, including an explicit statement of the indigenous right to self-determination, and those, particularly the employers and a segment of governments, who saw any mention of self-determination as potentially destructive of the sovereignty of nation-states (Swepston 1990: 223–24). This controversy emerged most sharply in what Lee Swepston, human rights coordinator of the ILO, described as "an arcane international battle akin to debating the shape of the table" (228). Meetings on the ILO convention struggled for three years over replacing the word "populations," in the Convention No. 107 of 1957, with "peoples" in the instrument being developed. A conference on the document was reduced to using the term ["peoples"/"populations"], with brackets reducing its potency. The issue was resolved with the unhappy compromise of using the term "peoples" in the ILO convention, but with a proviso placed in Article 1.3 intended to remove its legal authority: "The use of the term 'peoples' in this Convention shall not be construed as having any implications as regards the rights which may attach to the term under international law." In effect, the ILO, in the interests of realizing a convention that would meet the immediate needs of indigenous peoples, postponed the debate on indigenous self-determination by handing it over to its parent body, the United Nations.[2]

In the context of Cree opposition to the proposed terms of Quebec secession, the "S" issue has been more contentious in Canada than elsewhere for two related reasons. First, Canada's constitution, revised and repatriated in 1982, makes reference to "aboriginal peoples." This gave prominence to Canada's rejection of the "S" in the context of international human rights standards for indigenous peoples, making the reluctant states appear inconsistent and hypocritical. Second, the likely motives for Canada's position on the "S" also emerged with particular clarity—relating to concerns about possible Quebec secession—thus confirming the idea that the position of governments on the "S" had little to do with justice or consistency in law and a great deal to do with vested state interests. For these reasons the government of Canada was a primary target when indigenous delegates realized the significance of the "S" and began to challenge states on their position toward it.

In annual meetings of the Working Group on Indigenous Populations, Canada used and supported phrasings that avoided the "S," including "populations" (as in the name of the Working Group), "groups," and "people" in the singular. In a paper submitted to the 1987 Working Group, some of the thinking behind this approach was made explicit: "It should be noted that references made to Canada's Aboriginal 'peoples' are consistent with the terminology of the Canadian Constitution with respect to Canada's domestic situation. They should *not* be interpreted as supportive of the notion that Canada's Aboriginal groups are 'peoples' in the sense of having the right to self-determination under international law [emphasis in original]" (Canada 1987:1).

At the 1993 World Conference on Human Rights in Vienna, indigenous delegates became aware that some states, including Canada, were avoiding using the "S." In response, they drew large "S"s on sheets of paper and pinned them to their clothing. When Canada's delegates spoke, they removed the sheets and raised them over their heads, a gesture that underscored the absence of the word "peoples" from everything being said.

It was only after the narrowest possible victory of the "No" vote in Quebec's 1995 referendum on secession that Canada began to revise its position on the "S." On October 31, 1996, at the 53rd session of the Working Group on the Draft Declaration on the Rights of Indigenous Peoples, a qualified recognition of indigenous self-determination was presented in which the government of Canada (1996a) accepted "a right of self-determination for indigenous peoples which respects the political, constitutional and territorial integrity of democratic states" (2). (It is worth noting that the qualification "which respects" gives Canada room to maneuver in the event that a secessionist province were to claim indigenous territories as part of a new state.)

This did not by any means put an end to the general controversy at the United Nations. Although such states as Australia, Denmark, and Canada changed their positions, other states, such as India, China, and the United States, have remained adamantly opposed to use of the term "indigenous peoples" in any official UN document. This focal point of state/indigenous disagreement finds its way into almost every conceivable issue under discussion. On the first day of the 1999 World Health Organization Consultation on the Health of Indigenous Peoples, indigenous delegates made a connection between their health conditions, their control of land and resources, and therefore their need, above all else, for self-determination. At the 2000 meeting of the ad hoc working group on a new permanent forum, controversy flared up, among other things, over the name to be given the forum. When some states made it clear that they would not accept the word "peoples" in the name of the forum, and proposed instead that it be called the "Permanent Forum for Indigenous Issues," some indigenous delegates placed yellow signs with bold letters in front of their desks reading "WE ARE PEOPLES, NOT ISSUES." Milelani Trask (representing Na Koa Idaika O Ka Lahui Hawai'i), seated behind such a sign, stated, "The chair is conceding and caving in to the states that are twisting his arm," and a representative of the Assembly of First Nations said, "It is a shame that the state governments cannot recognize the world's indigenous peoples as such.... We are peoples, not issues. Issues may go away, but peoples do not."

After these statements had been heard, a proposal was made by the International Indian Treaty Council to draft a clause that would limit the implications of the word "peoples" in international law, thus meeting state concerns, while acting to "preserve position" for the indigenous delegates. An IITC spokesman cited the precedent set by Article 1.3 of ILO Convention No. 169 and suggested the following wording: "As it is beyond the mandate of this Working Group to provide judicial interpretation, the interpretation of the word 'peoples' and its meaning under international law should be left to competent UN bodies."

A resolution sent by the Commission on Human Rights (United Nations 2000b) for adoption by the Economic and Social Council two months after this meeting took place made no reference to this debate or the proposed compromise on "peoples," but referred in its heading to "Establishment of a Permanent Forum on Indigenous Issues." This veto by the Human Rights Commission of the indigenous position lends credence to the kind of frustration expressed by a Lakota elder: "[T]he work is dictated, without the indigenous peoples' input even being given consideration, with changes made outside of public discussion.... It is cruel to invite input and then completely disregard it" (Tail 2000: 1). At the same time, it reveals a continuing caution on the part of the United Nations toward the issue of indigenous self-determination. Such contests over sovereignty, if we look more closely, can be found throughout many of the discussions that take place under other headings.

DIALOGUE ON SELF-DETERMINATION

Battlefields, legislatures, and courts, with so much hidden behind their main adversarial goals, do not reveal human interests quite so clearly as tasks of cooperation. When people resist one another while pursuing a supposedly common purpose, the tensions revealed usually tell us something about their characters, the core of their personalities, what makes them tick. When we see political organizations resist one another in a cooperative venture, we usually know we have found something that can reveal their basic motives and orientations.

When indigenous and state delegates sat together for 10 days at the UN headquarters in Geneva during February 2000, they had such a common purpose, revealed in the name given to the meeting in a UN document: "the ad hoc working group established pursuant to Commission on Human Rights resolutions ... to consider the establishment of a permanent forum and to submit concrete proposals to that effect" (United Nations 2000b: 2). The permanent forum is to be the centerpiece of the International Decade of the World's Indigenous People and the principal mechanism for "furthering partnership between Governments and indigenous people" (2).

The question of self-determination for indigenous peoples pervaded the discussions of this meeting, not just in the explicit controversy over use of the word "issues" rather than "peoples" in the name to be given the forum but in matters related only indirectly to concerns about sovereignty. The methods by which indigenous representatives would be elected or appointed to the forum, for example, fed directly into indigenous claims to self-determination. Indigenous delegates were concerned that too much involvement from states in the procedures for appointing indigenous representatives would emasculate the forum by making its principal decision-makers reliant upon state authority. The very discussion of state proposals for election or appointment of indigenous representatives seemed to be understood by indigenous delegates as an inappropriate intrusion into matters of concern to indigenous peoples as self-determining nations.

A Spanish proposal for setting up the indigenous representation at a permanent forum, for example, contained one element that provoked disapproval from many indigenous delegates: "Each Member State having indigenous populations on its territory will accredit two delegates for the plenary meetings: one representing the government and the other freely designated in an autonomous way by the Indigenous Peoples" (United Nations 2000a: 3). Indigenous delegates almost uniformly reacted with concern to this aspect of the proposal, seeing in it an attempt to "domesticate" and control state relations with indigenous peoples. The issue of representation was, for them, deeply implicated with self-determination. A representative of the Teton Sioux Nation thanked the Spanish delegation for presenting a concrete proposal for the membership of the forum but then offered a blunt criticism of the idea that indigenous members should be accredited by states: "Any attempt at linking membership in the forum with some sort of a formula between nation states and indigenous cultures from within the borders of those nation-states would be a real problem for us. This is the same kind of paternalism and the same kind of dominance that has brought us to the United Nations in the first place." Spain's position paper was probably not intended to weaken indigenous representation at the United Nations. It was a set of proposals to facilitate the establishment of a new forum in an organization dominated by states. Nevertheless, the suggestion that states should accredit the forum's indigenous representatives was broadly rejected by the indigenous caucus. The subtext of their objections seemed to be that indigenous sovereignty would not be secure in a system in which state governments had any part in the process of approving indigenous representatives.

The matter did not end here. A few state delegations grew impatient with the apparent inability of the indigenous caucus to arrive at a concrete, uniform system for electing or appointing indigenous representatives to the future permanent forum. Argentina's representative clearly felt that states were the most experienced at the international political game and should be closely involved in the appointment of indigenous members to the permanent forum: "What we want is for these communities to be properly represented. And the formula that we propose is the one which we think would best ensure representation for those communities."The government of Venezuela recommended the "homogenization of indigenous election procedures in order for there to be transparency," and others called for the indigenous caucus to arrive at the election procedures before the meeting's end. One indigenous delegate, however, shifted the blame for the slow progress being made on the election procedures by recalling the global impacts of colonization on indigenous political systems: "Governments are already highly organized.... But indigenous peoples are not in that situation. In fact, if we had been allowed to practice our own indigenous social, political structures, then maybe we would be in that state also. But those were the things that had been destroyed during colonization ... and nation-state building. We have not been allowed to really develop and nurture our own indigenous social structures and political structures." An indigenous spokesperson from Bangladesh pointed to the practical and financial constraints of formal elections of indigenous representatives, modeled on the procedures of democratic states: "Are we going to say that each community is going to vote? Who is going to organize this kind of nomination procedure? Is there an election commission in the country which is going to nominate these kind of indigenous representatives? If that is the procedure, then we are talking about financial constraints. If the state wants to ensure that [all indigenous communities participate in the election process and is] willing to contribute money ... the same money could be used for development of the indigenous communities."

The Commission on Human Rights, following up on this meeting, decided that the permanent forum would consist of 16 members, eight to be nominated by governments and elected by the Economic and Social Council, and eight indigenous members "to be appointed by the President of the Council ... on the basis of broad consultations with indigenous organizations taking into account the diversity and geographical distribution of the indigenous people of the world as well as the principles of transparency, representativity and equal opportunity for all indigenous people" (United Nations 2000b: 2). The United Nations was apparently neither in a position to accede to the will of some states to control indigenous representation nor able to recognize indigenous claims to complete control over procedures for determining indigenous membership of the forum. It gave ultimate authority over representation to the Economic and Social Council and left to one side the question of democratic mechanisms.

Another revealing difference between states and indigenous peoples that arose in discussions on the establishment of a permanent forum centered upon reference to the Charter of the United Nations in the mandate of the forum. The chairman of the previous year's meeting on the permanent forum pointed in his report to Articles 62 and 63 of the charter for possible guidance in setting out this mandate. Article

62 in particular points, in an apparently innocuous way, to the power of the Economic and Social Council to "make or initiate studies and reports with respect to international economic, social, cultural, educational, health, and related matters" and says that it "may make recommendations with respect to any such matters to the General Assembly, to the Members of the United Nations, and to the specialized agencies concerned." More of the same apparently bland material is found elsewhere in these articles, nothing that could easily be seen as a threat to state interests. But the prospect of referencing the Charter of the United Nations in the mandate of the permanent forum for indigenous people did indeed become contentious for some states. Their objections were not expressed so much in open plenary sessions as in the behind-the-scenes work of state and indigenous "facilitators," appointed to summarize the conclusions reached in closed caucus meetings. One indigenous delegate objected to this procedure, calling it "bad faith" on the part of governments to use facilitators to make objections to the indigenous peoples' positions without putting them on the floor. "They're not being forthright," he protested, "and they're saving their objections for the facilitators. We believe that's a corruption of the process." An indigenous delegate from Bangladesh insisted on the reasonableness of the indigenous position: "We're not at this meeting asking for a buffalo and hoping to get a goat," he said. "We want a goat and are asking for a goat."

As with many seemingly arcane but hard-fought controversies, the real issues of contention are general and far-reaching. Those states that objected to the very idea of an indigenous forum in the first meetings on the issue were faced with a growing consensus in its favour that they were no longer able to obstruct. With the forum itself now apparently a *fait accompli,* the strategy that remained to them was to limit its powers in every way possible. For some states, therefore, it became important to prevent the establishment of a forum with a mandate that could establish policy in the UN system, that could create compulsory instruments or standards, or that was able to intervene in internal violent conflicts. For these states, reference to the Charter of the United Nations invoked such possibilities. For the indigenous delegates, on the other hand, the charter embodied their most cherished aspirations. The goals set out in the preamble of the charter, "to save succeeding generations from the scourge of war" and "to promote social progress and better standards of life in larger freedom," seemed to resonate with particular force for one of Hawai'i's indigenous delegates, Milelani Trask, who stated in a plenary session, "For [states] to object to peace and prosperity, that leaves us with war and poverty." In an indigenous caucus meeting, one participant suggested that the indigenous delegates walk out of the meeting and call a press conference and urged others to "be strong and stand up against it" and to "fight for peace now, before they come with guns on our land." Others, who argued against a boycott of the meeting, prevailed.

A compromise between the indigenous and state positions was eventually achieved in a report of the facilitators with their recommendation that reference to Articles 62 and 63 of the Charter of the United Nations should be situated in the preamble of the document that would establish the indigenous forum. In this way, the mention of the charter would not be binding or operative. The states would be free of the risk of an indigenous forum with the power to intervene in violent conflicts.

Despite numerous disagreements between indigenous peoples and states, the 2000 meeting on the permanent forum brought out important points of agreement between the indigenous and state caucuses. The first of these was the general will to establish a permanent forum. This had not been a given in previous years, and the near-consensus among states that it be given a green light was something that caught some indigenous delegates by surprise, as though they had been bracing themselves for more confrontation than they actually encountered. Further, it was generally agreed that it be established as a subsidiary organ of the Economic and Social Council, putting it at a very high level within the UN system, as a body on the same administrative level (though not with the same power) as the High Commission on Human Rights. This would give the permanent forum an authority of its own, an ability to be seen and heard within the UN system, and therefore in the world at large. It would be in a position to attract requests for its help—from indigenous peoples, certainly, but also from governments and other agencies within the UN system. The dialogue on the permanent forum revealed deep differences between indigenous peoples and states, the expression of which indeed showed the United Nations to be largely controlled by states; but the points of consensus and compromise that were established showed the indigenous peoples' movement to be succeeding, in its own manner, in making the United Nations, as one indigenous delegate put it, "more human."

THE POLITICS OF SHAME IN INTERNATIONAL FORUMS

One of the creative uses to which the human rights forums of the United Nations are being put is as a launching point for the politics of shame. The release of information and opinions from the offices and press rooms of UN organizations can greatly raise the profile of a cause—so much so that UN agencies have taken to putting their facsimile cover sheets under lock and key to prevent NGOs (not just indigenous ones) from using their letterhead to command the attention of journalists.

The connection between UN meetings and indigenous lobbying is nowhere more apparent than at the annual gatherings of the Working Group on Indigenous Populations. Here attendance is open, and a wide variety of indigenous peoples and organizations, not just those experienced in standard setting, come to present information to the gathering. A broad base of attendance is also ensured by the establishment, as part of the International Decade, of a Voluntary Fund, which pays for those from indigenous organizations with small budgets to attend UN meetings, albeit on a shoestring. (The Office of the Secretariat notes the frequent incidence during the working group meetings of inappropriate requests for coffee and doughnuts, a sign of the relative inexperience of those in attendance.) And the broad topics covered by the working group—such as indigenous peoples and land, treaties, and indigenous children—provide wide latitude for the expression of grievance and opinion.

A large and varied attendance at working group meetings is further encouraged by an open definition of "indigenous peoples," essentially allowing any to speak who define *themselves* as indigenous. I witnessed only one instance in which an exception was made to this openness. In the 1996 working group meeting a Hutu delegate took the floor and spoke—off the topic—about the circumstances and causes of the genocide in Rwanda. He was "gavelled" by the chairperson, ostensibly because his case was already being considered, as a matter of great urgency, by the International Tribunal for Rwanda.

One of the appeals of working-group meetings, especially to delegates experienced in lobbying, is the international attention given to news that emerges from the UN headquarters. Information, views, pamphlets, petitions, and copies of submissions presented to the Secretariat are circulated by indigenous organizations to others in the room, and occasionally to the press. Tables at the back of the meeting room contain pamphlets for distribution to delegates. By the end of the first of two weeks, newspaper articles begin to appear, based on interventions made earlier. Press releases and telephone interviews have by this time already begun to work their magic.

Occasionally meetings concerned with developing human rights standards or institutions become, outside the main meeting room, focal points for information and censure. This usually relates to developments unfolding in the indigenous world, events that have already garnered some notice. Such an event reached an indigenous caucus meeting at the UN headquarters in Geneva on February 15, 2000. Four days earlier, the Colombian army fired tear gas on a group of U'we protesters who had set up roadblocks on a road used by Occidental Petroleum in the remote rainforest that they claimed as ancestral land. The U'we are a small people, with only 5,000 members, but their alliance with lawyers, human rights organizations, and environmental groups in Colombia and the United States had begun to raise the profile of their conflict with Occidental and the government of Colombia. As part of their protest strategy, they had threatened to commit mass suicide if a proposed exploratory well was drilled on land they considered sacred. The threat harkens back to an event during Spanish colonization in the 17th century in which scores of U'we walked off the top of a 1,400-foot precipice (Chang 2000).

Some might see this as idle posturing, an empty threat of the ultimate publicity stunt, with little connection to the act committed by some of the U'we's ancestors. But if indeed this was a serious expression of their desperation, the early morning raid of February 11 pushed the U'we closer to such an act and in the process resulted in the deaths of four infants who drowned as the protesters fled across a river. Probably because of the remoteness of the event, this information took four days to reach the indigenous caucus meeting, but once there it spread quickly. The same afternoon a declaration of protest was drafted in Spanish, hastily translated into English to reach a wider base of support, and presented to indigenous delegates for signature. A press conference was then called by the Latin American delegation to denounce the actions of the Colombian government. Emerging as it did from a meeting already under way at the United Nations, the information presented to the press had the imprimatur of truth and significance.

Media attention is not an end in itself, and the effects of this kind of organized protest that actually make a difference in people's lives are rarely immediate. But a critical mass of such notice is sometimes enough to bring reluctant governments to the table, and very occasionally—often enough at any rate to make the effort more than worthwhile—a contract will be cancelled, a project shelved, or an agreement with states and industry undertaken that improves conditions in indigenous communities and raises the stature of the leaders who brought it into effect.

In the politics of shame, international organizations have become the most important conduits of information filtered to the public via the press. The judgments of international panels of experts add to (or take away from, depending on the conclusions) the credibility of a grievance or cause. It is not just the interested parties, usually an indigenous organization in a relationship of conflict with a state or corporation, vying for public approval in a contest of popular support, but an independent evaluation of the merits of each story. The James Bay Crees, for example, were one of 10 plaintiffs in the 1992 hearings of the International Water Tribunal (IWT) in Amsterdam, the Netherlands, convened to consider the worst violations of water rights from around the world. The Cree delegation to the hearings did not attend passively but used the opportunity of their presence in Amsterdam to bring their case directly to the public. They flew a large canoe to Amsterdam—or, rather, a hybrid canoe/kayak, which they called an *odeyak* (from the Cree word *uut* and Inuit *qayak),* as a symbol of the Cree and Inuit peoples affected by hydroelectric development in northern Quebec—and paddled it through the canals of Amsterdam, speaking to the curious crowds and giving interviews to the press. They thus raised the profile of their case even before their testimony before the IWT was heard.

Such lobbying, of course, rarely goes unopposed. Jacques Finet, vice-president of Hydro-Quebec, for example, accused the Crees of using their concerns about the environment as a way of gaining control over the resources of the North so that they could act, not as environmental stewards, but as profiteers, no different from the enterprises that extracted resources: "The Cree's environmentalism is just a façade.... It wouldn't be six months before you would see bulldozers in the area if it was their country and they had control over natural resources" (*Gazette* 1992). Counterlobbying of this kind usually invokes imagined threats to national prosperity: a lack of jobs, insufficient energy resources, and loss of export revenue.

This might be one reason why indigenous lobbying is more effective when exported. In western Europe especially (perhaps with the exception of the Nordic countries, home to the Saamis), few of the concerns usually invoked as consequences of indigenous claims can have much effect. The people and land in question are simply too far away to be seen as a threat to jobs and prosperity.[3]

It is, of course, difficult to determine if the press attention briefly given to the Crees in Europe had any influence on the outcome of the IWT hearings. In its ruling, however, the jury expressed surprise at the inconsistency between Canada's reputation as a country that respects human rights and its insensitivity to the rights of the Crees. It also called on Hydro-Quebec to find alternatives to large dams in its energy policy, including a reduction of wasteful consumption (Niezen 1998:119). Cree delegates considered this a breakthrough in their campaign to stop the second phase of hydroelectric development in northern Quebec: "The jury's ruling was a great victory for our people. The ruling was unambiguous and clear: the International Water Tribunal determined that the first phase of the James Bay mega-project was imposed on the Crees, and that the devastating impacts on our health and the environment were never taken into account" (Grand Council 1992: 9). There can be little doubt that an accumulating mass of such publicity had a part in New York Governor Mario Cuomo's decision in 1992 to drop contracts for the purchase of electric power from Quebec. And there is similarly a likely connection between such loss of contracts in New England (potentially amounting to some 10 percent of Hydro-Quebec sales) and the 1994 decision by Quebec Premier Jacques Parizeau to shelve a proposed multi-billion-dollar hydroelectric project on the Great Whale River (Niezen 1998: 120).[4]

Despite such occasional success, the politics of shame has several unfortunate side effects. One of these derives from a condition in which indigenous formulations of tradition and nationhood require some degree of public approval. It is not enough that peoples and communities are destroyed, removed from the land, politically marginalized, unemployed in an unfamiliar formal economy, exposed to addictions, and educated in a way that convinces many individuals of their innate inferiority. To satisfy the public that can help them—the audiences most concerned with human rights and the environment—they must also be noble, strong, spiritually wise, and, above all, environmentally discreet. The reality of destroyed communities, however, is rarely consistent with the expectations placed upon them. There can be little nobility, wisdom, or environmental friendliness where addictions are rampant, economic desires are unfulfilled, and political frustration pushes regularly against the barriers preventing violence.[5]

This is an example of a phenomenon that has broad implications for the indigenous peoples' movement. Indigenous nationalism is shaped more significantly by the demands of consumer export than are other forms of group identity. This is so because indigenous peoples represent "a way of life" that is disappearing and embody features that are increasingly absent from the lives of those being carried along by the main current of modernity.[6]

Indigenous nationalism thus usually shapes itself around those core values that resonate most strongly with the non-indigenous public. And there is some comfort to be taken in this. Surely there can be little harm in an identity based largely on environmental wisdom. The harm comes more from public disapproval of necessary things, like legal knowledge and resource extraction. An artificial boundary is sometimes erected around indigenous communities that limits their options and inhibits their prosperity.

A second drawback of the need for public support is its tendency to weaken with use. "Compassion fatigue" is the term sometimes used to describe the reaction of the public in democratic countries against too many issues thrown at them for too long. Sympathy has a tendency to focus on the most immediate crises, the human rights catastrophes with the highest body count, the greatest evidence of horror and mass suffering. The human rights abuses that leave only trails of torment but little or no blood are difficult to bring to public notice. One of the secondary evils of genocide is that it disproportionately draws upon a finite reserve of public compassion, reducing lesser causes to the level of the "ordinary," the tacitly accepted.

Even those states that strive toward pluralism and cultural tolerance find it difficult to go much beyond the accommodation of recreational diversity, the celebration of differences through such things as sporting events, arts, and festivals. The subtext of state-sponsored celebrations of difference is usually a variation of the idea that, despite a variety of human appearances, languages, and cultures, all citizens are in one important sense the same: all are subject to the same law, the same constitution, the same rights, loyalty to the same state. In the histories of many states, blood has been shed in liberation struggles to establish and safeguard higher standards of such diversity within equality.

Indigenous peoples are problematic for many states because they stand outside the accepted protocols of cultural difference. The rights that have accrued to indigenous peoples do not correspond to those of peoples who are culturally distinct but constitutionally equal.

The pursuit of self-determination is the focal point of indigenous peoples' participation in human rights meetings and processes, but it means something different for each representative of the various internationally active indigenous peoples—or rather, the hopes and aspirations attached to it vary from one people or organization to the next. For many, the importance of self-determination is that it represents control of land, resources, and livelihood. For others, it provides an opportunity to redress systemic injustice in state judicial systems. For still others, it represents above all new opportunities to express culture and language without the expectation that these will be systematically maligned, suppressed, and extinguished by state-sponsored programs. The emphasis placed on such aspirations may vary, but all would probably agree that each of these things is an important dimension of indigenous self-determination.

The point at which indigenous self-determination has become entangled in the development of human rights standards is where its implications in international law come to the fore, implications that associate self-determination with a right, under conditions of extreme and systematic human rights violations, of secession from a nation-state. To some extent, state concerns over indigenous peoples' status as "peoples" have not been allayed by the fact that indigenous self-determination is often couched in nationalist terms. In their development of an identity that fits within the framework of international organizations, and that at the same time provides collective sources of esteem, indigenous leaders have made ready use of the symbols and structures of nation-states. At the same time, it is still possible to see that the social realities behind such symbols are usually not consistent with independent statehood and that some states, moreover, are using their concerns over indigenous nationalism as a means of obstructing the development of human rights standards specific to indigenous peoples. The human rights agenda, which has in recent decades come to include indigenous peoples, has built into it a form of age-old contest between states pressing for uniform political control and cultural domination, and minority peoples with their own claims of sovereignty, attachment to territory, and cultural integrity.

The claims (and exercise) of self-determination by the James Bay Crees tell us something about the relationship between self-determining indigenous peoples and states. The James Bay Crees, politically represented by the Grand Council of the Crees, have a highly developed system of regional autonomy functioning within a multicultural state. Yet the government of Canada was long opposed to recognition of indigenous peoples' rights of self-determination as "peoples" in international law. By presenting a strong argument for the rights of Aboriginal peoples living within the province of Quebec to decide for themselves their territorial and political affiliation in the event of Quebec's secession, presenting their arguments in international forums, the Canadian courts, and to the public, the Crees, Inuits, Naskapi, and other Aboriginal groups in Quebec could well have influenced the outcome of the 1995 referendum on Quebec independence and contributed to the subsequent declining fortunes of the province's separatist agenda. In this case, arguments for indigenous self-determination have meant, not the division of a nation-state, but concrete support for its unity.

The new politics of resistance connects indigenous leaders with national and international laws that provide legitimacy for local expressions of self-determination through written laws and formal procedures. The worlds of Montesquieu and Maine do not just quietly come together through this phenomenon; they collide with a force that produces uncomfortable juxtapositions and fragments of incoherence. Each step toward the use of written laws as an expression of indigenous self-determination is understandable in itself: it makes sense that, confronted by the mechanisms of state domination, indigenous leaders would try to reconstitute their sovereignty in terms easily interpreted by state officials, and it is equally understandable that reconstituting the values of oral societies in the form of written legal codes might carry more authority with states and international organizations than the mere assertion of oral traditions, often inaccessible to bureaucracies. Indigenous laws in this sense carry a message that is otherwise difficult to get across: "We are a sovereign people. We have always governed ourselves, and here is the evidence that we continue to do so. The laws that you make as a state presume to control us, to take away our land, to diminish who we are as a people, but these laws were not made by us. We have our own laws, made by the will of our people. You have made a promise that we should be able to govern ourselves. International law tells us that we should be allowed to govern ourselves. And here is the result of our governance." Such reasoning goes some way toward explaining the reluctance of states and international organizations to go further in their recognition of indigenous rights of self-determination. The main disincentive to recognition of indigenous rights of self-governance is not so much the Swiss-cheese effect of empty, ungovernable spaces in the states' constitutional frameworks as the loss of control over territory and natural resources that would result from it.

At the same time, as a strategy of cultural preservation—or at the very least of protection against change that is rapid, far-reaching, and potentially socially dislocating—inherent-jurisdiction law-making is a more dubious strategy. While ostensibly derived from practices and values that predate the imposition of colonial sovereignty, it requires the development of institutions, technologies, and procedures that are quintessentially modern. Of course it can be argued that indigenous societies have long histories of adaptation, of innovating in their use of the tools and institutions of other societies to advance their ability to pursue forest-based or pastoral subsistence. It remains to be seen, however, to what extent indigenous peoples' use of formal laws and procedures furthers their stated goal of preserving their cultural distinctiveness or contributes to their assimilation, perhaps not within states, but within a global pattern of cultural and institutional similarity.

The new politics of resistance also connects indigenous societies, more than ever before, with the "outside" world, with international networks consisting of other indigenous organizations, non-indigenous support groups, and more passively sympathetic audiences. On the face of it, this has tremendous advantages over "ordinary resistance." Although local acts of noncooperation, mendacity, and sabotage can exert upon states a cumulative burden of administrative inconvenience and even regional gridlock, they do not have the same implications for state power as the coordinated activities of indigenous peoples organizations engaged in the "politics of shame." New strategies of and resources for information gathering and dissemination make it more often problematic for state governments, especially liberal democracies, to appear callous and indifferent to the welfare of indigenous communities. It is a well-recognized principle of liberal states, though by no means always followed, that no minority group can be visibly neglected or victimized by the state without in some way compromising the rights of all citizens, especially the members of other minorities. There is thus a connection between the geographical and political isolation of indigenous societies. If their misery were encountered daily by others, above all by citizens of the state, such visibility would translate readily into greater political will to respond. The technology of travel and communication is to some extent having the effect of bringing conditions in isolated communities to the attention of a wider public, presented mainly through the lenses of activist lobbying and journalism. This requires a cultural presentation of self, a reflection upon what is important to communicate about a society unknown (it is usually assumed) to a mutually unknown audience. This encounter of strangers is predicated upon assumptions of vaguely similar values: environmental preservation, appreciation of "different" cultures, and rejection of poverty, misery, and illegitimate death.

Indigenous peoples are unlike other ethnic minorities in the extent to which they must rely upon such presentations of collective self to achieve a desired degree of political influence, to have an impact on decision-making in industry, state governments, and international organizations. Indigenous identity is thus not a simple reflection of timeless values and practices; it is based in large measure on a compendium of cultural facts and artifacts intended for consumption within a dominant national society and an international audience. Indigenous lobbying is inseparable from the cultural and spiritual trends within its audiences, trends that seek some form of perfection or ancestral source of wisdom from the native, Aboriginal, or indigenous "others." From the point of view of indigenous lobbyists, this is as much a source of constraint as influence. The realities of collective suffering in their communities intrude upon their presentation of a cultural ideal, and the expectations of those from a dominant culture seeking indigenous wisdom as a corrective to their own lives intrude upon the abilities of indigenous peoples to adapt, to develop their economies, and to move beyond compelling cultural images as the source of their entry into global society.

NOTES

1. Some material in this chapter consists of informal statements made by delegates in plenary sessions of international meetings. In some instances I recorded and transcribed these statements, in others I wrote them verbatim into my notes during the meeting. In both instances I have adjusted the spoken version of these statements to eliminate repetitions and minor grammatical errors. They should be taken as fragments of dialogue, not as formal policy statements emerging from governments or indigenous peoples' organizations.

2. The Organization of American States (OAS) currently faces the same controversy in the process of drafting a proposed American Declaration on the Rights of Indigenous Peoples. The working document for a January 2001 meeting on the proposed declaration consistently situates the words "peoples"/"populations" in square brackets, indicating that consensus had not been reached. The notion of equality, by contrast, expressed as antiracism and antidiscrimination, is not controversial, as in the draft Article 4 of the preamble: "Reiterating the responsibility incumbent upon all states to combat racism and all forms of discrimination with a view to eliminating them" (OAS 2001b). Equality and antidiscrimination, applied in particular to indigenous peoples, continue to be less controversial for state governments than the distinct rights of "peoples."

3. The cultural imaginings and longings of the European New Age movement appear strongest in Germany, possibly because its colonial entanglements with living, breathing, rights-seeking Aboriginal people are not as immediate as those of many other European nations. The *Gastarbeiter* are closer to home as targets of intolerance.

4. Similarly, the Arun III Hydroelectric Project in Nepal came under the scrutiny of the World Bank's Inspection Panel, largely through the lobbying activities of residents in harm's way of the project, who created the Arun Concerned Group. The World Bank can experience loss of legitimacy and the projects they sponsor can even lose profitability if they are the cause of social conflict, litigation, and embarrassing media coverage. Projects are assessed by the Inspection Panel according to the criteria of the policies and procedures of the World Bank itself, without direct reference to human rights treaties. The Inspection Panel, after investigating the impact of the Arun III project on the ethnic groups in the area to be impacted by the project (whether or not they were labeled "indigenous"), recommended strict social-impact monitoring, environmental-impact assessments, and informed public participation in the project. Given the extent of measures required to prevent the project's interference with vulnerable populations, the president of the Bank decided not to proceed with the project and recommended that the World Bank support the government of Nepal in seeking an alternative energy strategy. This decision was taken even though discontinuation of the project was not a recommendation of the Inspection Panel (Scheinin 2000:186–90).

5. Martin Scheinin (2000) emphasizes the need for a judicial approach to cultural rights in which even modern forms of economic activity, such as running casinos, should require protection as Aboriginal rights if they provide an economic foundation for self-government and hence the preservation of an indigenous culture. He argues that "the ultimate outcome of affording protection only to economic activities that were practiced 'at the time of contact' will, in many cases, be the extinction of the culture" (197–98). A variety of economic opportunities is called for, especially in "pathological" situations in which cultures have already been largely destroyed.

6. State judiciaries have also promulgated conceptualizations of indigenous cultures that stress their core value as being stagnantly "distinctive." In Canada this is exemplified by a "species-by-species" approach to hunting and fishing rights emerging from Supreme Court rulings. In *Van der Peet v. R.* (1996), for example, the Musqueam Indians' right to participate in British Columbia's salmon fishery was predicated upon their ability to demonstrate that the activity was for them "an element of a practice, custom or tradition integral to [their] distinctive culture" (para. 46). Rights, in other words, must be subject to tests of cultural authenticity, based largely upon ethnohistorical accounts of Aboriginal societies at the time of European assertion of sovereignty. Such a "frozen-in-time" approach to subsistence rights does not take into account the need of all societies to use new technologies, or harvest new species, in adaptation to economic, social, and cultural challenges. The Court's requirement of authenticity overlooks the basic kinds of adaptations societies engage in during such events as migration or the introduction of revolutionary technologies. The motivations behind judicial stereotyping are clearly different from the romantic impulses of the New Age movement or the environmental lobby, although some trace of cultural romanticism in the judiciary cannot be altogether ruled out. It is clearer that "distinctive" cultural rights are less of a burden on the state than general political rights; cultural rights break indigenous claims of sovereignty into manageable pieces. The alternative—recognizing Aboriginal political rights—would, as Michael Asch (2000) points out, "produce a fundamental challenge to Canada's claim to have secured legitimate sovereignty in the absence of treaties or adhesions in which Aboriginal peoples voluntarily surrendered their sovereignty, jurisdiction, and underlying title. Such assumptions would raise serious questions about the jurisdictional arrangements between First Nations and various levels of Canadian government" (135). The antiquated approach to culture on the part of the judiciary is more an outcome of the containment of political claims than a longing for a better world, at least not a world in which indigenous cultures are the repositories of the political rights of peoples.

In one respect, however, the "frozen-in-time" judicial conceptualization of culture has a similar effect to that of popular romanticism. Both impose definitions and expectations of culture that in some ways limit the manner in which indigenous societies can present themselves. They both curtail the range of choices to be drawn upon in making adaptations to rapidly changing circumstances. Whether or not an indigenous society chooses to assert its sovereignty, it is called upon by many, from a variety of sources, to diminish it.

REFERENCES

Anaya, James. 1996. *Indigenous Peoples in International Law.* Oxford, England: Oxford University Press.

Canada. 1987. "Evolution of Standards Concerning Indigenous Populations." Unpublished statement to the UN Working Group on Indigenous Populations, 5th Session, Geneva.

Chang, Chris. 2000. "A Leap of Faith." *Audubon* 102 (1):14.

Grand Council of the Crees. 1992. *1991–1992 Annual Report.* Nemaska, Québec: Grand Council of the Crees.

Kingsbury, Benedict. 2000. "Reconstructing Self-Determination: A Relational Approach." In *Operationalizing the Right of Indigenous Peoples to Self-Determination*, edited by Pekka Aikio and Martin Scheinin. Turku, Finland: Åbo Akademi University.

Moses, Ted. 1996. "Customary Law and National/ International Law." Statement presented at the International Encounter of Amerindian Communities, Paris, June 19–21.

Moses, Ted. 2000. "The Right of Self-Determination and Its Significance to the Survival of Indigenous Peoples." In *Operationalizing the Right of Indigenous Peoples to Self-Determination*, edited by Pekka Aikio and Martin Scheinin. Turku, Finland: Åbo Akademi University.

Nettheim, Garth. 1988. "'Peoples' and 'Populations': Indigenous People and the Rights of Peoples." In *The Rights of Peoples*, edited by James Crawford. Oxford, England: Clarendon.

Niezen, Ronald. 1998. *Defending the Land: Sovereignty and Forest Life in James Bay Cree Society*. Needham Heights, Mass: Allyn & Bacon.

Raymundo, Francisco. 1997. "Justicia en el Area Ixil." *Chuj Wallijo'q; Information Mensuel de la Defensoría Maya* 1 (1):4–6. Also available at http://www.derochos.net/ngo/defe-maya/feb97.txt

Swepston, Lee. 1990. "The Adoption of the Indigenous and Tribal Peoples Convention, 1989 (No. 169)." *Law and Anthropology* 5:221–35.

Tail, Eli J. 2000. "Address to the Government and Indigenous Representatives at the Working Group on the Permanent Forum for Indigenous Peoples." Unpublished document. Geneva, February 22.

Tetuwan, Oyate. 2000. "Pine Ridge Takeover: Statement of the Tetuwan Oyate, Teton Sioux Nation Treaty Council." Unpublished document. Geneva, January 25.

United Nations. 2000a. *Document Presented by the Delegation of Spain for the Permanent Forum*. Commission on Human Rights. UN doc. no. E/CN.4/AC.47/2000/CPR.5

United Nations. 2000b. *Indigenous Issues: Resolution to the Economic and Social Council*. UN doc. no. E/CN.4/2000/L.68. April 18

CHAPTER 19

POLITICS WITHIN THE METIS

ASSOCIATION OF ALBERTA

Joe Sawchuk

An entirely new political arena—that of Native politics and Native politicians—was created by the advent of government funding in the 1960s, and it in turn developed many new patterns in the lifestyles of Native people in Canada. The Native leader formed an important part of a new phenomenon, the rising of a Native middle class. A new career, that of Native politician, is now open to people of Native ancestry, and there are hundreds of Natives pursuing this career in Canada today. This new political arena is an interesting phenomenon, forming as it does a satellite of the major political system of this country. It is in some ways a self-contained unit. The politicians are elected, usually by secret ballot, from a select portion of the population (the Native population). The political system that generates these Native leaders has usually grown up independently from mainstream politics and often unofficially, within the various provinces. It is manifested by the Native organizations, some of which in their constitutions, bylaws, and so on resemble the voluntary organizations of the dominant society; others of which have unique organizational structures.

THE METIS POLITICAL ARENA

If the years I have worked for Metis political organizations in Manitoba and Alberta have taught me anything, it is that the Metis (and indeed all Native people in Canada) have their own politics. When one visits a Metis assembly and sits in a smoke-filled room watching hopeful candidates campaign for the position of president or vice-president of a national or provincial organization, or the chair of a local of one of the provincial political organizations, one quickly becomes aware that more is at stake than simply resistance to the political domination of the larger society.

Not only are these people advancing their own visions of their place in Canadian society, but also they are operating in a separate political and social sphere. They are redefining themselves on a personal and on a national basis.

Whether the location for the assembly is a convention centre in downtown Winnipeg or Edmonton, a friendship centre in Brandon, or a small auditorium in

Lac La Biche, the issue of government programs and financing often fades away. What becomes important are the issues of being Metis. Part of this involves purely internal matters. There are the interpersonal conflicts between political rivals or between politicians and the audience—who did what while in office, what was done with bingo funds, who was hired by the local, who was hired by the head office? But part of this also involves the Metis defining themselves in relation to other Native Peoples and other Canadians—Metis versus non-Native, Metis versus Status, Metis versus Non-Status. What we are seeing here are Metis politicians operating in their own social sphere, self-defined and self-defining.

This internal political field encompasses a wide range of arenas, in the form of associations, agencies, boards of service organizations, friendship centres, and business incentive programs. The field draws on a surprisingly small pool of Native politicians and professionals to staff and direct their operations. Most professional politicians have had at least some experience working for or directing several of these associations. One sign of a successful politician is how well he or she can manoeuvre between the various arenas—using a position on the board of the friendship centre as a launching pad for a place on the board of the Metis association, using that as a springboard for a run at the presidency, and so on. What follows is a description of the political field as it existed in Alberta in the 1980s. While many of the organizations are specific either to Alberta or the time period, the principles of operation remain the same to this day.

THE IMPORTANCE OF POSITIONS

A consideration of any prominent Metis politician's career over a five-year period would reveal directorships on several boards of organizations such as the Metis Association of Alberta (MAA), the Alberta Native Communications Society, Native Outreach, or a staff position in one of these organizations while serving as an officer of another.

Elected Positions

Individuals are usually discouraged from holding directorships on the boards of two Native organizations at the same time. For example, the 1977 constitution of the Metis Association of Alberta (MAA) stated in article IX(6) that a member of the board of the association could not hold an elected position in any other provincial Native organization, nor could a board member be an elected member of a political party. The Alberta Native Communications Society (ANCS) had a similar proviso. Article V(ll) of its constitution stated: "No full member of the Society who is President or Board Member in any Native organization of a provincial or national organization is eligible to become a member of the Board of Directors of the Society."

Nevertheless, several of the more active leaders have, in fact, held memberships on two or more boards simultaneously. In most cases it may simply be because no one challenged them on this fact, or because not all the positions were considered political or conflicting. In 1979, one individual was a board member for the MAA, Native Outreach, and the friendship centre simultaneously.

The variety of positions generated by the organizations and associations serve many functions. They serve as training grounds for neophytes, introducing them to the structure and function of the different organizations, and to the network of politicians and government officials who people the two spheres of Native politics in the province. The more experienced politicians, including many who have been board members for even presidents of the MAA or the association of the Metis Nation of Alberta, use some of these other positions as holding patterns, bases from which they can show that they are still politically active and from which they can build support and strategies for re-election to more prestigious positions.

The career of Stan Daniels is a particularly good example of this strategy. Daniels was president of the MAA on three separate occasions. During one period between presidencies, he got himself elected as a member of the board of directors of the association. He was able to use this position to keep abreast of events in the association and to keep in the Metis public eye, gathering information and ammunition to use against the current president in the next election. He was able to gain re-election in 1976. After his last defeat in 1978, he attempted to repeat his earlier strategy of getting a seat on the board of the association. He lost this election bid by a small margin, but this did not totally block his participation in the political arena. A few months later he successfully ran for the board of the ANCS. He was able to use that position as a jumping-off place for his next campaign, using a television program on provincial Native affairs produced by the ANCS to announce his candidacy for the 1981 election for president of the MAA.

There are several other strategies with which recently defeated or out-of-power politicians can maintain a semblance of activity. The former vice-president of the MAA, Joe Blyan, was defeated in his bid for president in 1981. This defeat left him temporarily without an official position in the political field. While political inactivity prior to running does not totally preclude one's chances for election to the presidency of the MAA—or other political plums such as president of the Native Council of Canada or the Federation of Metis Settlements—it is felt to be a genuine setback. Also, it is a frustrating experience to be totally without a vehicle for participation in the political scene (other than as a grassroots member) once one has been an active member able to wield some power. Blyan quickly made his intention of staying in the field clear by reorganizing and then getting himself elected as president of an Edmonton local of the MAA in early 1982.

This was a particularly effective way for Blyan to stay on the scene, since most of his support came from the younger urban-based Metis and he had made the urban setting his turf. At the first official meeting of the local, Blyan used this base to launch an attack on the MAA and its leadership, stating that Metis living in urban centres did not receive sufficient information about the MAA's activities because of poor organization and communications. Demands were made for information from the president on matters such as to how constitutional recognition of the Aboriginal rights of the Metis would affect urban Metis.

Even prior to becoming president of the local, Blyan had made some efforts to stay active in politics. These were interesting because he first attempted to do this without occupying any of the official positions allowing political activity. Relying on an obscure section of the MAA constitution, which states that a special assembly can be called if it is requested by at least 25 percent of the membership,[1] Blyan headed up a group of seven presidents from various locals who in late September and early October 1981 (scarcely six weeks after his electoral defeat) presented a petition that demanded a special assembly of the MAA to discuss an alleged lack of policy and position papers in health, economic development, communications, education, housing, land claims, and other areas. The petition stated that not only was there a lack of clear-cut policy in these areas, but also there was no mechanism for the general membership of the association to have any input into the policy-making process *(Native People* 1981).

Blyan, as spokesperson for the group, of course denied that they were protesting the election he had just lost, or the right of the present leadership to run the association, but the potential political benefits to Blyan were obvious, since an accusation of a lack of policy was tantamount to an accusation of incompetence on the part of the board and the president, and would be grounds for impeachment if that were possible under the MAA constitution.

However, this bid for the political limelight from outside the system was short-lived and easily subverted (demonstrating to Blyan his need to get back into some sort of official position) when the board of the MAA simply decided to reject the call for a special assembly. The president, Sam Sinclair, publicly based that decision on the fact that it would cost the MAA "at least $100,000" *(Native People* 1981b) to hold a special assembly (actually the cost would be closer to $65,000, based on figures from the previous assembly), and that the association simply did not have the money to pay for it. However, the protest did force the board to make some overt moves in reaction to the petition, such as giving each board member certain portfolios, such as health, the constitution, land claims, housing, communications, and so on, corresponding to the major areas the petition claimed were being ignored.

PAID POSITIONS

Another means of keeping within the orbit of Native political affairs, at least indirectly, is by working for one of the associations as an employee. This has the advantage of having a salary attached to the position, something not all political positions have (board members of the MAA, for example, were unpaid except for travel expenses or special services) There is a fair amount of switching back and forth between the roles of employee and politician. For example, Clifford Gladue, one of the field directors who was fired after a new administration was elected in 1979, became chair of the settlement he lived in and a member of the board of the Federation of Metis Settlements (FMS). He later became president of the FMS, but resigned his position to run (unsuccessfully) for the New Democratic party in the provincial elections of 1978. There was some resentment over the settlements of his resignation (it had come only a short time after he had become president) and this contributed to his defeat in his next political bid, for the presidency of the Metis Association of Alberta (MAA) in 1979. Nevertheless, shortly after he became an employee of the MAA, as an economic development officer. When that position ended, he became a board member of the Alberta Native Communications Society (ANCS).

It was mentioned earlier that there is a relatively small pool of professional politicians for the various organizations to call on. Family and marriage ties tend to tie the small number of Natives working for the organizations into an even more tightly woven group. This tendency can be seen in both Status and Metis circles. The daughter of the president of Indian Rights for Indian Women was a long-time personal secretary to the president of the MAA. The daughter of Stan Daniels, one of the more prominent Metis politicians, was on the board of the friendship centre and used to write the MAA newsletter, which appeared regularly in *The Native People* while her father was president. The wife of an ex-president of the ANCS worked in the housing department of the MAA.

This concentration of family and marriage ties in the organization has had some predictable results as far as the effectiveness of the organization's daily administration is concerned. The executive director of the MAA (a non-Native) once complained to me that she couldn't discipline or fire any of MAA's employees because "you always find out later that they're somebody's cousin or sister."

INTERORGANIZATIONAL RIVALRY

Part of what defines Metis politics as a separate arena is the relationship or division between Status Indian and Metis. In Alberta, this was illustrated by the relationship between the Metis Association of Alberta (MAA) and the Indian Association of Alberta (IAA). Although the two organizations share a common history (Joe Dion, one of the founding members of the MAA, was also responsible for later founding the IAA), the two organizations have not always been able to cooperate effectively.

One matter that caused a particular strain between the two organizations came in February 1981, during the early debates on the Canadian Constitution. The president of the IAA, plus many of the member chiefs, publicly condemned an early draft of the Constitution that promised to recognize the Aboriginal rights of the Metis. They declared that the Metis did not deserve any special status "because their forefathers gave up their land for money." Conflating treaty rights with Aboriginal rights, they insinuated that this inclusion would give the Metis the same status as Treaty Indians, and that their already overpopulated reserves would be overrun by Metis newcomers. However, the Metis were not being offered an adhesion to any treaties and so could not affect the Indians' treaty rights in any way. The matter caused some ill feeling between the two associations (and between the IAA and the Federation of Metis Settlements). The president of the IAA at the time had a well-known and often publicly stated antipathy toward the Metis, and this did not make for much cooperation between the two organizations.

There was a coolness between the organizations at the best of times, since many issues divided them (such as the Indian Rights for Indian Women movement, officially opposed by the IAA but supported by the MAA). Under one administration, there was some attempt on the part of a vice-president of the IAA to get the MAA to cooperate with the IAA in the Isolated Communities and their land claims,[2] but this didn't go very far, due to a lack of interest on the part of the MAA. But the leaders of the two organizations would meet in formalized situations, such as the boards of the friendship centre, the Alberta Native Communications Society, and so on.

ELECTIONS

Metis politics most obviously comes into its own when elections are held to choose new officers for the association. The patterns have changed slightly over the years, as the number of vice-presidents or methods of voting have been modified, but the principles have remained the same.

When the Metis Association of Alberta (MAA) had only one vice-president, each presidential candidate was expected to have a more or less official running mate for vice-president. In actuality, the candidates for president and vice-president rarely mentioned each other in their campaigns, although it was generally known whether two individuals were allies or could work together harmoniously. The presidential candidate might have indicated that he favoured one particular individual over another, but any alliances were extremely tentative, for there was no guarantee that both members of a team would be elected. Since the elections were held in a set order, with first the board members being chosen, then the vice-president, and finally the president, no one knew who the new president would be until after the vice-president had already been chosen. Thus, it was difficult for a voter to choose a vice-president on the basis of compatibility with the president, and it is unlikely that one would have wanted to choose a president on the basis of who had just been chosen vice-president.

At least twice in the history of the MAA, the voters elected a president and vice-president who were the bitterest of enemies. One could almost suspect the electorate of deliberately choosing individuals unwilling or incapable of working together, or of viewing any evidence of an unusually close relationship between the president and vice-president with suspicion or alarm. It may well have been a way of deliberately limiting the power of the president, since if he had the automatic backing of the vice-president in all matters, he could exercise his will over the board much more easily. In fact, in the last few administrations where I was present, the president had a running battle with the vice-president, severely limiting his success in putting through projects he was interested in. The dynamics are somewhat more volatile now there are six vice-presidents, allowing for a much more complex pattern of alliances and negotiation between the presidential and vice-presidential candidates.

In Manitoba, two presidents have been ousted by their boards in disputes that ended up in court: Ernie Blais in 1993 and Billyjo De La Ronde in 1996. The constitution of the Manitoba Metis Federation (MMF), as amended on July 30 and 31, 1992, allows the board to demand the resignation of the president if there is a policy dispute, although in that case all board positions become vacant from the date of the president's resignation. Likewise, the president can dismiss the entire board in the case of a policy dispute, but his position also becomes vacant from the date of such dismissal. The constitution also allows for the removal or suspension of any director by a simple majority. The board consists of 18 members, three from each region, plus the president.

De La Ronde attempted to dismiss part of the board, 12 members, through the MMF Membership Appeal Tribunal (Kuxhaus 1996). This tribunal, which consists of three Aboriginal persons, including at least one Metis, is appointed by the MMF board of directors to hear appeals of membership decisions by the board. The court eventually ruled that the tribunal had no authority to remove an MMF director and returned the ousted board members to office (Robertson 1996). This cleared the way for the board to remove De La Ronde, which they eventually did. An interim board ran the MMF until the elections in 1997, when David Chartrand was elected president (Martin 1997). Removing a president or vice-president was much more difficult under the old MAA structure; one attempt at removing Vice-President Joe Blyan from office failed even though the board voted for it unanimously.

VOTERS

The first issue the organization must resolve when holding elections is who can or cannot vote. This question is, of course, tied to the issue of who is or is not a Metis. Typically, only bona fide members of the association are entitled to vote. This leads to the development of some method for scrutinizing potential voters.

In Alberta, the candidates nominated two or three scrutineers to protect their interests at the polls, making sure that only bona fide Metis Association of Alberta (MAA) members were allowed to vote and that these people voted only once. Each member's card was punched to make sure he or she could not vote more than once. However, despite the efforts of the scrutineers (or because they were mainly concerned with checking the bona fides of those members they knew or suspected were voting for their rivals), there were still irregularities at the voting booths. Many people who held invalid MAA membership cards were able to cast ballots; for example, it was common for Status Indians to be in possession of membership cards and vote illegally. This has continued to be an issue. In 1993, five of the presidential candidates charged that election fraud was rampant. They claimed that Status Indians were offered membership cards in exchange for voting for the incumbent, and that other people were told that they couldn't have membership cards unless they voted for a particular candidate (Fuller 1993a).

In Alberta, attendance figures at the annual assembly varied between 1,600 to 3,000 from 1978 to 1981, but the number of those present who participated in the elections was much smaller—consistently between 800 and 900.[3] Generally, interest in the political aspects of the assembly ran higher during those years a president was to be elected. On the alternate years, when the election involved only half the board of directors, the voting population was even smaller. But in either case, the actual number of voters that determined the officers of the MAA represented a very small percentage of the total Metis population of the province.

The MAA claimed over 30 locals, but many of these were inactive or moribund. However, even the most inactive communities had some representatives at the annual assembly, and it was these people, the members who attended, who determined who were to become officers of the association. Unlike some other Metis or Non-Status Indian organizations (for example, the Manitoba Metis Federation [MMF]), the MAA did not use a delegate system of voting, where each local would send one or two representatives to the assembly, empowered to vote on behalf of the entire community.[4] The election was run on the system of one person one vote, and any full-fledged member was entitled to vote. Since members attending the assembly were entitled to travelling expenses, and accommodation in the form of free tents was provided as well, the assembly usually attracted a certain following even from those communities that demonstrated relatively low levels of political activity for the rest of the year.

Sporadic or minimal interest at the local level has been common for years. In Manitoba in the late 1960s, I participated in a survey of several local Metis communities that indicated a very small active participation in MMF locals. One or two influential families or individuals controlled the activities of the MMF in these communities. The membership and participation would swell if an issue that was of vital interest to the community came up, such as the possibility of the MMF bringing in or administering a government-sponsored housing project or economic development plan. If it then became obvious that the program in question would not be coming to that particular community, interest in and attendance at local meetings would drop off sharply (Sawchuk 1978).

Most Metis people in the community knew the MMF only as the organizer of local Friday night bingo games, and attendance at these games was the limit of their official involvement in the association. Many of these people did not even know what the MMF was, and this was in some of the most active locals in Manitoba. The situation in Alberta is similar. The largest local meetings were those involving "gut issues": the possibility of launching land claims, discussions on improving housing, visits by the Land Tenure Secretariat, and so on. Otherwise, months or years would go by without much local activity, and the relatively small turnout at the assemblies (despite the payment of expenses) was indicative of the level of interest of the population as a whole.

POLITICKING AT THE ASSEMBLY

There were a great many variables at work in the elections that could determine the final outcome—or at least were thought to determine the outcome by the participants. Whether these variables had any significant effect or not, they caused the candidates to behave in certain ways.

INFLUENCING VOTERS

The relatively small voting population made it susceptible to some simple techniques for swaying the results, such as bussing in supporters and "packing" the election hall. This could be particularly effective in the case of the election of board members, since a small number of voters was involved. Only actual residents of a zone were allowed to vote for the board member representing their district. This resulted in a voting population of no more than 150 people for each zone, and even 10 or 20 extra people bussed in could make a significant difference to the final result. Not everyone bothered to vote for board members, so there *was* always a pool of eligible voters for the energetic politician to draw on and try to convince to vote for him. Family ties and friendship were two important drawing cards used to get votes at the board level. If it appeared that not enough supporters were going to be around, efforts were made to bring more in.

In the 1980 elections for board members, the ex-president of the Metis Association of Alberta (MAA), Stan Daniels, ran for the position of director in zone 4. The incumbent vice-president, Joe Blyan, did not regard this with equanimity. Daniels was a bitter enemy of his, and Blyan was having trouble with the board of directors as it was: they had just unanimously voted to expel him from the board and terminate his position as vice-president. It turned out that the board was powerless to force his resignation, since the constitution of the MAA at the time had no provision for impeaching either the president or the vice-president. Blyan realized he desperately needed support on the board and that Daniels would be a significant opponent. Fortunately for Blyan, a close political ally won the seat over Daniels.

Daniels, generally an astute politician, was caught completely off guard. He later admitted that he did not know that his opponent was a friend of Blyan's, and he had underestimated the amount of campaigning and planning this man had done. Daniels had not done much campaigning on his own, relying instead on his long-established reputation among the Metis and his record as a former president of the association to see him through. It was very nearly enough; he lost by only one vote. However, that one vote was a significant one as far as the operation of the association for the next year was concerned. Blyan now had at least one person on the board who could be counted to support him and the programs that formed part of Blyan's ultimate campaign for president. Daniels learned a lesson from this election. A few months later he ran successfully for the board of the Alberta Native Communications Society. He ensured his election there by packing the meeting with a large number of supporters. "A real case of overkill," one of his disgruntled opponents said later.

One of the reasons Daniels lost out in his bid for the MAA board membership was that the older voting population was split between him and another long-time worker for the association. Blyan's man had garnered most of his votes from the younger population and from Blyan's supporters. Had Daniels realized the strength of his opponent in time, he could easily have gathered more support, either by convincing the third man (a sometimes willing ally) to drop out, throwing his support to Daniels, or by persuading a few more people to vote for him. However, he did neither and lost. It is likely that this loss, which was widely perceived as the second time Blyan had "beat him out" (Daniels had lost to Blyan the year before in the vice-presidential race) contributed to Daniel's poor showing the next year when he ran unsuccessfully for president, trailing both Sam Sinclair and Blyan. Daniels was beginning to acquire an image that was quite foreign to him, but which was becoming increasingly difficult to shake off.

LOCATION OF THE ASSEMBLY

A completely different set of variables can affect the outcome of the presidential and vice-presidential races. One of the most important factors was thought to be where the assembly was being held. Support for a candidate was often manifested on a regional basis. That is, if a candidate's home territory was in zone 6, it could be expected that a majority of zone 6 electors would support him. This could be turned to advantage if the assembly was held in zone 6, especially if it was being held close to the community or district where the candidate's major support lay (that is to say, where the candidate had family and close relatives) and if there was no other credible candidate from the same zone, because a large local attendance could always be counted on. If the candidate had a demonstrable interest in some program or issue of local interest (such as supporting the local firefighters or bringing in a local community project), this could also be of considerable advantage.

Thus the selection of the assembly site was crucial in a presidential election year and was the subject of much political manoeuvering by any of those on the board of directors, or the executive, who intended to run for president or vice-president. The choice of High Prairie in the election of 1981 was a good one for Sam Sinclair, and the local support undoubtedly helped him win re-election.

There are, of course, other matters that determined the selection of an assembly site than strictly political convenience, such as the amount of cooperation the association could expect from local town councils and merchants. Some communities were much more cooperative and demonstrated a much more positive attitude towards the association than others. The location of the assembly did not usually matter for the election of board members, since only their own zone members could vote for them, no matter where the assembly was being held. Since the assembly was invariably held somewhere north of Edmonton, it was always in zones 1, 4, 5, or 6. Still, for board members representing one of those zones, one location might be more advantageous than another, especially if it was near his or her home territory and the corresponding support group of friends and relatives.

TIMING OF THE ELECTION

Another way officers of the association could attempt to sway the results of an election was by the scheduling of the election itself. In several assemblies, the elections were scheduled to take place early on the first day of the assembly (usually on Friday or even on Thursday afternoon) Since most working people did not get to the assembly until Friday evening or Saturday morning, this tactic was widely regarded as an attempt by the board members to restrict voting to the supporters they had brought to the assembly ahead of time.

Whether or not this was the reason behind the timing of the election (it may simply have been an attempt to get the elections out of the way so that the regular business of the assembly could be attended to), it was widely regarded as an attempt to manipulate the election, and motions were usually put to the floor to revise the schedule, moving the elections to Saturday afternoon. This generally meant the elections didn't get completed until some time on Sunday, leaving little time for the regular business of the assembly. This last-minute revision of the schedule happened so many times that the board finally became resigned to the inevitable and automatically scheduled the elections for Saturday.

The next step was to eliminate voting from the annual assembly entirely, replacing it with polling stations at each Metis local. While moving elections away from the annual assembly eliminated some of the above-mentioned opportunities for manipulation, it opened the doors for other forms, including fraud. In 1993, it was reported that candidates campaigned openly at the Lac La Biche polling station on election day, that liquor flowed freely, and that the polls allegedly remained open for at least thirty minutes past the 8:00 P.M. deadline (Fuller 1993a).

Last-Minute Deal-Making

The attempts at gaining an advantage in the elections by influencing the location of the assembly and the schedule of the elections were, of course, limited in scope and were only part of the candidate's overall strategy. Furthermore, these tactics were only available to someone who was already an officer of the association or who had an ally on the board. A much more vital part of a candidate's campaign was the face-to-face politicking on the floor of the assembly or out in the campground. This was where the last-minute deals were made, where candidates made the final decisions to drop out, to join forces with another to ensure the defeat of a particular rival, or to stay in for another ballot.

Candidates sometimes went to extraordinary efforts to head off the election of a particularly disliked rival. It is likely that one of the reasons Daniels stepped down as president to run as vice-president in his last election was that he hoped to head off Blyan for the vice-presidency when it became obvious there was a good chance Blyan was going to win. Apparently the thought of being vice-president under somebody else was preferable to being president with Blyan as vice-president. Also, Daniels was confident he would be strong enough to control the association even as vice-president. However, his bid failed. Blyan won the vice-presidency, and Daniels was left out completely that year.

When the pursuit of votes became particularly hectic, as between the first and second ballots, the would-be president or vice-president often found himself making promises (political favours or support, jobs, or money) that could be embarrassing to fulfill if he did get elected. Almost anyone who got elected found he had several political debts due, many which were inconvenient or even impossible to repay. The question the new incumbent had to ask himself was "Which promises or debts can I safely renege on, and which ones are too costly or dangerous to ignore?" This question was particularly important for an incumbent seeking re-election, as his supporters had to decide if they had been sufficiently rewarded for their support in the past and what they could expect if they offered their support again.

Political debts tended to be paid when it was likely that payment would ensure continued support. When Daniels stepped down as president to run unsuccessfully for vice-president in the same election that gave Sinclair the presidency, he threw his support behind Sinclair. This may or may not have helped Sinclair to win, although Daniels' loss points out again how candidates for president and vice-president who supported each other were not necessarily both going to get elected. Daniels then ran for president against Sinclair and Blyan in the next presidential election. He was eliminated in the first round, but again threw his support behind Sinclair. Not all his votes went to Sinclair,[5] but enough did to give Sinclair the election.

Shortly after the election, Daniels was working for the association as a field-worker, even though that position had been officially eliminated when Sinclair had first taken office two years previously. With a man as politically influential as Daniels, Sinclair evidently felt that he would be an asset to his administration. He was a good ally and a tough opponent, and since he was well qualified to be a fieldworker for the association (in fact, it was an ideal use of his talents), it was both advantageous and appropriate to repay his political support. It was probably regarded as appropriate by the members of the association as well.

SUMMARY

When we look at Metis political activity from within, it is obvious that there is much more to it than resistance to state domination, and that it is not simply a microcosm of the larger Canadian political process. These political activities are part of a whole subset of activities that make up the Canadian Metis experience. At this level, the politics are not about boundary maintenance—the activity of defining who is or who is not a Metis in relation to the rest of Canadian society. That activity is part of another arena: association-government negotiations, or Metis-Status or, Metis-Non-Status negotiations. Inside the boundaries, there is no need to define who is a Metis or when a person is a Metis; everyone knows everyone else.

Interestingly, this political field, although it may be a vital part of the Metis experience, is not defined by much cultural content either. The face-to-face election-eering seen on the floor of the annual assembly is not so different from the behaviour one would see at a leadership convention for one of the major Canadian political parties—a further indication of how Native political organizations replicate the

larger political structures that surround them. But what separates local Metis political activity from mainstream political activity is not how the action is structured,
but between whom it takes place and around what prizes the competition is
centered. And in this microcosm, it is Metis-to-Metis; the wider Canadian spectrum is ignored.

This is not to deny that the political activity of the organizations as a whole is
not a statement of otherness or resistance. The arena is clearly one of negotiation
with and reaction to the larger society, and it is heavily influenced by prevailing
trends. We have already seen how, at this level, the goals and activities of the organizations and their leaders have been affected by outside influences. The repatriation
of the Canadian Constitution is one such influence. Since repatriation in 1982,
there has been heavy pressure to define all political activities of the Metis (and of
all Aboriginal Peoples in Canada) in terms of nationhood rather than in terms of
accommodation to the Canadian state. This had its beginnings in the recognition
of Aboriginal rights and of the Metis themselves in section 35 of the *Constitution
Act, 1982*. While on one level it could be argued that nationhood has always been
the objective of the Metis organizations, from the beginnings of the Metis Association
of Alberta in the 1930s to the present day, negotiations and the whole structure of
the language surrounding negotiations (even the whole idea of "nation") have been
affected by the Constitution. This can be seen clearly in the split of Metis and Non-
Status organizations into separate organizations in the 1980s.

But none of that is of much import to the political activity in this other area—
local politics—where one's identity is not questioned and where acceptance of the
idea of Metis has always been taken for granted. Further, we need not find grassroots resistance in all day-to-day life of people, even in the political sphere. The
organizations are more than arenas for political competition. They provide services
and cultivate intergroup cooperation. Housing programs, after all, do provide housing for people in need, and getting on the board of a Metis housing program does
allow an individual to serve his or her own community as well as bolstering the
individual's political career. Remembering this is a useful antidote to the prevailing anthropological perspective of interpreting everything in the political arena as
"resistance" (Brown 1996).

NOTES

1. Article VII(8) of the 1977 MAA constitution states, "A special Meeting of the members shall be
    called by the Secretary upon receipt by him of a Petition signed by one-fourth of the member-
    ship at large setting forth the reasons for calling such a Meeting and notice of such a Meeting
    shall be given in the manner hereinbefore provided by these By-Laws" (at least 21 days notice:
    Article VII, Section 1).
2. The Isolated Communities of north-central Alberta consist of a number of small communities
    located directly north of Lesser Slave Lake, east of Peace River, and west of Fort McMurray. They

are characterized by their small size, relative isolation, and mixed population of Treaty Indians, Non-Status Indians, and Metis. They have been involved in land-tenure disputes with the Province of Alberta since 1975, when they proclaimed unextinguished Aboriginal titles to their territory.

3. For example, in the 1979 election for president, a total of 909 votes were cast in the first ballot, and this was the highest number cast in this (or the preceding) election. In the second and final ballot, a total of 788 votes were cast. The figures for the vice-presidential contest are similar. In 1979, 850 ballots were cast in the first round and 776 in the second. In 1981, the total votes cast in the first round for president were 878 and 734 for the second. The vice-presidential race showed 875 total votes in the first round and 824 in the second. Attendance figures were quoted as over 2,500 for 1981.

4. The MMF no longer uses a delegate system.

5. In the first round, the vote distribution was as follows: Sam Sinclair 351 votes, Joe Blyan 270, and Stan Daniels 257. After Daniels withdrew, Sinclair received 477 votes and Blyan 336.

REFERENCES

Brown, Michael F. 1996. On Resisting Resistance. *American Anthropologist* 98 (4): 729–49.

Fuller, Patty. 1993a. Mayhem Among the Metis: The Metis Nation of Alberta faces membership-fixing and corruption changes. *Alberta Report* 20(42):16

Kuxhaus, David. 1996. Metis Alliance in chaos: Judge scraps corporation, tells MMF to "start over." *Winnipeg Free Press*, July 7.

Martin, Nick. 1997. Election roils MMF waters, Chartrand wins; McKay says vote "flawed." *Winnipeg Free Press* May 17.

Robertson, Bud. 1996. MMF court decision reversed: Board members returned to office. *Winnipeg Free Press*, June 22.

Sawchuk, Joe. 1978. *The Metis of Manitoba: Reformulation of an Ethnic Identity.* Toronto: Peter Martin Associates.

CHAPTER 20

"SOVEREIGNTY"—

AN INAPPROPRIATE CONCEPT

Gerald Taiaiake Alfred

My principal cause is freedom. I'm old enough to remember what it was like to be free. Free from harassment by police, free from harassment by fisheries. And so it's difficult for me to give up the struggle because I want to be there when we win our freedom. When I speak about freedom, that means I want the recognition of our sovereignty, as the first people not only of Canada but of the States. I believe that we should be recognized as indigenous people, with the right to make our own decisions and govern ourselves. To once again take control of our lives, our lands, and our resources.... People talk about this country being a free country. They have no idea of freedom. If you ever had the taste of freedom that I have known, you would never give it up, you'd fight for it like I do.

— THOWHEGWELTH, HAIDA (JOHNSON, *The Book of Elders,* 190–3)

THE CONCEPT OF SOVEREIGNTY as Native leaders have constructed it thus far is incompatible with traditional indigenous notions of power. Nevertheless, until now it has been an effective vehicle for indigenous critiques of the state's imposition of control; by forcing the state to recognize major inconsistencies between its own principles and its treatment of Native people, it has pointed to the racism and contradiction inherent in settler states' claimed authority over non-consenting peoples. In fact, it has become obsolete mainly because of the success the best Native leaders have had in creating the space required for greater assertion of self-governing powers.

Even so, the suitability of sovereignty as the primary political goal of indigenous people has gone largely unquestioned. It is taken for granted that what indigenous peoples are seeking in recognition of their nationhood is essentially what countries like Canada and the United States possess now. In fact, most of the current generation of Native politicians see politics as a zero-sum contest for power—just the way non-indigenous politicians do.

There is real danger in the assumption that sovereignty is the appropriate model for indigenous governance. The Canadian scholars Menno Boldt and Tony Long have described that danger in the context of their work among the Blood and Peigan peoples:

> by adopting the European-Western ideology of sovereignty, the current gener-
> ation of Indian leaders is buttressing the imposed alien authority structures
> within its communities, and is legitimizing the associated hierarchy comprised
> of indigenous political and bureaucratic elites. This endorsement of hierarchi-
> cal authority and a ruling entity constitutes a complete rupture with traditional
> indigenous principles.

Traditional indigenous nationhood stands in sharp contrast to the dominant under-standing of "the state": there is no absolute authority, no coercive enforcement of decisions, no hierarchy, and no separate ruling entity. In accepting the idea that progress is attainable within the framework of the state, therefore, indigenous people are moving towards acceptance of forms of government that more closely resemble the state than traditional systems. Is it possible to accomplish good in a system designed to promote harm? Yes, on the margins. But eventually the grinding engine of discord and depri-vation will obliterate the marginal good. The real goal should be to stop that engine.

Instead of treating nationhood as a value rooted in traditional indigenous philos-ophy, many Native politicians seem to regard it as a lever to gain a better bargain-ing position. As the former Assembly of First Nations' head Ovide Mercredi said in 1996, "I'm not going to allow my philosophy of sovereignty to interfere with the working relationship that can produce the results we're working for. That's all it is, a philosophy." For such politicians, there is a dichotomy between philosophi-cal principle and politics. They don't really believe in a sovereign right for indige-nous peoples; it is simply a bargaining chip, a lever for concessions within the established constitutional framework. The problem is that if Natives don't believe in it, no one else will—which explains the consistent failure to achieve recogni-tion of a "sovereign" Native power.

Because shallow-minded politicians do not take the concept of sovereignty seri-ously, they are unable to grasp that asserting a right to sovereignty has significant implications. In making a claim to sovereignty—even if they don't really mean it—they are making a choice to accept the state as their model and to allow indige-nous political goals to be framed and evaluated according to a "statist" pattern. Thus the common criteria of statehood—coercive force, control of territory, population numbers, international recognition—come to dominate discussion of indigenous peoples' political goals as well.

This is not only a movement away from traditional indigenous philosophies and values, but transparently disingenuous in the terms of the sovereignty model itself.

Who would believe that indigenous nations could ever successfully challenge Canada and the United States to win their sovereignty? No one, apparently, because even those who advocate sovereignty as a goal seek only a limited form of autonomy, not independence; the goal relates only to powers of self-government within a framework of constitutional law and authorities delegated by the state. Canada's Mercredi has described his goal of sovereignty in terms of the limited authority granted to American Indian tribes by the US Congress:

> We are not talking about secession. We are talking about essentially gaining and regaining control of our lives. American Indians do not have to negotiate their powers of self-government because their internal political authority is recognized by the Supreme Court of the land.

Thus the Native sovereigntist must modify the concept of sovereignty to fit his limited goals. But the simple act of framing the goal in terms of sovereignty is harmful in itself. "Sovereignty" implies a set of values and objectives in direct opposition to those found in traditional indigenous philosophies. Non-indigenous politicians recognize the inherent weakness of assertions of a sovereign right for peoples who have neither the cultural framework nor the institutional capacity to sustain it. The problem is that the assertion of a sovereign right for indigenous peoples continues to structure the politics of decolonization, and the state uses the theoretical inconsistencies in that position to its own advantage.

A case in point is the issue of "land claims." The resolution of such claims (addressing the legal inconsistency of Crown or state title to indigenous lands) is generally seen by progressive non-indigenous people as a step in the right direction. But without a fundamental questioning of the assumptions underpinning the state's approach to power, the counterfactual assumptions of colonialism will continue to structure the relationship between the state and indigenous peoples. Within this framework, any progress made towards justice will be marginal; in fact, it will be tolerated by the state only to the extent that it serves, or at least does not oppose, the interests of the state itself.

In Canada, for example, the ongoing definition of the concept of "Aboriginal rights" by the Supreme Court since the 1980s is widely seen as progress. Yet even with a legal recognition of collective rights to certain subsistence activities within certain territories, indigenous people are still subject to state control in the exercise of their inherent freedoms and powers; they must also meet state-defined criteria for Aboriginal identity in order to gain access to these legal rights. Given Canada's shameful history, defining Aboriginal rights in terms of, for example, a right to fish for food and traditional purposes is better than nothing. But to what extent does that state-regulated "right" to food-fish represent justice for people who have been fishing on their rivers and seas since time began?

To argue on behalf of indigenous nationhood within the dominant Western paradigm is self-defeating. To frame the struggle to achieve justice in terms of indigenous "claims" against the state is implicitly to accept the fiction of state sovereignty. Indigenous peoples are by definition the original inhabitants of the land. They had complex societies and systems of government. And they never gave consent to European ownership of territory or the establishment of European sovereignty over them (treaties did not do this, according to both historic Native understandings and contemporary legal analysis). These are indisputable realities based on empirically verifiable facts. So why are indigenous efforts to achieve legal recognition of these facts framed as "claims"? The mythology of the state is hegemonic, and the struggle for justice would be better served by undermining the myth of state sovereignty than by carving out a small and dependent space for indigenous peoples within it.

The need to perpetuate a set of fictive legal premises and fact-denying myths is apparent in every legal act of the state. To justify the establishment of non-indigenous sovereignty, Aboriginality in a true sense must necessarily be excluded and denied. Otherwise it would seem ridiculous that the original inhabitants of a place should be forced to justify their existence to a crude horde of refugees from another continent. As the European scholar Fae Korsmo has pointed out, the loss of collective memory is an essential requirement for creating a colonial reality:

> The people already living in or near the area have no role in the new myths, except perhaps as enemies or a dying race. They represent a noble yet doomed past that must be prevented from becoming a present-day threat. Insofar as the colonial mythology has put the burden on the indigenous societies to justify their claims in terms of their origins and hardy continuity, the doctrine of Aboriginal title is part of colonialism and therefore dooms the indigenous claimants to failure.

To summarize the argument thus far, sovereignty is an exclusionary concept rooted in an adversarial and coercive Western notion of power. Indigenous peoples can never match the awesome coercive force of the state; so long as sovereignty remains the goal of indigenous politics, therefore, Native communities will occupy a dependent and reactionary position relative to the state. Acceptance of "Aboriginal rights" in the context of state sovereignty represents the culmination of white society's efforts to assimilate indigenous peoples.

Framing indigenous people in the past as "noble but doomed" relics of an earlier age, allows the colonial state to maintain its own legitimacy by preventing the fact of contemporary indigenous peoples' nationhood to intrude on its own mythology.

Native people imperil themselves by accepting formulations of their own identities and rights that prevent them from transcending the past. The state relegates indigenous peoples' rights to the past, and constrains the development of their societies by allowing only those activities that support its own necessary illusion: that indigenous peoples today do not present a serious challenge to its legitimacy. Thus the state celebrates paint and feathers and Indian dancing, because they reinforce the image of doomed nobility that justified the pretence of European sovereignty on Turtle Island. Tribal casinos, Indian tax-immunity, and Aboriginal fisheries, on the other hand, are uncomfortable reminders that—despite the doctrine of state sovereignty—indigenous identities and rights continue to exist.

Native leaders have a responsibility to expose the truth and debunk the imperial pretense that supports the doctrine of state sovereignty and white society's dominion over indigenous nations and their lands. State sovereignty depends on the fabrication of falsehoods that exclude the indigenous voice. Ignorance and racism are the founding principles of the colonial state, and concepts of indigenous sovereignty that don't challenge these principles in fact serve to perpetuate them. To claim that the state's legitimacy is based on the rule of law is hypocritical and anti-historic. There is no moral justification for state sovereignty. The truth is that Canada and the United States were established only because indigenous peoples were overwhelmed by imported European diseases and were unable to prevent the massive immigration of European populations. Only recently, as indigenous people have learned to manipulate state institutions and gained support from other groups oppressed by the state, has the state been forced to change its approach. Recognizing the power of the indigenous challenge, and unable to deny it a voice, the state has attempted to pull indigenous people closer to it. It has encouraged them to re-frame and moderate their nationhood demands to accept the *fait accompli* of colonization, to collaborate in the development of a "solution" that does not challenge the fundamental imperial lie.

By allowing indigenous peoples a small measure of self-administration, and by forgoing a small portion of the money derived from the exploitation of indigenous nations' lands, the state has created incentives for integration into its own sovereignty framework. Those communities that cooperate are the beneficiaries of a patronizing false altruism that sees indigenous peoples as the anachronistic remnants of nations, the descendants of once-independent peoples who by a combination of tenacity and luck have managed to survive and must now be protected as minorities. By agreeing to live as artifacts, such co-opted communities guarantee themselves a role in the state mythology through which they hope to secure a limited but perpetual set of rights. In truth the bargain is a pathetic compromise of principle. The reformulation of nationhood to create historical artifacts that lend legitimacy to the political economy of the modern state is nothing less than a betrayal.

What do traditionalists hope to protect? What have the co-opted ones forsaken? In both cases, the answer is the heart and soul of indigenous nations: a set of values that challenge the destructive and homogenizing force of Western liberalism and free-market capitalism; that honour the autonomy of individual conscience, non-coercive authority, and the deep interconnection between human beings and the other elements of creation.

Nowhere is the contrast between indigenous and (dominant) Western traditions sharper than in their philosophical approaches to the fundamental issues of power and nature. In indigenous philosophies, power flows from respect for nature and the natural order. In the dominant Western philosophy, power derives from coercion and artifice—in effect, alienation from nature.

A brief detour to consider the relationship of human beings to the earth may serve to illustrate the last point. Indigenous philosophies are premised on the belief that earth was created by a power external to human beings, who have a responsibility to act as stewards; since humans had no hand in making the earth, they have no right to "possess" it or dispose of it as they see fit—possession of land by man is unnatural and unjust. The stewardship principle, reflecting a spiritual connection with the land established by the Creator, gives human beings special responsibilities within the areas they occupy as indigenous peoples, linking them in a "natural" way to their territories.

The realities of capitalism make this concept problematic both for the state and for indigenous peoples. But the perceptions of the problem are different. Non-indigenous people may suspect that traditionalist Natives would oppose the types of uses and activities promoted by the state in their nations' territories. In fact this is not the case; most Native people do not reject modernization or participation in larger economies. However, traditionalists recognize a responsibility to participate in the economy with the intent of ensuring the long-term health and stability of people and the land; in this context, development for development's sake, consumerism, and unrestrained growth are not justifiable. It is the intense possessive materialism at the heart of Western economies that must be rejected—for the basic reason that it contradicts traditional values aimed at maintaining a respectful balance among people and between human beings and the earth.

The form of distributive or social justice promoted by the state today depends on the development of industry and enterprises to provide jobs for people and revenue for government institutions. Most often—especially on indigenous lands—those industries and enterprises centre on the extraction of natural resources. Trees, rocks, and fish become commodities whose value is calculated solely in monetary terms without reference to the spiritual connections between them and indigenous peoples. From a traditional point of view, this is an extreme devaluation of nature.

Yet in a world economy dependent on "resource" exploitation, and structured so that such exploitation seems the only means of survival, what are indigenous peoples committed to traditional values to do? All societies must take their sustenance from the land; however, we must also recognize that the earth has an inherent value, beyond human needs. The situation now, and in the framework of conventional economic development models, is that a small minority of the white population of the earth go far beyond sustenance to take extravagant wealth from indigenous lands. Very little in terms of either employment or wealth comes back to the indigenous people themselves. The modern reality demands that indigenous people use the land much more intensively, and in very different ways, than their ancestors did. However, traditionalists believe that Native people must assert their consciousness of nature and power by demanding that their territories be used in ways that respect indigenous notions of justice, not simply for the short-sighted generation of wealth for others.

The only position on development compatible with a traditional frame of mind is a balanced one, committed at once to using the land in ways that respect the spiritual and cultural connections indigenous peoples have with it and to managing the process so as to ensure a primary benefit for its natural indigenous rewards. The primary goals of an indigenous economy are to sustain the earth and to ensure the health and well-being of the people. Any derogation of that principle—whether in qualitative terms or with reference to the intensity of activity on the land—should be seen as upsetting the balanced ideal that lies at the heart of Native societies.

Returning to the issue of nationhood, we must acknowledge that, unlike the earth, social and political institutions were created by men and women. From the indigenous perspective, this means that people have the power and responsibility to manipulate those institutions. Whereas the human-earth relationship is structures by the larger forces in nature, beyond the capacity of humans to change, the human-institution relationship gives rise to an active responsibility in human beings to use their own powers of creation to achieve balance and harmony. Governance structures and social institutions should be designed to empower individuals and reinforce tradition in order to maintain the balance found in nature.

In this view, sovereignty is not a natural phenomenon but a social creation—the result of choices made by men and women located in a particular social and political order. The unquestioned acceptance of sovereignty as the framework for politics today reflects the triumph of a particular set of ideas over others—and is no more natural to the world than any other man-made object.

The kind of justice that indigenous people seek in their relations with the state has to do with restoring a regime of respect. This ideal stands in clear contrast to the statist notion, still rooted in the classical notion of sovereignty, which, in the name of equity, may direct more material resources to indigenous people, but which preserves the state's superior position relative to them and to the earth. The indigenous conception of justice builds a framework of respectful coexistence on the fundamental acknowledgement of the integrity and autonomy of the various elements that make up the relationship. It goes far beyond even the most liberal Western ideas of justice in advancing the cause of peace, because it explicitly allows for difference while promoting the construction of sound relationships among autonomous elements.

The Western view of power and human relationships is so thoroughly entrenched that it appears valid, objective, and natural; it has become what Jens Bartelson has called "the unthought foundation of political knowledge." The challenge, then, is to de-think the concept of sovereignty and replace it with a notion of power that is based on more appropriate premises.

One of the most progressive liberal thinkers today, James Tully, has recognized the obstacle to reconciliation posed by intellectual demands for conformity to a single language and way of knowing. In his view, the "imperial" demand of uniformity is obsolete and unachievable in the (ethnically, linguistically, racially) diverse social and political communities characteristic of modern states. Justice demands recognition—intellectual, legal, and political—of the diversity of languages and knowledge that exists among people, indigenous peoples' ideas about relationships and power commanding the same respect as those that used to constitute the singular reality of the state. Creating a legitimate post-colonial relationship means abandoning notions of European cultural superiority and adopting a mutually respectful stance. The idea that there is only one right way to see or do things is no longer tenable:

> one of the important discoveries of the 20th century is that such a comprehensive language or point of view is an illusion. There is no view from no where. No matter how comprehensive such a language may appear to be ... it will always bring to light some aspects of the phenomenon it is employed to comprehend at the expense of disregarding others.

In recent years, indigenous leaders from around the world have had some success in undermining the intellectual credibility of state sovereignty as the only legitimate form of political organization. Scholars in international law are now beginning to see the vast potential for peace in indigenous political philosophies. The international attention focused on the Rotinohshonni *Kaienerekowa* (Great Law of Peace) is indicative of the growing recognition given to indigenous models as post-colonial alternatives to state sovereignty. According to the most comprehensive and authoritative legal text on indigenous peoples in international law:

The Great Law of Peace promotes unity among individuals, families, clans, and nations while upholding the integrity of diverse identities and spheres of autonomy. Similar ideals have been expressed by leaders of other indigenous groups in contemporary appeals to international bodies. Such conceptions outside the mold of classical Western liberalism would appear to provide a more appropriate foundation for understanding humanity.

But the state will not easily release its grip on control-power and accept the alternative of knowledge-power. The traditional values of indigenous peoples directly threaten the monopoly of control-power currently enjoyed by the state. Some scholars have interpreted the violence that occurs when the state confronts indigenous traditionalism as a natural statist reaction to such threats. For example, Arthur Kroker believes that the state is determined to eliminate the intellectual threat posed by the idea of a politics beyond state sovereignty, and to that end is prepared to use terror—including not only physical force but the intellectual violence inherent in state policies. In the wake of Canada's conflicts with the Kanien'kehaka and other indigenous nations in the 1990s, Kroker asked whether "the indefinite occupation ... and the ceaseless police raids into other aboriginal territories [were] not an indefinite preparation for war in another way ... a violent warning to all First Nations people?" The same question might be posed with respect to the intellectual violence done to indigenous people through the continued denial of their reality in the dominant mythology.

Hope for moving beyond the intellectual violence of the state is offered by the emerging concept of legal pluralism, which is reflected in the limited recognition afforded indigenous principles in recent legal argumentation. That concept must be taken to its logical conclusion. As the Canadian legal scholar Alain Bissonnetie has put it, the courts must develop the ability to think "in multiple terms." In other words, they must develop what Native people have maintained all along is the necessary precondition to peace and justice: respect for others. Bissonnette sees great potential for preserving the Canadian state's legitimacy in the respect and recognition of indigenous rights:

> judges should break with a knowledge of the law that does not allow them to assimilate or master this new legal reality, especially since the recent constitutional recognition ... informs them that over the years, these rights "were virtually ignored" and, on the other hand, requires them in future to protect these rights by using a form of legal reasoning different from that which prevailed before.... If they take this approach they will no doubt gradually be able truly to legitimize the whole of the Canadian legal system, which in future will be based on the recognition or

creation of a common cultural code that rejects in advance any symbolic violence against the historical, social and cultural reality of the Aboriginal peoples.

Within Native communities themselves, people are seriously questioning the identities shaped by the colonial reality, in an effort to construct intellectual and political strategies that will both resonate within the communities and present an effective challenge to the state's latest strategies to perpetuate its dominance. I asked Audra Simpson, a 29-year-old Kanien'kehaka graduate student in anthropology, to comment on some of these issues. Her responses shed light on the depth of the examination now under way, as well as the significance attached to the process of constructing a post-colonial identity among politicized people in our communities.

Is there a difference between the Native concept of "nationhood" and "sovereignty" in the legal sense, or as you understand it?

These concepts are quite different. I find it hard to isolate, define, and then generalize what a "Native" concept of nationhood would be without its sounding contrived. This is a tired point: we are all different people, different nations, and would have different ideas about what nationhood is and what it means to us. The Sechelt conception or Northern Cree conception will certainly depart from Mohawk ideas about who we are. Each people will have a term in their own language that will mean "us." I think that is what our concept of nationhood is.

My opinion is that "Mohawk" and "nationhood" are inseparable. Both are simply about *being*. Being is who you are, and a sense of who you are is arrived at through your relationships with other people—your people. So who we are is tied with what we are: a nation.

Now, sovereignty—the authority to exercise power over life, affairs, territory— this is not inherited. It's not a part of being, the way our form of nationhood is. It has to be conferred, or granted—it's a thing that can be given and thus can be taken away. It's clearly a foreign concept, because it occurs through an exercise of power—power over another.

This is not to say that the valuing of sovereignty, of having control over territory, has not been indigenized. We've used it in a rhetorical and political way time and time again. But I think there is a difference between the *being* of who we are— Mohawk—and the defence mechanisms that we have to adopt in the neo-colonial context—sovereignty.

But in terms of the substance of who we are, the nature of our "being," is it necessary to be self-conscious in defining and maintaining our tradition as a support for either cultural nationhood or political sovereignty?

This "self-conscious traditionalism," like the culture concept, cannot be thought about, or written about, enough. To be Native today is to be cultured: to possess culture, to exercise it, to proclaim it, to celebrate it. But we cannot have just any culture; it has to be "traditional" culture—defined, isolated, reflected upon, relearned, and then perfected. Our very sovereignty—in the European sense—depends on it, as we must continually prove our difference in order to have our rights respected. We see this with land-claims cases and in day-to-day life—our day-to-day experiences do not suffice when making claims to difference, as these claims are always made to others outside of our communities.

This traditionalism is therefore very important in the context of the neo-colonial present, because it is the basis of our claim to difference, and difference is tied to sovereignty. However, I fear that in the long run we might lose who we really are in order to perfect a dance that looks great, feels good at the time, but is done largely for the benefit of others—to meet somebody else's standards of Indianness.

I sought an alternative perspective on these same questions from Vine Deloria, Jr, the highly influential Lakota scholar and American Indian activist.

Is there a difference between the Native concept of nationhood and "sovereignty" in the legal sense?

I think that "sovereignty" was a European word that tried to express the nationhood of a people who could think with one mind. Since the king was the ruler, he was sovereign in the sense that he was supposed to represent what the people of his nation wanted. Indians had spread out the idea of governing to include all activities of life—thus at times medicine people would be influential and at other times warriors, or hunters, or scouts would be influential. Many tribes did not have "laws" or "religion", but a single belief system that was described as "our way of doing things."

Sovereignty today, unfortunately, is conceived as a wholly political-legal concept. I would prefer that social processes determined how the people feel about things and whether they are willing to act as a single unit. If they could all boycott a store, bank, or social function of the whites and just be content with a more closed society, people would have to pay attention to them.

The Six Nations' [Rotinohshonni] arrangement of chiefs in their meetings is a very good way of ensuring that real sovereignty exists and is protected—that the political actions of a people reflect their consensus. We should think about the process they developed a lot more. The Sioux used to be more formal and dignified, but now they shout and carry on in meetings until you don't want to attend them anymore!

What about the "co-optation" of Native leaders, both in their minds and as a process?

It's relatively easy to co-opt Indian leaders—but it's easy to co-opt everyone else also. The problem people face is gaining access to the levers of power, and that requires cooperating with the people who control things. You have to have an enormous amount of power to oppose co-optation. Indians could do a lot more for themselves if they stood by certain principles. It is noteworthy that in those instances where Indians have stood firm on something, they have been more successful.

One of the loosely related problems is that Indians won't criticize other Indians no matter how bad they are. This enables people who are basically rip-offs to have the same kind of status as devoted leaders. So there is a group of Indians frantically trying to buy into the system, and they clog up the analysis of our problems because they seem to be co-opted, but they are really just selling out. One way to avoid that is to have a council governing the tribe and have it choose a particular person as spokesman for different occasions. Many tribes practiced that successfully with similar institutions. The Sioux used to appoint people to make different speeches, without vesting the power to negotiate in any of them. The Cheyenne had peace chiefs and war chiefs—no warrior as such was allowed to be either, as I understand it.

I agree that we need to return to a traditional mode. Has your experience given you any ideas on how to make the first practical steps toward that goal?

Since we live in a world that has many forms of communication, it is impossible to speak to a small group—like the old tribal circles—without everyone knowing what you are saying. So I think we should institute new customs, and have some nights set aside to do storytelling, some to discuss the future of the tribe or community, every so often. We should also teach the old clan and kinship responsibilities, and make deliberate efforts to carry them out, perhaps even set up deadlines to accomplish certain kinds of goals—calling people within the family by the relative name, like "father" or "sister," and reviving the customs of doing things for them. Then we can move on to more complicated things. There was a sense of civility that the old traditional ways brought that we do not have now, and we should return to them.

What is the role of a leader in this? Or more generally: what are the duties and traits of a real Native leader?

Well, in the old days a leader made certain that the camp, or longhouse, did not have petty problems that festered. Many a chief called the two parties who were quarrelling together and tried to get them to make up. Sometimes he had to give them his own horses or some other gift to put everything right.

So I think that the Indian leader, insofar as possible, should be a figure of reconciliation and futuristic vision. And I think we are getting some people elected now who are acting that way. But a leader also should look at the community, evaluate where the strengths and weaknesses are, and develop a cadre of people who can work together on things—making sure that everyone comes together once in a while to get the general feeling that the community as a whole is moving forward. A leader probably ought also to be someone who enables processes to happen, who realizes that sometimes people are not ready to do things, and [will take the time] to gently educate them, to prepare them. Many of the old tribal chairmen of the 1960s did that, and they were very powerful leaders.

Is it still possible to hold our current leaders to a traditional standard of "accountability" to the people?

Well, before Western individualism took over, people were held accountable by their family, clan, and community; and they used shame to bring people around. As you know, the Cherokees executed some of their chiefs who signed away lands—an extreme form of accountability. Today we are so polarized between Indian and white that no one dares criticize an Indian leader publicly, so we let them get away with murder.

Back in the 1960s, when I first got into this stuff, there was a core group at NCAI [the National Congress of American Indians] that had worked together for years, through the hardest years of termination [the former US policy aimed at extinguishing indigenous nations]. They acted as a committee to enforce accountability. Unfortunately, after we had rebuilt the NCAI in 1967, the "out" group won the election, and then corruption on a large scale set in. I remember some of the crooks asking some of us who had lost the election to help throw out the others. But the honest elected officers wouldn't take action against the crooks for fear they would lose the next NCAI election. So we began to lose accountability, at least on the national level, around 1969–70. I think that's when AIM [the American Indian Movement] came to prominence, because tribal leaders wouldn't speak out. Poverty funds ruined integrity at the national and tribal level and we have never been able to restore much of it—people would do anything for a dollar, or an appointment to a national committee.

Maybe once the funds dry up and we have to live by our wits, people will take offence at the squandering of tribal assets and demand accountability again. But look at the Navajos: Peter McDonald was looting the tribe, trying to skim millions from his own people, and now the Navajos have petitioned for [President] Clinton to pardon him. If we don't want to punish anyone for wrongdoing, how can we have accountability?

In spite of their national, gender, experience, and age differences (and very different styles), both Deloria and Simpson express the same core critique of "sovereignty," the colonial power structure, and the intellectual justifications that have been used to perpetuate it. Their views represent those of many indigenous people who have managed to see through the state's facade of legitimacy, and recognize the destructive implications—both intellectual and political—of remaining within a colonial structure and mindset.

[Publisher's Note: Reference markers for notes were missing from the original text, which has been faithfully reproduced here.]

NOTES

1. "By adopting the European-Western ideology…": M. Boldt and J.A. Long, "Tribal Traditions and European Political Ideologies: The Dilemma for Canada's Native Indians," *Canadian Journal of Political Science* 17 (1984), 548.

2. On the notion of sovereignty, and the difference between sovereignty and nationhood: T. Andersen, *Sovereign Nations or Reservations?* (1990); J.G. Biersteker and C. Weber, eds, *State Sovereignty as a Social Construct* (1996); Boldt and Long, "Tribal Traditions," 537-53; J.R. Wunder, ed., *Native American Sovereignty* (1996).

3-4. Mercredi on sovereignty ("I'm not going to allow…"; "We are not talking about succession…") *Globe and Mail*, 11 July 1996, A8.

5. "The people already living on or near the new area…": F. Korsmo, "Claiming Memory in British Columbia: Aboriginal Rights and the State," *American Indian Culture and Research Journal* 20 (4), 72.

6. On sovereignty as a concept, and its effect on knowledge and politics: J. Bartelson, *A Genealogy of Sovereignty* (1995), 3-7.

7. "One of the important discoveries of the twentieth century…": J. Tully, *Strange Multiplicity* (1995), 56. On accommodating indigenous nationhood within the state paradigm, see also R.L. Barsh and J.Y. Henderson, *The Road* (1980); V. Deloria, Jr., and R.M. Lytle, *American Indians, American Justice* (1983); C.F. Wilkinson, *American Indians, Time and the Law*. And for a post-colonial perspective on the state: see F. Buell, *National Culture and the New Global System,* 217-62.

8. "the Great Law of Peace promotes unity…": S.J. Anaya, *Indigenous Peoples in International Law* (1996), 79.

9. "The indefinite occupation…": A. Kroker, *The Possessed Individual* (1992), 48.

10. "Judges should break with a knowledge of the law…": A. Lajoie et al., *Le Statut juridique des peuples autochtones* (1996), 265 (translation provided by the authors).

REFERENCES

Anaya, S.J. *Indigenous Peoples in International Law.* New York: Oxford University Press, 1996.

Barsh, R.L., and J.Y. Henderson. *The Road: Indian Tribes and Political Liberty.* Berkeley: University of California Press, 1980.

Bartelson, J. *A Genealogy of Sovereignty.* Cambridge: Cambridge University Press, 1995.

Biersteker, J., and C. Weber, eds. *State Sovereignty as a Social Construct.* Cambridge: Cambridge University Press, 1996.

Buell, F. *National Culture and the New Global System.* Baltimore: Johns Hopkins University Press, 1994.

Deloria, Jr., V., and R.M. Lytle. *American Indians, American Justice.* Austin: University of Texas Press, 1983.

Johnson, S., ed. *The Book of Elders: The Life Stories of Great American Indians.* New York: HarperCollins, 1994.

Kroker, A. *The Possessed Individual: Technology and the French Postmodern.* Montreal: New World Perspectives, 1992.

Lajoie, A., J.M. Brisson, S. Normand, and A. Bissonette. *Le Statut juridique des peuples autochtones au Québec et le pluralisme.* Cowansville: Éditions Yvon Blais, 1996.

Tully, J. *Strange Multiplicity: Constitutionalism in an Age of Diversity.* Cambridge: Cambridge University Press, 1995.

Wilkinson, C.F. *American Indians, Time, and the Law: Native Societies in a Modern Constitutional Democracy.* New Haven: Yale University Press, 1987.

Wunder, J.R., ed. *Native American Sovereignty.* New York: Garland, 1996.

CHAPTER 21

INDIGENEITY AT THE EDGE:

TOWARDS A CONSTRUCTIVE ENGAGEMENT

Roger C.A. Maaka and Augie Fleras

"WALKING UP A DOWN ESCALATOR"

HOW DO WE ASSESS THE HEALTH of the indigenous rights movement at the end of the International Decade of World Indigenous Peoples? Have the settler societies of Canada and Aotearoa addressed the many injustices foisted on their indigenous peoples, particularly injustices that ignored their constitutional status as nations, abrogated their right to self-rule, eroded their culture and identity, and bypassed their consent to be ruled (Tully, 1995)?

To some extent, yes. Indigenous challenges to the national agenda have yielded positive responses and progressive changes. Several approaches have been explored to improve indigenous peoples–Crown relations, including an increased indigenization of policy and administration, restitutional settlements such as comprehensive and specific land claims, statutory amendments, devolution of power, decentralization of service delivery structures and limited self-government arrangements. In recent times there have been shifts in the indigenous affairs agenda to include

(a) government promotion of indigenous-driven capacity building rather than state determined disparity-reduction programmes;

(b) government negotiation *with* indigenous peoples rather than *for* indigenous peoples;

(c) government reparations to improve economic development rather than to simply right historical wrongs; and

(d) government promotion of self-governance initiatives rather than more of the same (Loomis, 2000).

Indigenous peoples–state relations in New Zealand and Canada may be in better shape at present than at any time prior to colonization, but constitutional adjustments to indigenous peoples–Crown relations have proven a major disappointment as well. Reforms to re-design the social contract tend to be reactive, motivated by political ambition or conflict management, focus on superficiality rather than substance, and are aimed at cooling out "troublesome constituents" rather than changing the relationship. Relationships continue to be framed within the discourse and structures of 19th-century colonialism—albeit with a more human face—with the supremacy of Crown sovereignty and veto power firmly in place. Government policy tends to remain stuck around perceptions of indigenous peoples as a "problem people" with "needs" requiring solutions (Humpage and Fleras, 2001). Indigeneity as principle and practice is rarely taken seriously as a basis for living together differently, resulting in a corresponding diminishment of indigenous claims to self-determining autonomy.

The cumulative effects of positive changes in redefining indigenous peoples–state relations is offset by the failure to think outside a conventional constitutional box. A colonial constitutional order persists, with its monocultural focus on controlling the rules and standards by which power is shared, relations constructed, rewards allocated, decisions made, and issues resolved. In that sense, any further change will be akin to walking up a down escalator whose speed is controlled by entrenched interests and hidden agendas.

Two oppositional forces are clearly in play: Crown resistance to foundational changes is matched by the intensity of indigenous struggles to sever the bonds of colonialist dependency and under-development. There is mounting pressure to transcend orthodox ways of "doing" indigenous peoples–Crown relations and establish a just social contract that acknowledges indigenous claims to joint sovereignty as a precondition for living together differently. A more inclusive constitutional approach is endorsed that emphasizes engagement over entitlement, relationships over rights, interdependence over opposition, cooperation over competition, reconciliation over restitution, and power-sharing over power conflict (Maaka and Fleras, 1998; Coates and McHugh, 1998).

But is it possible to reconcile stubbornly sovereign and fundamentally different peoples into a mutually acceptable constitutional framework? The enormity of the challenge should never be underestimated, as noted by Daniel Salée:

> The points of contention between First Nations and non-Aboriginals do not simply consist of irritants that might be overcome by mere good will, or of territorial claims that might be satisfied if one or the other party showed flexibility or compromised. As the conceptual differences over land partly revealed, the two parties operate within institutional parameters and sociocultural systems which have nothing in common ... The contention between Aboriginals and non-Aboriginals rests in fact on a paradigmatic contradiction of which the poles are, *a priori,* logically irreconcilable (Salée, 1995:291).

These logically irreconcilable differences will prove nettlesome even under the best of circumstances. No more so than at constitutional levels where the *status quo* prevails. Nevertheless, a constitutional *modus vivendi* may be possible if these divergences are approached not as a problem to be solved, but as an opportunity to explore in the spirit of a creative tension. A resilient outlook may yield exciting new opportunities for living together differently.

This article explores the possibility of a new constitutional order based on the foundational principles of constructive engagement. A constructive engagement model is proposed as an innovative paradigm for re-constitutionalizing the social contract between indigenous peoples and society at large. Constructive engagement is predicated on the premise that a new constitutional order must reflect, reinforce, and advance the principles and practice of indigeneity, indigenous rights, indigenous difference, and indigenous models to self-determining autonomy. A commitment to process is no less critical in advancing constructive engagement. A post-colonial social contract implores both indigenous peoples and central authorities to engage constructively as constitutional partners in sharing the land. The challenge will lie in transforming the balancing act between mutually opposed yet equally valid rights—indigenous self-determining rights versus Crown rights to rule and regulate—into a viable constitutional package.

Certainly, the real world of indigenous peoples–state relations is too messy to reduce into a single solution. To assume the existence of such a grand narrative in a world of multiple discourses and diverse publics may induce serious intellectual entanglements. Nevertheless, the emergence of a constructive engagement model may provide a respite from the interminable bickering over "who owns what." Such a commitment may also broker a constitutional framework for bridging the gap in deeply divisive societies.

JURISDICTIONAL WRANGLES: UNPRODUCTIVE DISENGAGEMENT

Indigenous struggles to sever the bonds of colonialist dependency and under-development appear to be gathering momentum. Several innovative routes have been explored for improving indigenous peoples–state relations, most of which involve debates over ownership and control (Fleras, 1996; 2000). Treaty settlements in both Canada and New Zealand are predicated on the need to define "who controls what" for righting historical wrongs. Not surprisingly, both government policy and indigenous politics revolve increasingly around the issue of what is mine, what is yours, and what is ours.

There is much to be gained from debating jurisdiction over the allocation of land, identity, and political voice, yet the politics of jurisdiction are not without its costs and consequences. Confrontational models for dividing jurisdiction may prove counterproductive without a unifying constitutional vision to soften or absorb competing demands. The adversarial thrust of jurisdictional politics may inadvertently reinforce the very colonialisms that indigenous peoples are seeking to escape. A confrontational approach to indigenous peoples–state relations generates unhealthy competition over who gets what. The end result is nothing less than "unproductive disengagement" between the constitutional partners. Ongoing debate about divvying the spoils makes it doubly important to re-visit the politics of jurisdictions with respect to treaty settlements.

Treaty Settlements

A growing reliance on restitution-based settlements represents a striking development in jurisdictional politics. The logic behind a restitution-based approach (or "treaty settlements" in New Zealand or "comprehensive land claims agreements" in Canada) is relatively straightforward. In an effort to right historical wrongs by settling outstanding complaints against the state for breaches to indigenous rights, the government offers a compensation package of cash, land, services, and controlling rights to specific indigenous claimants in exchange for "full and final" settlements of treaty-based grievances (Office of Treaty Settlements, 2002).

On the surface, restitution-based agreements appear to be a win–win situation. Governments approve of regional agreements as one way of establishing certainty in land titles and access to potentially lucrative resource extraction (Jull and Craig, 1997). Not only is the honour of the Crown restored in compensating historically disadvantaged peoples for unwarranted confiscation of land, but also these settlements are endorsed as restorative justice (Humpage and Fleras, 2001). For indigenous peoples, these agreements are critical for advancing their interests. A resource base is procured that offsets the social and cultural dislocations created by colonization (see Wilson, 1995).

In Canada, this process revolves around comprehensive land claims settlements. Comprehensive settlements resemble 19th-century treaties which involved an exchange of rights, resources, and obligations between Aboriginal peoples and the Crown. Each of these agreements—from James Bay–Cree settlement of 1975 to the Nisga'a Final Agreement in 2000—entail extinguishment of Aboriginal title in a region in exchange for a package of

(a) perpetual Aboriginal rights to various categories of land;
(b) co-management and planning in various socio-economic and environmental issues;
(c) hefty compensation payouts to foster Aboriginal economic development and political infrastructures; and
(d) various self-management arrangements, with near-exclusive jurisdiction over internal affairs (Gallagher-Mackay, 1997).

The situation in New Zealand is slightly different. There are no formal treaties in the transactional sense of land for goods and services, rather, Maori land was acquired by individual freehold purchase. Treaty settlements are focused on the Treaty of Waitangi, which promised much but did not always deliver. Thus, Treaty settlements between the Crown and Maori tribes are driven by a commitment to right Treaty wrongs. The objective is compensation for Crown violations of its promises to Maori under the Treaty of Waitangi. Financial compensation is a key to these settlements, in addition to receipt of an apology, return of sacred sites or traditional fishing grounds, and co-management rights in conservation.

SETTLEMENTS AS DOUBLE-EDGED

There is much to commend the Canadian and New Zealand governments for transferring wealth to indigenous peoples. Identity-building and resource mobilization are but two benefits that accrue from the exchange. However, critics and supporters disagree about the benefits of the claims-making activity. Are restitution agreements a catalyst for crafting a new political order or little more than an administrative quick-fix to make the "indigenous problem" go away? Is the claims-making process conducive to creating a genuine partnership or does it foster closure and separation? Will it bring about supra-tribal harmony or is it a recipe for bickering and divisiveness between competing claimants?

Reactions to restitution settlements vary because of different perspectives. Supporters point to these agreements as an innovative, even unprecedented, process where two peoples negotiate the basis by which to share territories, public revenues, decision-making, and economic development through a mix of pragmatism, recognition, accommodation, and tolerance (Jull and Craig, 1997). Critics prefer to point at the unintended consequences of a restitutional claims-making process. A claims-making approach embraces an underlying agenda, which has transformed the politics of partnership into a zero-sum game of winners and losers. However unintended, the consequences of a claims-making process foster an adversarial mentality between the state and indigenous peoples. No less disabling are the rivalries among indigenous tribes who compete for scarce government resources.

Additional problems can be also discerned. A reliance on contractual obligations for framing indigenous peoples–Crown relations elevates litigation to the preferred method of resolving differences (Spoonley, 1993). A preoccupation with the past takes precedence over the present need for constructive living relationships (Coates and McHugh, 1998). Fixating on results does little to advance a sharing of the land on a principled basis (see also Mulgan, 1998). Disputants are drawn into a protracted struggle for scarce resources, rather than focusing on the structures that created the scarcity in the first place (Humpage and Fleras, 2001). Issues become occluded inside a rigid format that complicates the ability to compromise without losing face. Levels of rhetoric under a claims-making model are stretched to the breaking point, as each party attempts to out-manoeuvre the other for maximum effect. Rhetoric tends to be blown out of proportion to get media attention. The claims-making competition compels indigenous peoples to articulate their aspirations in the language of the protagonist, with the result that indigenous aspirations are crammed into a Eurocentric framework (Tully, 1995).

Difficulties are further intensified when central authorities and indigenous peoples operate at cross-purposes in the claims-making process (Minogue, 1998). Governments prefer a full and final settlement for past injustices, if only to eliminate uncertainty from any further governance or development (Graham 1997). This misreads indigenous perceptions of settlements as prescriptions for co-operative co-existence (Coates and McHugh, 1998). For indigenous peoples, the resolution of claims is not an end in itself, but one stage in an evolving and ongoing relationship between partners. The attainment of indigenous autonomy is not about a farewell, but the onset of a new relationship. Indigenous demands are not about closure, but about inclusion and co-operation as a basis for living together differently.

So restitution-based claims-making is a double-edged sword that can be swung in different directions. The government and indigenous peoples compete for scarce resources, often culminating in antagonistic positions of mistrust or hostility that trap groups into confrontational politics at the expense of relations-repair. Worse still, indigenous peoples bicker among themselves in the division of the spoils, as evidenced by the proposed allocation of fisheries assets in New Zealand (Inns and Goodall, 2002).

To sum up, the politics of jurisdiction by way of restitution-based settlements are exacting a toll on indigenous communities. The domain of indigenous peoples–state relations is experiencing stress as well. However well intentioned and valuable, jurisdictional politics tend to induce an unproductive disengagement rather than a blueprint for living together differently. Of course, restitution is critical if indigenous peoples are to reclaim the land and resources unfairly confiscated or stolen; after all, the control of land and resources is crucial in driving economic development, cultural survival, and political influence. But without an overarching constitutional framework to transform competition into co-operation, the possibility for productive engagement is diminished. A commitment to engaging constructively may provide a constitutional framework model for unblocking the gridlock.

INSIGHT
The Politics of Reconciliation: "Talking Past Each Other"

Using the same words is no guarantee that people are speaking the same language. Breakdowns in communication are often caused when people use similar words with substantially different meanings that can vary from context to context. "Reconciliation" has become a core phrase in righting historical wrongs. Both indigenous peoples and central authorities make repeated references to reconciliation, but mean something different by it, with the result that they literally end up talking past each other.

In general, reconciliation is about atonement and renewal—atonement for historical wrongs, renewal as improvement. Beyond this, meanings vary. For some, especially non-indigenous individuals, reconciliation is about saying "sorry" for the past and moving on. A practical reconciliation means delivering services like clean water or clinics to remote indigenous communities (Jull and Bennett, 2001). Others believe reconciliation is about land rights and compensation, or about rewriting settler history. For some, reconciliation means nothing without restoring indigenous peoples to their rightful status as a constitutional partner (McIntosh, 1999). Predictably, then, conflicts over reconciliation are inevitable, as long as indigenous peoples continue to identify with the past as a springboard for the future, while the mainstream wants to put the past behind by getting on with the present.

"Reconciliation" can vary with differing perceptions of colonial history (Mulgan, 1998; Jong, 1998). For many indigenous groups, the historical past is a source of anger and resentment because of dispossession, relocation, and servitude, which will remain a sore point unless there is some sense of closure through restitution. The past provides a basis for demanding redress and reparations as a matter of right rather than as an act of benevolence. In other words, a sense of historical grievance underlies indigenous hopes and aspirations, and any attempt to deny or gloss over this history may be interpreted as yet another denial or putdown.

While indigenous peoples often embrace history, there can be non-indigenous aversion to it. The colonial past is often a source of guilt because of settler mistreatments that include genocide, forced assimilation, expropriation of land and resources, and the destruction of culture and authority. When the past is viewed as an embarrassing blot, there is an urgency to "put it behind" in order to move forward into the future. For others, there is nothing embarrassing about a colonial past or carrying out the "white man's burden." They are proud of the colonizing (civilizing) mission that not only developed the country, but also brought so-called civilization to allegedly primitive peoples. But the past has passed by, according to this line of thinking, and dwelling on it serves no purpose in getting on with the present, especially since the present generation bears no responsibility for historical indiscretions. Nor should incidents or omissions from the past be judged by modern sensibilities. Only historical context matters.

The contrasts could not be more sharply etched. For non-indigenous peoples, reconciliation symbolizes a closing of the books on colonial history. For indigenous peoples, reconciliation is about acknowledging the past as a precondition for living in the present. A commitment to reconciliation not only concedes Orwell's prescient notion that whoever controls the past controls the present, but clearly exposes the damaging legacy of colonization, reinforcing the connection between present disadvantage and past dispossession. Reconciliation is premised on the assumption that colonialism was inherently unfair, insofar as the process forcibly imposed settler regimes on indigenous peoples (Mulgan, 1998). Without reconciliation, in short, there is no justification for non-indigenous presence. The legitimacy of the state (or crown), its laws and institutions, and the right of settlers to claim citizenship depends on it.

For indigenous peoples, then, reconciliation is an exercise in co-operative co-existence. It includes a multi-textured process that addresses

(a) the righting of historical wrongs by way of reparations;
(b) new partnerships as a basis for interaction;
(c) full and equal participation in decisions that affect them;
(d) working through differences rather than closing doors when things do not proceed smoothly; and
(e) taking indigeneity seriously by taking it into account for recognition or rewards.

According to Gatjil Djerrkura, Chair of ATSIC, the principles of respect, recognition, and rights are central to any notion of reconciliation:

At the heart of reconciliation is the co-existence of rights, along with respect for different values, and acceptance that different sectors of the community can share resources with beneficial results ... For Aboriginal and Torres Strait Islander people, reconciliation means respect for our cultures, recognition of our prior occupancy, and regard for the rights that result from that history. We want to be certain that we are not missing any of the rights and opportunities that other members of the Australian community enjoy to maintain our cultural values, to pursue our spiritual beliefs, to maximise our scope for improving the lives of our families and children (Djerrkura, 1997:17).

Others concede the possibility of different levels of reconciliation (Dodson, 2000). The interpersonal level of reconciliation proposes encounters that are free of racism but reflect understanding, empathy, and inclusiveness. At the social level, reconciliation involves the construction of inclusive social policies pertaining to health or education. At the governance level is a re-distribution of powers between the elected and non-elected. And the final level involves the recognition of the intrinsic sovereignty and self-determining rights of indigenous peoples. For any meaningful reconciliation to take place, all aspects must be incorporated (also Council for Aboriginal Reconciliation, 1997).

In short, reference to reconciliation provides the framework for a new social contract. Reconciliation secures a foundational principle for a post-colonial constitutional order based on recognition of indigenous peoples as autonomous and self-determining political communities (nations or peoples). To be sure, there is no guarantee that reconciliation will improve meaningful dialogue. The reality gap between indigenous peoples and central authorities may be too divergent for clear communication to be possible. Perhaps a version of reconciliation is required that acknowledges the inevitability of creative conflict implicit within any process of compromise, accommodation, and negotiation. In other words, tensions and disagreements are not something that must be avoided, but actively nurtured in exploring opportunities for living together differently.

CONSTRUCTIVE ENGAGEMENT: A NEW CONSTITUTIONAL BLUEPRINT

Proposed solutions for breaking the constitutional impasse for the most part tend to be piecemeal, sectoral, superficial, and modest in scope, with a tendency to paper over flaws within the existing arrangement. However beneficial and overdue, these modifications are unlikely to bring about the constitutional space for living together differently.

A constructive engagement model proposes a constitutional alternative to a colonial social contract. Within the model is a new social contract that transcends both the legalistic (abstract rights) and restitutional (reparations) as a blueprint for engaging indigeneity. A new constitutional order will be constructed that secures and promotes indigenous rights, including the right to indigenous models of self-determining autonomy without, however, denying the equally legitimate claims to Crown rule and authority. In this "middle way," indigenous difference is taken seriously without undermining Crown rights to govern and regulate on behalf of all citizens (see also Cairns, 2000). Put simply, then, constructive engagement is about rethinking the basis for living together differently, in part by emphasising the importance of the "differently" without reneging on a need for the "together."

There are two dimensions to constructive engagement as a constitutional blueprint. In terms of content, a constitutional framework provides a template for a post-colonial social contract. The foundational principles of a settler social contract, with their focus on assimilation and hierarchy, are discarded, and in their place is a new post-colonial constitutional order whose foundational principles include partnership, equity, and inclusiveness as part of the social contract. The normative framework envisaged by constructive engagement is grounded on several principles: both colonizer and colonized are here for the long haul; there is no choice but to acknowledge each other's permanence; each partner and their cultural background has a legitimate right to be here; and finally, the claims of both must be treated as equally valid. Process is also important. Constructive engagement establishes a meeting ground for negotiating a broader framework of co-operative co-existence. Under constructive engagement, mechanisms are set in place to foster a "dialogue between sovereigns" that ensures open lines of communication for negotiation, compromises, and adjustment. These mechanisms also provide a safety valve for blowing off steam when tensions mount (Thakur, 2001).

For our purposes, constructive engagement can be defined as a principled pattern of interaction between constitutional partners, consisting of a social contract whose foundational ("first") principles are anchored in a new constitutional order. The necessary preconditions for living together differently in deeply divided societies are also secured, at least in principle. The following first principles provide the inventory of constructive engagement. They also draw together the many issues raised in this book.

THE "SOVEREIGNS WITHIN"

Constructive engagement is anchored on the principle that indigenous peoples are sovereign peoples. Indigenous peoples do not aspire to sovereignty *per se*. Strictly speaking, they already *have* sovereignty by virtue of original occupancy, never having relinquished this independence by explicit agreement. Sovereignty already exists; it only needs to be lived (Monture-Angus, 2001). The fact that indigenous peoples *are* sovereign for purposes of entitlement or engagement puts the onus on creating a constitutional framework to put principle into practice (Reynolds 1996; Jackson, 2000).

RELATIONS REPAIR

Constructive engagement is not about separation, secession, or independence. A commitment to engaging constructively secures a co-operative co-existence by establishing relationships of relative and relational autonomy within a non-dominating context between interconnected peoples (Young, 1990; Scott, 1996). Relations-repair is the key, rather than "throwing money at the problem." A treaty-based relationship provides the constitutional grounds for a government-to-government (or nation-to-nation) relationship embracing mutual consent between equal sovereign powers (Tully, 2000). In acknowledging the inescapable fact that "let's face it, we are all here to stay," is there any other option except to shift from the trap of "who gets what" to the primacy of "how to relate" (McHugh, 1998)?

PEOPLES WITH RIGHTS, NOT MINORITIES WITH PROBLEMS

Indigenous peoples are neither a problem requiring solution nor a need to be met. Nor are they an ethnic minority to be appeased with multicultural concessions. They are peoples with inherent rights to define who they are, what they want, and how they plan to get there. A constructive engagement approach does not deny the existence of problems within indigenous communities. However extensive and debilitating, these problems must be addressed within a principled rights-based framework rather than from the default position of needs or disadvantage (see also Durie, 2000).

INDIGENOUS MODELS OF SELF-DETERMINING AUTONOMY

A constructive engagement approach endorses an inalienable right to indigenous self-determination. But a distinction is critical: to one side are government-defined models of state-determination as essentially an exercise in self-sufficiency. To the other side are indigenous models of self-determining autonomy over land, identity, and political voice that reflect and reinforce indigenous realities, experiences, and aspirations. Problems arise when this distinction is not acknowledged.

INDIGENOUS PEOPLES AS POLITICAL COMMUNITIES

Constructive engagement defines indigenous peoples as relatively autonomous political communities who are sovereign and share joint sovereignty. Indigenous peoples' aspirations and demands for political recognition are consistent with the principled discourses of a political community rather than the pragmatic frameworks of ethnic struggles (Chartrand, 1996). Crafting a new constitutional order must acknowledge the political rights of indigenous peoples as independently sourced, not shaped for the convenience of the political majority or subject to unilateral override (Asch, 1997).

TAKING INDIGENEITY SERIOUSLY

Constructive engagement acknowledges the indigeneity principle for what it really is: a politicized ideology of challenges, resistance, and transformation. Rather than looking for space within the existing constitutional framework, indigeneity is challenging the foundational principles of a settler constitutional order, resisting state-defined solutions to self-determination, and looking to transform society along post-colonial lines.

PRIMACY OF INDIGENOUS DIFFERENCE

It goes without saying that indigenous peoples are different and want to remain different for political, cultural, and economic reasons. Reference to indigenous difference goes beyond a "celebrating diversity" model, but acknowledges that indigenous peoples embrace a unique constitutional status with a special relationship to the Crown; indigenous difference must be taken seriously in securing the legitimacy of indigenous claims and entitlements; and indigenous difference must be taken into account in constructing a new constitutional order for living together differently.

POWER-SHARING

A commitment to power-sharing is pivotal in advancing co-operative engagement and co-existence. All deeply divided societies that have attained some degree of stability embrace a level of governance that connotes a sharing of power based on consensual rather than adversarial terms (Linden, 1994). Structural and constitutional changes must be implemented to include indigenous peoples within institutions of power (Green, 2002). Precise arrangements for rearranging power distributions are varied, of course, but invariably embrace the notion that power must be shared rather than fought over (Thakur, 2001).

RETHINKING CITIZENSHIP: BELONGING TOGETHER BY STANDING APART

Innovative patterns of belonging are integral to constructive engagement. Indigenous proposals for belonging to society are anchored in a primary affiliation with the ethnicity or tribe rather than as individual citizens (Ladner, 2003). The implications are far-reaching. Indigenous peoples can belong to society in different ways, without necessarily rejecting a sense of citizenship or loyalty to the whole (Kymlicka, 2001). The challenge rests in creating a constitutional order around a citizenship that is both inclusive yet customized, without compromising commonalities (Fleras and Elliott, 2003).

NEW GAME, NEW RULES, NEW OUTCOMES

Placing constructive engagement at the centre of a relationship entails a fundamental rethink in terms of how resources are distributed. As with dispute resolution in general, engaging constructively eschews any winner-takes-all game that pits the powerful against the weakest, but advocates a problem-solving exercise in which both sides have a stake in sharing an agreement (see Campbell, 1998). A relational framework must be negotiated not on the basis of jurisprudence but on the grounds of justice, not by cutting deals but by formulating a clear vision, and not by litigation but by listening.

CONSTITUTIONAL PARTNERSHIP

Constructive engagement upholds the principle of equal and meaningful partnership as the framework for renewing the relationship. Indigenous peoples should not be considered a competitor to be jousted with or a junior partner to be consulted. They embody a constitutional player to work with to resolve differences in a spirit of partnership.

MULTICULTURALISM WITHIN A BI-NATIONALISM FRAMEWORK

Constructive engagement endorses the principle of bi/multiculturalism within a bi-national framework. A commitment to multiculturalism or biculturalism may provide a useful framework for institutional accommodation, particularly for immigrant minorities who are looking to settle down, but such a political framework does not address the realities of indigenous peoples. As self-determining peoples who want to establish nation-to-nation relationships, indigenous peoples require a constitutional framework that reflects, reinforces, and advances their status as "nations within" who are independently sourced and sovereign for purposes of reward, recognition, and relations.

JURISDICTIONS WITH A VISION

A commitment to constructive engagement involves a division of jurisdiction that acknowledges shared yet exclusive control. In the final analysis, all successful relations are based on balancing the "you" with the "me" and the "us" in terms of defining what is "yours," what is "mine," and what is "ours." The challenge lies in creating constitutional space that allows the autonomy of the other in certain spheres and shared jurisdiction in others (Tully, 2000). This division of society into "who controls what" cannot be conducted in a ruthless manner but on a principled basis. Without a unifying vision, the politics of jurisdiction divide rather than unite.

CREATIVE OPPOSITION

Constructive engagement goes beyond the dualities that polarize and provoke conflicts between two entities, thereby disallowing the possibility of drawing upon the supposed opposite for meaning and relevance (Fay, 1996; Meredith, 1998). A dialectical mode of thinking is proposed that avoids the "politics of polarity" in which differences are perceived not as absolute or antagonistic, but as deeply interconnected and existing in a state of creative tension with potential opportunity. A commitment to constructive engagement parlays this ongoing tension into an opportunity as a basis for living together differently; with Crown rights to rule and regulate in creative opposition to indigenous rights to self-determining autonomy.

RECONCILIATION

Reconciliation is central to any constructive engagement. This involves two dimensions. To one side are expressions of sorrow or regret for the deplorable acts of a colonial past. To the other side is an acknowledgement that Crown sovereignty and settler prosperity owe their origins to a colonization process that assumed the inferiority of indigenous peoples and systematically denied their rightful place within the national framework. An apology acknowledges how the legacies of the past continue to inform the injustices in the present.

A DIALOGUE BETWEEN SOVEREIGNS

Settler societies were grounded in discourses that endorsed a "white is right" mentality. This openly racist stance is no longer politically or socially acceptable, despite the continuing colonialist legacy of "we know what is right for you." Constructive engagement challenges this patronizing superiority and proposes a constitutional relationship based on a dialogue between sovereigns (see also Boast, 1993). That is, both indigenous peoples and the state interact as partners who are equally sovereign in defining a new constitutional order.

The principles of constructive engagement provide a principled approach for living together differently in deeply divided societies. Constructive engagement goes beyond the realm of rights or restitution, notwithstanding their importance in securing co-operative co-existence. Rather, this model hopes to carve out a new constitutional space. The challenge lies in acknowledging the legitimacy of indigeneity without destroying the integrity of the whole or interconnectedness of its parts. The focus is on creating a new social contract by sorting out who controls what, in a spirit of give and take. Process is no less important. As a "meeting" ground for exploring a "middle" way, constructive engagement draws energy and strength by incorporating two equally valid yet competing rights: Crown rights to rule and regulate with the right of indigenous peoples to self-determining autonomy.

To be sure, biases are implicit in a constructive engagement discourse. First, the value and validity of the existing nation-state is accepted as a given. But who says the state must take precedence over indigenous nationhood as a basis for global order? Second, and following upon this, constructive engagement explores how to balance indigenous rights with Crown rights, but why is it not the case of balancing Crown rights with indigenous rights? Third, the politics of jurisdiction are inescapable; a sorting out of rights, powers, and resources is critical and inevitable in any proposal for living together differently (Fleras, 1999; Maaka and Fleras, 2001). But the wheeling-and-dealing approach to jurisdiction by jurisprudence cannot be viewed as final or authoritative, any more than it can be preoccupied with "taking" or "finalizing." Any sorting-out process must be situated within the context of "sharing" and "extending." Wisdom and justice must precede power-politics, in other words, rather than vice versa (Cassidy, 1994).

LOOKING FORWARD, LOOKING BACKWARDS: RE-PRIMING THE SOCIAL CONTRACT

Indigenous politics and the politics of indigeneity have leapt to the forefront in the unfolding of national constitutional dramas. Indigeneity as discourse and transformation has proven a key dynamic in reshaping the political contours of contemporary society. Energies are focused on contesting the foundational principles that govern a mono-constitutional order by advancing an indigenous agenda that sharply curtails state jurisdictions, while enhancing indigenous models of self-determination over land, identity, and political voice.

But a proposed re-constitutionalizing of indigenous peoples–Crown relations will fail unless those foundational principles that systemically erode, deny, or exclude indigenous peoples are revoked. Constructing a post-colonial social contract between the colonizer and the colonized is a more formidable constitutional challenge than the decolonization of the Third World. The challenge lies in creating consensual ways of sharing the land and citizenship, rather than following the power of the stronger (Niezen, 2003). Proposals for meaningful change are undermined by a stubborn Crown insistence on

(a) needs-oriented policies over a rights-based relationship;
(b) bi/multicultural accommodation over bi-nationalism engagement;
(c) ethnic minority discourse over the language of nationhood;
(d) junior partner over equal partnership;
(e) conformity and universalism rather than indigenous difference as a politicized ideology for constitutional change; and
(f) a universal ("one size fits all") citizenship over an inclusive citizenship as basis for belonging (Maaka and Fleras, 2001).

Crown reluctance to endorse constitutional change goes beyond arrogance or pigheadedness. A refusal to take indigeneity seriously has reinforced the very paradoxes at the heart of the constitutional impasse. A proposed restructuring of indigenous peoples–Crown relations remains trapped inside a (neo)colonialist constitutional framework, despite modest success in eradicating the most egregious expressions of colonial discrimination, such as broken promises, unwarranted confiscation, discriminatory barriers, and socio-economic disadvantages. Failure to move beyond a mono-constitutional discourse has had the unintended yet controlling effect of reinforcing a colonial social contract. Only a paradigm shift toward the principles of "constructive engagement" may secure a blueprint for transcending the constitutional gridlock that currently engulfs indigenous peoples–Crown relations.

But what sounds good in principle may not always be possible to implement or work in practice. Yes, constructive engagement models may provide a principled approach to redefining indigenous peoples–Crown relations, but putting these principles into practices may be something else, as the following passage indicates:

> The federal government has rejected the concept of Aboriginal peoples as "sovereign" in international law. Aboriginal peoples, however, maintain that government must recognize their claims to sovereignty before any true discussions occur. Hence, there is a political stalemate, creating a serious obstacle to negotiations on self-government. No aboriginal chief or representative wants the legacy of signing away aboriginal claims to sovereignty; no governing political party will sacrifice its political future by embracing sovereignty (Noah Augustine, *Toronto Star,* 11 January 2000).

Moreover, the gap between a colonial constitutional order and a constructive engagement contract may be impossible to reconcile or implement without substantial controversy and conflict. But acknowledging the mutually opposed yet concurrently valid claims of both indigenous peoples and the state provides a useful starting point. Constructive engagement provides a blueprint for exploring the middle in a way that is workable, necessary, and fair. Time will tell if a constructive engagement model can absorb these oppositional dynamics in opening up creative opportunities for living together differently.

What does the foreseeable future hold? Indigenous peoples in the settler societies of Canada and Aotearoa New Zealand are in the process of disengaging their linkages with a colonial past. But the re-constitutionalizing process has not happened as smoothly as many would like. Politics and expediency continue to tarnish the process of de-colonizing those foundational principles that empower some, disempower others. Central authorities bristle at the prospect of moving over and making constitutional space for indigenous peoples for fear of jeopardizing the paramountcy of an indivisible state with its time-honoured rights to establish agendas, conduct business, demand compliance, and enforce laws. Fears persist that taking indigeneity seriously could endanger national unity, by transforming society into an archipelago of indigenous nations without a unifying centre to hold it together (Epp, 2003). Settler states remain suspicious of any fundamental restructuring, preferring instead to deflate indigeneity by channelling it into institutional inclusion or delegated self-governing arrangements. Preferences are geared toward rearguard actions that evade, deny, or suppress any move toward a dispersal of power or localization of autonomy. Not unexpectedly, government initiatives for engaging indigeneity continue to miscalculate the enormity of the indigenous challenge.

Global changes are also creating obstacles because of conflicting forces.

Fundamental and yet-to-be-resolved contradictions reflect tensions between indigenous peoples and the forces of globalization with their tendency to commodify and commercialize life, relations, and environment around the discipline of a global market (Kelsey, 2002). In contrast to colonialism, which imposed foreign values and expropriated indigenous property, globalization is proving more insidious (Greenshill, 2001). Economic globalization looks for profit maximization for trans-capitalists by creating a global free market in which investment and capital can move freely to secure the highest return with the least impediment or cost. International agreements are in place that compel governments to remove barriers that impede the entry of capital, while prohibiting governments from discriminating in favour of local interests. Indigenous rights are deemed to create costs that must be subordinated to the market. Yet indigenous peoples promise to be the buffer that ensures global capitalism does not run roughshod over state sovereignties.

Despite overwhelming odds, the politics of indigeneity are challenging the foundational pillars of a settler constitutional order. A proposed paradigm shift is gathering momentum because of a growing crisis in state legitimacy. But the widely heralded realignment of indigenous peoples–Crown relations is riddled with inconsistencies and contradictions as competing interests clash over a new indigenous agenda, with colonial paradigms grating against post-colonial realities.

The muddle in the models is clearly evident. This should come as no surprise since the birthing phase of a new era is always messy, infused with contradictory and awkward hybrids of old and new (Walker-Williams, 2001). To one side, the old assimilation paradigm with its roots in the "old rules of the game" appears to be drawing to a close, but not without a struggle (Borrows and Rotman, 1997:31). Colonialism has moved underground in that its most oppressive features have been masked by a carefully crafted narrative that champions indigenous causes while simultaneously subverting Aboriginal aspirations (Christie, 2002). To the other, a new post-colonial paradigm based on empowerment and renewal through constructive engagement has not yet taken hold. Indigenous peoples lack the political power and critical mass to force the kind of constitutional change that would entrench an inherent right to self-determining autonomy based on unextinguished political sovereignty (Schouls, 2002).

Instead of a paradigm shift, in other words, what is emerging is a paradigm muddle. Indigenous peoples–state relations are imbued with an air of ambivalence as colonialist paradigms grind up against an emergent post-colonialism. The old ("colonialism") is colliding with the new ("post-colonialism") without either displacing the other. The "old" model talks about the need to build capacity and partnership but isn't prepared to give up much control, preferring, instead, to impose changes it thinks are best for Aboriginal peoples (Barnsley, 2002). The new model says "give us the tools and we will do the job," yet runs into timid and distrustful decision-makers. The new seeks to dismantle the old, but the old guard is digging in its heels in a last-ditch effort to preserve the *status quo*.

Metaphors borrowed from the theory of continental drift may help. Just as plate tectonics collide and displace, so too the clash of paradigms suggests diverse viewpoints on a collision course, as perspectives slide into each other, past each other, around each other, and over or under each other. Each of the "plates" tends to "talk past the other" by using the same words, but speaking a different language. Neither colonization nor the partnership paradigm is compelling enough to dislodge its conceptual opponent, with the result that the renewal process is enlivened by discordant amalgams of progress and reaction. Such a state of uncertainty and expediency is likely to persist until such time as a seismic shift embraces a new social contract involving a constitutional covenant between consenting political communities, each of which is autonomous and self-determining in its own right, yet which are inextricably interlocked as partners in jointly exploring a post-colonial alternative for living together differently without drifting apart.

REFERENCES

Asch, Michael, ed. 1997. *Aboriginal and Treaty Rights in Canada. Essays on Law, Equity, and Respect for Difference.* Vancouver: UBC Press.

Barnsley, Paul. 2002. "How Much Goes to Indians?" *Windspeaker*, March 6–7.

Boast, Richard P. 1993. "The Waitangi Tribunal: Conscience of the Nation, or Just Another Court?" *University of New South Wales Law Journal*, 16(1): 233–44.

Borrows, John and Rotman, Leonard. 1997. "The *Sui Generis* Nature of Aboriginal Rights: Does it Make a Difference?" *Alberta Law Review*, 36: 9–45.

Cairns, Alan. 2000. *Citizen Plus: Aboriginal Peoples and the Canadian State.* Vancouver: UBC Press.

Campbell, Murray. 1998. "Mediation Suggested in N.B. Forest Dispute." *The Globe and Mail*, 27 April.

Cassidy, Frank. 1994. "British Columbia and Aboriginal Peoples. The Prospects for the Treaty Process." *Policy Options*, March: 10–13.

Chartrand, Paul L.A.H. 1996. "Self-Determination without a Discrete Territorial Base?" In D. Clark and R. Williamson, eds. *Self-Determination: International Perspectives.* Basingstoke: Macmillan, 302–12.

Christie, Gordon. 2002. "Challenges to Urban Aboriginal Governance." Report, Osgoode Hall Law School, October.

Coates, Ken and McHugh, P.G., eds. 1998. *Living Relationships, Kokiri Ngatahi: The Treaty of Waitangi in the New Millennium.* Wellington: Victoria University Press.

Council for Aboriginal Reconciliation. 1997. *The Path to Reconciliation: Issues for a People's Movement.* Canberra: Australian Government Publishing.

Djerrkura, Gatjil. 1997. "The Meaning of Reconciliation." *Walking Together*, 18.

Dodson, Pat. 2000. "Until the Chains are Broken." *Australian Indigenous Law Reporter*, 5(2): 70–89.

Durie, Mason. 2000. "Contemporary Maori Development: Issues and Directions." Working Paper, School of Maori and Pacific Development, Hamilton: University of Waikato.

Epp, Roger. 2003. "We are all Treaty People: History, Reconciliation, and the 'Settler Problem'": In Prager and Govier, 223–44.

Fay, Brian. 1996. *Contemporary Philosophy of Social Sciences*. Oxford: Blackwell.

Fleras, Augie. 1996. "The Politics of Jurisdiction." In David A. Long and Olive Dickason, eds. *Visions of the Heart*. Toronto: Harcourt Brace, 241–98.

Fleras, Augie. 1999. "Comparing Ethnopolitics in Australia, Canada, and Aotearoa." In Paul Havemann, ed. New *Frontiers First Nation Rights in Settler Dominions in Canada, Australia, and New Zealand*. Auckland: Oxford University Press, 133–65.

Fleras, Augie. 2000. "The Politics of Constructive Engagement." In David A. Long and Olive Dickason, eds. *Visions of the Heart,* 2nd edition. Toronto: Harcourt Brace, 241–98.

Fleras, Augie and Elliot, Jean Leonard. 2003. *Unequal Relations: An Introduction to Race, Ethnic, and Aboriginal Dynamics in Canada*. Scarborough ON: Pearson/Prentice Hall.

Gallagher-Mackay, Kelly. 1997. "Interpreting Self-Government: Approaches to Building Cultural Authority." *Canadian Native Law Reporter*, 4: 1–19.

Graham, Douglas. 1997. "Treaty Process at Turning Point says Graham." *Dominion,* 2 August.

Green, Joyce. 2002. "Decolonizing in the Era of Globalization." *Canadian Dimension.* March/April 3–5.

Greenshill, Angeline. 2001. "Balancing Hapu and Iwi (Central and Local) Interests." In E. Te Kohu Douglas and M. Robertson Shaw, eds. *Ngai Tatou 2020*. Vol. 2. *Governance and Accountability*. Auckland: Published by FIRST (Foundation for Indigenous Research on Society and Technology).

Humpage, Louise and Fleras, Angie. 2001. "Intersecting Discourse, Closing the Gaps, Social Justice, and the Treaty of Waitangi." *Social Policy*, 14:37–53.

Inns, Justine and Goodall, Anake. 2002. Fisheries Allocation—Where is it at? *Te Karaka,* Autumn: 14–15.

Jackson, Moana. 2000. "Where Does Sovereignty Lie." In C. James, ed. *Building the Constitution*. Wellington: Institute of Policy Studies, 196–201.

Jong, Alice de. 1998. "The Human Rights of Indigenous Peoples, in Papua New Guinea." In C. Cohen, ed. *Human Rights of Indigenous Peoples*. Ardsley, New York: Transnational Publishers, 127–51.

Jull, Peter and Craig, Donna. 1997. "Reflections on Regional Agreements: Yesterday, Today, and Tomorrow." *Australian Indigenous Law Reporter*, 2(4): 475–93.

Jull, Peter and Bennett, Kathryn. 2001. "Stop the World, We Want to Get Off." *Indigenous Affairs*, 1:34–8.

Kelsey, Jane. 2002. "Old Wine in New Bottles: Globalisation, Colonisation, and Resource Management and Maori." In M. Kawharu, ed. *Whenua: Managing our Resources*. Auckland: Reed Publishing, 372–96.

Kymlicka, Will. 2001. *Politics in the Vernacular*. Don Mills: Oxford University Press.

Ladner, Kiera L. 2003. "The Alienation of Nation. Understanding Aboriginal Electoral Participation." *Electoral Insight*, 5(3): 21–6.

Linden, Wilf. 1994. *Swiss Democracy*. New York: St. Martins Press.

Loomis, Terrence. 2000. "Government's Role in Maori Development. Charting a New Direction?" Working Paper no. 6, Department of Developmental Studies. Hamilton, University of Waikato.

Maaka, Roger, and Fleras, Augie. 1998. "Rethinking Claims-Making as Maori Affairs Policy." *He Pekenga Korero,* 3(2): 43–51

Maaka, Roger and Fleras, Augie. 2001. "Realigning Relationships: From Indigenous Self Determination to Indigenous Models of Self-Determination." Paper presented to the Rethinking Indigenous Self-Determination Conference. School of Political Science and International Studies. Queensland University, Brisbane. 25–28 September.

McHugh, Paul. 1998. "Aboriginal Identity and Relations—Models of State Practice, and Law in North America and Australasia." Paper presented to the Ministry of Justice, Wellington. Subsequently published in Ken Coates and P.G. McHugh, eds. 1998. *Living Relationships, Kokiri Ngatachi: The Treaty of Waltangi in the New Millennium,* Wellington Press: Victoria University Press.

McIntosh, Ian. 1999. "Australia at the Crossroads." *Cultural Survival Quarterly*, 24(4): 43–51.

Meredith, Paul. 1998. "Hybridity in the Third Space: Rethinking Bi-cultural Politics in Aotearoa / New Zealand." A paper delivered to Te Oru Rangahau Maori Research and Development Conference. Massey University. July 7–9.

Minogue, Kenneth. 1998. *Waitangi: Morality and Reality.* Wellington: Business Roundtable.

Monture-Angus, Patricia. 2001. "Citizens Plus: Old Debates, New Understandings." In Andrew Parkin, ed. *Bridging the Divide between Aboriginal Peoples and the Canadian State.* Montreal: Centre for Research and Information, 8–14.

Mulgan, Richard. 1998. "Citizenship and Legitimacy in Post-Colonial Australia." In Peterson and W. Sanders, eds. *Citizenship and Indigenous Australians. Melbourne, Cambridge University Press,* 179–95.

Niezen, Ronald. 2003. *The Origins of Indigenism: Human Rights and the Politics of Identity.* Berkeley: University of California Press.

Office of Treaty Settlements. 2002. *Healing the Past, Building a Future: A Guide to Treaty of Waitangi Claims and Negotiations with the Crown.* Wellington.

Reynolds, Henry. 1996. *Aboriginal Sovereignty: Three Nations, One Australia?* Sydney: Allen and Unwin.

Salée, Daniel. 1995. "Identities in Conflict: The Aboriginal Question and the Politics of Recognition in Quebec." *Racial and Ethnic Studies*, 18(2): 277–314.

Schouls, Tim. 2002. *The Basic Dilemma: Sovereignty or Assimilation?* In J. Bird et al, eds. *Nation to Nation.* Toronto: Penguin, 12–16.

Scott, Craig. 1996. "Indigenous Self-Determination and Decolonization of the International Imagination." *Human Rights Quarterly*, 18: 815–20.

Spoonley, Paul. 1995. *Racism and Ethnicity in New Zealand.* Auckland: Oxford University Press.

Thakur, Ramesh. 2001. "Why Peace Exceeds our Grasp." *The Globe and Mail*, 14 July.

Tully, James. 1995. *Strange Multiplicity: Constitutionism in an Age of Diversity*. Cambridge: Cambridge University Press.

Tully, James. 2000. "A Just Relationship between Aboriginal-and Non Aboriginal Peoples of Canada." In C. Cook and J.D. Lindau, eds. *Aboriginal Rights and Self-Government*. Montreal/Kingston: McGill-Queen's University Press, 39–71.

Walker-Williams, Meaghan. 2001. "Our own native Hong Kong." *National Post*, 5 January.

Wilson, Margaret. 1995. "Constitutional Recognition of the Treaty of Waitangi: Myth or Reality?" In M. Wilson and A. Yeatman, eds. *Justice & Identity*. St. Leonards: Allen and Unwin, 1–17.

Young, Iris. 1990. *Justice and the Politics of Difference*. Princeton: Princeton University Press.

CRITICAL-THINKING QUESTIONS

CHAPTER 16 *by Anthony J. Hall*

1. Why do you think that in Mexico and Australia, Indigenous Peoples are supported by some non-indigenous people and opposed by others?
2. How is the struggle of Indigenous Peoples for their rights interconnected with globalization?
3. Describe the difference between the approaches of the Australia and New Zealand governments to the Indigenous Peoples of their respective countries.

CHAPTER 17 *by Trond Thuen*

1. What are the common bonds that bind the Saami together as a people?
2. What are the obstacles to pan-Saami development?
3. Why do you think that the Saami people would consider the King of Norway as their King, when they do not want to be considered Norwegians?

CHAPTER 18 *by Ronald Niezen*

1. How is the concept of self-determination understood in this reading?
2. What is the difference between the terms "indigenous people" and "Indigenous Peoples"?
3. In what ways is the indigenous struggle an international movement?

CHAPTER 19 *by Joe Sawchuk*

1. Why you think the experience of the Metis of Alberta does, or does not, resonate with other Indigenous Peoples?
2. Why do you think a study of the internal political development of a specific indigenous group is important in understanding the indigenous struggle for rights?
3. What evidence does the author give to support his argument that Metis political activity is more than "simply a microcosm of the larger Canadian political process"?

CHAPTER 20 *by Gerald Taiaiake Alfred*

1. What is the problem with Aboriginal leaders espousing sovereignty as the aim of their people's struggle for indigenous rights?

2. How does the indigenous concept of nationhood differ from sovereignty?

3. What, according to the author, are differences between indigenous and Western notions of power?

CHAPTER 21 *by Roger Maaka and Augie Fleras*

1. Why do you think that constructive engagement between Indigenous Peoples and the State entails a rethinking of citizenship?

2. What is the new constitutional order that is described in this reading, and how does it differ from the present colonial constitutional order?

3. Why are Treaty settlements in Canada and New Zealand not the complete answer to the indigenous struggle for rights?

FURTHER READING

Alfred, Taiaiake. 2005. *Wasase: Indigenous Pathways of Action and Freedom.* Guelph, ON: Broadway Press.

This book addresses the intellectual aspect of the indigenous struggle, confronting the colonization of the mind to which Indigenous Peoples have been subjected. In the author's own words, "This book traces the journey of those Indigenous people who have found a way to transcend the colonial identities which are the legacy of our history and lives as *Onkewehonwe*, original people."

Durie Mason. 2005. *Nga Tai Matatu: Tides of Maori Endurance.* Melbourne: Oxford University Press.

Using the traditional metaphor of the tide for the resilience of Maori, who in spite of the colonial experience have not only survived but also begun to flourish, the author offers a comprehensive and detailed overview of contemporary Maori society. The author's final words in the preface epitomize the indigenous struggle: "In writing about endurance, I had in mind our *mokopuna*, our grandchildren, and our belief that they should be able to grow up as Maori, as healthy New Zealanders, and as global citizens."

Garroute, Eva Marie. 2003. *Real Indians: Identity and the Survival of Native America.* Berkeley, University of California Press.

Identity is central to the contemporary indigenous struggle, and this book addresses the complexities of Native Americans' identity. The book contains an interesting section on "radical indigenism" where the author argues the case for the construction of theory and notions of identity to come from the Native American experience rather than from Western European ideologies.

Peterson, Nicholas and Will Sanders, eds. 1998. *Citizenship and Indigenous Australians.* Melbourne: Cambridge University Press.

A book of readings on Australian Aboriginal people that covers a wide range of historical, contemporary and future issues of concern to both Aboriginal and non-Aboriginal Australians.

APPENDIX: RELEVANT WEBSITES

http://www.hrweb.org/legal/genocide.html
This UN website on genocide lays out the conventions on the prevention of genocide, and the punishment of anyone found guilty of participating in or conspiring to participate in genocidal activities.

http://www.ahf.ca/
This is the website of Aboriginal Healing Foundation, an organization set up to deal with the legacy of Canada's residential schools on the Aboriginal people who attended them. The foundation's primary goal is to provide resources for healing initiatives, and to facilitate public awareness of the effects of residential schools and their intergenerational effects.

http://www.who.int/about/en/
The World Health Organization website is extremely useful for understanding the global reach of disease epidemics and our reactions to them. Although this website may seem out of place in this text, the reality is that indigenous societies are still among the most likely to be affected by disease outbreaks and to suffer their worst effects.

http://www.amnesty.org/results/is/eng
A subsection of the larger Amnesty International website, the Indigenous Peoples' section contains a wealth of information on the human rights abuses that Indigenous Peoples around the globe continue to suffer. It lists a wide range of media releases and publications that deal with the impact of economic and cultural globalization on the sustainability of indigenous collectivities.

http://www.webster.edu/~woolflm/holocaust.html
This reference-oriented site contains a wealth of information on what genocide is, how it has been used, and where it has occurred over the past four or five hundred years. Especially useful is the website's inclusion of numerous academic references referring back to the larger study of genocide.

http://lanic.utexas.edu/la/region/indigenous/
Latin American Network Information Centre

http://www.genocidewatch.org/iceg/

http://www.un.org/rights/indigenous/mediaadv.html
Gives information about the Decade for Indigenous Peoples.

http://www.unhchr.ch/indigenous/main.html
Website containing information on Indigenous Peoples and conflict resolution.

http://www.unhchr.ch/html/menu2/ind_main.htm
Website for information regarding the UN and Indigenous Peoples.

http://www.cwis.org/fwdp/un.html
A direct link to accessing UN documents.

COPYRIGHT ACKNOWLEDGEMENTS

CHAPTER 19 by Joe Sawchuk, "Politics Within the Metis Association of Alberta," from *The Dynamics of Native Politics* (Saskatoon: Purich Publishing, 1998): 117–133. Reprinted by permission of Purich Publishing.

CHAPTER 20 by Gerald Taiaiake Alfred, "Sovereignty: An Inappropriate Concept," from *Peace, Power and Righteousness: An Indigenous Manifesto* (Don Mills: Oxford University Press, 1999): 55–69. Copyright © Oxford University Press Canada 1999. Reprinted by permission of Oxford University Press.

CHAPTER 21 by Roger Maaka and Augie Fleras, "Indigeneity at the Edge: Towards a Constructive Engagement," from *The Politics of Indigeneity Challenging the State in Canada and Aotearoa New Zealand* (Dunedin: Otago University Press, 2005): 283-300.

FIGURES AND MAPS

FIGURE 2.1: "The monuments of Easter Island," from Voyage de La Pérouse Autour du Monde. Paris: Imp. De la Republique, 1797. Reprinted by permission of Linda Hall Library of Science, Engineering & Technology.

FIGURE 2.2: "Trade, slavery and colonialism," from A. Pinart, 1878, "Voyage à l'île de pâques," *Le Tour du monde,* no. 36: 225–240.

FIGURE 3.1: "Ainu hunting a bear," from *Tōkai Yawa*. Reprinted by permission of Tokyo National Museum and Hokkaido University Library.

FIGURE 3.2: "A spring-bow trap," from *Ezoto kikan*. Reprinted by permission of Tokyo National Museum and Hokkaido University Library.

FIGURE 3.3: "The ecology of Ainu autonomy and dependence," from *The Conquest of Ainu Lands: Ecology and Culture in Japanese Expansion*. Copyright © Tokyo National Museum.

FIGURE 3.4: "Archaeological remains from the old port at Matsumae (Fukuyama)," from *The Conquest of Ainu Lands: Ecology and Culture in Japanese Expansion*.

FIGURE 3.5: "The inside of an Ainu home," from *Ezo fuzokuzu*. Reprinted by permission of Tokyo National Museum and Hokkaido University Library.

FIGURE 14.1: "Manco Inca, raised up as Inca king," from *Nueva corónica y buen gobierno,* 1615.

FIGURE 14.2: "The Xiu family tree," probably by Gaspar Antonio Chi, 1557. Updated by don Juan Xiu, 1685. Reprinted by permission of Tozzer Library of Harvard College Library.

FIGURE 15.1: "Cree camp near Saskatoon, c. 1990," from Saskatchewan Archives Board, R-B1016.

FIGURE 15.2: "Native farmers c. 1906–10," from Archives of Manitoba, Edmund Morris Collection, G11-510.

MAP 15.1: "Saskatchewan and Assiniboia Districts," from *Native Peoples: The Canadian Experience*, R. Bruce Morrison and C. Roderick Wilson, eds. (Toronto: Oxford University Press, 2004): 325. Copyright © Oxford University Press Canada, 2004. Reprinted by permission of Oxford University Press Canada.